DEBT, DEVELOPMENT, AND DEMOCRACY

DEBT, DEVELOPMENT, AND DEMOCRACY

MODERN POLITICAL ECONOMY AND LATIN AMERICA, 1965–1985

Jeffry A. Frieden

PRINCETON UNIVERSITY PRESS   PRINCETON, NEW JERSEY

Copyright © 1991 by Princeton University Press
Published by Princeton University Press, 41 William Street,
Princeton, New Jersey 08540
In the United Kingdom: Princeton University Press, Oxford
All Rights Reserved

Library of Congress Cataloging-in-Publication Data

Frieden, Jeffry A.
Debt, development, and democracy : modern political economy and
Latin America, 1965–1985 / Jeffry A. Frieden.
p. cm.
Includes bibliographical references and index.
ISBN 0-691-07899-8 (alk. paper)
1. Latin America—Economic policy—Case studies. 2. Debts,
External—Latin America—Case studies. 3. Latin America—Economic
conditions—1982– —Case studies. 4. Latin America—Politics and
government—1980– —Case studies. I. Title.
HC125.F69 1991
338.98'009'046—dc20   91-12106 CIP

This book has been composed in Linotron Sabon

Princeton University Press books are printed
on acid-free paper and meet the guidelines
for permanence and durability of the Committee
on Production Guidelines for Book Longevity
of the Council on Library Resources

Printed in the United States of America by
Princeton University Press, Princeton, New Jersey

10 9 8 7 6 5 4 3 2 1

Contents

List of Tables and Figure   vii

Preface   ix

Abbreviations   xiii

Introduction   3

PART I: THE ARGUMENT

1. Modern Political Economy and Latin American Borrowing   15

2. The Setting: Latin American Political Economies and
International Financial Trends   42

3. The Response: Economic Policies and Politics in Borrowing
and Financial Crisis   67

PART II: FIVE CASE STUDIES

4. Debt, Economic Policy, and Politics in Brazil   95
   Appendix   138

5. Debt, Economic Policy, and Politics in Chile   143

6. Debt, Economic Policy, and Politics in Mexico, Venezuela,
and Argentina   178

PART III: IMPLICATIONS

7. Observations and Implications   233

8. Conclusions   254

Select Bibliography   257

Index   275

Tables and Figure

Table 2.1	Selected Latin American Economic Indicators, 1965–1973	52
Table 2.2	Latin American International Financial Indicators, 1973–1986	60
Table 2.3	Net Flow of Foreign Resources to Latin America, 1961–1986	62
Table 3.1	Credit and Foreign Credit in Five Latin American Borrowers, 1972–1982	76
Table 3.2	External Debt of More than One-Year Maturity Owed by Public and Private Sectors, 1981	76
Table 3.3	Foreign Debt and Public Spending	77
Table 3.4	Foreign Debt and Public-Deficit Financing	78
Table 3.5	Debt, Investment, Manufacturing, Finance, and Imports	79
Table 3.6	Efficiency of Investment in Latin America	80
Table 3.7	Real Effective Exchange Rates and Capital Flight	81
Table 3.8	Summary Regressions for Five Latin American Borrowers	84
Table 3.9	The Debt Crisis and Political Regimes in Latin America	86
Table 4.1	Brazil: Selected Economic Indicators, 1970–1985	108
Table 4.2	Brazil: Foreign Borrowing and the Financial Sector	110
Table 4.3	Brazil: Loans Approved by the National Bank for Economic and Social Development System, by Economic Activity, 1964–1981	113
Table 4.4	Brazil: Borrowing by Manufacturing Sectors	114
Table 4.5	Brazil: Financial Data on Selected Parastatals, 1980	121
Table A4.1	Brazil: Concentration Ratios of Manufacturing Sectors	140

Table 5.1   Chile: Macroeconomic Data, 1970–1985   154

Table 5.2   Chile: External Debt, 1973–1985   161

Table 5.3   Chile: Sectoral Economic Trends, 1974–1982   163

Table 6.1   Mexican External Debt Outstanding, End-1981   191

Table 6.2   Venezuelan External Debt Outstanding, End-
              1982   201

Table 6.3   Argentine External Debt Outstanding, 1975–
              1982   208

Figure 1.1   Stylized Evolution of Crisis Politics   37

Preface

BETWEEN the late 1960s and the middle 1980s, the disparate nations of Latin America experienced very similar external financial conditions. They gained access to previously unavailable foreign loans, first in a trickle and eventually in a torrent. As they borrowed, the interest rates they were charged rose and fell in lockstep. Then, within the space of a few months in 1982, foreign financiers decided that loans to Latin America were a bad bet, and lending shut down almost completely.

The Latin American responses to these international conditions varied widely on both economic and political dimensions. During the borrowing period, some governments took advantage of the newly available money to expand their economic activities, augment subsidies to the private sector, increase trade protection, and fund public investment. Other countries, however, embarked on unprecedented attempts to decrease government involvement in the economy, reduce subsidies, liberalize trade, and sell off existing state enterprises. The loan cutoff of 1982 and the ensuing continent-wide economic crisis, similarly, had widely varied political effects. In many nations, long-established military dictatorships were replaced by elected civilian governments. In others, by contrast, repressive dictatorships held onto power with little apparent difficulty.

When similar conditions lead to different outcomes, social scientists reach for their pens.[1] Different analysts give different explanations for variation in national reactions to similar international events. Some look to distinct cultural, ideological, or political traditions. Others focus on historically established institutions of governance in individual countries. Still others search for diverse international economic or strategic positions to explain divergent outcomes.

In this study, I base my explanation of economic and political reactions

---

[1] Or, as Peter Gourevitch wrote about an enterprise similar to this one, "For social scientists who enjoy comparisons, happiness is finding a force or event which affects a number of societies at the same time" (Peter Alexis Gourevitch, "International Trade, Domestic Coalitions, and Liberty: Comparative Responses to the Crisis of 1873–1896," *Journal of Interdisciplinary History* 8, no. 2 [Autumn 1977]: 281). Gourevitch has expanded on this in *Politics in Hard Times: Comparative Responses to International Economic Crises* (Ithaca: Cornell University Press, 1986). My study owes a great conceptual debt to that of Gourevitch, and to two prior analyses of the great depression of the late nineteenth century: Charles Kindleberger, "Group Behavior and International Trade," *Journal of Political Economy* 59, no. 1 (February 1951): 30–46, and Hans Rosenberg, "The Depression of 1873–1896 in Central Europe," *Journal of Economic History* 13 (1943): 58–73.

to international economic conditions on the economic interests of groups within Latin American societies. I look at Latin America's five biggest borrowers—Argentina, Brazil, Chile, Mexico, and Venezuela—and compare their economic policies during the borrowing period that began in the late 1960s and early 1970s. I then compare the political fallout of the crisis that followed the loan cutoff of the early 1980s.

Economic policies during the borrowing episode, I argue, can be explained as the outcome of group pressures on policymakers. Generally, the interests of concentrated, specific economic sectors led governments to channel borrowed money directly or indirectly to them. In a few instances, conflict between classes overrode sectoral pressures and pushed governments toward more market-oriented policies.

On the political front, the crisis of the early 1980s heightened interest-group pressures on policymakers. Where governments faced sectoral demands that they were unable or unwilling to meet, these sectors defected to the political opposition and strengthened movements for a change in the government or the regime, often with success. Where, again, sectoral demands were counterbalanced by class tensions, pressure for political change was dampened.

The presentation, application, and defense of this analytical perspective in the present study may be too single-minded for the taste of many. I ignore important issues and factors. I do this, however, in the interest of explanatory and expository power and simplicity, and the effort should be judged by the extent to which the results meet these standards. If this framework sheds light on the causes of Latin American economic and political developments in the 1970s and 1980s, and if its conclusions have implications for further analyses and policies, the heroic simplifications involved will have been justified.

In the process of defining and refining this study, the advice of friends and colleagues has been invaluable. Barbara Geddes and David Lake had the extraordinary patience and forbearance to review successive drafts of all or part of the book. A hardy few commented on a draft of the full manuscript: Richard Baum, Barry Eichengreen, David Felix, Miriam Golden, Sylvia Maxfield, George Tsebelis, and three anonymous reviewers. Others gave important suggestions on the basis of portions of the study at various stages in its progress: Mônica Baer, León Bendesky, Luiz Carlos Bresser Pereira, Anabela Costa, James De Nardo, Robert Devlin, Carlos Díaz Alejandro, David Dollar, Ricardo Ffrench Davis, Albert Fishlow, Stephan Haggard, Nora Hamilton, Roger Haydon, Peter Katzenstein, Robert Kaufman, David Mares, Timothy McKeown, Moisés Naím, Sule Ozler, Angel Palerm, Manuel Pastor, Miguel Rodriguez, Jack Snyder, Michael Waldman, and Michael Wallerstein. Scott Bruckner and Carlos

Juarez provided expert research assistance. Malcolm DeBevoise and Walter Lippincott helped guide the manuscript through the publication process.

While doing research for this volume, I received financial assistance from the Institute for the Study of World Politics, the Tinker Foundation, the UCLA Academic Senate's Committee on Research, and UCLA's International Studies and Overseas Programs. On the ground in Latin America, the hospitality of many research institutions was extremely helpful. I was fortunate to be affiliated with the Instituto de Planejamento Econômico e Social in Rio de Janeiro, the Centro Brasileiro de Análise e Planejamento in São Paulo, the Instituto Latinoamericano de Estudios Transnacionales in Mexico City, and the Instituto de Estudios Superiores de Administración in Caracas. I also benefited from the assistance of the Centro de Estudios de Estado y Sociedad and the Centro de Investigaciones Sociales Sobre el Estado y la Administración in Buenos Aires, the Corporación de Investigaciones Económicas para Latinoamérica and the Economic Commission for Latin America in Santiago, and the Centro de Estudios Monetarios Latinoamericanos in Mexico City. Finally, the study would have been impossible without the cooperation of hundreds of current and past government officials, businessmen, politicians, scholars, and journalists all over Latin America.

Abbreviations

AD	Alianza Democrática (Democratic Alliance, Chile)
AD	Acción Democrática (Democratic Action, Venezuela)
ARENA	Aliança Renovadora Nacional (National Renovation Alliance, Brazil)
BHC	Banco Hipotecario de Chile (Mortgage Bank of Chile)
BNDES	Banco Nacional de Desenvolvimento Econômico e Social (National Bank for Economic and Social Development, Brazil)
CEBRAP	Centro Brasileiro de Análise e Planejamento (Brazilian Center for Analysis and Planning, São Paulo)
CEDES	Centro de Estudios de Estado y Sociedad (Center for Studies of State and Society, Buenos Aires)
CEMLA	Centro de Estudios Monetarios Latinoamericanos (Center for Latin American Monetary Studies, Mexico City)
CFE	Comisión Federal de Electricidad (Federal Electricity Commission, Mexico)
CIEPLAN	Corporación de Investigaciones Económicas para Latinoamérica (Corporation for Economic Research for Latin America, Santiago)
CISEA	Centro de Investigaciones Sociales Sobre el Estado y la Administración (Center for Social Research on the State and Management, Buenos Aires)
COPEI	Comité de Organización Política Electoral Independiente (Committee for Independent Electoral Political Organization, Venezuela)
CORFO	Corporación de Fomento (Development Corporation, Chile)
CPI	Consumer price index
ECLA	Economic Commission for Latin America (Santiago, Chile)
FDI	Foreign direct investment
FDN	Frente Democrático Nacional (National Democratic Front, Mexico)
FIESP	Federação das Indústrias do Estado de São Paulo (Federation of Industries of São Paulo State, Brazil)
GATT	General Agreement on Tariffs and Trade
GDI	Gross domestic investment
GDP	Gross domestic product
IESA	Instituto de Estudios Superiores de Administración (Institute for Higher Management Studies, Caracas)

ILET   Instituto Latinoamericano de Estudios Transnacionales (Latin American Institute for Transnational Studies)
IMF   International Monetary Fund
IPEA   Instituto de Planejamento Econômico e Social (Institute for Economic and Social Planning, Rio de Janiero)
ISI   Import-Substituting Industrialization
LDC   Less developed country
LIBOR   London inter-bank offer rate
MAS   Movimiento al Socialismo (Movement for Socialism, Venezuela)
MDB   Movimento Democrático Brasileiro (Brazilian Democratic Movement)
MDP   Movimiento Democrático Popular (Democratic Popular Movement, Chile)
ORTN   Obrigação Reajustável do Tesouro Nacional (readjustable obligation of the National Treasury, Brazil)
PAN   Partido de Acción Nacional (National Action Party, Mexico)
PDC   Partido Democrático Cristiano (Christian Democratic Party, Chile)
PDS   Partido Democrático Social (Democratic Social Party, Brazil)
PMDB   Partido Movimento Democrático Brasileiro (Brazilian Democratic Movement Party)
PND   Plano Nacional de Desenvolvimento (National Development Plan, Brazil)
PRD   Partido de la Revolución Democrática (Party of the Democratic Revolution, Mexico)
PRI   Partido Revolucionario Institucional (Institutional Revolutionary Party, Mexico)
SOFOFA   Sociedad de Fomento Fabril (Society for Manufacturing Development, Chile)
UCR   Unión Cívica Radical (Radical Civic Union, Argentina)
UP   Unidad Popular (Popular Unity, Chile)

DEBT, DEVELOPMENT, AND DEMOCRACY

Introduction _____

IN THE 1980s Latin America went through a devastating depression. Output per person dropped 10 percent during what Latin Americans called the lost decade, and by 1990 per capita income was still below 1975 levels. Meanwhile, and to the surprise of most observers, the region experienced a wave of democratization. While in the late 1970s South America had only two elected civilian regimes, by the late 1980s virtually all the military dictatorships had been swept from power.

The decade brought to popular attention two enduring enigmas: why Latin America is poor and why it is so seldom democratic. On the first count, the region's persistent poverty despite remarkable natural resources is especially puzzling. Indeed, around the turn of the century, Argentina was one of the world's five or six richest nations, well ahead of most of Western Europe in income per person; the continent as a whole was as developed as was Central Europe. Today, Argentina ranks far behind Europe, while Latin America has dropped back to the middle rungs of the developing world. It appears difficult to understand how a continent endowed with ample natural and human resources, skilled and entrepreneurial immigrants, and substantial foreign capital has managed to stagnate economically.

On the second count, Latin American political systems are among the most unstable in the world; when they are stable, it is often due to the brutal repressiveness of military dictators. If this were simply the residue of decolonization, as in much of Africa, it might be easier to understand. But the Latin American nations have been politically independent since the 1820s, longer than almost all developing—and even many developed—countries. In 170 years, the region has not generated the sturdy political institutions that we might expect to arise with long experience. Again, it is reasonable to ask why a region with long-standing political independence, a tradition of Western philosophical and sociopolitical influences, and mature mass organizations has so often found itself ruled by petty despots.

This book is an attempt to explain crucial aspects of this dismal economic and political picture. Such sweeping categories as "poverty" and "democracy" are too broad for nuanced analysis, and it would be foolish to claim a full-blown explanation of them. I focus on more modest and tractable objects of examination, the making of economic policy by government officials and the process of engaging in political activity by social groups. Indeed, much of what interests scholars and other observers is captured in the analysis of patterns of economic policy and political activity.

The economic performance of Latin American countries is closely related to the economic policies pursued by their governments. This is perhaps a more popular assertion now than it was twenty years ago, when many believed that the international economy largely determined national development paths. More recent experiences have refocused attention on the ways national governments can affect patterns of national economic growth. A major motivation for this study is the belief that economic policies make a crucial difference to the character and success of national economic development.[1]

In fact, government policy enters virtually all explanations of why countries develop differently.[2] In some accounts, powerful groups whose immediate interests would be harmed by modern economic growth deliberately manipulate the state apparatus to retard growth.[3] This might be

[1] A seminal book along these lines is Robert Bates, *Markets and States in Tropical Africa: The Political Basis of Agricultural Policies* (Berkeley: University of California Press, 1981). An excellent review of the literature is Stephan Haggard, "The Newly Industrializing Countries in the International System," *World Politics* 38, no. 2 (January 1986): 343–70. Haggard continues and extends this work in *Pathways from the Periphery: The Politics of Growth in the Newly Industrializing Countries* (Ithaca: Cornell University Press, 1990).

[2] This is as good a place as any to note that throughout this book I ignore the enormous debate over the relationship between economic growth and development. There are some who argue that sheer growth in per capita income is not the same as development, which must involve social improvements for the entire population and the equitable distribution of the benefits of growth. This is an important moral point, for it is clearly socially undesirable for aggregate per capita income growth to mask declines for the majority and increases only for a minority. Nevertheless, there are strong analytical and empirical reasons to focus on economic growth for our purposes. It is, after all, clearly impossible to undertake an equitable distribution of the fruits of economic growth if there is no economic growth to start with; thus economic growth is a *necessary* condition for broad-based socioeconomic development, although it is certainly not sufficient to ensure it. It is certainly the case that economic growth does not *inevitably* lead to broad and equitable development; thus economic growth is not a *sufficient* condition for social development. Some developing countries have extremely unequal income distribution and indefensible social indicators (infant mortality and illiteracy rates, for example), while others have both patterns of income distribution and social indicators that rival the developed world; most of this variation seems due to domestic political differences. The two processes—economic growth and broader social development—thus appear to be analytically distinct, although clearly interrelated. Since my task is not to explain differential patterns of income inequality and social development, but rather to explain differences in economic growth and political development, I ignore the social dimension to economic growth. While this will not please some, it at least allows for a more manageable analytical focus. In any case, the political results I attempt to explain themselves have an important bearing on the ultimate distribution of economic benefits, and in this sense my discussion may be of some interest and use even to those concerned only about social and distributional outcomes.

[3] This is the approach of the stream of Marxist thought that emphasizes the antidevelop-

the case for societies ruled by planters who depend on cheap labor, are unable to diversify their operations, and would be hurt by the flood of migrants from countryside to city that would accompany industrial development.[4] In other accounts, the process might be less conscious: interest groups obstruct structural change because the transition costs of modernization appear higher to them than expected benefits.[5] The culprits here could be Luddite craftsmen or protectionist rye farmers, but the result is that economically efficient activities are not pursued and output is lower than it could be. In some views, foreigners are central: colonial rulers representing their manufacturers restrict competing local industrialists.[6]

Whether the cause of economic retardation is defined as rent-seeking or class struggle, analysts implicitly agree that government economic policy is a crucial link in the chain of causation. Oligarchic landowners use government policies to retard labor mobility; foreign capitalists and their domestic accomplices use government policies to enrich themselves at the expense of local society; interest groups use government policies to extract rents from the rest of society; classes use the state apparatus to further their own interests. There may be differences about the results of various government policies, about whether government intervention helps economic growth, but there is agreement that the policies themselves play an important role in determining economic outcomes.

If economic success or failure is in large part a result of economic policies, the logical next step is to ask from what the policies result. My argument is that government actions are the response of policymakers to

mental interests of preindustrial (or even pre-capitalist) classes or class fractions; this strain is strong in Marx's own writings on Ireland. Marx wrote that the English bourgeoisie had "a common interest with the English aristocracy in turning Ireland into mere pasture land," and Engels concluded that "Ireland has been stunted in its development by the English invasion and thrown centuries back" (Marx and Engels, *On Colonialism* [Moscow: Progress, 1968], 336, 334). A modern neo-Marxist variant associated with the dependency school is represented by Celso Furtado, *Economic Development of Latin America* (New York: Cambridge University Press, 1970).

[4] Important elements of this are present in the works of Hans Singer and W. Arthur Lewis that emphasize the "enclave" character of modern economic activities in certain developing areas. See, for example, passages in Hans W. Singer, "The Distribution of Gains between Investing and Borrowing Countries," *American Economic Review* 40, no. 2 (May 1950): 473–85; and in W. Arthur Lewis, *The Evolution of the International Economic Order* (Princeton: Princeton University Press, 1978).

[5] Mancur Olson, *The Rise and Decline of Nations: Economic Growth, Stagflation, and Social Rigidities* (New Haven: Yale University Press, 1982).

[6] Paul Baran, *The Political Economy of Growth* (New York: Monthly Review Press, 1957), is the classic statement of the early dependency neo-Marxist view of this relationship. A more recent, less mechanistic, interpretation is that of A. G. Hopkins, *An Economic History of West Africa* (New York: Columbia University Press, 1973).

sociopolitical pressures brought to bear upon them by interest groups. The specifics of this argument are detailed later, but the general line of causation is straightforward: political pressures lead politicians to pursue policies that affect economic activity. Identifying the pressures and their policy effects is the first task of this study.

The second task, and a component part of a political economy of Latin America, is to explain the varied political fortunes of the region. I am interested in explaining why and how individuals and groups interact in the political arena: why and how existing coalitions or institutions persist or are changed, why and how political forms endure or deteriorate. This is, in fact, a focused way of exploring regime formation and decay, authoritarianism and democracy.

Democracy is, after all, a set of formal and informal institutions that regularize political interaction: coalition formation, voting, the judicial system, regulation of public speech and of the press. All involve implicit or explicit agreement to work within these institutions or to change them within established parameters and procedures. Such agreement entails willingness to admit defeat in one election in the hope of future victories, to compromise on policies with the calculation that while one alternative to compromise might be total victory, another might be total defeat.[7]

If enough or powerful enough social actors decide that existing institutions do not sufficiently serve their interests, they can try to change the institutions. This can involve electoral reform, building new coalitions, or, in extreme cases, overthrowing the government and replacing it with a more pliable one. Social support for a military coup, for example, might come from those who regard the prevailing system of governance as so inimical to their interests that the cost of changing it is lower than the cost of accepting it; this could include those who lose electoral battles, economic interests underrepresented in the political system, or the military itself. Similarly, a democratic movement might try to replace an authoritarian regime since its demands have little prospect of being met under authoritarianism. The task under this rubric is to understand the forces that lead individuals and their organized social groups to take the political positions they do, both toward specific policies and toward institutional formation and change.

To understand the origins of regime change, then, we need clear explanations of the behavior of important sociopolitical actors. We also need to explore the impact of political institutions themselves on political in-

[7] An outstanding discussion of the issues is Adam Przeworski, "Some Problems in the Study of the Transition to Democracy," in *Transitions from Authoritarian Rule*, ed. Guillermo O'Donnell, Philippe Schmitter, and Laurence Whitehead (Baltimore: Johns Hopkins University Press, 1986), 3:47–63.

teraction—how the party system affects coalitions, for example—and, pari passu, how political activity affects political institutions.

Here, again, my argument is that political outcomes are the result of choices made by social groups. Individuals may not be conscious of the effects of their behavior on democratization, or on the collapse of democracy, but in the end the political activity of groups and individuals determines the evolution of political institutions. As above, I argue that the economic interests of social groups are central to their political choices. Once more, and without details, the causal arrows are straightforward: economic interests lead groups to engage in political behavior that affects the evolution of national politics. The second task of this book is to specify the links between economic interest, political behavior, and political outcomes.

The Latin America described in this book is peopled by interest groups whose activities are crucial determinants of economic and political development. Groups pressure governments as they make economic policies, and these policies affect economic activity. Groups enter the political arena in pursuit of their interests, with major effects on political outcomes.

Analytical Puzzles and Proposed Solutions

The things to be explained, then, are patterns of economic policy and political activity. This book compares five countries—Argentina, Brazil, Chile, Mexico, and Venezuela—which faced similar external financial conditions during the 1970s and 1980s, but whose economic policies and politics diverged in important ways.

What determines economic policy? What determines political change? I propose one set of answers to both questions: the character of socioeconomic interest groups and their patterns of cohesion and conflict. I incorporate two cross-cutting sets of economic interests into the analysis, sectors and classes, but for reasons specified below I regard sectoral divisions as the norm over which class divisions prevail only in unusual circumstances.

The starting point of the analysis is the time in Latin America's recent past when the floodgates of international financial markets began to open to the region's borrowers. At this point, policymakers found themselves with substantial new resources at their disposal. Politicians used these new resources to protect and defend their domestic political positions— but, of course, what this implied varied with the domestic political lineup. In some countries, especially Brazil, Mexico, and Venezuela, borrowing was associated with a flurry of public investments and major industrialization drives. In others, especially Argentina and Chile, borrowing went hand in hand with large-scale privatization and "deindustrialization."

My analytical expectation is that policymakers provided more resources to those who exerted more pressure on them, and that economic interest groups exerted pressure on policymakers in direct proportion to what they had to gain or lose from policy and to the ease with which they could mobilize. This implies that economic policies were tailored to the desires of well-organized interest groups with a great deal at stake. I attempt to capture these factors with summary measures, or shorthand expressions: asset specificity and concentration. Policy can more easily enhance the fortunes of economic actors when their assets are more specific to their current use, that is, the more costly it is to move them into or out of that use. In parallel fashion, the more concentrated a sector is—the fewer economic agents there are in it—the easier it is for it to mobilize politically.

In general, then, economic policies were designed to channel the newly available financial resources directly or indirectly to specific and concentrated sectors. This is my explanation of the patterns of economic policy in Brazil, Mexico, and Venezuela.

Although sectoral pressures are the norm, other political divisions may cut across or against them. Foremost among these, at least in the Latin American context, are class divisions that call into question the distribution of national income between wages and profits. Where class conflict was prevalent, sectoral pressures were muted, and governments stood back from sector-specific intervention in favor of more general policies typically aimed at protecting or reconstructing the general investment climate. This is my broad explanation of the economic policies undertaken by the goverments of Argentina and especially Chile during the borrowing period.

Moving to explanations of political activity, I concentrate on the early 1980s, a period of crisis precipitated and exacerbated by the drying up of foreign finance in 1982. The sudden change in the international economic environment confronted governments with a serious dilemma. Previous access to external finance had allowed them to expand the benefits they extended to constituents, but the end of lending forced major retrenchments; debtor governments had to *take* resources from society rather than distribute them. Governments inevitably failed to meet all of the social demands they faced during the crisis.

The new resource constraints led to conflict over who would bear the brunt of adjustment to financial stringency. In this context, my interest is in the political fallout of the economic crisis. I examine whether groups supported the government or opposed it, whether they clamored for regime change (i.e., democratization) or opposed it, whether opposition to the government or to the form of government (democracy, dictatorship) was successful. This eventually leads to an analysis of why regimes changed or did not change; why, for example, democratization did or did not take place.

Here my analytical expectation is that opposition to existing governments came primarily from those whose economic demands were not met by these governments. Where an established opposition stood a chance of taking office, disgruntled groups looked to the opposition for assistance. Where the best hope of a change in policy implied a change in regime (such as democratization), dissatisfied sectors supported such a regime change. Once again, where class conflict was rampant, I expect this dimension to override more sector-specific policy and political preferences.

In this study, then, I rely on economic interest groups in Latin American societies as the principal determinants of both economic policies during the borrowing years and the political results of the financial crisis of the early 1980s. The policy and political concerns of specific and concentrated economic sectors are expected to dominate in most instances. Where class conflict was important—in Chile almost always and in Argentina much of the time—it overrode such sectoral policy and political demands in favor of more general attempts to safeguard the business environment.

Issues of Theory and Evidence

The analyst of Latin American politics and economics confronts a wide variety of theoretical perspectives and a great paucity of relevant data. Every analyst must develop a strategy to deal with these two problems.

As regards contending theoretical frameworks, my approach here is to focus single-mindedly on developing and applying an analysis based on the economic interests of domestic groups. When I develop the logic of my analysis, I do not counterpose it to other potential logics. There is no head-to-head, country-by-country confrontation between my approach and that of others. Certainly this is not to imply that there are no perspectives contending with, or complementary to, my own; I ignore them for the purposes of this study for two reasons.

First, there is rarely consensus *within* theoretical schools of what to expect in the cases at hand. The broad schools of thought in development studies—such as modernization, dependency, bureaucratic authoritarianism, or postimperialism—do not readily translate into predictions about national economic policy responses to an increase or decrease in the supply of external financial resources. Nor do they predict national political responses to financial crisis. I could be bold and project from scattered citations what one or another theory might predict, but partisans of the theory would immediately, perhaps with reason, accuse me of misinterpreting the implications of their theory for the case at hand. In other words, while I can be confident of having formulated my own hypotheses in ways that express my views, I have no such confidence about formulating the hypotheses of other theoretical schools—and such alternate hypotheses have not, to my knowledge, been formulated by adepts of the other schools. So I will leave it to them to present and defend their alternative explanations of the cases discussed here.

Second, even if I could present consensual alternative hypotheses, the state of the evidence does not allow for systematic enough testing of these hypotheses to satisfy serious scholars. Latin American data of interest to political economists are scarce and frequently unreliable. Often the kinds of information needed to evaluate contending perspectives do not exist. In an ideal world, propositions about the effects of economic interests on policies, for example, could be investigated with a wide range of evidence. This might include the economic characteristics of different groups, the political and other influence organizations in existence, the attempts to exert influence by groups and organizations, the response of policymakers, and the step-by-step formulation of policy. Many quantitative measures could be useful: private expenditures on lobbying and other attempts to influence public opinion, politicians, and policymakers; campaign contributions; and characteristics of electoral or other political constituencies.

Such information is rarely available in the most open societies. In Latin America, especially in countries under military dictatorship, there is often *no* directly observable information about the connection between interest groups, political pressures, policymakers, and policies. Because there is no ironclad way to confront the hypotheses without such evidence, alternative hypotheses cannot be tested in a way that would satisfy their partisans enough to warrant the effort.

This leads to questions about how I deal with the lack of data on the Latin American political economies as I present and defend my own interpretations. There are a few, not fully satisfactory ways of dealing with the evidentiary problem.

In this study, a first strategy for approaching the scarcity of hard data is to use whatever statistical evidence may be available. This is easier for purely economic factors than for political trends, where statistics are often nonexistent. Even the economic measures are generally collected for reasons that have little to do with political-economy analysis, and fitting them to my purposes was often difficult. I attempted a series of statistical tests of some of my hypotheses. In every instance, there were too few observations, and their reliability was too suspect, to justify the attempt (although one set of indicators is reported in the appendix to chapter 4).

Given the limited nature of statistical information, a second evidentiary strategy is to rely on "softer" data. These include interviews with participants and observers, contemporary and retrospective market and political commentary, journalistic accounts, and scholarly studies. Of course, the softer the data the less well they lend themselves to the rigorous evaluation of explanations. In addition, some of the information most useful to me was provided in confidential interviews, so I cannot report its source to allow for independent evaluation. Nevertheless, soft data are better than no data at all.

A third strategy shifts the focus from unobservable indicators of cause or effect toward more directly observable ones. In other words, while we may not be able directly to observe how X affects Y, we can logically deduce how the more observable T should affect X and how the more observable Z should be affected by Y. From this we can infer that the correlation of T and Z follows a chain of causation that includes X and Y. To take one of the cases in point, my principal argument as to economic policy is that economic interest groups bring political pressure to bear on policymakers, and that policy formulation reflects these pressures. We cannot directly observe the process by which political pressure is exerted and policies are made. However, we can deduce what factors would lead economic interest groups to exert more or less political pressure—for example, the intensity of their policy preferences and their organizational capacity—and we can observe the policy outcomes. Where we see policy favoring interest groups that logic and theory tell us are most likely to bring pressure to bear on policymakers, it is appropriate to infer, at least provisionally, that there is a line of cause and effect that relates lobbying pressure and policy.

This method, put differently, involves the choice of more observable proxies for variables that cannot be directly observed. Because asset specificity and concentration logically imply greater interest in and ability to exert pressure on policymakers, I use them as proxies for the unobservable exertion of pressure. This approach is not without potential pitfalls—the "black box" between the proxy measures may not contain what I think it does, for example—but, again, in the absence of more reliable evidence it is acceptable.

None of this should be taken as an argument that the analysis presented here is all-encompassing. A full explanation of politics and economics in Argentina, Brazil, Chile, Mexico, and Venezuela would include many more factors than interest groups. Most of these factors could be incorporated into an explanation in which interest groups played an important role. The point is not to argue for one force as the exclusive cause of Latin

American politics and economics, but to understand the effects of many forces. Clearly I believe that economic interest groups are extraordinarily important, indeed dominant, factors; but other factors are significant. Although generally I ignore them in this book, in chapter 7 I do return to speculate on how some of the more important neglected variables might be incorporated into a fuller analysis.

These methods will not convince all readers. But this book is at best an opening salvo in an analytical assault on problems of explanation and interpretation that will last a long while, and that will require more complex and nuanced tools than are generally used here. I believe, nonetheless, that the framework presented here stands up to the test of the cases I examine.

The task of the study is to use the tools of political economy to analyze the economic policies and politics of Latin American borrowing. It attempts to apply a clear-cut framework to a set of problems in the study of economics and politics in Latin America, and to employ the framework to shed light both on Latin American development and on the practice of political economy more generally.

Chapter 1 summarizes the political-economy approach used here. Chapter 2 begins with a survey of the historical background to the Latin American experience so as to provide a base on which to build my analysis. It also specifies the features of the external financial environment that provide the shocks to the five national systems. Chapter 3 examines the record of Latin American economic policies and political behavior during borrowing and financial crisis, presenting the "stylized facts" of the cases we examine. Chapters 4, 5, and 6 go through the five country case studies to apply the analytical framework and causal arguments in detail. Chapter 7 summarizes the case studies and the theoretical, analytical, and policy "lessons" that can be gleaned from them. Chapter 8 is the conclusion.

Part I

THE ARGUMENT

1

Modern Political Economy and Latin American Borrowing

THIS BOOK examines development and democratization in Latin America by focusing on two issues: government economic policies and the political behavior of social groups. The first is key to understanding economic development, for most differences among developing economies' structure and performance are in the final instance due to variations in economic policy. The second issue is pivotal to understanding political development, for political change in developing societies at one point or another involves the mobilization or demobilization of sociopolitical groups.

The tools used here belong to what I call modern political economy. This approach assumes that actors are rational and self-interested. For this study, I focus on the *economic* interests of firms and individuals to explain their actions. Within this framework, the study examines the impact of economic interests on economic policy and political mobilization.

I argue that conflict and cooperation among economic sectors, and at times among social classes, was the principal determinant of government economic policies and of political trends. This chapter summarizes the approach used, some of its implications for the study of economic policy and politics, and my specific application of the approach to Latin America.

The Method of Analysis: Modern Political Economy

The framework used here is what I call modern political economy. The book's principal analytical goal is to examine the usefulness and implications of modern political economy for the study of politics and economics in the developing world.

Modern political economy, as I use the term, is a general designation covering a wide variety of analytical approaches. Members of the category, which comprises a group of interrelated and complementary schools, include conservative neoclassical economists, liberal institutional economists, and classical Marxists.[1] I ignore the differences among

[1] For representative examples of the three schools, see respectively Gary S. Becker, *The*

schools and distill the mode of analysis down to its essentials. Modern political economy, simply put, studies how rational self-interested actors combine within or outside existing institutional settings to affect social outcomes. Despite variations, members of the school share the view that individuals can be assumed to act rationally to maximize their utility within constraints.

The term *modern political economy* may be contentious. I use it primarily because the approach is a direct descendent of the classical political economy of such authors as Adam Smith, John Stuart Mill, and Karl Marx, enhanced by recent developments in social science. Others within this tradition use different names for what they do, all of which I find too limited. Rational choice or rational-choice Marxism misleadingly implies a focus on the choice process itself rather than social outcomes. Public choice or social choice again misleads by implying that the public as a whole or society as a whole is choosing a strategy or an outcome. Rationalist political economy is descriptive but ugly; neoclassical Marxism is oxymoronic. I choose to use modern political economy to avoid some of the limitations of other appellations. This will anger people who consider themselves political economists and modern but who reject some or all of the precepts I ascribe to modern political economy. I believe, nonetheless, that the method described here can be considered the modern social scientific heir to classical political economy. This assertion will no doubt lead to charges of taxonomic imperialism, but semantic debates should not impede serious consideration of the approach itself.

Modern political economy as used here has four component parts: defining the actors and their goals, specifying actors' policy preferences, determining how they group themselves, and following their interaction with other social institutions. In what follows the applications given are to interest groups rather than state actors (bureaucrats and politicians), for interest groups are the focus of this study. In other words, here I emphasize the demand side of interest-group–government interaction. I return to the role of the government, the supply side, further on.[2]

Economic Approach to Human Behavior (Chicago: University of Chicago Press, 1976), and George J. Stigler, ed., *Chicago Studies in Political Economy* (Chicago: University of Chicago Press, 1988); Douglass C. North, *Structure and Change in Economic History* (New York: W. W. Norton and Company, 1981); and John Roemer, ed., *Analytical Marxism* (Cambridge: Cambridge University Press, 1986). Good textbook-style surveys include Bruno Frey, *Modern Political Economy* (New York: John Wiley and Sons, 1978); James Alt and K. Alec Chrystal, *Political Economics* (Berkeley: University of California Press, 1983); and Edmund S. Phelps, *Political Economy: An Introductory Text* (New York: W. W. Norton and Company, 1985).

[2] The method presented here is probably most closely paralleled by the literature on the political economy of trade policy. Representative studies include Robert Baldwin, *The Political Economy of U.S. Import Policy* (Cambridge: MIT Press, 1985); Richard Caves, "Economic Models of Political Choice: Canada's Tariff Structure," *Canadian Journal of Eco-*

Definition of Actors and Their Objectives

Actors are assumed to maximize utility, and to make cost-benefit calculations of how best to achieve this end. In this study, I also assume that actors maximize income. The desire to maximize income says only that workers prefer higher to lower wages, and capitalists prefer higher to lower profits.[3]

The objective of income maximization leads actors to a variety of subsidiary concerns, including preferences for certain government policies. While capitalists and workers are assumed to have the same *objective* of earning as much as possible, their *policy preferences* may be different: capitalists might prefer taxes to be paid entirely by workers, while workers might prefer all taxation to be on capital. Changed conditions can lead actors to change their policy preferences (but not their income-maximization objective!): free-trade steelworkers might, with the rise of imports, become protectionist. However, individuals and firms, in my analysis, rationally calculate their policy preferences as a function of their goal of maximizing their incomes given their positions in the economy.

The assumption that actors are utility maximizers is straightforward. Analysis based on rational self-interested individuals and firms is common to neoclassical economics, its public-choice/rational-choice offspring, and classical Marxism. However, criticism of models of social behavior that assume self-interested rationality are common.[4] It would be impossible to engage all but the most widespread such objections.

Perhaps the most frequent charge leveled at those who assume rationality is that people do lots of irrational things. This can be distilled into two points. It might mean that there is a systematic bias to individual decision making—caring more about losses than about gains, for example[5]—in which case analysts simply need to control for this bias.

---

nomics 9 (May 1976): 279–300; Howard P. Marvel and Edward J. Ray, "The Kennedy Round: Evidence on the Regulation of International Trade in the United States," *American Economic Review* 73, no. 1 (March 1983): 190–97; Timothy McKeown, "Firms and Tariff Regime Change: Explaining the Demand for Protection," *World Politics* 36 (January 1984): 215–33; Helen Milner, *Resisting Protection: Global Industries and the Politics of International Trade* (Princeton: Princeton University Press, 1988); Edward John Ray, "The Determinants of Tariff and Nontariff Trade Restrictions in the United States," *Journal of Political Economy* 89, no. 1 (1981): 105–21.

[3] A number of potential qualifiers might be added for full accuracy, such as the possibility of a trade-off between higher wages or profits now and in the future.

[4] Interesting debates on the problem of rationality are in Robin Hogarth and Melvin Reder, eds., *Rational Choice: The Contrast between Economics and Psychology* (Chicago: University of Chicago Press, 1986).

[5] The work of Amos Tversky and Daniel Kahneman, as in their "The Framing of Decisions and the Psychology of Choice," *Science* 211 (1981): 453–58, is exemplary of this view.

Alternately, it might mean that people make decisions at random, with no predictable pattern, in which case there is no room for social scientific analysis. Neither point invalidates the rationality assumption for those interested in normal social science.[6]

A second common protest is that the world is so complex that even the most rational of individuals does not have enough information to make rational decisions. This misunderstands the issue: the rationality assumption means that people do their best given their circumstances, not that they are omniscient. Indeed, much modern game theory investigates the effects of different informational environments on social interactions.[7]

A third mistake is to assert that rationality is the same as economic interest. Many critics object to the assumption of rationality because they believe that it implies assuming that all people care about is their income. They are mistaken. Rationality means only that individuals attempt to achieve whatever goals they have by the best means at their disposal. Politicians, for example, might be assumed to maximize the probability of being elected. It so happens that in this study I assume that income maximization drives economic policy preferences, but this is not inherent in the rationality assumption. My restrictive income-maximization assumption should not be confused with the much less limiting assumption of utility maximization.

Finally, many argue that the focus on individual choice—methodological individualism—is not adequate for explaining social outcomes; that the social whole is greater than the sum of its parts and that looking at the parts will not allow us to understand the whole. This may well be the case, but it is not an argument *against* understanding the parts and how they interact, and its validity depends on a demonstration that it is impossible to build an explanation from the bottom up, on firm microfoundations. Indeed, most modern political economists believe that many social outcomes are in some sense greater than the sum of their parts, inasmuch as they are not the intentional result of individual actions but rather the aggregation of individual behavior into unintended consequences.[8] We need a baseline from which to begin this analysis, and the assumption of rationality provides such a baseline. There can hardly be a strong case made *against* wanting to build coherent arguments from elemental units up to final consequences.

[6] For an interesting exploration of apparently irrational behavior that may in fact serve actors' objectives, see Robert Frank, *Passions within Reason: The Strategic Role of the Emotions* (New York: W. W. Norton and Company, 1988).

[7] See, for an introductory example, Eric Rasmusen, *Games and Information* (New York: Basil Blackwell, 1989).

[8] For a Marxist argument to this effect, see John Roemer, " 'Rational Choice' Marxism: Some Issues of Method and Substance," in *Analytical Marxism*, 191–201.

Ultimately this is the simplest reason for the core assumptions of modern political economy: they allow us to develop logically consistent analyses, starting with the basic entities that compose society. They give us the opportunity to derive testable propositions about the behavior of individuals, firms, and groups, and about how their interaction produces social effects. Many objections are misguided, irrelevant, or not motivated by concern with the pursuit of social science. The modern political economy assumption that individuals rationally attempt to maximize their utility allows for the incorporation into analysis of confused or inadequate information, goals other than wealth or income, and social complexity. It provides a fruitful starting point for subsequent analysis.

Specification of Actors' Policy Preferences

In this framework, all else equal, social actors prefer public policies that maximize their incomes. Purely economic characteristics of the actors, therefore, determine whether they will seek government policies and what sort of policies they will seek.

Given stable property rights, economic actors—individuals and firms—earn income from their assets, and what their assets earn is a function of relative prices. The assets in question can range from the right to mine gold on a particular plot of land to a steel mill, from a technical skill to the exclusive right to import Scotch whiskey.

Assets perform better when their output prices rise and their input prices decline, and their owners prefer policies that effect this change in relative prices. However, the degree to which governments can alter relative prices varies, as does the degree to which owners of assets can profit from relative price changes. This leads to differences in what is sometimes called preference intensity. Leaving aside for now problems of collective action, the extent to which an asset-holder tries to influence policy depends on how policy will affect returns on the asset, and on the availability of other uses to which the asset might be put. Both of these are a function of asset specificity.

First, an actor's policy preferences are a function of the susceptibility of the actor's assets to policy. The less policy can change the return on the asset—change the relevant relative prices—the less incentive the asset's owner has to try to affect policy. If firms can easily enter an industry, for example, benefits to pre-existing firms of changes in relative prices will be lost through competition from new entrants. On the other hand, the more barriers there are to new entrants, the more existing producers profit from a change in relative prices. This means that those in industries characterized by significant scale economies, sunk costs, reputational costs, or other barriers to free entry will, other things equal, be more concerned to influence policy toward their industries.[9]

Second, an actor's policy preferences are a function of the degree to which his asset has an available alternate use in which it earns a similar rate of return. The harder it is to move an asset from use to use, the more closely its owner is wedded to its current activity and the greater the incentive to obtain policies to favor this activity. At one extreme, if an asset can be transferred without cost from one activity to another, its owner has no reason to lobby for sector-specific policy, since the asset can be redeployed to earn the highest available rate of return. At the other extreme, if an asset is fully specific to a sector and cannot be employed in *any* other activity, its owner is completely dependent upon the sector's fortunes. By the same token, the more diversified an actor's asset portfolio, the less susceptible the actor is to policy. At the extreme, someone with equal shares of all firms would be indifferent among policies that take from some firms and give to others. The point is that if the owner of an asset can easily shift the asset from one activity to another, or is fully diversified, the owner has no incentive to support sector-specific policies. Other things equal, this means that those in industries characterized by specialized skills, machinery, supply and distribution networks, or other barriers to easy exit will be more motivated to influence policy toward their industries.

This discussion, in more rigorous terms, concerns asset specificity and quasi-rents.[10] Asset specificity is the degree to which the return on an asset depends on its use in a particular circumstance; a quasi-rent is the difference between the asset's return in its best use and in its best alternate use. The more specific an asset, the larger the quasi-rent and the greater the loss to the asset's owner if forced to use it in some other activity. A machine that can only make Ford Escort nameplates is highly specific: its

---

[9] It is also the case that policy will depend on the industry's price elasticities. Where demand is completely elastic, whatever positive (negative) effects altered relative prices might have will simply be counteracted by the negative (positive) effect on the level of demand. The corresponding, possibly positive, effects of inelastic demand, however, will be negated if entry into the sector is free. We therefore focus on entry rather than demand or supply elasticities, recognizing that this glosses over one potentially important set of issues.

[10] Representative statements are in Benjamin Klein, Robert Crawford, and Armen Alchian, "Vertical Integration, Appropriable Rents, and the Competitive Contracting Process," *Journal of Law and Economics* 21, no. 2 (October 1978): 297–326; and Oliver Williamson, *The Economic Institutions of Capitalism* (New York: The Free Press, 1985). Attention to asset specificity and the related problems of transactions costs and incomplete contracts are central to modern industrial organization; see, for example, the surveys by Bengt Holmstrom and Jean Tirole, "The Theory of the Firm," and Martin Perry, "Vertical Integration: Determinants and Effects," in *Handbook of Industrial Organization* (Amsterdam: Elsevier, 1989), 1:61–133 and 1:183–255.

value to Ford may be great as long as Ford makes Escorts, but if Escorts are discontinued the machinery's next best use may be as scrap. The quasi-rent is the difference between the machine's value in current use and its salvage value, a very large difference in this case. Assets can be specific for many reasons, from mechanical or technical factors to less tangible personal contractual ties with suppliers or even less tangible reputations with consumers.

The more dependent an asset's rate of return on public policy, the greater the asset-holder's incentive to lobby for policy. Asset specificity captures both the amenability of relative prices to policy—the more specific an asset, the less relative price changes will be washed out by new entrants—and the redeployability of assets—the more specific an asset, the more costly its transfer to another use.

Expressed as a continuum, the returns to lobbying for specific government policies increase with asset specificity (quasi-rents). Owners of assets in an industry will expend resources to influence government policy toward their industry up to the point where it would make more sense for them to find another use for their resources. The greater the potential influence of policy on their earnings, the greater the incentive to lobby. The greater the cost of moving their human or physical assets to other activities, the greater the incentive to lobby.[11]

This abstract discussion can be made more concrete by describing the range of asset specificity found in the real world. Assets that are not specific at all are those that can easily be redeployed—demand deposits, financial assets more generally. Holders of completely liquid assets are indifferent to policy, for they can move their funds to whatever activity is earning the highest rate of return. Of course, these asset-holders have an incentive to oppose policies that repress the return to financial investments—interest-rate ceilings, for example—but beyond this they are indifferent as to the relative price structure. Similarly, physical capital of a standardized nature is relatively unspecific; if the machinery in a firm can easily be converted to another equally profitable use, its owner will have less incentive to lobby for government support.[12]

---

[11] This discussion, and the book as a whole, focuses on sector-specific economic policies as opposed to the provision of such public goods as education or the transportation infrastructure. It may well be that many problems of development are due to the undersupply of public goods, insufficient public performance of socially desirable activities. The issue merits more attention, but most observers would probably agree that it has been at best a secondary factor in Latin American economic development. Explicit attention is paid to the problem in Barbara Geddes, *Politician's Dilemma* (Berkeley: University of California Press, 1991).

[12] Robert Bates and Da-Hsiang Donald Lien, "A Note on Taxation, Development, and Representative Government," *Politics and Society* 14, no. 1 (1985): 53–70, argue on the contrary that owners of more liquid assets will have more influence over policy. Their as-

Asset specificity is generally associated with industries with high barriers to entry and unique technology, skills, and networks. A firm producing turbines for a Venezuelan hydroelectric power plant is likely to have a larger proportion of its assets tied up in things specific to this use than a firm producing men's clothing or bricks. Industries to which entry is difficult—those using specialized technologies or specialized networks of suppliers or customers—typically have the most specific assets, and therefore the greatest incentive to lobby for industry-specific policies.

I use asset specificity to include features of economic activities that are often thought of separately. One such feature is the existence of entry barriers to a particular industry. Another is the undiversified nature of an asset portfolio. Some might prefer to separate these attributes of economic actors, but I believe that they can be subsumed usefully under the rubric of asset specificity.[13]

The general point is that economic characteristics of assets determine the policy preferences of their owners. Such are, then, the purely economic determinants of pressure brought to bear on policymakers; and these determinants can usefully (although not exhaustively) be understood as a function of asset specificity. The incentive to lobby increases with the specificity of the asset.

Aggregation of Actors into Groups

It is not enough for actors to have an incentive to lobby; they must organize to exert effective political pressure. The above discussion concerns economic determinants of policy preferences, but we also need to discuss the political determinants of the translation of these policy preferences into pressure on policymakers. This involves the organization of individuals and firms into groups.

Once the policy preferences of social actors are determined, the next step is to figure out how these actors work with others to reach their goals. Indeed, political activity is generally carried out by or on behalf of groups, not individuals, and there are many ways in which the same in-

---

sertion is that the threat of exit that liquid asset-holders can bring to bear will lead policymakers to respond to their needs. This ignores—curiously for an article on politics—the role that political action would play, relying entirely on the policymakers' anticipation of the long-term economic effects of their policies. For this reason it seems to me inadequate as a predictor of economic policies in general; it may be more useful in analyzing long-term evolutionary pressures on policy or politics.

[13] See Williamson, *Economic Institutions of Capitalism*, 373–76. By the same token, asset specificity is the flip side of the contestability of markets, as in William Baumol, John Panzer, and Robert Willig, *Contestable Markets* (New York: Harcourt Brace Jovanovich, 1982).

dividuals and firms could be aggregated. A Mexican oil worker is also an oil consumer, as well as a taxpayer. These various attributes of an individual oil worker might pull him in different directions, and the analyst must make some determination of how the crosscutting interests can be weighted.

Two complementary tools can be used to predict how socioeconomic actors combine in the political arena. The first is purely economic and groups individuals and firms by shared economic characteristic, similarity of asset. Those with like assets are affected analogously by relative price changes. Individuals and firms facing equivalent economic conditions share interests that distinguish them from others: they, unlike others, care strongly about the fate of their industry, region, or sector. Those with like assets in the oil industry, for example, favor a higher price for oil and may tend to come together in defense of these interests. In this sense, group formation flows from the interaction of those with similar assets and interests. Oil workers cohere more naturally with each other than with other taxpayers or consumers; they share assets associated with their economic activity, while their experiences as taxpayers or consumers differ from those of other taxpayers and consumers. Individuals or firms tend to come together with others holding similar assets.

A second tool to determine what kinds of groups are likely to cohere is the logic of collective action.[14] The literature on collective action is based on such observations as, for example, that while all workers may gain from a strong union, union membership may be irrational for each individual worker. A worker benefits from union strength but incurs costs in joining the union, and union strength appears independent of one individual's actions. After all, one member less or more makes no difference. The rational action for the individual can be to "free ride," take the benefits without incurring the costs. Thus no worker may have a reason to join the union.

Some groups unite more easily than others. Organizations can come and stay together by overcoming the contradictions of collective action, especially the free-rider problem. The literature on collective action suggests that cohesion depends on such factors as the size of the group (the smaller the group, the easier to police its membership) and its ability to provide selective benefits to members (health plans only for union members). More generally, better information or enforcement mechanisms make it easier to sustain an organization. The point is that we cannot assume that individuals or firms with similar assets will automatically

[14] Mancur Olson, *The Logic of Collective Action: Public Goods and the Theory of Groups* (Cambridge: Harvard University Press, 1965), is the classic statement.

come together, and collective-action considerations illuminate who will organize more easily.[15]

The success of collective action depends in many ways on characteristics of industries that parallel the previous discussions of asset specificity and similar assets. The more concentrated the industry, the easier we would expect it to be able to exert political pressure. The greater the entry barriers, the more easily the industry will be able to avoid free riding by new entrants. The more similar the assets, the greater the ease of communication—including monitoring agreements—among those in the industry. As with asset specificity, then, we expect more concentrated industries able to exclude (or selectively include) members to be more politically influential.

Groups and Their Relations with Other Social Institutions

Once the policy preferences of socioeconomic interests are determined and their pattern of internal political organization is understood, the next step is to discover how organized interests work within or against existing institutions to achieve their goals. Here we define institutions broadly, to include all long-term agreements about patterns of social behavior—formal or informal social contracts. Groups themselves are thus institutions, but we treat them separately (as above) as building blocks for other social institutions. Such other institutions include lobbies and political parties: members abide by formal and informal rules in return for assistance from fellow members. Governmental structures are institutions: they exist only as social actors consent to observe their constraints. Specific public agencies are institutions: their employees, constituents, and targets all concede authority over some realm to the agency.

Organized groups can combine to work within existing institutions or to build new ones in a variety of ways. The same interest group, for example, could tie itself to several different parties. To return to the earlier case, even if we know that the economic interests of Mexican oil workers are dominated by their condition as oil workers rather than by their status as consumers or taxpayers, we still do not know how they will associate their interests with those of others. The oil workers might determine that they are best able to accomplish their goals in a class-based party, focusing on their common interests with other workers whose principal asset is their labor power. Alternatively, they might decide that their best po-

---

[15] This cursory discussion does not do justice to the rich literature on collective-action problems and glosses over such important considerations as the size of the stakes in question and actors' time horizons. For a classic exposition of the issues in question see Russell Hardin, *Collective Action* (Baltimore: Johns Hopkins University Press, 1982).

litical bet is a sectoral alliance with their managers and employers, as workers whose skills and seniority are industry-specific and whose income thus depends on the vicissitudes of the oil industry. In the former case, oil workers would ally politically with other workers, while in the latter they would associate with management in the oil sector. The political combinations and permutations relevant to the analysis of real-world political and economic problems are not inherently obvious, and energy must be devoted to exploring and comparing the various possible associations of interests.

In the first instance, we take prevailing institutions as given and explore how rational self-interested actors use these institutions to satisfy as many of their needs as possible. With a given party structure, an interest group must determine which party or faction is most likely to champion successfully its policy preferences. With a given bureaucratic design, a group must decide which agency is most amenable to its demands and best located to meet them. The members of organized interest groups can carry out cost-benefit calculations as they weave their way through existing institutions in pursuit of their goals.

In this "static" picture, with institutions held constant, interest groups can strategize to form coalitions. If several weak groups ally against a strong group, they may prevail and obtain policies to their liking. Protectionist lobbies, each of which cares only about its own product, can support each others' demands in return for votes; the result might be that a free-trade group larger than any other *single* group is defeated by an alliance of all other groups united only by the logic of log-rolling. Political influence depends on coalition-building.

In the second instance, we relax the assumption that institutions are static and evaluate the determinants of institutional change. Even those with strong preferences and extensive alliances can be stymied by institutions biased against them. Literacy requirements inflate the impact of some groups or regions and reduce that of others; many parliamentary structures overrepresent rural voters. Restrictive labor or voting laws curtail the influence of the working class, while such ethnic restrictions as apartheid and Jim Crow impede political action. Biased institutions lead victims of bias to weigh the possibility of changing the institutions, although this may involve a long, hard struggle, as in the American South and South Africa.

In this "dynamic" picture in which institutions can be changed, socioeconomic groups evaluate whether complying with the requirements of existing institutional structures is in their interest.[16] The first impulse is to

---

[16] It should be noted that, at least in the cases examined here, these costs and benefits are almost never truly measurable. All that we hope to do—and all that we expect the individ-

abide by strictures imposed by an existing party, bureaucratic, or other arrangement, because the cost of destroying old structures and building new ones is usually considerable. But if the costs of *obeying* existing strictures is high, it may be more attractive to consider changing the institutions. Calculation of the costs of institutional stasis and the benefits of institutional change may lead a group to try to eliminate and replace the institution. Parties split, interest-group pressure leads to the creation of new agencies, elite discontent takes the form of support for the military elimination of democratic political systems.

The responsibility of the analyst here is to explain how the constraints set by existing institutions affect the political activities of socioeconomic interests. This involves illuminating the process by which social actors work through markets, parties, bureaucracies, and political systems to obtain as many of their goals as possible. It also involves exploring the circumstances under which social actors attempt to change, eliminate, or replace prevailing institutions.

As promised, the above exposition of the method used in this book focuses on interest groups, who demand policy, rather than the government, which supplies it. This is appropriate, for the study directs most of its analytical attention to groups whose interests can be determined or inferred from socioeconomic indicators and theory rather than to policymaking processes that are generally opaque. However, nothing inherent in modern political economy precludes incorporation of—or, indeed, explanatory primacy for—the role of politicians and bureaucrats in affecting economic policy and political change.[17]

We could include government explicitly in this approach, for example, by assuming that politicians maximize the probability of staying in office. The next step is to examine policies most likely to improve a politician's chances. These policies might involve responding to special interests, playing to broader public opinion, or some mix. The specifics presumably vary according to the issue and the political system. The rational politician then weighs the political benefits of a particular policy against the political (or other) costs incurred by supporting it, and acts accordingly.[18]

One implication of an assumption that politicians are trying to maximize political support, which I use here, is that an increase in the avail-

---

uals and groups in question to do—is calculate the sign and general magnitude of the effect of institutional change on them.

[17] In fact, one of the fastest-growing areas of interest in American Political Science is in the application of economic models to the political process. A seminal article is Kenneth Shepsle and Barry Weingast, "Structure-Induced Equilibrium and Legislative Choice," *Public Choice* 37, no. 3 (1981): 503–19.

[18] In the Latin American context, this approach is reflected in Barry Ames, *Political Survival* (Berkeley: University of California Press, 1987), and in Geddes, *Politician's Dilemma*.

ability of resources to the government leads to increased government spending as politicians attempt to improve their political standing. However, I do not explore the full implications of this supply side of the story; I simply assume that in order to maximize their political survival politicians and policymakers must respond to politically powerful groups in society. This ignores such considerations as public opinion and bureaucratic politics in the interests of analytical and expository simplicity.

Policies and Politics

The above overview of the analytical framework used in this study can be brought to bear on two outcomes of interest. First, we are interested in *policy outcomes*, what government policies are adopted. Inasmuch as actors accept the institutional restrictions upon them, we want to know how their interaction leads to the dominance of the policy preferences of one group or coalition over another. This tries to explain what economic policies governments undertake. Second, we are interested in *political outcomes*, in whether, how, and when actors decide to reject, reform, or build political institutions. This tries to explain, most centrally, when democratic political forms come under attack and when authoritarian regimes collapse.

Where seeking to explain government policy toward a particular group, we begin with the costs and benefits to the government of supplying the policy. These costs are a function of the resources the government must expend to supply the policy; they decline as more resources become available. Taxes may increase; more important for our purposes, the interest rate charged to the government may drop. If interest rates fall and borrowing becomes easier, other things equal, we expect government to supply more of the policies demanded by society.

The benefits to the government of undertaking policies vary with the political pressure exerted by groups that stand to gain. This pressure is, as discussed above in detail, a function of economic and political characteristics of members of the various groups. On the economic side, the more specific a group's members' assets are to particular activities amenable to policy intervention, the more incentive they have to lobby for favorable policies. On the political side, the better able the group's members are to overcome collective action problems, the better able they will be to lobby for favorable policies. These are related to the level of asset specificity and concentration.

Where the thing to be explained is social behavior toward political institutions, we look at the costs and benefits to socioeconomic groups of accepting or rejecting existing political organizations. The less existing institutions provide the benefits a group demands, the more incentive it has to alter the institutions. The easier it is to alter an institution, the likelier it is that a disgruntled group will try to do so.

The method outlined above is continuous; effects in one time period feed back to causes in the next time period. Government economic policies alter economic conditions and change the economic interests of existing social groups—even create new economic interests. Trade liberalization may strengthen firms with free-trade interests; trade barriers may reinforce uncompetitive firms and intensify their protectionism. Alternatively, trade liberalization may lead to such a surge in imports that latent protectionist forces mobilize; or the proliferation of trade barriers may create such costs for unprotected industries and consumers that they mobilize and form a countervailing free-trade coalition. Similarly, social pressures that succeed in changing political institutions or building new ones affect future political interaction. Groups that prevail on the military to overthrow a democratic system they find unsatisfactory and replace it with a more amenable dictatorship may at some future point find that the insulation of the dictatorship is now working *against* rather than for them.

The general method to be used in this study can be summarized in four steps. The first step is to identify the policy preferences of individuals and firms, based on their position in the economy. The second step is to determine how they are grouped into politically relevant social forces, on the basis of both common economic interest and ability to overcome problems of collective action. The third step is to trace the aggregation of organized interests in the context of existing institutions, as they seek to obtain their preferred policies. The fourth step is to determine and trace the pressures for institutional change. The result is a series of new government policies and political institutions that create a new environment within which socioeconomic interests continue to contend.[19]

Examination of this process must start somewhere, and it is convenient to use as an analytical entry point changes in relative prices. The economic interests of social actors are a function of how their assets are influenced by the economic environment, and the most important component of the economic environment is the price of output and inputs. The relationship between the price of labor (wages) and the price of consumer

---

[19] It should be noted that this approach ignores most strategic aspects of political behavior, a topic that has attracted a great deal of attention among political scientists in recent years. This is not to deny the importance of strategic considerations in conflict and cooperation among social groups; the issue is neglected only for the sake of simplicity. The analytical structure presented here could easily be made far more complicated and more complete with the addition of such matters; we prefer to keep it as simple as possible at the starting point.

goods determines the living standard of workers; the relationship between the cost of labor plus raw materials and product prices determines the profit earned by capitalists. Changed prices are thus the crucial indicators (although not necessarily the underlying causes) of changed economic conditions.

The application of modern political economy developed here traces the effects of relative price changes induced by cross-border capital flows on the political economies of the five largest Latin American debtors. In so doing, it explores the characteristics of the central socioeconomic actors in the five countries, and how the interests of these actors were changed by the economic trends brought on by external borrowing and the financial crisis. It then investigates the politico-institutional setting within which these economic interests contended, in order to understand the policy and political outcomes. It thus analyzes the effects of foreign debt on economic interests, political behavior, policy outcomes, and political institutions in Argentina, Brazil, Chile, Mexico, and Venezuela during borrowing boom and bust.

The Application of Modern Political Economy to Latin America

The application of modern political economy in this study attempts to show how economic sectors and classes affected the different patterns of economic policy and political change in the five major Latin American borrowers. Here I present the principal divisions used in the analysis, a summary of how they fit into the framework discussed above, and a sketch of how I apply modern political economy to explain policies and politics of five Latin American debtors during borrowing and financial crisis.

I start by differentiating between two essential building blocks of my analysis, sectors and factors or classes.[20] In neoclassical economic terms all resources are factors of production, and individuals can be grouped either on the basis of their factor endowments or by the sector in which they employ their factor endowments. The definition of a factor is loose

[20] There are long traditions in economics of both factoral and sectoral interpretations of the interests of producers. The best-known of the former is the Stolper-Samuelson theorem, which identifies the interest of factors in trade policy; the best-known of the latter is the specific-factors approach, which focuses on sectoral interests in trade policies. For the former, see W. Stolper and P. Samuelson, "Protection and Real Wages," *Review of Economic Studies* 9, no. 1 (November 1941): 58–73; for the latter, see R. W. Jones, "A Three-Factor Model in Theory, Trade, and History," in *Trade, the Balance of Payments, and Growth*, ed. Jagdish Bhagwati (Amsterdam: North-Holland, 1971), 3–21. For one particularly imaginative application of the factoral approach to political economy, see Ronald Rogowski, *Commerce and Coalitions* (Princeton: Princeton University Press, 1989).

and can be as detailed as land fit for growing rice or technology to produce aspirin. It is more common, however, to define three or four principal factors of production—land, labor, capital, and sometimes human capital or skills. These factors overlap the classes and strata central to Marxist analysis—capitalists, proletarians, peasants, the petite bourgeoisie, and intelligentsia. Where factor endowment is the relevant grouping, the analysis is similar to Marxist class analysis: owners of capital act alike, owners of labor power act alike. However, many factors are specific as to use—physical capital to the steel industry, land to rice farming—and in this case the analysis looks at the sector to which the factor is specific. The two units of analysis employed, then, are classes (nonspecific factors), and sectors (sector-specific factors).

Classes

The distinction between those whose principal asset is capital and those whose principal asset is the ability to work—between capitalist and worker—is an important dividing line in all capitalist societies. The central difference between labor and capital, for the purposes of political economy, is in their interests in regard to the property right of the other, and more generally to income accruing to the other out of joint production. Since the returns to labor and capital are divided between the two, the income of one can be increased at the expense of the other. Workers thus have no immediate reason to respect private property rights for capital, since expropriation of the capital they work with would allow them to control distribution of the firm's income, presumably in their own favor. Of course, worker hostility to private property in capital can be tempered by many things: coercion, "false consciousness," or the conviction that the long-term costs of expropriation would outweigh short-term benefits.[21] Capitalists, on the other hand, have an obvious interest in protecting their own property rights.

Labor and capital may exert opposing pressure in the political arena inasmuch as property rights and the division of national income between wages and profits are concerned. In extreme instances, workers as a class may call for expropriation of capital, or of specific capitalists; they are more likely to raise demands that call into question profits to capital. This might include lobbying for increased wealth taxes, or for the nationalization of utilities or public transportation.

[21] For an exploration of this last possibility, see Adam Przeworski, "Material Interests, Class Compromise, and the Transition to Socialism," *Politics and Society* 10, no. 2 (1980): 125–53.

However accurate the stark divide between labor and capital may be in describing economic positions and interests in the last instance, it is far too stark for most analyses of modern political economies, which rarely approach the last instance. As even the above examples indicate, at all but the most extreme levels, the demands of workers, even when they endanger property rights in capital, are not necessarily inimical to those of capitalists as a class. Workers lobbying for nationalization of a utility to reduce residential electricity rates might be joined by capitalists who see an opportunity to reduce commercial rates. By the same token, capitalist resistance to attacks on property rights might well be joined by employees of the capitalists under attack, if the attack were motivated by a desire to liquidate the firm or sector as a whole. If workers in a power plant felt that nationalization and rate reductions would entail wage cuts for them, they might prefer to support private ownership.

This is not to imply that the labor-capital divide is never important. Varying attitudes to property rights, and to government policies toward the "investment climate," can separate capitalists and workers. Sometimes these differences are important enough to dominate other cleavages in society. Often they form an important backdrop to sectoral, regional, and other divisions. At times they fade into insignificance when compared to more immediate social conflicts.[22]

Sectors

Inasmuch as labor and capital cannot move without cost from sector to sector, from the steel industry to dairy farming, both factors of production in a sector have an incentive to try to maintain the economic attractiveness of the sector. Steelworkers and steel industrialists can make common cause in forming private cartels, demanding government subsidies

[22] One potential interpretation of the relationship between class (factoral) and sectoral interests is that the former tend to prevail in the long run, while the latter tend to prevail in the short run. If political horizons were characteristically shorter-term than economic, this would make factor endowments the predominant determinant of broad patterns of economic activity, and sectoral characteristics the predominant determinant of pressures on policy. Alternately, class issues would tend to increase in political importance over sectoral issues as actors' time horizons lengthen. The classic attempts to integrate sectoral and factoral considerations (specific and nonspecific factors, in more traditional economic terms) in the analysis of international trade are Wolfgang Mayer, "Short-Run and Long-Run Equilibrium for a Small Open Economy," *Journal of Political Economy* 82 (1974): 955–67; Michael Mussa, "Tariffs and the Distribution of Income: The Importance of Factor Specificity, Substitutibility, and Intensity in the Short and Long Run," *Journal of Political Economy* 82 (1974): 1191–1203; and J. Peter Neary, "Short-Run Capital Specificity and the Pure Theory of International Trade," *Economic Journal* 88 (1978): 488–510.

or seeking trade protection. Analysis based on the policy preferences of relatively united economic sectors has a long history in the study of Latin American political economy.[23]

Economic sectors are defined by output rather than by broadly defined factor endowment. The blue-collar workers, technicians, managers, and owners of a copper mine share an interest in the price of copper, even though they may be divided over how to allocate the returns to the firm among wages, salaries, and profits.

Identifiable sectors have played a major role in Latin American development. Perhaps the most famous such sectors are the export-oriented primary producers that were central to the continent until the onset of modern industrial development, and that remain important. Export-oriented primary producers were at the core of the "landed oligarchy" that is often associated in Latin America with antidemocratic, anti-urban, and anti-industrial trends. Another complex of sectors central to Latin American political economies is modern industry. Tertiary ("service") sectors have also been significant in Latin America, most prominently trade, finance, and government services.

Sectoral interests are complex and crosscutting. Each sector can be divided into sub-sectors; each sub-sector can be further divided until we reach the level of the firm. The difficulty of tracing and understanding the relevant divisions and preferences calls for the use of as systematic an analytical method as possible; the discussion above of asset specificity and concentration describes the method used here.

Explaining Economic Policies in Latin America

The easy availability to Latin America of foreign finance after 1965 presented governments with policy options. When financial markets opened, policymakers had to decide how the new resources would be allocated.[24] Governments determined whether to allow access to foreign funds to all who could borrow, only to the government itself, or to a favored few. If the government borrowed, it had to decide what to do with the new re-

---

[23] Sectoral analyses are to be found in virtually all modern treatments of Latin American politics and economics. For explicit examples, see Markos J. Mamalakis, "The Theory of Sectoral Clashes," *Latin American Research Review* 4, no. 3 (1969): 9–46, and Markos J. Mamalakis, "The Theory of Sectoral Clashes and Coalitions Revisited," *Latin American Research Review* 6, no. 3 (1971): 89–126; and Dale Story, *Sectoral Clash and Industrialization in Latin America* (Syracuse, N.Y.: Maxwell School, 1981).

[24] It should be noted that the five Latin American countries had all made a prior decision to *allow* foreign borrowing by private or public actors. A few developing countries chose not to borrow at all, although they had access to international financial markets. This choice was very rare, however, and certainly not characteristic of Latin America.

sources; if it limited private-sector foreign borrowing, it had to decide who would be permitted to borrow and how much.

The modern political economy framework developed above leads to a series of analytical propositions about the determinants of government policies in circumstances such as these. To start with, political support-maximizing policymakers, faced with growth in the resources available to them, increase their aid to political supporters. The next step is to determine which groups are more likely to be politically important to policymakers. Three central propositions drive my explanations of Latin American economic policy during the borrowing period.

1. **The more specific a sector's assets, the more political pressure it exerts and the more influence it has on government policy.** The specificity of the sector's assets affects what is often called the intensity of its preferences: the more tied to its current activities, the greater the intensity of the sector's preferences. Put another way, the higher the opportunity cost to a sector of not obtaining favorable government policies, the more likely the sector will be to seek these policies. This compares the return on sectoral assets in the absence of policy with the value of favorable policies (the cost of lobbying is assumed to be constant for all sectors): the less successful the sector would be without public support, and the more costly it would be for it to redeploy its assets, the more likely it is to lobby for this support.

A subset of this category is sectors whose profitability is dependent upon existing government policies, the specificity of whose assets thus depends directly upon government action. Sectors that are relatively indifferent to government policy will be less willing to spend energy on political mobilization than those whose interests are very dependent upon policy. Our principal indicator here is the ability of sectoral asset-holders to prosper without government support.

Pressure for government support will come primarily from those sectors in which firms and individuals are "caught" in highly specific assets, especially if returns to these assets can be strongly affected by government policies. The prediction here is that sectors with more specific assets—higher entry barriers, less diversified portfolios—exert more pressure on policymakers and obtain more favorable policies.

2. **The greater the internal cohesion of a sector, the more political pressure it can bring to bear and the more influence it has on policy.** The more successful a sector is in coming together to make common demands on policymakers, the more powerful will be the pressure it can exert. Sectoral cohesion flows both from cooperation among capitalists and among laborers, and from cooperation between labor and capital in the sector: the more disunited owners and workers or the more hostile labor-management relations, the weaker the sector's political cohesion.

One determinant of sectoral cohesion is the level of concentration of the sector. The fewer the firms in the sector—that is, the more oligopolistic the sector—the more likely they are to be able to cooperate in the political arena. Another determinant of sectoral cohesion is the character of relations between labor and capital, specifically whether workers and capitalists unite in making sectoral demands or divide along class lines. Where conflict dominates, the sector will not formulate unified demands on policymakers and will be less likely to achieve its goals. The prediction here is that more concentrated and united sectors will be more effective in obtaining favorable policies.

These two propositions imply that government economic policies of Latin American borrowers are expected to favor more concentrated sectors with more specific assets. Such sectors generally include sophisticated manufacturing, such as the automotive, chemicals, and machinery sectors; in some societies they include technically advanced modern agribusiness. Indeed, during the borrowing period in Brazil, Mexico, and Venezuela, governments expended or directed enormous subsidies and incentives, funded directly or indirectly by foreign borrowing, toward such manufacturing and agribusiness sectors. To some extent, such patterns were observed in Argentina and Chile, but politics in these two countries was dominated by class cleavages, which overrode sectoral demands. The following proposition makes the difference explicit.

3. Where class conflict is salient, it overrides sectoral demands, and policy focuses on the general investment climate. An important determinant of a sector's internal cohesion is the character of relations between labor and capital, specifically whether workers and capitalists unite in making sectoral demands or divide along class lines. Where conflict dominates, the sector will not formulate unified demands on policymakers and will be less likely to achieve its goals.

To generalize this to society as a whole, inasmuch as class conflict is the principal consideration of capitalists and workers, issues of property rights, wages, and profits dominate concerns over the return to specific activities. In these circumstances, capitalists press government to maintain or restore an attractive climate for investment, often against labor, rather than unite with labor for sectoral demands. Put another way, where the predominant social cleavage is factoral (between labor and capital), the central policy issues are the distribution of income between wage and profits rather than the allocation of resources to sectors.

In the Latin American context, policy to restore or safeguard the investment climate for capital as a class has tended to take on market-oriented characteristics as opposed to more interventionist sectoral policies. This has to do with historical properties of the Latin American political economies that will become evident in the chapters that follow. It is not to imply that the market is inherently antilabor, only that in the Latin American context organized labor's interests were closely tied to past patterns of sectoral intervention. By the same token, I do not purport to explain the prevalence or absence of class conflict in the societies under study at the point when borrowing began; I simply take it as given.

The prediction here is that in societies where disputes between labor and capital are of particular importance, the government concentrates on restoring or maintaining the general investment climate and ignores or opposes sectoral demands for specific policy intervention. In this context, the salience of labor-capital conflict in Chile and Argentina during the borrowing period explains the broad tendency of their governments to pursue market-oriented policies with few sector-specific features. Chile, where class cleavages were deeper and more hostile, was more extreme in this than Argentina, but both differed noticeably from the other three.

My explanation of the type of government economic policies pursued in the allocation of external financial resources in Latin America after 1965 thus rests on the interaction of sectoral and class forces. The norm is a country in which sectoral cleavages dominate, in which the division of national income between profits and wages or property rights are not at issue. In this case, policymakers are expected to pursue the administrative allocation of resources in line with the political influence of the various sectors. In other words, the political weight of each sector—a function of the specificity of its assets and its concentration—determines the degree to which the sector will be favored by policy. However, in societies characterized by serious class conflict, whether over the division of national income between profits and wages or over property rights, sectoral cleavages are expected to be overridden by factoral cleavages, and governments are expected to pursue more market-oriented policies.

Explaining the Political Effects of the Debt Crisis in Latin America

As for domestic *political* responses to external financial trends, I focus on the crisis after 1981. International financial events in the early 1980s led to political upheaval in all five nations, with very different eventual outcomes.

When the financial crisis hit, governments suddenly had fewer resources available to allocate. Worse, debtor societies had to undertake real resource transfers abroad. Real wages and consumption had to be reduced in order to increase exports and reduce imports, so that foreign exchange could be channeled to foreign creditors. Government revenues had to rise and expenditures had to fall to free up resources for debt service payments. The resulting economic crisis in Latin America rivaled that of the 1930s in severity.

The ready availability of funds during the borrowing period provided a permissive environment for the typical Latin American government. It could take advantage of foreign finance, or not, as it wished. But the elimination of the borrowing option imposed a severe constraint: the government had no choice but to reduce spending and, in most instances, increase its income. This made it impossible for policymakers to satisfy as many of the political pressures as they had while borrowing. While the pie was growing, there was little conflict over its distribution; once it began to shrink, political strife erupted.

In this context, socioeconomic actors contended in the battle to maintain access to reduced government resources. In some countries, this pressure flowed through existing political structures; in others, it turned into demands for a change in the political system itself, which sometimes led to regime change, especially democratization. My concern is to understand the reasons for the different political outcomes during the crisis.

I explain patterns of political activity in the crisis on the basis of the previous discussions of factoral and sectoral pressures for policies and of the sources of institutional change. The central policy issues in the debt crisis had to do with which groups governments would continue to assist and which would find public support curtailed or eliminated. These issues became eminently political when existing political regimes were unable to satisfy new social demands, and major socioeconomic actors turned from pressures for policy changes within existing institutions toward pressures for new institutions altogether.

When the policy demands made by those affected by the crisis are not met by existing political institutions, I expect the sectors involved to demand institutional change, such as democratization. The insistence, power, and success of these demands for political change depend, as above, on the social groups' internal cohesion and the intensity of their policy preferences. The general view proposed is that institutional changes—especially altered political structures and regimes—are not the result of demands for these changes per se, but rather are "tools" of socioeconomic actors who find that they cannot achieve their policy goals within existing institutions.

Figure 1.1 is a simple representation of how a crisis might affect political behavior. The crisis begins (1) with different effects on different groups (2). On some, the crisis has a positive or neutral impact, and they are expected to exert no pressure on the government for relief. On other groups, however, the crisis has a negative effect, and they are expected to pressure policymakers for government support (3). The government responds to the crisis and accompanying social pressures with a set of pol-

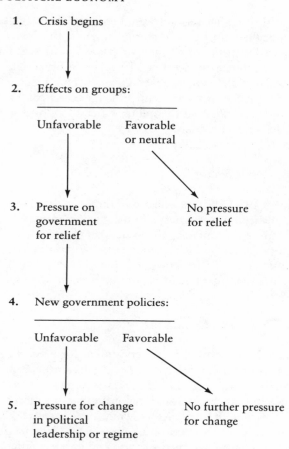

1.   Crisis begins

2.   Effects on groups:

     _____

     Unfavorable   Favorable
                      or neutral

3.   Pressure on   No pressure
     government   for relief
     for relief

4.   New government policies:

     _____

     Unfavorable   Favorable

5.   Pressure for change   No further pressure
     in political   for change
     leadership or regime

Figure 1.1. Stylized Evolution of Crisis Politics

icies (4). These policies alleviate the distress of some, who cease their lob-bying for government support. The policies do not offer relief or offer insufficient relief to others, and these groups consider working for a change in *policymakers* (5) to some more favorably disposed. This takes the form of pressure for institutional change if the possibilities of replacing policymakers are slim within the current political system. In all these steps, the class and sectoral determinants of political influence discussed above are important.

The predictions flow from this discussion. The most powerful demands for relief from the crisis come from concentrated sectors with specific assets. Sectors whose demands are not met by governments move to support for a viable political opposition, where one exists, or to support for a change in political regime. As before, in societies where class cleavages are paramount, they mute such sectoral demands. In Mexico and Venezuela disgruntled sectors shifted their support to parties and movements out of power, with varying degrees of success. In Brazil and Argentina, sectoral dissatisfaction led to successful demands for a change in regime, from military to civilian government. In Chile, class conflict dampened sectoral complaints, allowing the military dictatorship to stay in power throughout the economic crisis.

The Role of Other Factors

The framework of modern political economy can, and in the hands of others does, incorporate a variety of other factors into analysis. My application of it to Latin America, however, is quite restricted in its reliance on the economic interests of private actors. Without addressing objections from outside the orbit of modern political economy, I can indicate several variables that might be incorporated into the analysis.

International Economic Conditions

Although financial conditions were very similar for the five countries under study, as will be discussed in chapter 2, other aspects of their international economic relations differed. This is simply an example of the general principle that the international economic position of a country includes a very wide variety of factors, which may not move together. Nor do the less developed countries (LDCs) in general face identical international economic conditions; their exports and imports differ, as do their underlying endowments and their historically established ties with other nations. All of these can be expected to affect national economic policies.

Institutions

It is widely recognized that sociopolitical institutions can have a significant effect on social interaction. Because there is a cost to ignoring or changing an institution, most actors most of the time play by the existing rules of the game. For this reason, political institutions can affect both the content of policy and the outcomes of political behavior. This fact has given rise to an enormous literature within modern political economy.[25]

[25] Douglass C. North, "The New Institutional Economics," *Journal of Institutional and Theoretical Economics* 142 (1986): 230–37, is a good survey of the state of the art.

Nonetheless, I generally ignore the independent explanatory effect of institutions and focus on the direct influence of economic interest groups.

Political and Bureaucratic Interests

I focus almost entirely on political pressures brought to bear on government by private groups and individuals. I downplay the possibility that a significant set of pressures may have emanated from the bureaucratic or political institutions of the government itself. The most obvious candidate for inclusion is the military, which played a major role in three of the five countries. Military organizations may have interests of their own, from larger budgets to control over resources; they may also have strong preferences about issues with potential military implications such as strategic doctrine, diplomatic alliances, and protection for national armaments manufacturers.[26]

The economic bureaucracy, which in my analysis is essentially a reactor to private demands, may also have interests of its own. Ministry officials and employees, parastatal managers and workers, and central bank officers may all have stakes in policy disputes different from those of their constituents in the private sector. Most obviously, they seek to maximize the resources available to the bureaucracy and control over their use.[27] Politicians may use policy to divert resources toward them, either for simple pecuniary reasons or because they can use these resources to strengthen their own political position.[28]

Ideology

What interest groups demand, and what governments are willing to supply, may depend on ideological views prevalent among the relevant population. General ideological acceptance of the military dangers of communism may predispose public opinion to look favorably upon military demands for more weaponry; ideological belief in the moral superiority of laissez faire may favor support for trade liberalization.

[26] See, for example, Alfred Stepan, *Rethinking Military Politics: Brazil and the Southern Cone* (Princeton: Princeton University Press, 1988), especially 66–127.

[27] The classic statement of this case in general is William Niskanen, *Bureaucracy and Representative Government* (Chicago: Aldine, 1971). Barbara Geddes evaluates the evolution and activities of more or less autonomous bureaucracies in "Building 'State' Autonomy in Brazil, 1930–1964," *Comparative Politics* 22, no. 2 (January 1990): 217–35; and Geddes, *Politician's Dilemma*.

[28] This is the thread running through Barry Ames, *Political Survival*.

In a view consonant with modern political economy, for example, ideology can serve as a signal among potential transactors. Shared ideologies can help hold disparate coalitions together and can transmit useful information among members of coalitions.[29] This approach can probably be applied fruitfully to Latin American politics and economic policy, where ideological lines are often well-defined.[30]

Strategic Interaction

Game-theoretical approaches to politics and political economy highlight the potential importance of strategic interaction among forward-looking agents. There is little doubt that the degree to which political actors take the response of others into account in formulating their strategies has a major impact on these strategies.[31] "Strategic" interest groups can misrepresent their interests, log-roll, and bargain in ways that severely complicate the translation of economic interest into policy position, and I generally ignore this possibility. I similarly ignore the possibility that existing political institutions might lead economic interest groups to alter their publicly expressed policy preferences.

Omnipotence

The argument presented here explains only a portion of the reality it examines. The variables used to explain economic policies and political activity are themselves the result of socioeconomic and political processes, and there is no theoretical justification for cutting into the problem at an arbitrary midpoint. For example, I argue that the asset specificity and concentration of sectors are major determinants of the demand and sup-

[29] North, *Structure and Change in Economic History*, 45–58, contains an interesting discussion of ideology. Of course, in the presence of uncertainty, ideological blinders might lead to otherwise undesirable outcomes, as in Timur Kuran, "The Tenacious Past: Theories of Personal and Collective Conservatism," *Journal of Economic Behavior and Organization* 10 (1988): 143–71.

[30] A good example of the application of modern political economy to ideological variables is the so-called reputational or partisan approach to political business cycles, in which politicians have an incentive to favor one group or ideology over another for self-interested electoral reasons. See, for instance, Douglas Hibbs, *The Political Economy of Industrial Democracies* (Cambridge: Harvard University Press, 1987); Alberto Alesina and Jeffrey Sachs, "Political Parties and the Business Cycle in the United States, 1948–1984," *Journal of Money, Credit, and Banking* 20 (1988): 63–82.

[31] George Tsebelis, *Nested Games* (Berkeley: University of California Press, 1990), is an application of models of strategic interaction to comparative politics.

ply of policy; but I do not explain *why* some sectors' assets are more specific than others, or why some sectors are more concentrated than others. More broadly, I argue that the level of class conflict is related in the Latin American context to the degree to which policy will be market-oriented; but I do not explain why class conflict is more bitter in some countries than in others.

All of these variables and more would have to be incorporated into a complete explanation of the recent Latin American experience. The fact that I choose to leave them aside at the outset does not mean that I "censor" them from the case studies; where they are empirically important, I discuss them. It does mean that I assert that economic interest groups are the most compelling explanation of the outcomes examined here. In chapter 7 I return to these omitted variables to see what the case studies can tell us about their implications.

Summary

This is a study of the response of five Latin American countries to changes in the international financial environment from about 1965 until 1985. It focuses on explaining patterns of economic policy and political activity in the countries in question; its explanations rely on the interaction of sectoral and class conflict within the borrowing countries. The method used assumes that individuals and firms act rationally to maximize their economic well-being, and explores how socioeconomic groups cohere, form alliances, bargain, and work through existing institutions or create new ones in pursuit of their goals. It attempts to explain why the five countries in question undertook the types of economic policies they did during the financial expansion of the 1970s, and why their political systems responded as they did to the financial crisis of the 1980s.

2

The Setting: Latin American Political Economies
and International Financial Trends

THE RESPONSES of the five major Latin American debtors to external financial conditions in the 1970s and 1980s provide an excellent opportunity to study the politics of economic development and the economics of political development. At the outset of the period, although differences among them should not be minimized, the five nations were similar enough to allow comparison. The international financial conditions they faced were largely out of their control and broadly similar for all five. However, their economic policies during the borrowing period and subsequent financial crisis and their political behavior during the economic turmoil of the crisis varied widely. The episode is probably as close to laboratory conditions as we are likely to find for the issues at hand, as several crucial variables can be held constant. The level of economic development and external financial "shocks" are roughly comparable for all five countries, so that differences in their economic policy and political responses to international financial events can usefully be contrasted. Our goal is to identify the variables that explain the variety of economic policies pursued in the borrowing period and the contrasting political results of the financial crisis that began in 1982.

This chapter sets the basis for the investigation that follows by explaining domestic conditions at the start of the analysis and the character of external financial events. I begin with discussion of the baseline, the general socioeconomic and political situation within the five countries at the outset of the study. This requires a very brief sketch of modern Latin American economic and political history. I then describe the evolution of the international financial environment after 1965. Here I explain why I regard the international financial relations of the five countries as driven by external factors rather than by decisions made within the countries themselves. The section includes a description of international financial trends since 1965. The chapter thus summarizes the domestic and international baselines for the five-country comparison.

The Domestic Setting: A Survey of Modern Latin American Economic and Political Development

In this section I describe schematically the economic and political history of Latin America before 1965 in order to present a rudimentary picture of the "starting point" for our analysis. Discussions of specific countries are left for the case studies, and there is no pretense that the treatment here is anything but indicative; indeed, it purposely glosses over many national differences. Nor is this an attempt to apply the analytical arguments developed in chapter 1 to Latin American history, for this would be too controversial. Its objective is to describe in very broad outline, and in ways that reflect the scholarly consensus, the contours of economic and political activity at the time external borrowing began.[1]

Modern Latin American economic growth began in the 1860s, after the turmoil of the independence and postindependence periods settled. The continent was pre-industrial, and growth was concentrated in the primary sectors, especially mining and agriculture. Although there is some dispute about how crucial foreign trade was at the outset of the modern era,[2] by the late nineteenth century international trade and finance were at the center of the area's economic life, and the most dynamic sectors and regions were tied to rapidly growing international markets.

[1] It would be foolish to try to list full references for so broad-gauged a discussion of modern Latin American economic history. A good start is the *Cambridge History of Latin America*; a more superficial account is Celso Furtado, *Economic Development of Latin America* (New York: Cambridge University Press, 1970). Important country sources include Annibal Villela and Wilson Suzigan, *Government Policy and the Economic Growth of Brazil, 1889–1945*, Brazilian Economic Studies no. 3 (Rio de Janeiro: IPEA/INPES, 1977); Nathaniel Leff, *Underdevelopment and Development in Brazil*, vol. 1: *Economic Structure and Change, 1822–1947* (London: George Allen and Unwin, 1982); Werner Baer, *The Brazilian Economy: Growth and Development*, 2d ed. (New York: Praeger, 1983); Markos Mamalakis, *The Growth and Structure of the Chilean Economy: From Independence to Allende* (New Haven: Yale University Press, 1976); Leopoldo Solís, *La realidad económica mexicana: Retrovisión y perspectivas*, 16th ed. (Mexico City: Siglo Veintiuno, 1987); Roger D. Hansen, *The Politics of Mexican Development* (Baltimore: Johns Hopkins University Press, 1971); Ramón J. Velásquez et al., *Venezuela moderna: Medio siglo de historia 1926–1976*, 2d ed. (Caracas: Editorial Ariel, 1979); Oscar Echevarría, *La economía venezolana 1944–1984* (Caracas: FEDECAMARAS, 1984); Carlos Diaz Alejandro, *Essays in the Economic History of the Argentine Republic* (New Haven: Yale University Press, 1970); and David Rock, *Argentina, 1516–1982: From Spanish Colonization to the Falklands War* (Berkeley: University of California Press, 1985). More detailed historical references are found in the country chapters.

[2] For a well-known attack on those who give primacy to external economic ties, see D. C. M. Platt, "Dependency in Nineteenth-Century Latin America: An Historian Objects," *Latin American Research Review* 15, no. 1 (1980): 113–49.

Primary exports to and capital imports from the developed countries were especially important to the region. Argentine beef and wheat, Brazilian coffee, Mexican copper, and Chilean nitrate all found their principal markets in Europe and North America. Finance to import capital equipment, expand transportation systems, and build new urban centers flowed to Latin America, especially from London.[3]

Not surprisingly, domestic social groups tied to exports and foreign finance came to dominate the continent's political economies. The groups varied from country to country, but almost everywhere they included major primary producers—Argentine cattle ranchers, Brazilian coffee planters, Mexican miners—as well as those in foreign trade, finance, and related sectors. The region's political systems were dominated by the primary producers and their allies.[4]

The political economy of these export-led economies matured after 1890 as economic and social diversification proceeded. Urban centers grew, and more varied productive structures developed. Industrialization began, as production for local markets became more attractive. Economic and social deepening had political effects, and in some countries (especially Argentina and Uruguay) governing coalitions expanded to include middle classes and portions of the urban working classes.[5]

By the early 1900s, despite general economic prosperity, social and political strains began to appear. The first major indication of their depth was the Mexican Revolution of 1910–1920. The economic implications of World War I had further social and political consequences.[6] What sociopolitical harmony was restored by the export boom of the 1920s dis-

[3] Among the many studies of European–Latin American economic relations in the late nineteenth and early twentieth centuries are Roberto Cortés Conde and Shane Hunt, eds., *The Latin American Economies: Growth and the Export Sector, 1880–1930* (New York: Holmes and Meier, 1985); H. S. Ferns, *Britain and Argentina in the Nineteenth Century* (Oxford: Oxford University Press, 1960); A. G. Ford, *The Gold Standard, 1880–1914: Britain and Argentina* (Oxford: Oxford University Press, 1962); Richard Graham, *Britain and the Onset of Modernization in Brazil, 1850–1914* (Cambridge: Cambridge University Press, 1968); D. C. M. Platt, *Latin America and British Trade, 1806–1914* (London: A. and C. Black, 1972); and D. C. M. Platt, ed., *Business Imperialism 1840–1930: An Enquiry Based on British Experience in Latin America* (Oxford: Clarendon Press, 1977).

[4] Excellent case studies are Warren Dean, *The Industrialization of São Paulo, 1880–1945* (Austin: University of Texas Press, 1969); Theodore Moran, *Multinational Corporations and the Politics of Dependence: Copper in Chile* (Princeton: Princeton University Press, 1974); and Peter Smith, *Politics and Beef in Argentina: Patterns of Conflict and Change* (New York: Columbia University Press, 1969).

[5] For example, David Rock, *Politics in Argentina, 1890–1930: The Rise and Fall of Radicalism* (New York: Cambridge University Press, 1975).

[6] For a survey of the important new work on the impact of World War I on the Latin American economies, see Rory Miller, "Latin American Manufacturing and the First World War: An Exploratory Essay," *World Development* 9, no. 8 (August 1981): 707–16.

solved as foreign markets collapsed with the Great Depression. The dislocations of the 1930s and 1940s accelerated Latin America's economic, social, and political evolution.

After 1929, a succession of trade and financial, supply and demand shocks spurred industrial development and social change. They also contributed to the rise of nationalist populism throughout the continent.[7] The first disturbance was the collapse of trade that began in 1929, which caused massive declines in export earnings. The region's terms of trade, the relationship between prices earned by its exports and prices paid for its imports, fell disastrously; between 1929 and 1932 Mexico's terms of trade dropped 40 percent, Chile's 45 percent. Although export prices rose gradually after 1934, by 1939 the continent as a whole had seen its terms of trade deteriorate by 32.5 percent from their 1929 level.

As foreign demand for Latin American exports declined and prices for these export products went down, the ability of Latin America to import plummeted. To take the most extreme case, the volume of Chile's exports dropped by over 70 percent between 1929 and 1932; this, combined with the decline in world prices for Chilean products, meant that the country's exports went from $283 million in 1929 to $20 million in 1931. As import prices fell more slowly than export prices, the purchasing power of Chilean exports in 1932 was 85 percent below what it was in 1929.

The effects of the crisis varied from country to country, but all of Latin America faced a combination of declining demand and falling terms of trade that seriously reduced its ability to import goods. In addition, foreign financial markets dried up after 1930. Before the crash, Latin America had financed many of its imports by borrowing abroad; after the crash, not only did export earnings decline, but the option of borrowing foreign currency in order to import disappeared.[8]

Despite national variations, the general effect of the crisis of the 1930s was that Latin America earned far less on its exports and had to pay far more for its imports. This inevitably meant that the continent would shift

[7] On the economic trends of the 1930s in Latin America, see especially Carlos Diaz Alejandro, "Stories of the 1930s for the 1980s," in *Financial Policies and the World Capital Market,* ed. Pedro Aspe Armella, Rudiger Dornbusch, and Maurice Obstfeld (Chicago: University of Chicago Press, 1983), 5–35; Carlos Diaz Alejandro, "Latin America in Depression, 1929–39," in *The Theory and Experience of Economic Development: Essays in Honor of Sir W. Arthur Lewis,* ed. Mark Gersovitz et al. (London: George Allen and Unwin, 1982), 334–55; Rosemary Thorp, ed., *Latin America in the 1930s* (New York: St. Martin's Press, 1984); Angus Maddison, *Two Crises: Latin America and Asia, 1929–38 and 1973–83* (Paris: OECD, 1985); and Furtado, *Economic Development of Latin America,* 54–57. Figures used here are from Maddison.

[8] A good survey of the financial experiences of the 1920s and 1930s is in Carlos Marichal, *A Century of Debt Crises in Latin America* (Princeton: Princeton University Press, 1989), 171–228.

its economic activities away from production for export and toward production to satisfy domestic demand that could no longer be met by expensive imports. The process of import substitution—the replacement of previously imported goods by local production—went on naturally, even where governments did nothing to encourage it, driven by the skyrocketing domestic price of imported goods. The export-oriented agricultural and mining sectors were in disarray, while the production of industrial and agricultural goods for local markets grew rapidly.[9]

Import substitution was reinforced by war in Europe and the Pacific. If the depression increased the domestic price of foreign goods, World War II made many of them unavailable. Traditional suppliers of manufactured goods to Latin America were preoccupied with war production, and even essential capital equipment was hard to come by. At the same time, the war increased demand for some Latin American exports, especially raw materials and agricultural products essential to the war effort. The result was something of an export boom along with a considerable improvement in the terms of trade.[10] This boom continued through European reconstruction and the Korean War; Latin American exports went from $1.6 billion in 1940 to $7.8 billion in 1951, while the region's terms of trade improved by 62 percent.[11] Since the range of foreign goods available during the war was small, most Latin American countries simply accumulated foreign currency, which they used to buy capital equipment and other necessities after the war ended. International economic trends in the 1940s and early 1950s intensified the inward orientation of the Latin American economies by reducing the availability of foreign manufactured goods.

The economic shift away from an emphasis on exports to the satisfaction of domestic demand had inevitable social and political repercussions. By the late 1940s and early 1950s, the major Latin American countries had gone quite far on the road to urbanization and industrialization. The continent as a whole produced over 90 percent of what it consumed, including most industrial goods. Manufacturing was 19 percent of the combined Latin American gross domestic product (GDP), ranging in the major nations from 19 percent in Mexico to over 23 percent in Argentina and Chile. The portion of the male labor force employed in manufacturing in

[9] An outstanding study of the Brazilian process is Pedro S. Malan, Regis Bonelli, Marcelo de P. Abreu, and José Eduardo de C. Pereira, *Política econômica externa e industrialização no Brasil (1939/52)* (Rio de Janeiro: IPEA/INPES, 1980).

[10] Carlos Diaz Alejandro, "The 1940s in Latin America," in *Economic Structure and Performance: Essays in Honor of Hollis B. Chenery*, ed. Moshe Syrquin, Lance Taylor and Larry Westphal (New York: Harcourt Brace Jovanovich, 1984), is a comprehensive survey.

[11] Barbara Stallings, *Banker to the Third World* (Berkeley: University of California Press, 1987), 364–71.

the two last countries, about one-fifth, was similar to that in the United States in the 1890s. By 1950 over one-quarter of the continent's people lived in cities of more than twenty thousand, a level reached by continental Europe only after 1900. The literacy rate was over 80 percent in Argentina and Chile and over 50 percent in most of the rest of the region. National income per person, after growing by 22 percent between 1900 and 1929, rose by 39 percent from 1929 to 1952, by which time it was nearly half that of Western Europe.[12]

Urbanization and industrialization reinforced the influence of new social groups whose political power was soon felt. Pressures from industrial entrepreneurs, small businessmen, urban middle classes, government functionaries, and industrial workers came to dominate the political systems of the continent's major nations. In many countries, the formative political mobilization of these groups came in the interwar years, when they fashioned social coalitions to oppose the political power of traditional elites tied to primary production for export. The resultant pattern of political participation varied from country to country, but it generally included a mixture of nationalism, developmentalism, and populism. The typical model was a multiclass alliance aimed at protecting the domestic economy from a hostile external environment, encouraging the growth of national industry, and redistributing income away from traditional sectors toward the modern urban economy. In one way or another—most notably under the aegis of Vargas in Brazil, Perón in Argentina, and Cárdenas in Mexico—politics was remade in the context of an implicit or explicit alliance of domestically oriented businessmen with the urban working and middle classes.[13]

World trade and payments returned to relative normalcy after the Korean War, but Latin America did not revert to previous patterns of economic activity. To be sure, export markets were expanding and foreign capital was again available—now primarily in the form of North American multinational corporations—but the previous twenty-five years of

[12] Figures, which are meant only to be illustrative, are from Paul Bairoch, *The Economic Development of the Third World since 1900* (Berkeley: University of California Press, 1977), 79–82, 136, 149–51, 191; and from *Statistical Abstract of Latin America (SALA)* (Los Angeles: UCLA Latin American Center), various issues.

[13] Representative studies include Charles C. Mueller, *Das oligarquias agrárias ao predomínio urbano-industrial* (Rio de Janeiro: IPEA/INPES, 1983); John D. Wirth, *The Politics of Brazilian Development, 1930–1954* (Stanford: Stanford University Press, 1970); Carlos Waisman, *Reversal of Development in Argentina* (Princeton: Princeton University Press, 1987); Kenneth Erickson, *The Brazilian Corporative State and Working-Class Politics* (Berkeley: University of California Press, 1977); Nora Hamilton, *The Limits of State Autonomy: Post-Revolutionary Mexico* (Princeton: Princeton University Press, 1982); and Paul Drake, *Socialism and Populism in Chile, 1932–1952* (Urbana: University of Illinois Press, 1978).

inward-oriented development had strengthened opposition to a return to the "Golden Age" of export-led growth. Industrial development had taken place very largely free from international competition, and prices, wages, and profits prevailing in Latin American industries were well above those prevailing on world markets. In this context, national governments, along with industrialists and industrial workers, were generally unwilling to revert to free-trade liberalism.[14]

As international commerce and investment were restored, government policy evolved to protect the industries that had grown up. Most Latin American governments embraced import-substituting industrialization (ISI), the development of domestic industries to satisfy local demand for manufactured products.[15] ISI involved quantitative restrictions and tariffs on imports, multiple exchange rates that made it expensive to import finished goods in competition with local producers but cheap to import the capital equipment and inputs that local manufacturers needed, government credit or fiscal subsidies to domestic industrial investment and production, public-sector provision of subsidized inputs to industry, and government controls on the activities of foreign-owned corporations.

Latin American industrial growth in the 1950s and 1960s was impressive, spurred by pent-up demand, government support, and foreign investment. By 1970, manufacturing was 25 percent of the region's combined GDP.[16] The continent's major nations produced almost all of the manufactured goods they consumed, including such consumer durables as household appliances and automobiles. Only more complex capital equipment continued to be imported, and even here domestic capital goods industries were growing rapidly.

Industrial development policies adopted after World War II had important effects on Latin American social structures. The region's pattern of development tended to strengthen labor and capital in modern industry

[14] On postwar trade policies, see Joel Bergsman, *Brazil: Industrialization and Trade Policies* (London: Oxford University Press, 1970); Jere R. Behrman, *Foreign Trade Regimes and Economic Development: Chile* (New York: Columbia University Press, 1976); and Timothy King, *Mexico: Industrialization and Trade Policies since 1940* (London: Oxford University Press, 1970).

[15] The notion that conscious government policies to encourage import-substituting industrialization date to the 1930s is a common misperception. Some incipient pro-industrial policies were pursued during the depression, but they were of little importance compared to the *natural* process brought on by trends on international markets. Concerted and explicit policies for ISI were seldom pursued during the 1930s simply because they were unnecessary; they were only demanded, and obtained, by domestic industrial sectors once they became relevant in the late 1940s and early 1950s. The general process is summarized in Werner Baer, "Import Substitution and Industrialization in Latin America," *Latin American Research Review* 7, no. 1 (Spring 1972): 95–122. A good study of the Brazilian experience is Malan et al., *Política Econômica Externa e Industrialização no Brasil.*

[16] *SALA* 23:415.

and a middle class based in public employment—at the expense of agriculture and the urban "marginals," the underemployed and unemployed. Put simply, the political bargains worked out among urban businessmen, industrial workers, and the middle class served to safeguard their living standards at the expense of other groups.[17] It is not surprising that policy tended to reinforce the position of the politically powerful, but some of the results were especially perverse.

Protection of domestic industry indeed turned the "internal terms of trade" against agriculture, as manufactured goods became more expensive. Chronic currency overvaluation, which provided industries with cheap imported capital equipment, exacerbated the problem by pricing primary producers out of world markets. The resultant agricultural stagnation drove millions of rural dwellers off the land and into the cities.

Displaced peasants might have found jobs in new factories, but industrial protection and subsidization had made it relatively unattractive for manufacturers to use labor-intensive production methods. On the one hand, the experience of the 1930s and 1940s, reinforced by postwar policies, had "locked in" relatively high industrial wages. Manufacturers might, and some did, try to force wage cuts on their employees, but it was generally easier simply to lobby for government protection. On the other hand, government loans that cheapened credit and overvalued currencies that cheapened imported capital equipment made capital relatively inexpensive to industrial entrepreneurs. Above-market labor costs in protected industries, and below-market credit and capital goods, induced capitalists to use more labor-saving devices than the countries' supply of labor and capital would have indicated, and as Latin American industry became increasingly capital-intensive it was unable to provide jobs for the millions of displaced peasants flooding to the cities. The consequence was an increasing divide between formal and informal sectors, and especially between relatively well paid organized workers in modern industries and urban workers with such "marginal" jobs as construction day labor and domestic service, often earning below the legal minimum wage.[18]

---

[17] Some examples of the enormous literature on the heyday of ISI are Sylvia Hewlett and Richard Weinert, eds., *Brazil and Mexico: Patterns in Late Development* (Philadelphia: ISHI, 1982); Ricardo Ffrench-Davis, *Políticas económicas en Chile 1952–1970* (Santiago: Ediciones Nueva Universidad, 1973); Barbara Stallings, *Class Conflict and Economic Development in Chile, 1958–1973* (Stanford: Stanford University Press, 1978); Hansen, *Politics of Mexican Development*; José Luis Reyna and Richard S. Weinert, eds., *Authoritarianism in Mexico* (Philadelphia: ISHI, 1977); Guillermo O'Donnell, "State and Alliances in Argentina, 1956–1976," *Journal of Development Studies* 15 (1978–1979): 3–33; Guido di Tella and Rudiger Dornbusch, eds., *The Political Economy of Argentina, 1946–83* (London: Macmillan Press, 1989); and Gary Wynia, *Argentina in the Postwar Era* (Albuquerque: University of New Mexico Press, 1978).

[18] The issue of the employment effects of ISI is controversial. Representative articles in-

Another predictable result of protection for domestic industry was the proliferation of multinational corporate affiliates. Foreign corporations unable to export to Latin America set up branch plants there, where government policy permitted; the number of Latin American affiliates of the largest U.S. multinational corporations went from 276 in 1939 to 950 in 1957 and 1,757 in 1967. By the late 1960s, affiliates of foreign firms accounted for between one-fifth and one-third of manufacturing production in all major Latin American countries.[19]

The pattern of industrial protection was sometimes self-reinforcing. Firms that received government subsidies or trade protection had little incentive to become more efficient and often responded to competitive pressures simply by demanding more government subsidies or protection. In some instances, the result was extremely inefficient industrial firms that existed solely because of their ability to extract resources from the government or, via government policy, from captive consumers.

Major tensions developed in the various Latin American political systems. Rapid but unbalanced growth, with swollen urban centers and serious urban underemployment, put pressure on governments to increase social spending. Protected firms demanded ever-larger government subsidies. Tax collections lagged, with most governments unwilling or unable to increase taxes on the middle and upper classes. All of these pressures and more led to stubborn budget deficits and inflationary pressures in many of the region's countries. They also led to increasingly polarized political conflicts, which took different forms in different countries. Bitter battles between Peronists and their opponents in Argentina, the populism of the Goulart regime in Brazil and its military overthrow, tensions within Mexico's ruling Partido Revolucionario Institucional (PRI), and the growing divisiveness of Chilean politics all reflected the social pressures built up in the twenty-five years after World War II.[20]

---

clude David Morawetz, "Employment Implications of Industrialization in Developing Countries: A Survey," *Economic Journal* 84, no. 335 (September 1974): 491–542; William R. Cline, "Distribution and Development: A Survey of the Literature," *Journal of Development Economics* (1975): 359–400; and William P. Glade, "The Employment Question and Development Policies in Latin America," *Journal of Economic Issues* 3, no. 3 (September 1969): 43–62. Recent scholarly attention to the distributional consequences of trade policies is reflected in the studies in Anne Krueger, Hal Lary, Terry Monson, and Narongchai Akrasanee, eds., *Trade and Employment in Developing Countries* (Chicago: University of Chicago Press, 1981).

[19] United Nations, *Multinational Corporations in World Development* (New York: United Nations, 1973), 156–57; United Nations, *Transnational Corporations in World Development: A Re-Examination* (New York: United Nations, 1978), 263–71.

[20] The classic study of these pressures, whose conclusions are controversial but provocative, is Guillermo O'Donnell, *Modernization and Bureaucratic Authoritarianism* (Berkeley: Institute of International Studies, 1973). Further evaluations are in David Collier, ed., *The New Authoritarianism in Latin America* (Princeton: Princeton University Press, 1979). Other specific studies include the articles in Juan Linz and Alfred Stepan, eds., *The Break-*

Table 2.1 presents indicators of socioeconomic conditions in Latin American in the 1960s. Variations are obvious: Mexico and Brazil were more rural than the others, and income distribution there was more unequal. Venezuela was less industrial and faced fewer balance-of-payments constraints, due to petroleum revenue. Inflation was not serious in Mexico and Venezuela. Despite the usual problems with data unreliability, the table illustrates the broad contours of the five countries' political economies.

The "baseline" of our study in the late 1960s thus reflects this inheritance of modern Latin American industrial development. Its prominent features can be summarized as follows:

1. *The economy.* Growth had been rapid but sectorally and regionally unbalanced. Macroeconomic strains were growing.
   A. The industrial structure was quite "deep," with substantial production of consumer durables and capital goods. Affiliates of foreign corporations were important. Yet there were increasing problems of industrial inefficiency as protected firms relied on political lobbying rather than modernization to overcome competitive pressures.
   B. Agriculture and other primary producing sectors were often hampered by economic policies that penalized exporters and favored the manufacturing sector.
   C. Policies biased against exports, and tolerant of uncompetitive industries, led to repeated shortages of foreign exchange and balance-of-payments crises.
   D. Insistent demands for government spending, coupled with low levels of tax collection, led to chronic government budget deficits and inflationary pressures.
   E. The cities and parts of the countryside were flooded with a mass of economically "marginal" workers who did not participate in the modern industrial economy.
2. *Politics.* Alliances formed between World War I and the 1940s defined the contours of political activity. Strains within these coalitions were growing, as were pressures from outside them.
   A. The dominant political forces continued to be broad coalitions of urban groups, including in various combinations modern-sector businessmen, the middle classes, and the organized working class.

down of Democratic Regimes: Latin America (Baltimore: Johns Hopkins University Press, 1978); Alfred Stepan, ed., *Authoritarian Brazil: Origins, Policies, and Future* (New Haven: Yale University Press, 1973); Paul Sigmund, *The Overthrow of Allende and the Politics of Chile* (Pittsburgh: University of Pittsburg Press, 1977); and Arturo Valenzuela, *The Breakdown of Democratic Regimes: Chile* (Baltimore: Johns Hopkins University Press, 1978).

Table 2.1
Selected Latin American Economic Indicators, 1965–1973

	Argentina	Brazil	Chile	Mexico	Venezuela
Per capita GDP, 1970, in 1986 dollars	$2,531	$1,382	$2,275	$1,940	$3,066
Urban population as % of total, 1965	76	51	72	55	72
Industry as % of GDP, 1965	42	33	40	31	23
Industry as % of labor force, 1965	34	20	29	22	24
Agriculture as % of GDP, 1965	17	19	9	14	7
Agriculture as % of labor force, 1965	18	48	27	50	30
Exports as % of GDP, 1965	8	8	14	9	31
Manufactured exports as % of exports, 1965	5	9	5	17	2
Current acct. deficit as % of reserves, 1970	24	70	23	141	10
Average annual rate of inflation, 1965–1973	24.1	23.2	50.3	4.8	3.3
Public-sector spending as % of GDP, 1970	33	28	41	21	32
Public-sector deficit as % of GDP, 1972	1	2	5	2	3
Income distribution	(1970)	(1972)	N.A.	(1977)	(1970)
Share of top 10% of households	35	51		41	36
Share of bottom 60% of households	28	16		22	23

Source: World Bank, *World Development Report 1986* (Washington, D.C.: World Bank, 1986), except for per capita GDP, which is from Inter-American Development Bank, *Economic and Social Progress in Latin America 1987 Report* (Washington, D.C.: IDB, 1987), 426, and public finances, from Bela Belassa et al., *Toward Renewed Economic Growth in Latin America* (Washington, D.C.: Institute for International Economics, 1986), 126.

N.A. = Not available.

   B. There was much sectoral cooperation in the pursuit of favorable policies ("rent-seeking"). Capitalists and workers in specific industries tended to work together in demanding government support, while traditional rural and other groups were less well organized and influential.
   C. Political tensions were mounting over such issues as land reform, social programs, and labor relations. Such conflicts frequently pitted industrial labor against industrial capital, and the urban middle classes against urban modern-sector workers. Uncharacteristically for the region, the normally passive "marginals" sometimes mobilized in concert with other lower-income groups. In some instances class conflict prevailed over sectoral conflict, against a backdrop of real or potential social unrest.

The region's major nations were thus characterized by a series of crosscutting sectoral and class cleavages, against a backdrop of growing economic, social, and political problems. This is the starting point of our analysis, the political economy that external financial trends acted upon.

External Variation: The Price and Supply of International Finance

It is important to my analytical purpose to establish the essential exogeneity of international financial trends in the analysis of Latin American political economies in the last twenty years. The study's central organizing principle is that the five countries in question faced externally given financial conditions to which they formulated responses. If, on the other hand, the supply of funds available to an individual Latin American nation and the price at which funds were available to it were driven by the policies of the country itself, we could not take the external financial conditions faced by the country as given. If the Latin American countries had on their own been able to affect the supply and price of finance to them, international financial flows to the region and interest rates charged would be the *result* of trends in the Latin American economies, not a cause. Many discussions of foreign borrowing, indeed, assume that the accumulation of foreign debt is driven entirely by the borrowing nation, as when, for example, a country chooses to run a trade deficit and then goes about financing it.

My purpose is not to deny the importance of macroeconomic imbalances in foreign borrowing—without them borrowing would be unnecessary—but to argue that the *possibility* of foreign borrowing is not constant. In other words, the presence or absence of a borrowing option is exogenously determined, because borrowers on international financial markets are "credit-rationed" or "supply-constrained"; the amounts they can borrow are set by lenders, not by market-clearing prices. This assertion can be supported on theoretical and empirical grounds.

The argument that Latin America was for all intents and purposes a passive taker of both the quantities of international finance available to it and the interest rates at which it was available is meant as a general rule, not an absolute precept. Had a Latin American country not wanted to borrow, no lender could have forced it to do so. By the same token, just as domestic sociopolitical turmoil could drive potential lenders away, the restoration of stability could bring them back—and in some sense governments might be able to impose stability, as indeed the Chilean and Argentine military regimes attempted to do. The point is a simpler one: Latin American debtors could not control the international financial market they operated within to any appreciable degree. The relevant variables out of their control were international interest rates, interest-rate spreads beyond a certain margin, and quantities supplied.

The assertion that borrowers could not control international interest rates is not particularly controversial. Virtually all commercial bank loans to the less developed countries (LDCs) from the 1960s onward have been in the form of Eurocurrency credits whose interest rate is pegged to the London inter-bank offer rate (LIBOR), the cost of funds to banks on the London Eurocurrency market. As with American home mortgages tied to, say, the Treasury bill rate, the interest rate on Latin American external bank debt moves up and down with LIBOR. This last rate in turn reflects similar interbank rates in the home country of the currency in question: LIBOR for Euro-dollar loans follows American interest rates, LIBOR for Euro-sterling loans follows British interest rates, and so on. When interest rates go up or down in the United States, LIBOR for Euro-dollars goes up or down, and Latin American borrowers cannot affect this any more than home-owners can affect the Treasury bill rate that leads their mortgage-rate fluctuations. After all, even at the height of Third World lending, from 1979 to 1981, no Latin American nation ever accounted for more than 2 or 3 percent of total international borrowing.

While LDC borrowers cannot affect LIBOR, the interest rate to which their debt is pegged, they can conceivably affect how much more than LIBOR they have to pay. International banks typically lend at LIBOR plus some margin, or spread. An attractive borrower might be able to borrow at LIBOR plus ¼ percent, while an unattractive borrower might have to pay LIBOR plus 2 percent. International lenders distinguish among countries in this way, and by pursuing policies that lenders like, potential borrowers can reduce the spread they have to pay.

Although borrowers can affect the spreads above LIBOR that they pay, especially by pursuing policies desired by lenders, the impact of the borrowers policy is limited by the peculiar nature of the international financial market. In most markets prices tend to adjust until supply equals demand; if consumers want more shoes they pay a higher price, and eventually the supply of shoes increases. If international loans were negotiated in a market in which supply and demand responded smoothly to price differences, most countries could borrow at *some* interest rate, and could borrow as much as they wanted, again at *some* interest rate.[21] Such an international financial market would clear as borrowers and lenders made deals for more or less money at higher or lower interest rates. A country that could not borrow at LIBOR plus 2 percent could offer to pay LIBOR plus 5 percent, and the loans would be supplied.

International financial markets, however, unlike most other markets, operate on the basis of both price and control by lenders of the supply of funds offered to borrowers. Quantitative controls, usually known as credit-rationing, mean that prices (spreads) are only one factor in clearing the market. The difference among spreads offered to countries, indeed, is a less accurate reflection of the differences among countries' creditworthiness than is the simple ability to borrow. Some countries cannot borrow anything, no matter how high an interest rate they are willing to pay, while other countries can borrow virtually unlimited amounts at rates that appear to be too low by most measures. While borrowers do have some control over the spreads they are charged, this control is limited by the credit-rationing characteristic of international financial markets.

Although they may disagree on the exact mechanism, almost all analysts agree that international banks rationed credit to LDC borrowers, that is, would not lend to some would-be borrowers at any price, and restricted the amounts they would lend.[22] The reasons have to do with the

---

[21] This assumes that the supply curve is not backward-bending, which may not be justified in the ideal-typical non–credit-rationed financial market under discussion. The point is however a minor one.

[22] The literature is not solely, or primarily, applied to sovereign lending. See, for example, Dwight M. Jaffee and Thomas Russell, "Imperfect Information, Uncertainty, and Credit Rationing," *Quarterly Journal of Economics* 90, no. 4 (November 1976): 651–66; Joseph Stiglitz and Andrew Weiss, "Credit Rationing in Markets with Imperfect Information," *American Economic Review* 71, no. 2 (June 1981): 393–410; and Stephen Williamson, "Costly Monitoring, Financial Intermediation, and Equilibrium Credit Rationing," *Journal of Monetary Economics* 18 (1986): 159–79. Some examples of the enormous number of applications to international lending are Vincent Crawford, *International Lending, Long-Term Credit Relationships, and Dynamic Contract Theory*, Princeton Studies in International Finance no. 59 (Princeton: International Finance Section, 1987); Jonathan Eaton and Mark Gersovitz, "Debt with Potential Repudiation: Theoretical and Empirical Analysis," *Review of Economic Studies* 48 (April 1981): 289–309; Jeffrey Sachs, *Theoretical Issues in International Borrowing*, Princeton Studies in International Finance no. 54 (Princeton: International Finance Section, 1984); and Jonathon Eaton, Mark Gersovitz, and Joseph Stig-

environment within which international lending takes place, especially its incomplete information and unreliable enforcement mechanisms.

Lenders to foreigners face default risk, that is, the possibility that the debtor will not make prompt debt-service payments. Of course, the lender has no way of knowing beforehand whether the borrower will default; leaving aside the borrower's honesty, the lender also does not have as full a picture as the borrower of the uses to which borrowed funds will be put and how successful the projects financed are likely to be. To complicate matters, there is no effective way of enforcing contracts in international lending, since creditors can hardly foreclose on a country and no international judicial or police system has the power to force an errant debtor to comply with a loan agreement.

In this context, lenders may find that charging high interest rates on new loans can reduce the likelihood of being repaid. On the one hand, very high interest rates may induce borrowers to engage in riskier projects than they had originally planned, thus increasing the prospects of inability to pay. On the other hand, because higher interest rates increase the cost of servicing the loan, they increase the debtor's incentive to default. A domestic example might be the case of a bookmaker with large loans outstanding to a particular gambler; if the bookie extends new loans to the debtor at a much higher interest rate, the higher rate might drive the gambler either to wager the new loans on high-risk bets or to take the money and skip town.

International lenders are thus unwilling to offset their distrust of a potential borrower by charging it a significantly higher interest rate and would rather simply refuse to lend to the borrower. This means that lenders ration credit; they determine that there are some borrowers to which they will not lend. They also may set limits on the quantities they lend to individual borrowers, for similar reasons: the more lent to one borrower, the higher its incentives to default and the greater its ability to hold heavily committed lenders hostage. Borrowers find themselves constrained by the unwillingness of international markets to lend beyond a certain point or above a certain interest rate. There is very little that a potential borrower can do consciously to counteract banks' unwillingness to lend: professions of good intentions are not credible. Of course, a wide variety of borrower characteristics might affect that country's credit ration, but most of them—the level of development and political stability, for example—are outside of the direct control of policymakers.

A number of related theoretical suggestions have been made about other features of international financial markets, especially their tendency to engage in cycles of boom and bust. One hypothesis is that bankers tend

litz, "The Pure Theory of Country Risk," *European Economic Review* 30, no. 3 (June 1986): 481–513.

to underestimate the likelihood of major financial problems as financial crises recede into the past, and that this bias itself leads to overlending. A similar dynamic might be at work on the downswing, in which bankers overreact to financial crisis by pulling out of risky markets altogether. Such interpretations reflect the common notion that financial markets are driven by a herd instinct or, in the words of two analysts, by "disaster myopia."[23] Similar observations help explain why bankers tend to change spreads for all countries, and/or quantities offered to all borrowers, together, rather than differentiating among borrowers: "new information" that appears to increase (decrease) the general riskiness of the international environment leads all international lenders en masse to raise (lower) prices and/or lower (raise) quantities offered.[24]

Other analysts argue that overlending and underlending can be ascribed to institutional characteristics of international banking. International financial markets are dominated by very large banks that invest in information gathering, cooperation with other banks and with lenders, and a wide variety of costly measures that increase the immediate cost of lending but decrease its risk. Smaller banks are unwilling or unable to bear the informational or other costs shouldered by major international banks, but they can "piggy-back" on work that the major banks do. In this scenario, large banks pay to gather information about which borrowers are more creditworthy and to develop ties with debtors to reduce the risk of default; the small banks simply "follow the leaders" and lend to those countries that the large banks' behavior has indicated are safe. Small banks thus "free ride" on the research, diplomatic, and lobbying expenses borne by the large banks. In the upswing, large banks blaze trails but are followed by a flood of opportunistic small banks; in the downswing, amid great uncertainty, the small banks exit the market, while the large banks maintain their presence in order to reap the full benefit of their prior efforts.[25]

Some of these characteristics of international lending are seen in the

[23] Jack Guttentag and Richard Herring, "Credit Rationing and Financial Disorder," *Journal of Finance* 39, no. 5 (December 1984): 1359–82; Jack Guttentag and Richard Herring, *Disaster Myopia in International Banking*, Essays in International Finance no. 164 (Princeton: International Finance Section, 1986). Charles Kindleberger, *Manias, Panics, and Crashes*, draws on the work of Hyman Minsky to develop similar points.

[24] Evidence of the importance of information to the pricing of international loans—although not precisely along the lines developed here—can be found in Sule Ozler, "Evolution of Commercial Bank Lending to Developing Countries" (mimeo, 1988).

[25] This approach is presented in William Cline, *International Debt: Systematic Risk and Policy Response* (Washington, D.C.: Institute for International Economics, 1984). It is developed and applied, along with other arguments about institutional characteristics of international lending, in Robert Devlin, *Debt and Crisis in Latin America: The Supply Side of the Story* (Princeton: Princeton University Press, 1989); and Mark Spiegel, "International Lending with Heterogenous Banking Firms," unpublished paper, Los Angeles, 1987.

historical record, especially the cyclical nature of credit-rationing to developing-country borrowers as a group. International lending to underdeveloped areas has gone through phases of booms, crises, and dormancy.[26] In the modern era, the sequence began with British overseas lending in the 1820s, largely to new nations in the Western Hemisphere; defaults ensued in the late 1830s. Borrowing picked up in the 1840s and collapsed with the crisis of 1847; similar cycles led to crises in 1873 and 1890. British net foreign investment thus moved in waves, from £12 million in 1861 to £97 million in 1872, down to £10 million in 1877, back up to £107 million in 1890, to £19 million in 1901, then up to £234 million in 1913.[27]

More recent experience with this cycle confirms the general trend. Lending to the developing world—including Central and Eastern Europe—boomed in the 1920s, from both New York and London. The crisis of the 1930s ended the boom, and although negotiated settlements had generally been reached by the late 1940s, virtually no new foreign lending by either bondholders or commercial banks was undertaken until the mid and late 1960s. By one measure, as late as the early 1960s, private lending to Latin America was less than 7 percent of total capital flows to the region, as compared to over two-thirds in the late 1970s.[28] The reasons for not lending in the 1930s are obvious—many potential borrowers were in default—but in the 1950s and 1960s Latin American nations were creditworthy by most indicators, yet lenders were uninterested. The general consensus among scholars is that potential lenders did not distinguish among countries that had maintained good financial records and those that had not, and regarded Latin America as a whole as a bad bet so long as memories of the defaults of the 1930s lingered.[29] The region remained supply-constrained until the mid-1960s.[30]

[26] A good survey is Charles Kindleberger, "The Cyclical Pattern of Long-Term Lending," in *The Theory and Experience of Economic Development*, ed. Mark Gersovitz, Carlos Diaz Alejandro, Gustav Ranis, and Mark Rosenzweig (London: George Allen and Unwin, 1984), 300–312. The articles in Barry Eichengreen and Peter Lindert, eds., *The International Debt Crisis in Historical Perspective* (Cambridge: MIT Press, 1989), give more in-depth information on these issues.

[27] Michael Edelstein, *Overseas Investment in the Age of High Imperialism* (New York: Columbia University Press, 1982), 313–14.

[28] Devlin, 24. Devlin, *Debt and Crisis in Latin America*, contains a detailed account of modern international lending to Latin America, along with his supply-driven explanation of the experience. Stallings, *Banker to the Third World*, pp. 58–106, looks at a longer historical period from a similar perspective.

[29] For example, Barry Eichengreen, "The U.S. Capital Market and Foreign Lending, 1920–1955," in *Developing Country Debt and Economic Performance*, Vol. 1: *The International Financial System*, ed. Jeffrey D. Sachs (Chicago: University of Chicago Press, 1989), 107–55.

[30] The several exceptions generally involved loans secured by gold or by implicit or ex-

International bank and bond lending in the past twenty years has followed the same path as that observed in the past 150 years: Funds are readily available for some time. A debt crisis follows, after which funds are not available at any price to a whole class of potential borrowers.[31] Even during periods of financial expansion, some countries are unable to borrow at any interest rate. The point, then, is that from 1965 until 1985 the quantities that Latin American countries could borrow were largely determined by forces they did not control.

In summary, Latin American borrowers could not affect three crucial variables they faced on international financial markets. They did not control that portion of the interest rate charged them that was determined internationally, and that portion was generally more than four-fifths of the total cost of borrowing.[32] Borrowers did have some control over the spread they were charged, but this too was limited. Most important, the supply of funds available to an individual Latin American nation was largely beyond the control of the individual borrower.

Trends on International Financial Markets after 1965

This section describes the evolution of the global financial environment in the period under study. It recounts the sequence of international financial developments between 1965 and 1985, especially changes in the supply of funds available to Latin America and the cost of these funds (the interest rate).

Main financial indicators for the 1973–1986 period are in table 2.2; data before 1973 are not reliable. Postwar international lending to Latin

---

plicit U.S. government guarantees. Thus a New York bank consortium lent $200 million to the Brazilian government and rolled the loan over in 1958 and 1960; another American bank consortium lent $54 million to Argentina in 1958. In the former case the loan was against gold held in the Federal Reserve Bank of New York; the latter loan was part of a stabilization program for which $75 million came from the International Monetary Fund and $175 million from the U.S. government. Neither episode was remotely comparable to previous or subsequent international lending. Archives of the Superintendência de Moeda e Crédito (Brazil), "1002ª Ata, 8 Nov. 1961," 9; Fred Klopstock, "A New Look at Foreign and International Banking," in Paul Horvitz et al., *Private Financial Institutions* (Englewood Cliffs, N.J.: Prentice-Hall, 1963).

[31] Charles Kindleberger, "Historical Perspective on Today's Third-World Debt Problem," in his *Keynesianism vs. Monetarism and Other Essays in Financial History* (London: George Allen and Unwin, 1985), 190–209.

[32] Some might argue that the spread is the only relevant variable here, since Latin American countries can earn LIBOR on their overseas deposits. However, the borrowers are generally major net capital importers, whose reserves are substantially below their overseas liabilities; the potential for public borrowers, the vast majority, to hedge is thus very limited.

Table 2.2
Latin American International Financial Indicators, 1973–1986
(Billions of dollars, percent, and years)

	Latin American External Debt[a]			
	All Creditors		Private Creditors	
	Current $s	1982 $s[b]	Current $s	1982 $s[b]
1973	40	81	28	57
1974	56	104	42	78
1975	75	126	59	99
1976	98	155	80	127
1977	116	172	95	141
1978	161	223	135	187
1979	197	251	167	213
1980	241	281	207	242
1981	294	313	259	275
1982	331	331	291	291
1983	355	342	305	294
1984	374	346	322	298
1985	384	344	330	296
1986	395	346	340	298

	Capital Inflow[c] (Billion 1982 $s)	LIBOR[d] (%)	Real LIBOR[e] (%)	Avg LDC Spreads[f] (%)	Avg LDC Maturities[g] (Years)
1973	17.5	9.3	3.1	1.0	9.6
1974	25.5	11.2	0.2	1.0	8.2
1975	27.8	7.6	−1.5	1.6	5.2
1976	26.0	6.1	0.3	1.6	5.4
1977	23.2	6.4	−0.1	1.4	6.2
1978	33.5	9.4	1.7	1.1	8.1
1979	34.1	11.9	0.6	0.9	8.7
1980	40.9	13.9	0.4	0.9	7.7
1981	52.2	16.7	6.3	1.0	7.8
1982	27.6	13.6	7.5	1.1	7.0
1983	5.8	9.9	6.7	1.7	7.0
1984	9.7	11.3	7.5	1.3	8.5
1985	3.0	8.6	5.6	0.9	8.4
1986	5.5	6.9	4.3	0.6	8.2

Table 2.2 (*cont.*)

Source: Debt before 1978, Carlos Massad, "External Financing in Latin America," in Economic Commission for Latin America and the Caribbean, *Latin America: International Monetary System and External Financing* (Santiago: ECLAC, 1986), 356. Debt 1978–1986, Inter-American Development Bank, *Economic and Social Progress in Latin America*, various issues. There are only marginal differences between the two series. Net balance on capital account is also from Inter-American Development Bank, *Economic and Social Progress in Latin America*, various issues. Financial data before 1978, R. C. Williams et al., *International Capital Markets: Recent Developments and Short-Term Prospects*, IMF Occasional Paper 1 (Washington, D.C.: IMF, 1980), 26. Financial data 1978–1983, Maxwell Watson et al., *International Capital Markets: Developments and Prospects*, IMF Occasional Paper 43 (Washington, D.C.: IMF, 1986), 98. Financial data 1984–1986, Mark Allen et al., *International Capital Markets: Developments and Prospects* (Washington, D.C.: IMF, 1989), 116.

[a] All short-term debt is assumed to be owed to private creditors. Comparable figures for 1984 and 1985 debt to private creditors are not directly available; they were computed by extrapolating proportions for 1983 and calculating on the basis of total debt.

[b] Deflated by the U.S. GNP implicit price deflator.

[c] Net balance on capital account.

[d] Six-month Euro-dollar deposit rate, average for the year.

[e] Deflated by the U.S. Consumer Price Index.

[f] Average spreads (margins above LIBOR) charged to all nonoil developing countries.

[g] Average maturities (length of repayment) for all nonoil developing countries.

America began in the mid-1960s.[33] By then, memories of the defaults of the 1930s had begun to fade, Latin American economies were growing rapidly, and the presence of many multinational affiliates indicated the general attractiveness of the local economic environment. At the same time, major American banks had become interested in overseas expansion. While most initial lending to Latin America took the form of traditional bond flotations, the rise of the Eurocurrency markets in the early 1960s made them the market of choice for international lending, and since then most Latin American borrowing has been done from the offshore markets, whether in the form of syndicated Eurocurrency bank credits, Eurobonds, or a variety of other international financial instruments.[34]

[33] The literature on recent LDC borrowing and the subsequent crisis is by now so enormous that only a few representative samples can be cited: Edmar Lisboa Bacha and Carlos Diaz Alejandro, *International Financial Intermediation: A Long and Tropical View*, Princeton Essay in International Finance no. 147 (Princeton: International Finance Section, 1982); Carlos Diaz Alejandro, "Latin American Debt," *Brookings Papers on Economic Activity* 2 (1984): 335–89; Economic Commission for Latin America and the Caribbean, *External Debt in Latin America* (Boulder, Colo.: Lynne Rienner, 1985); Inter-American Development Bank, *External Debt and Economic Development in Latin America* (Washington, D.C.: IDB, 1984); Charles Lipson, "The International Organization of Third World Debt," *International Organization* 35, no. 4 (Autumn 1981): 603–31.

[34] On the Euromarkets, and the general principles of international lending, see Jeffry A.

In the late 1960s, Latin America borrowed, on average, more than $300 million a year from foreign private banks and bondholders. By the early 1970s, the trickle was becoming a flood, as several LDCs were regular Euromarket borrowers and total LDC debt to private financial markets was $34 billion.[35] As table 2.3 indicates, average annual foreign bank and bond lending to Latin America went from $115 million in the early 1960s to $313 million in the late 1960s. Although this was still equal to only about one-third of inflows in the form of foreign direct investment (FDI), a few countries in the region were large debtors as early as 1969: Mexico owed $1.6 billion to international financial markets, Brazil owed $604 million. Latin American borrowing grew very rapidly between 1969 and 1973, by which time Mexico's foreign bank debt was $4.2 billion and Brazil's was $2.8 billion.

LDC borrowing exploded in the 1970s, spurred partly by the "oil shocks" of 1973–1974 and 1978–1979, which both led OPEC members to deposit large amounts in the offshore markets and created major pay-

Table 2.3
Net Flow of Foreign Resources to Latin America, 1961–1986
(Annual averages in millions of current dollars)

	1961–1965	1966–1970	1971–1975	1976–1982	1983–1986
Net public inflow	948	1,059	1,902	3,305	8,344
Net private inflow[a]	637	1,562	5,622	19,124	9,753
Suppliers	123	365	174	444	627
Banks and bonds	115	313	3,463	14,061	5,592
Direct investment	399	884	1,985	4,619	3,534
Total	1,585	2,621	7,524	22,429	18,097

Source: Inter-American Development Bank, Economic and Social Progress in Latin America, various issues. For loan data after 1982, World Bank, World Debt Tables, various issues.

Note: There are some differences between World Bank and IDB data, but they do not affect the trends indicated here.

[a] Does not include nationalization credits.

Frieden, Banking on the World: The Politics of American International Finance (New York: Harper and Row, 1987), especially chap. 5.

[35] Jeff Frieden, "Third World Indebted Industrialization," International Organization 35, no. 3 (Summer 1981): 410.

ments deficits for the oil-importing LDCs that borrowing helped cover. The first oil shock of 1973–1974 indeed increased the need of such oil importers as Brazil to borrow and improved the creditworthiness of such oil exporters as Venezuela and Mexico. Private lending to the region went from $3.1 billion in 1973 to $5 billion in 1974 and $5.9 billion in 1975. Up until this point, virtually all loans were made by the very largest international banks that dominated the offshore markets.

The late 1970s were the heyday of private international lending to Latin America. The profitability of international lending drew hundreds of smaller banks into the market. Syndicated credits—in which a few very large banks arranged for a major loan, provided some of the funds themselves, then invited other banks to participate—gave internationally inexperienced banks an easy way into LDC lending. As international financial markets drew in deposits and banks, Latin American nations found it extraordinarily easy to borrow. Spreads fell, lenders rarely asked for detailed information about the purposes of the borrowing, and LIBOR was at or below international inflation. Between 1976 and 1982, private lending averaged $14.1 billion a year, more than three times the FDI inflow.

During most of the 1970s, international interest rates barely kept up with inflation. The international banking crisis in 1974, which involved the failure of two mid-sized Euromarket banks, helped drive LIBOR up from 9 percent to over 11 percent, but this was still barely equal to the increase in the American consumer price index (CPI) in 1974. LIBOR subsequently declined substantially, averaging barely 6 percent in 1975–1977, even as the American CPI was increasing at more than 7 percent a year. As the pace of price inflation quickened, interest rates drifted above 9 percent in 1978, to 12 percent in 1979, and to 14 percent in 1980. Still, they were barely keeping up with U.S. inflation.

Potential borrowers could sometimes affect spreads they were offered, and those which the banks trusted more got better deals.[36] However, spreads on international bank loans, like the quantity of lending itself, moved up and down for reasons that appeared to have little to do with individual country behavior. In the aftermath of the 1974 banking crisis, spreads charged to all borrowers, developed and developing, rose dramatically; those on loans to *developed* countries doubled. Developing-country spreads went from about 1 percent in 1973–1974 to 1.5 percent in 1975–1977. They then fell to a low of about 0.9 percent in 1979–1980, drifted upward above 1 percent in 1981–1982, then shot to 1.7

---

[36] Sebastian Edwards, "The Pricing of Bonds and Bank Loans in International Markets: An Empirical Analysis of Developing Countries' Foreign Borrowing," *European Economic Review* 30, no. 3 (June 1986): 565–89, discusses related issues.

percent in 1983, after the debt crisis hit. The behavior of spreads is consonant with a supply-driven process in which international financial markets largely determine both the price they charge borrowers and the quantities they make available.

Late in 1979, in a development of major importance to LDC debtors, the Federal Reserve began a systematic attempt to restrain inflation in the United States by way of monetary tightening. American interest rates shot above 20 percent for brief periods. LIBOR also soared in response to trends on American money markets, to 17 percent in 1981 and 14 percent in 1982. These rates were high even in nominal terms, but compared to the American CPI, which increased by 10 and 6 percent in the two years, they were astronomical. Real interest rates, the difference between nominal rates and inflation, went from near zero or negative in the 1970s to unprecedented levels after 1980. They have since stayed very strongly positive, with LIBOR remaining several percentage points above the American CPI.

The combination of the spectacular rise in international interest rates, eventual recession in the developed world, and the second oil shock caused major strains in international lending to Latin America after 1979. Increased oil prices put pressure on the Brazilian payments balance, while the growth of Mexican oil exports coupled with the price hikes encouraged both lenders and borrowers to be overly optimistic about the country's economic prospects. Shortly thereafter, as international interest rates rose and the developed countries fell into a steep recession, Latin America's need for funds grew rapidly: debt-service payments soared as interest rates rose, while the recession-induced decline in demand for Latin American goods exacerbated trade deficits. In 1981 and 1982, the region borrowed furiously, often at very short term. Despite the clear signs of distress, spreads remained very low and overseas borrowing was extremely easy. By one calculation, during the last half of 1981 Latin America borrowed an astounding $4 billion a month from international banks.[37]

When Argentina invaded the Falklands (Malvinas) in April 1982, it introduced more uncertainty into an international financial market already worried about the global recession and LDC debt. Some of the smaller banks began to leave the Latin American lending market. By summer 1982 it was clear that the major Latin American borrowers were in trouble, and in August Mexico declared that it would not service its international bank debt as agreed. Within a matter of weeks, lending to Latin American virtually ceased. The regional banks and other relatively small players in international financial markets fled immediately, while the major international financial institutions were left trying to piece together rescheduling agreements with the major debtors.

[37] Bank for International Settlements, *Fifty-third Annual Report* (Basel: BIS, 1983), 116.

After 1983 Latin America's debtors were driven into round after round of renegotiations with commercial bank consortia, the International Monetary Fund, and official creditors. Apart from "concerted" or "involuntary" loans that international banks made to debtor nations in the course of debt renegotiations, there was next to no new lending to the region after 1982. While in 1981 there was a net resource transfer of over $20 billion to Latin America, that is, new foreign lending and investment was $20 billion more than debt service and profit payments abroad, in 1983 the net resource transfer was negative: the region sent $20 billion more overseas to foreign creditors and investors than it received in new loans and investments. The latest round of Latin American borrowing had ended.

Through the 1970s and until 1982, then, Latin American countries could borrow virtually as much as they wanted. At the height of the boom, between 1979 and 1982, Latin America borrowed an annual average of $24 billion in long-term bank Eurocredits, and billions more in short-term credits. Late in 1982, the cycle came to a halt. In 1983 banks lent only $2 billion to Latin America, and after that virtually no new bank loans were extended to the region. The only exception was credits extended by banks in the process of debt renegotiation to allow countries to remain current with interest payments—that is, loans made to service outstanding debt.[38]

The availability of international finance to Latin America since 1965 has been essentially exogenous. Of course, the picture presented above is simplified; the process was two-sided. Countries could undertake actions that directly or indirectly reduced their foreign borrowing, whether this involved economic policies that lenders found distasteful or limits on capital inflows. Within a very limited range, public policy might affect the availability of funds. However, two crucial and interrelated variables— the availability of foreign loans, and the price of the loans—were fundamentally determined by features of and developments on international financial markets. For our purposes, the international financial environment that Latin American borrowers faced after 1965 was beyond their control, and it varied in much the same way for all countries in the region.

Summary

In 1965 the political economies of Latin America's major nations reflected over thirty years of import substituting industrialization, some natural and some policy-driven. From 1930 to 1950, as most foreign

[38] Maxwell Watson et al., *International Capital Markets: Developments and Prospects*, International Monetary Fund Occasional Paper 43 (Washington, D.C.: IMF, 1986), 38.

manufactured goods were unaffordable or unavailable, domestic economic activity shifted away from primary-goods production for export toward the production of industrial goods for home consumption. By 1950, political systems were dominated by urban groups, often in a formal or informal nationalist populist alliance that included modern-sector urban businessmen, labor unions, and middle classes. Economic policy making focused on subsidizing domestic industry, protecting it from foreign competition, and sometimes attracting foreign branch plants to complement domestic production. By the late 1960s the region was heavily industrial, but much of its industry had grown up behind trade barriers and was internationally uncompetitive.

In the late 1960s, international financial markets began to open to Latin America after over thirty years of dormancy. This process was almost entirely driven by developments on the markets themselves, not by decisions made in Latin America. The exogenous increase in the supply of foreign finance completely changed the structure of international economic constraints and opportunities available to the region; different nations responded differently, but all took advantage of cheap foreign finance in the 1970s. After 1980, however, developments on international financial markets dealt serious blows to Latin America: international interest rates rose dramatically, raising the cost of the continent's floating-interest debt, and in 1982 the supply of funds to Latin America was essentially cut off. The next chapter surveys the response of economic policy and political activity in Latin America's five major debtors to changes in international financial conditions.

3

The Response: Economic Policies and Politics in Borrowing and Financial Crisis

THIS CHAPTER summarizes the variation in economic policies and results and in political behavior and outcomes in Argentina, Brazil, Chile, Mexico, and Venezuela. It begins with an outline of the expected economic impact of a capital inflow in the absence of active government policy, discusses how government policies can alter the effects of a capital inflow, then examines the different ways in which the five governments under study did in fact respond to capital inflows after 1965.

The chapter also reviews the effects of the financial crisis that began in 1982 on domestic politics in the five major borrowers. It points to the varied political evolution of the five societies and their different institutional outcomes. The chapter presents the "stylized facts" of the five countries' experiences in the 1970s and 1980s, and sets the stage for case studies that analyze the process in more depth.

The Domestic Economic Impact of International Financial Flows

The first array of questions addressed in the case studies has to do with economic policies pursued by borrowing-country governments before 1982. The five governments had a wide range of choices open to them. They could let the market take its course or intervene in economic activity. If they chose the latter alternative, they had to decide how to intervene and to what end. Investigating their actual choices requires an analytical baseline of what economic theory would lead us to expect in a country whose government did nothing as capital flowed in. As well as providing a benchmark against which to measure national policies, this survey frames many of the economic issues that recur throughout the case studies.

In the absence of intervening policies, cross-border financial flows are expected to have relatively straightforward economic effects on capital-sending and capital-receiving societies. Foreign loans increase the local supply of capital and foreign currency; if extended to the public sector, they increase government resources. The effects are reversed in the case of a capital outflow or, of more relevance to Latin America, net resource outflows to service existing foreign debt.[1]

A capital inflow first of all increases the supply of funds to the local economy and tends to lower interest rates.[2] This normally promotes investment, as the cost of borrowing falls. It might also reduce saving, although national savings rates tend to adjust only very slowly to changes in interest rates.

An inflow of foreign funds also increases local availability of foreign currency, and cheapens its price. In other words, the national currency appreciates (goes up in value) against foreign currencies. Appreciation raises the price of domestic relative to foreign goods, tending to increase imports and reduce exports.

If, as is common in LDC borrowers, much of the capital inflow goes to the public sector, it increases the resources available to the government and generally leads to fiscal expansion as government spending rises.[3] For symmetry with the previous effects, a reduction in the price of capital and foreign exchange, this can be regarded as a reduction in the price of government services which causes the demand for, and supply of, these services to increase.[4]

---

[1] For an interesting survey and discussion of the issue, see Arnold C. Harberger, "Welfare Consequences of Capital Inflows," in *Economic Liberalization in Developing Countries*, ed. Armeane M. Choksi and Demetris Papageorgiou (New York: Basil Blackwell, 1986), 157–78.

[2] This effect will be felt only if the monetary authorities adopt an "accommodating" stance, allowing the money supply to increase with the financial inflow. This might be regarded as government policy, but for all intents and purposes it is only a passive response to the capital inflow, a willingness to allow the money supply to expand as borrowing increases local purchasing power. "Sterilization," in which the monetary authorities refuse to allow the money supply to grow and thus counteract the monetary effects of a financial inflow, is more properly regarded as an active policy. More generally, the discussion here avoids the many complex issues addressed by more detailed analysis of capital flows, which are outside the scope of the study. We focus on the consensus interpretation of the near-term effects of cross-border capital flows.

[3] The tendency of foreign loans to flow toward the public sector is not so obviously a result of government choices as it might seem. Political risk factors typically lead the public sector to be the most credit-worthy borrower in developing countries—the full faith and credit of the local government is generally more valuable than that of a local private enterprise. In these conditions, even if the government did not actively channel funds toward itself, foreign lenders would typically choose to extend many of their loans to the public sector. This, of course, assumes that the government is running a deficit, not too strong an assumption in most developing countries. The point could be discussed at much more length, but it is enough for our purposes simply to note the regularity with which foreign loans tend to concentrate in public sectors.

[4] This somewhat peculiar way of putting the matter implies that government employment is also a government service, and that as the public sector expands its payrolls, the "cost" of getting onto the government gravy train decreases while its benefits increase.

A capital inflow thus changes three sets of relative prices. First, it reduces interest rates, tending to increase investment. Second, it reduces the price of foreign currency, tending to increase imports. Third, it reduces the price of government services, tending to increase government activity. In times of easy international borrowing we expect these prices to fall, leading to increased investment, imports, and government spending; in times of international financial stringency we expect these prices to rise, leading to reduced investment, imports, and government spending.

This process can be restated using familiar balance of payments and national income accounting identities. These yield the relationships in equation 1:

$$\Delta NFA \equiv (X - M) \equiv (S - I) + (T - G) \qquad (1)$$

where

ΔNFA = Change in net foreign assets
X = Exports
M = Imports
S = Private savings
I = Private investment
T = Taxes
G = Government expenditures

The equation states two truisms. First, if a country imports more than it exports, it must borrow the difference (a decrease in net foreign assets is the same as borrowing). Second, if a country invests more than it saves and its government spends more than it takes in, the differences must be borrowed abroad.[5] This implies that a capital inflow, an increase in a country's foreign debt (decrease in its net foreign assets), is associated with an increase in imports and/or a decrease in exports, and an increase in investment and/or government spending.

This discussion leads by implication to the "textbook" picture of the beneficial effects of foreign borrowing. As the capital inflow lowers domestic interest rates, domestic investment increases. As the influx of foreign currency cheapens imports, producers are driven to modernize in order to face the stiffer import competition, but they can take advantage of cheaper imported capital equipment to do so. As foreign lending to the local government increases the resources at the government's disposal, the public sector can undertake investments in economic infra-

[5] We assume, as do most analyses, that savings rates and the government's ability to tax are constant. This is true *grosso modo*, for empirically they appear to change only very slowly.

structure to complement this process: new roads, power plants, port facilities.

Foreign borrowing makes sense if it goes directly or indirectly to increase society's ability to replace imports with local production or to increase exports. Debt-service payments can be met because greater production provides the domestic resources necessary, more exports and less imports provide the foreign exchange necessary, and overall economic growth increases government revenue. In reality, of course, there are many deviations from this ideal-typical path, most of which have to do with the effects of government policy on the distribution of external resources to domestic economic activities.

Distributional and Policy Issues

Government policies substantially affect the "natural" impact of a capital inflow, and these policies are precisely the topic of this study. By the same token, capital flows affect socioeconomic actors differently; it is their differential impact that politicizes capital flows, for the distributional consequences may be reflected or combatted in the political arena. The preceding discussion simply outlines the baseline from which these policies are taken.[6]

The actual results of capital inflows for the local economy are a function both of the economic considerations discussed above and government policies. Governments can affect the impact of a capital inflow on all three fronts, because they can control allocation of capital, foreign exchange, and government services. Groups in society have an interest in obtaining these resources, and as capital flows in, the government faces social demands for capital, foreign currency, and public spending.

From a distributional standpoint, the effect of capital inflows in increasing the local supply of funds is especially important to borrowers, whose borrowing cost is reduced. Domestic lenders may be harmed by the reduction in interest rates if foreign lenders undercut a domestic banking cartel. It is more likely that the capital inflow will benefit domestic financial intermediaries, since the increased supply of funds to the economy allows domestic banks to expand their operations.

From the standpoint of policy, all potential borrowers want to get ample funds as cheaply as possible. The allocation of foreign finance can therefore become highly politicized, with some firms or industries receiv-

---

[6] For one summary and application along these lines, see Rudiger Dornbusch, "External Debt, Budget Deficits, and Disequilibrium Exchange Rates," in *International Debt and the Developing Countries*, ed. Gordon W. Smith and John T. Cuddington (Washington, D.C.: World Bank, 1985), 213–35.

ing all of the foreign loans and others receiving none. The more government intervention in the allocation of capital, the more we observe otherwise unexplained differences in lending rates, and investment and growth, across sectors. Most generally, it is possible for central banks to "sterilize" a capital inflow by tightening monetary policy to offset the increased supply of funds; for every dollar turned in to the central bank for local currency, the central bank reduces the money supply by an equal amount of local currency. The net effect is to keep interest rates where they were.[7] The principal empirical questions here are whether the government intervenes in allocating credit from abroad and, if so, to whom; the principal analytical question is why these courses of action were chosen.

By the same token, the distributional effects of an inflow of foreign exchange and the resulting currency appreciation are especially favorable to consumers of imports, who can buy more as their currency appreciates, whether the imports are such consumer goods as clothing or such production inputs as machine tools. The stronger the local currency, for example, the cheaper imported capital equipment, raw materials, and intermediate inputs are to manufacturers. Of course, appreciation makes imported manufactured goods cheaper and can increase competition in product markets. At the same time, the international price of local goods is increased by currency appreciation, which may make it difficult for exporters to compete on foreign markets.

Because foreign exchange, like capital, is a precious commodity in Latin America, policies that affect its allocation can be hotly disputed. Each potential user of imported goods wants as much foreign currency as possible, as cheaply as possible. Producers of traded goods want to ensure that foreign currency is not allocated to import goods that compete with them. In this competition for foreign exchange, favored firms get more foreign currency, perhaps even at a lower price, than other, nonfavored, firms. So we want to know whether, how, and why the government intervenes in the allocation of foreign exchange.

The distributional effects of the increased government spending that a capital inflow generally brings depend on where the new resources are spent. It is safe to assume that government employees themselves benefit, along with private actors aided by government spending. These last include both users of government services and suppliers to the government; if borrowed funds are used to build public housing, the beneficiaries are both the residents of the housing and the construction firms that get the contracts. As governments decide how to spend the money that foreign

---

[7] In this case, the capital inflow would typically be counterbalanced by an increase in the central bank's foreign exchange reserves.

financiers lend the public sector, they pursue policies that favor some over others, supporting the government's employees, suppliers, and consumers.

There are many striking examples of the effects of government policies on an inflow of foreign resources. One of the best-known has to do with the allocation of spending among broadly defined tradeable and nontradeable sectors, and can be understood in the light of modern real exchange-rate analysis.[8] The real exchange rate (q) is generally defined[9] as in equation 2:

$$q = \frac{ep^*}{p} \qquad (2)$$

where

e = nominal exchange rate
p^* = world price level
p = national price level

The equation can also be seen as the price relationship between traded and nontraded goods and services within the home economy. This is because traded goods by definition are those readily available from abroad whose prices reflect the world price level plus tariffs (footwear, wheat), while nontraded goods and services are those that do not enter into world trade and whose prices are set domestically (haircuts, housing). Movements in the real exchange rate are equivalent to changes in the relative price of tradeables and nontradeables; if nontradeables become more expensive, producers of traded goods face higher input prices, since nontraded goods and services have important direct or indirect effects on the production costs of domestic producers. If construction gets more expensive, for example, shoe manufacturers have to pay more for factory buildings directly and for wages indirectly, since workers' higher rents will lead them to demand higher wages. Increased prices for nontradeables are equivalent to a real appreciation and vice versa; lower prices for non-

[8] For example, Arnold C. Harberger, "Economic Adjustment and the Real Exchange Rate," in *Economic Adjustment and Exchange Rates in Developing Countries*, ed. Sebastian Edwards and Liaquat Ahamed (Chicago: University of Chicago Press, 1986), 371–414; and Sebastian Edwards, *Real Exchange Rates, Devaluation, and Adjustment: Exchange Rate Policy in Developing Countries* (Cambridge: MIT Press, 1989).

[9] It should be noted that in traditional economic usage the exchange rate is expressed in units of home currency per unit of foreign currency, so that an *increase* in the exchange rate is a *depreciation* and vice versa. This is counter to everyday usage: when people say that the exchange rate went up, they generally mean that it appreciated. We will use common parlance here, implicitly or explicitly expressing the exchange rate as units of foreign currency per unit of home currency, so that an increase in the exchange rate implies an appreciation.

tradeables are equivalent to a real depreciation and vice versa. (Real traded goods prices cannot change, since they are set on world markets.)[10]

At one extreme, a government faced with a resource inflow may allow all the money to go to purchase nontraded goods and services and may not control the allocation of foreign exchange. As demand rises for housing, movie tickets, and restaurant meals, prices in the nontradeables sector increase. The nontradeables sector booms and spends much of its earnings to buy traded goods: barbers buy television sets, waiters buy clothing. Since domestic traded goods producers face rising production costs, they cannot compete with foreign producers, and spending on traded goods takes the form of a surge in imports of finished products. The result is that the appreciated real exchange rate increases demand for locally produced nontraded goods and services, while it confronts local producers of traded goods with stiff import competition. It is often argued that the "Dutch disease" that afflicted Holland after the discovery of natural gas there led to massive resource inflows and the economic experience of imperial Spain as resources flooded in from the New World are special cases of this phenomenon.[11]

At the other extreme, the government might channel newly available resources to the purchase of traded goods not made locally, to be used by domestic producers of traded goods. That is, government policy might only allow the resource inflow to be spent to import locally unavailable capital equipment and raw materials, for use in increasing domestic production of traded goods. In this case, since the inflow is spent entirely on foreign products, it has no immediate domestic price effect.[12] The result could be extremely rapid industrialization, with the underdevelopment of such nontradeable sectors as housing, public transportation, and leisure. This might describe a radical simplification of postwar Japanese development.

Government policies can have a significant effect on the economic impact of capital inflows. The same holds for government policy toward resource outflows, such as foreign debt-service payments. During the borrowing boom, governments in Latin America had to choose whether and how to apportion the increased supply of capital, foreign exchange, and

[10] Nontradability can be induced by policy. Indeed, in much of Latin America quantitative trade barriers have made much of the manufacturing sector nontradable.

[11] For a review, see W. M. Corden, "Booming Sector and Dutch Disease Economics: Survey and Consolidation," *Oxford Economic Papers* 36 (1984): 359–80. On the Spanish case, see Peter J. Forsyth and Stephen J. Nicholas, "The Decline of Spanish Industry and the Price Revolution: A Neoclassical Analysis," *Journal of European Economic History* 12, no. 3 (Winter 1983): 601–10.

[12] Over time, increased productivity in the traded goods sector will lead to gradual real appreciation, but this is a slow process.

government services to different groups. During the financial crisis, they faced similar choices about allocating the adjustment burden caused by the decreased supply of foreign capital, and the need to send resources abroad to service the foreign debt. In the first instance, the principal problem was whether and how to distribute the benefits of foreign borrowing; in the second instance, how to distribute the costs of debt service. There is an asymmetry in the comparison, as policymakers have many more options when foreign funds are available than when they are not. As money comes into the country, governments can pretty much choose to do what they want. However, once funds stop flowing in and net transfers become negative, the requirements of external balance become quite binding.[13]

The first set of dependent variables, things to be explained, is the variation among national economic policies in response to the increased supply of foreign capital before 1982. The second set of dependent variables is the variation among national political responses to the economic distress that the drying up of foreign capital entailed beginning in 1982. The following sections briefly summarize the range of outcomes observed in each dependent variable, starting with borrowing-period economic policies and moving on to crisis-era politics.

Summarizing Economic Policies in the Financial Expansion

Variations in economic policy during the borrowing period were of two general types. First, some governments chose a relatively market-oriented approach to the capital inflow, letting most or all funds go to whatever use private economic agents decided, while others intervened more in the markets for capital and foreign exchange. On this dimension, Chile is closest to the market-oriented position, with Argentina near it; Brazil, Mexico, and Venezuela are all far closer to the opposite pole. Chile and Argentina broke with previous import-substituting policies and liberalized their international economic relations, while Brazil, Mexico, and Venezuela continued along import-substituting lines developed in the postwar period.

Second, inasmuch as governments actively intervened in markets, they chose different economic activities to favor and disfavor. This dimension

[13] This helps explain why economic policies in the decade after the debt crisis tended to be more similar—trade and financial liberalization, privatization, reduction in government budget deficits—than in the prior decade of heavy borrowing. This point parallels the often-observed asymmetries in adjustment between surplus and deficit countries, on which see W. M. Corden, *Inflation, Exchange Rates, and the World Economy*, 3d ed. (Chicago: University of Chicago Press, 1986), 74–84.

is too multifaceted to summarize quickly, although probably the most visible contrast was between a general promanufacturing bias in Brazil, Mexico, and Venezuela and a general financially oriented, even antimanufacturing bias in Chile and Argentina. Indeed, the former three redoubled efforts to stimulate the growth of modern industry by means of trade barriers and government subsidies, while the latter two reduced import barriers and eliminated many subsidies to domestic industry. The details of variation on both dimensions are explored in the case studies; here a few summary descriptive statistics are presented for the sake of comparison.

Purely economic reasoning, as in equation 1 above, implies that the inflow of foreign finance to Latin American after 1965 should be associated with increased imports, investment, and government spending in the borrowing countries. In fact, one multicountry statistical study found a significant positive relationship between borrowing and investment, growth, and government budget deficits in the 1970s.[14] It is indeed evident that the 1970s heyday of Third World borrowing was associated with a general increase in the economic role of the state in most LDCs, while the virtual unavailability of foreign finance since 1982 has seen a reversal of this trend and a reduction in LDC public-sector involvement in direct economic activities, and even in economic regulation. In other words, access to foreign loans spurred LDC state capitalism and public-sector economic activism, while the drying up of these loans favored privatization and other such market-oriented policies.[15] Other implications suggest themselves. To the extent that manufacturing is protected by quotas and similar trade barriers that effectively make it a nontraded sector, the share of manufacturing in GDP will rise with the capital inflow. The more the capital inflow is channeled through the local financial system, the greater the rise in the share of financial activities in GDP.

The observed outcomes in Argentina, Brazil, Chile, Mexico, and Venezuela both fit and deviate from these trends in interesting ways. To set the stage, table 3.1 presents data that indicate how substantial the impact of foreign borrowing was on the domestic availability of funds. The borrowing periods for the countries were similar but not identical. Mexico got access to international financial markets in the mid-1960s, and Brazil followed around 1967. Venezuela's international creditworthiness was boosted by the 1973 oil shock, and the country's borrowing dates essentially from then. Although Chile and Argentina did some borrowing in

[14] As reported in World Bank, *World Development Report 1985* (New York: Oxford University Press for the World Bank, 1985), 50–51, 62.

[15] On the first phase of the process, see Jeff Frieden, "Third World Indebted Industrialization: International Finance and State Capitalism in Mexico, Brazil, Algeria, and South Korea," *International Organization* 35, no. 3 (Summer 1981): 407–31.

Table 3.1
Credit and Foreign Credit in Five Latin American Borrowers, 1972–1982
(Percent)

	Total Credit/GDP			Foreign Credit/Total Credit		
	1972	1979	1982	1972	1979	1982
Argentina	33.0	40.6	50.3[a]	32.6	41.7	51.7[a]
Brazil	34.9	43.7	38.5	43.5	66.9	76.9
Chile	32.9	58.6	71.3[a]	43.8	69.6	73.0[a]
Mexico	61.8[b]	53.6	93.7	N.A.	51.8	70.0
Venezuela	27.8	67.0	81.3	39.9	69.7	60.3

Source: World Bank, *World Development Report 1985* (Oxford: Oxford University Press
for the World Bank, 1985), 60.
N.A. = Not available.
[a] Data for 1981.
[b] Data for 1977.

Table 3.2
External Debt of More than One-Year Maturity Owed by Public and Private
Sectors, 1981
(Billions of dollars and percent)

	Total Medium and Long-Term Foreign Debt	Percent Owed by Public Sector[a]	Percent Owed by Private Sector
Argentina	22.7	46.3	53.7
Brazil	63.5	69.1	30.9
Chile	12.6	35.3	64.7
Mexico	52.8	80.7	19.3
Venezuela	19.9	56.9	43.1

Source: Inter-American Development Bank, *External Debt and Economic Development
in Latin America* (Washington, D.C.: IADB, 1984), 87–97, 151–92.
[a] Includes debt owed by the private sector but guaranteed by the government.

the 1960s, political turmoil in both countries effectively kept them out of
the Euromarkets until 1976, when respective military dictatorships were
firmly installed in power. In all cases, voluntary bank lending came to an
end in 1982–1983.

The experiences of the five countries during their borrowing periods
reflect their policy differences. Starting with the relationship between borrowing and state intervention in the economy, it is clear from table 3.2
that the great majority of foreign loans in Brazil, Mexico, and Venezuela
went to the public sector, while in Argentina and Chile most went to the
private sector. Table 3.3 shows that foreign borrowing was associated

Table 3.3
Foreign Debt and Public Spending (and investment)

	Public Spending as a Percent of GDP
Argentina	
1970–1973	32.38
1976–1981	38.64
Change	+ 19.3%
Brazil (public investment)	
1970–1973	5.93
1974–1979	8.55
Change	+ 44.2%
Chile	
1970	40.6
1976–1981	34.9
Change	− 14.0%
Mexico	
1970–1973	22.48
1974–1981	33.33
Change	+ 48.3%
Venezuela	
1970–1973	37.4
1974–1981	64.96
Change	+ 73.7%

Sources: Inter-American Development Bank, *External Debt and Economic Development in Latin America* (Washington, D.C.: IADB, 1984), 87–97, 151–92. Brazilian public investment is calculated from Thomas Trebat, *Brazil's State-Owned Enterprises* (Cambridge: Cambridge University Press, 1983), 121.

with significant increases in public spending as a share of GDP in Brazil, Mexico, and Venezuela; with some increase in Argentina; and with a *decline* in Chile. Not surprisingly, foreign loans (table 3.4) supplied most public deficit financing in Mexico and Venezuela and much of it in Argentina; the Chilean public sector was in surplus, and figures for Brazil are unavailable.

The association between foreign borrowing and domestic investment varied widely, as can be seen in table 3.5. The first column of the table shows the increase in each country's debt as a share of its gross domestic product (GDP) during its borrowing period; the second column shows gross domestic investment (GDI) as a share of GDP during the preborrowing and borrowing periods. Where many loans are used for investment, the GDI share of GDP should rise during the borrowing period over its previous level.

As can be seen from the table, foreign borrowing was accompanied by

Table 3.4
Foreign Debt and Public-Deficit Financing

	Percent of Public Deficit Financed Abroad
Argentina, 1976–1981	40.4
Brazil	Not available
Chile, 1976–1981	[Surplus]
Mexico, 1970–1981	59.8
Venezuela,[a] 1974–1981	88.8

Source: Inter-American Development Bank, *External Debt and Economic Development in Latin America* (Washington, D.C.: IADB, 1984), 87–97, 151–92.
   [a] Excludes "unidentifiable financing."

a *drop* in investment coefficients in Argentina and Chile, while investment rose substantially in Brazil, Mexico, and Venezuela. This difference is related to the difference in public spending policies, since in the latter three countries foreign loans were often used for public investment. It might be argued that these measures do not consider the relative efficiency with which the funds were used; Argentina might have invested less than before, but invested more wisely.[16] This can be assessed crudely with the data in table 3.6, which uses a Bank for International Settlements method to compare the share of GDP invested with the GDP growth rate that ensues; the higher the growth rate per percent increase in GDI as a share of GDP, the more efficient the investment is presumed to be (and the higher the "investment efficiency index" reported in the table). The last column converts this to show the percent of GDP that each country invested to obtain a one-percent increase in its GDP growth rate. By these measures, Argentina is terrible—it invested but obtained *negative* average annual growth rates. Chile invested quite efficiently, but not enough to make up for the decline in its investment coefficient. Venezuelan investment was quite inefficient, while Brazil and Mexico both increased their investment coefficients and invested relatively well.

Changes in the sectoral composition of output help reveal which sectors gained relative to others. The figures in table 3.5 show that manufacturing was an obvious loser in Argentina and Chile, a distinct winner in Brazil and Mexico, and grew slightly in Venezuela. This implies that protection, subsidies, and other support measures tended to divert spending

[16] There is also the possibility of measurement errors in these two cases. Specifically, some Argentine public investment in military industries may have gone unrecorded; and some of the Chilean purchases of imported consumer durables might economically be classified as investments for the purposes of future consumption. The issue is too complex to be evaluated here.

Table 3.5
Debt, Investment, Manufacturing, Finance, and Imports

	Change in Debt as % of GDP	Average GDI as % of GDP	Average Mfg. Value Added as % of GDP	Average Finance as % of GDP	Average Imports as % of GDP
Argentina					
1960–1969	—	18.4	23.0	4.2[b]	6.5
1976–1981	45.12	17.5	20.8[a]	7.1	8.9
Change		−4.9%	−9.6%	+69.0%	+36.9%
Brazil					
1960–1969	—	17.2	24.9	13.7[c]	5.9
1970–1981	20.07	23.5	31.3	15.1	8.0
Change		+36.6%	+25.7%	+10.2%	+35.6%
Chile					
1960–1969	—	18.7	24.2	11.5[b]	12.8
1976–1981	33.65	15.6	21.3[a]	14.4	22.3
Change		−16.6%	−12.0%	+25.2%	+74.2%
Mexico					
1960–1969	—	20.5	21.7	4.5	5.9
1970–1981	29.51	24.2	26.9	4.6	8.4
Change		+18.0%	+24.0%	+2.2%	+42.4%
Venezuela					
1970–1973	—	26.0	15.9	12.2	18.7
1974–1981	72.93	38.1	16.5	12.6	28.5
Change		+46.5%	+3.8%	+3.3%	+52.4%

Source: Except as noted below, Inter-American Development Bank, *Economic and Social Progress in Latin America,* various issues.

[a] Figures for borrowing-period manufacturing value added as a share of GDP for Argentina and Chile are for 1980–1981: IDB data for the entire period are not continuous.

[b] Figures for the financial sectors in Argentina and Chile are from Joseph Ramos, *Neoconservative Economics in the Southern Cone of Latin America, 1973–1983* (Baltimore: Johns Hopkins University Press, 1986), 142, 144. For Chile the benchmark is 1970; for Argentina the benchmark is 1970–1973. Continuous data are not available from the IDB, and comparable and continuous data for the 1960s are unavailable.

[c] Benchmark for financial sector in Brazil is 1971–1973; borrowing period is 1974–1981.

Table 3.6
Efficiency of Investment in Latin America

	Avg. GDP Growth[a]	Avg. GDI/GDP	Investment Efficiency Index[b]	GDI/GDP per 1% Increase in GDP Growth Rate[c]
Argentina				
1976–1982	−0.27	0.1749	−1.54	—
Brazil				
1968–1982	7.55	0.234	32.25	3.10
Chile				
1976–1982	3.89	0.1456	26.74	3.74
Mexico				
1970–1982	5.61	0.2396	22.79	4.39
Venezuela				
1974–1982	2.95	0.384	7.69	13.0
Latin America				
1970–1982	5.11	0.230	22.18	4.51

Source: For general method, Bank for International Settlements, *Annual Report 1988* (Basel: BIS, 1988), 42. For GDP growth rates and GDI/GDP, Inter-American Development Bank, *Economic and Social Progress in Latin America*, various issues.

[a] Five-year moving average of GDP growth rate over period.

[b] Average GDP growth rate divided by the average GDI share of GDP over the period. Higher numbers indicate a more efficient use of investment, i.e., higher growth rates with less investment.

[c] GDI as a percentage of GDP needed to obtain a 1 percent increase in the GDP growth rate; thus Latin American output grew 1 percent faster for each additional 4.51 percent of output invested.

toward manufacturing in the latter three, but not in the former two. On the other hand, finance grew substantially more rapidly in Argentina and Chile than elsewhere, indicating that more resources were channeled through the banking system here than elsewhere.

The trade dimension of borrowing-country policy also indicates some of the uses to which foreign finance was put. Table 3.5 indicates that all five countries increased imports as they borrowed; this is hardly surprising, since the added availability of foreign exchange sooner or later was likely to be reflected in greater imports. Chile experienced the largest import surge (in the context of a trade liberalization), followed by Venezuela. This measure is difficult to interpret, since increased imports could be paid for with increased exports as well as with borrowed funds; Mexican and Venezuelan oil exports probably had as much to do with their imports as did borrowing.

The degree of real appreciation during the borrowing period also indicates some of the policies pursued. Table 3.7 shows the evolution of real

Table 3.7
Real Effective Exchange Rates and Capital Flight

	Real Appreciation 1976–1978 to peak[a]	Real Appreciation 1976–1978 to 1979–1982	1976–1984 Capital Flight as % of 1984 Foreign Debt	
			1[b]	2[c]
Argentina	32.5% (1980)	16.5%	34.2	34.2
Brazil	2.7% (1982)	−11.2%[d]	8.7	0
Chile	24.7% (1981)	14.6%	0	0
Mexico	19.9% (1981)	4.8%	27.7	37.2
Venezuela	18.2% (1982)	6.5%	87.7	38.3

Sources: Real effective exchange rates—Bela Balassa et al., *Toward Renewed Economic Growth in Latin America* (Washington, D.C.: Institute for International Economics, 1986), 78–79. Capital flight—Donald Lessard and John Williamson, eds., *Capital Flight and Third World Debt* (Washington, D.C.: Institute for International Economics, 1987), 206. Total 1984 foreign debt—Inter-American Development Bank, *Economic and Social Progress in Latin America*, 1987 ed. (Washington: IADB, 1987), 463.

[a] Year of peak (i.e., most appreciated) real effective exchange rate in parentheses.
[b] As measured by Donald Lessard and John Williamson.
[c] As measured by John Cuddington in *Capital Flight* (see below).
[d] That is, real depreciation.

effective exchange rates during the late 1970s and early 1980s, when foreign finance was flowing into all five countries in large quantities. In all except Brazil, government policy led to substantial currency appreciation, typically reaching unsustainable levels and leading to major devaluations. The first column shows the highest level of appreciation achieved by the real exchange rate, and the year it was achieved. The second column shows the general exchange-rate trend between 1976–1978 and the period of greatest capital inflow, 1979–1982. Here it can be seen that the "overvaluations" of the Chilean and Argentine exchange rates were the most severe and sustained.

Exchange-rate movements are related to capital flight: investors respond to a real and unsustainable appreciation in the exchange rate by buying foreign currency in order to profit once devaluation occurs. It is not hard to explain why Argentine, Mexican, and Venezuelan investors engaged in massive capital flight, as shown in table 3.7, nor why Brazilian investors did so little. The Chilean case is a puzzle, dealt with in more detail in its case study; most of the explanation is that Chileans took advantage of the real appreciation not to buy dollar-denominated investments but to buy imported goods.[17]

[17] This simple discussion ignores the effects of interest rates. Capital might have remained

Table 3.8 displays another way of investigating the relationship between borrowing and other economic activity, by the use of regression analysis. In this instance the independent variable is the inflow of capital to each country, net of interest and profit payments. The regressions measure the change in imports, investment, and public spending (public investment, in Brazil) as a share of GDP, and movement in the real effective exchange rate (negative movement is appreciation) expected with a $1 billion capital inflow. For the three real variables capital inflow is lagged one year; in other words, the regressions measure the effect of a capital inflow in one year on investment, imports, and public spending the following year. This is justified because such decisions take time to make and implement; government budgets and investment and import plans do not adjust instantaneously to an inflow of capital. On the other hand, since the real exchange rate is a monetary variable that responds immediately to financial conditions, the regressions are for the same year. In addition to the usual regression results, the implications of the coefficients in percentage terms are also reported. That is, a $1 billion net inflow of capital to Argentina is associated with a 0.7995 percentage-point increase in imports as a share of GDP in the following year, which is equal to a 9.2 percent increase in the imports/GDP ratio.

The results confirm previous observations. Borrowing was associated with increased imports in all except Brazil, but the increase was larger in Argentina and Chile than in Mexico and Venezuela. Investment grew substantially in Venezuela and Brazil, somewhat less in Mexico; there was no discernible relationship between borrowing and investment in Argentina and Chile. Public spending was strongly correlated with borrowing in Brazil and Mexico, less strongly in Venezuela; there was no relationship in Argentina and Chile. In both Argentina and Mexico capital inflows were associated with real appreciation.[18]

---

at home if interest-rate differentials had compensated for expected devaluation. They may have in Chile, but they rarely did in Mexico and Argentina, and strong government controls on Venezuelan interest rates in 1981 were a major contributing factor to capital flight. John Cuddington's econometric analysis indeed finds a strong correlation between the real exchange rate and capital flight in Mexico, Argentina, and Venezuela; and between interest rates and capital flight in Venezuela. John Cuddington, "Macroeconomic Determinants of Capital Flight: An Econometric Investigation," in *Capital Flight and Third World Debt*, ed. Donald Lessard and John Williamson (Washington, D.C.: Institute for International Economics, 1987), 85–96; and John Cuddington, *Capital Flight: Estimates, Issues, and Explanations*, Princeton Studies in International Finance no. 58 (Princeton: International Finance Section, Princeton University, 1986).

[18] To some extent the Venezuelan results are contaminated by characteristics of the data used. In other countries that experienced capital flight, the figures are generally reported as residuals, under "errors and omissions" or some such category. The Venezuelan statistics, on the other hand, appear to include capital flight in the narrower measure of net capital inflows. This means that borrowing is substantially undercounted, since capital flight is sub-

A clear picture emerges from this survey of statistical evidence about the five borrowers in the 1970s and 1980s. Argentina and Chile, pursuing relatively market-oriented policies, experienced important increases in imports and the role of the financial sector; investment and manufacturing shares shrank in both. Public spending also shrank in Chile, and grew slowly in Argentina. On the other hand, Brazil, Mexico, and Venezuela pursued relatively interventionist economic policies, and investment, manufacturing, and public spending grew in all three; the latter two also increased their imports. Four of the borrowers, but not Brazil, experienced real currency appreciation, especially between 1979 and 1982; of these, all but Chile experienced capital flight as a result. Reality is far more complex than this simple taxonomy implies, and the five case-study chapters explore it in detail, but this summary clarifies the policy differences in need of explanation.

Summarizing Political Responses to the Debt Crisis

The second set of analytical issues addressed in this study involves the political consequences of the economic crisis that began around 1982 in all five debtors. The sudden cessation of foreign lending imposed serious adjustment costs on the heavily indebted nations. The reversal of capital flows—no new money flowed in, and debt service payments flowed out—reduced the local supply of capital, foreign currency, and public resources. Inevitably, government spending had to be cut and revenue increased, even as the region entered into a severe depression. This made it impossible for policymakers to continue to satisfy all of the groups that had benefited from borrowing-period policies. In the midst of this crisis, political protests swept the continent, leading to important political changes in many countries and, at the regional level, to a shift from a predominance of military dictatorships to an overwhelming commitment to civilian rule.

The trajectories and results of the political turbulence of the 1980s are summarized in table 3.9. The "Political Outcomes" columns present a very simple chart of the principal institutional characteristics of political activity in the five countries before the debt crisis, and the regime in place by 1988, after several years of crisis.

The remaining columns indicate the range of country experiences. "Change in Policy Orientation?" shows whether the government in office

---

tracted from it. Were Venezuelan figures fully comparable, it is likely that there would be a strong relationship between borrowing and real appreciation. This is symptomatic of the data problems encountered in compiling the statistical survey, but it is probably the only such problem with a systematic effect on the results.

Table 3.8
Summary Regressions for Five Latin American Borrowers

	Argentina	Brazil	Chile	Mexico	Venezuela
Imports/GDP					
Coefficient	0.7995	−0.0016	1.0849	0.1458	0.9519
R-squared	0.477	0.000	0.327	0.247	0.423
t-statistic	2.52*	−0.02	1.85*	2.07*	2.57*
Coeff. expressed as percent increase[a]	9.2	—	4.9	1.9	3.6
GDI/GDP					
Coefficient	0.0858	0.8052	0.7538	0.1741	1.8455
R-squared	0.002	0.488	0.075	0.226	0.474
t-statistic	0.11	3.52**	0.75	1.95*	2.85**
Coeff. expressed as percent increase[a]	—	3.5	—	1.1	5.4
REER[b]					
Coefficient	−5.6888	−0.5214	−1.6632	−1.0816	1.1792
R-squared	0.343	0.083	0.074	0.606	0.164
t-statistic	−1.91*	−1.09	−0.80	−4.47**	1.40
Coeff. expressed as percent increase[a]	−6.1	—	—	−1.1	—
Public spending/GDP[c]					
Coefficient	0.4819	0.3186	−0.3398	1.3010	0.8932
R-squared	0.119	0.398	0.051	0.620	0.375
t-statistic	0.74	2.15*	−0.46	4.04**	1.90*
Coeff. expressed as percent increase[a]	—	4.3	—	4.2	1.4

Sources: Inter-American Development Bank, *Economic and Social Progress in Latin America*, various issues; public spending from Inter-American Development Bank, *External Debt and Economic Development in Latin America* (Washington, D.C.: IADB, 1984), 151–92, except for Brazilian public investment, which is calculated from Thomas Trebat, *Brazil's State-Owned Enterprises* (Cambridge: Cambridge University Press, 1983), 121. Supplementary data graciously supplied by the Division of Statistics and Quantitative Analysis of the United Nations Economic Commission for Latin America.

Notes: Independent variable is net capital imports minus net outflow of interest and profit payments, expressed in billions of 1982 dollars, lagged one year (except for REER). Dependent variables are all expressed in percent of GDP (except for REER). The coefficient expresses the *percentage-point* increase in the relationship in question expected with a $1 billion net capital inflow. For example, a $1 billion net capital inflow was associated with a 0.7995 percentage-point increase in Argentina's imports as a share of GDP in the following year.

Time periods are as follows: Argentina, 1976–1984, except public spending, 1976–1982; Brazil, 1970–1985, except public investment, 1970–1979; Chile, 1976–1985, except public spending, 1976–1982; Mexico, 1970–1985, except public spending, 1970–1982; Venezuela, 1974–1985, except public spending, 1974–1982.

Asterisks indicate statistical significance at the 5 percent level (*) and the 1 percent level (**).

Table 3.8 (cont.)

ᵃ That is, coefficient as percent of average for the period; percentage increase in the relationship in question expected with a $1 billion capital inflow. For example, the 0.7995 percentage-point increase discussed the first note above is 9.2 percent of Argentina's average imports/GDP ratio (8.69 percent); a $1 billion net capital inflow was associated with a 9.2 percent increase in the country's imports/GDP ratio in the following year. These figures are reported only where the results are statistically significant.

ᵇ Real effective exchange rate, expressed in units of home currency per unit of (trade-weighted basket of) foreign currency. Negative numbers thus indicate real appreciation. Because this is a monetary rather than a real variable, unlike all the others considered here, in which price changes are expected to be nearly instantaneous, capital inflows are not lagged.

ᶜ For Brazil, public investment as a share of GDP.

responded to the debt crisis with a significant change in the general thrust of its economic policies—a subjective measure, to be sure, but one that can be checked against the more detailed case studies. The next column shows whether the government in power at the time of the crisis was able to weather the crisis. In the case of electoral systems, this would mean that the party in power in 1982 remained in power through the crisis; in the case of authoritarian systems, this implies no substantial change in the ruling faction or individual. The last column indicates whether the type of political system in place in 1982 lasted through the crisis—whether, most obviously, military dictatorship was replaced by democracy. The characterizations may be crude and controversial—some consider Mexico authoritarian and doubt the depth of democratization in Argentina and Brazil—but they help classify the five trajectories.

Argentina, Brazil, and Chile were military dictatorships on the eve of the debt crisis. In Brazil, a very gradual opening of the political system had begun in 1974, and the eventual end of military rule was under discussion, if not clearly in sight. In Argentina and Chile, although the most egregious abuses of human rights and civil liberties had been reduced, the military was solidly in command. By 1985 the Argentine and Brazilian military regimes had turned power over to the civilian opposition amidst great political turmoil. The Chilean dictatorship, in contrast, rode out popular unrest and maintained political control until the economic crisis was long past; only in the late 1980s did the military permit the election of a civilian president.[19]

---

[19] Some might object that Chile, like Argentina and Brazil, went through a crisis-induced democratization. The Chilean experience is in fact very unlike that of its Southern Cone neighbors. The military was able to weather serious crisis-era protests, which were larger than those in Argentina and even, perhaps, in Brazil. The gradual quasi-electoral victory of democratization came several years after the broad movement spawned by the crisis had subsided, and long after the economic crisis had passed and the economy had started growing quite rapidly. More details are set forth in chapter 5.

Table 3.9
The Debt Crisis and Political Regimes in Latin America

	Political Outcomes		Paths of Political Development		
	Regime before Crisis	*Regime after Crisis*	*Change in Policy Orientation?*	*Change in Government?*	*Change in Regime?*
Argentina	Military dictatorship	Multiparty civilian electoral	No	No	Yes
Brazil	Military dictatorship	Multiparty civilian electoral	No	No	Yes
Chile	Military dictatorship	Military dictatorship	No	No	No
Mexico	Civilian electoral, official party quasi-monopoly	Civilian electoral, single party dominant	Yes	No	No
Venezuela	Two-party civilian electoral	Two-party civilian electoral	No	Yes	No

The Brazilian political opening was overtaken and accelerated by the crisis. The economic downturn led to an outpouring of discontent. The military government struggled to ensure that the proregime party kept the presidency, but the opposition's ranks were swelled by general dissatisfaction and defections from the promilitary party. Despite the military's efforts, in 1984 an opposition president was elected by indirect vote and with the support of many former military supporters. A civilian president took power in March 1985.

The Argentine military was firmly entrenched when the crisis began. In March 1981, as the economy collapsed, a more moderate faction of the armed forces came to the fore briefly and attempted to open the political system and reverse the regime's previous economic policies. After just nine months, however, hard-liners forced the moderates out and resumed previous economic and political policies.[20] The ensuing Falklands (Malvinas) fiasco, coupled with continued economic distress, led to mounting opposition, and the armed forces left office in favor of an elected civilian government at the end of 1983.

The economic effects of the crisis were severe in Chile, and discontent was widespread. However, after a brief and partial relaxation of the regime's orthodoxy, economic policy returned to type. The armed forces in fact tightened their grip on power and reversed movement toward political liberalization. It was not until 1990, years after the economy had resumed growth, that the military ceded power to an elected civilian politician.

Mexico and Venezuela had long-standing civilian political systems when the crisis hit, and both country's systems remain in place. The Mexican political system has been controlled by the Partido Revolucionario Institucional (PRI) and its predecessors since the 1920s. The Venezuelan system since 1958 has been dominated by two parties, the vaguely social-democratic Acción Democrática (AD) and the vaguely christian-democratic Comité de Organización Política Electoral Independiente (COPEI). In both countries, there was some political change after the onset of the crisis: Mexico became a more or less multiparty system, while Venezuela saw electoral alternation of power.

In Mexico, when the crisis broke, the PRI administration initially swung toward economic nationalism and appealed for populist support. The most prominent policy measures taken were the nationalization of private banks and the imposition of capital controls in August–September 1982. The new PRI administration that took power in December 1982

[20] It is because the moderate junta was so short-lived, and its policies so thoroughly reversed by its successors, that I classify Argentina as having experienced no change in government or policy. This is of course a simplification to help fit the country into the overall classification scheme; chapter 6 explains the particulars of the process.

gradually moderated this policy stance. Meanwhile, the conservative opposition Partido de Acción Nacional (PAN) began to show unprecedented strength. As policy evolved toward commercial liberalization, nationalist and populist protests increased, both within the PRI and in the form of a new Frente Democrático Nacional (FDN), later transformed into the Partido de la Revolución Democrática (PRD). In the 1988 elections the FDN and the PAN combined won nearly half the seats in Congress.[21]

Venezuelan politics weathered the crisis without major institutional changes, as the rules of electoral alternation were respected. The AD's populist leader Carlos Andrés Perez had ruled from 1974 to 1979, when the party lost to COPEI. (Venezuelan presidents cannot succeed themselves.) When the crisis began COPEI pursued austerity measures that caused great distress. As a result, in the midst of the crisis in 1983 COPEI was voted out in favor of AD, and in 1988 AD's Perez was returned to power.

To summarize, Argentina and Brazil experienced the most striking political changes during the crisis: dictatorial military regimes gave way to civilian rule. In Venezuela, the political system remained intact, but the ruling party was voted out of office. Mexico's evolution was less dramatic, as the PRI held onto power; however, the unchallenged dominance of the official party ended and the country moved toward true multiparty competition. Neither the government nor the political system in Chile changed, as Pinochet maintained control.

The Explanatory Argument Recapitulated

Before moving to the case studies, it is useful to recall briefly the explanations given in chapter 1 of the variations described above. The choice between economic interventionism and market orientation, I argue, was determined largely by the character of labor-capital relations. Where these were relatively calm, asset-holders focused policy demands on their sectoral interests. Where class conflict was rife, capitalists reduced sectoral demands in favor of demands that the government protect or restore the overall investment climate. I argue that Brazil, Mexico, and Venezuela fit the first pattern, Chile and Argentina the second. These categories are not absolute, of course. Class conflict was more important in Brazil, for example, in the mid-1960s than afterwards, and policy was accordingly more aimed at general business conditions than it later became. The level

---

[21] The results of the election were hotly contested, with many insisting that a fair ballot would have shown a victory by Cárdenas. Whatever the reality, the unquestionable fact is that the political system has been mightily transformed.

of class hostility was lower in Argentina than in Chile, and the level of sectoral demands was thus higher in the former than in the latter.

Inasmuch as the government undertook to intervene in the economy, it chose groups to favor and hamper. I argue that the choice of distributional policies was driven by the political power of the groups involved and that this political power was in turn a function of the specificity of the sector's assets and the level of concentration of the sector. In Brazil, Mexico, and Venezuela, policy favored sophisticated manufacturing (and some agribusiness) with very specific assets and well-organized sectoral representation, largely at the expense of traditional manufacturing and agriculture with standardized assets and dispersed or competitive industrial structures. Although policy in Chile and Argentina was less interventionist, where it was undertaken (especially in Argentina) it also tended to favor the more concentrated sectors, especially in the financial system.

As for political activities of socioeconomic groups during the debt crisis, I argue that they flowed from desires for economically favorable policies. Where class conflict was predominant, it overrode sectoral demands for relief from the adjustment burden. This pattern applied pretty much only in Chile; by 1981 the threat of class conflict in Argentina had receded, and sectoral pressures came to the fore. In Chile, however, the business community's concerns about the military dictatorship's economic policies paled in comparison to its fear of a return of socialist rule.

In the other four countries, sectoral pressures dominated. Where the government did not meet sectoral demands for relief, the sectors in question defected to the political opposition; where opposition was unavailable or ineffectual, they called for a change in political regime. In Brazil and Argentina, politically powerful manufacturers and others pushed for a change in economic policy, and when they failed to obtain this, they threw their support to successful movements to end military rule. In Venezuela, the COPEI's failure to alter its policy course led to electoral defeat and replacement by the more responsive AD. The Mexican government, alone among the five, implemented new policies to support many affected groups. Although the PRI, over the ensuing several years, experienced major defections and the rise of an important opposition for the first time, it was able to hold onto the government. Detailed analyses, and support for these arguments, are presented in the case studies that follow.

Introduction to the Case Studies

The next three chapters are case studies of the five major Latin American debtors during the financial expansion of the 1960s and 1970s and the financial crisis of the 1980s. The purpose of the case studies is to demonstrate the explanatory power of modern political economy in the study of economic policy and politics in the countries in question.

The five cases presented allow three types of comparisons that address my analytical questions. First, because each nation responded differently to similar external financial developments, their experiences can be compared to one another to evaluate the explanatory power of my approach. For example, labor-capital relations in Chile and Brazil can be compared to see how well they explain differences between the two countries' economic policies. Second, methodical study of the history of each country allows for the evaluation of arguments about changes in national patterns over time. For example, the relationship between the deterioration of the economic position of Brazilian manufacturers after 1980 and their antigovernment and prodemocratization political position can be analyzed. Third, country studies permit the weighing of explanations of variation in the behavior of different groups or sectors. For example, comparisons can be made between the economic interests of various sectors of the Mexican economy and different patterns of political activity in the aftermath of the 1982–1983 crisis. The case studies allow comparisons among countries, within countries over time, and within countries among groups and sectors.

Case studies, of course, are not rigorous tests of hypotheses: the same event can be interpreted differently by different observers, and national peculiarities can distort or disguise the evidence. Yet they allow an exploration of how processes of interest develop over time, and discussion of nuances that can make statistical studies inadequate to some social-scientific tasks. Indeed, statistical data can be enriched by detailed case studies, just as case studies can be lent power by statistical tests. Perhaps more relevant is the paucity of reliable and comparable data in Latin America, which limits the potential for applying statistical techniques.

The structure of the five case studies is the same, although the Brazilian and Chilean cases are presented in separate chapters and the other three cases are grouped together in one chapter. Each case study begins with a brief summary of those features of the national experience with international financial flows in need of explanation, and of my explanation of these features; a synopsis, that is, of the dependent and explanatory variables. The case then summarizes the country's economic and political history before borrowing began. A detailed description of each country's development during borrowing boom and crisis follows. The case ends with a summary of the nation's patterns of economic policy and political participation in the period in question and with an evaluation of my analytical approach to explaining these patterns. The case studies highlight the features of interest in each country's economic and political development, and my interpretation of these features.

Summary

This chapter reviews patterns of economic policy and political activity in the five major Latin American borrowers during financial expansion and collapse. While external finance was available, national governments dealt very differently with these resources. The Chilean and Argentine regimes left most borrowing to the private sector and liberalized their international commercial and financial relations as finance flowed in. The Brazilian, Mexican, and Venezuelan governments intervened heavily in their economies, especially to promote import-substituting manufacturing.

The debt crisis reduced the resources available to governments, and also affected patterns of political behavior. The Argentine and Brazilian dictatorships gave way to civilian regimes; the Chilean dictatorship held onto power. The grip of Mexico's PRI on the country's political system was loosened, while the ruling party in Venezuela was voted out of office.

These condensed summaries of complex national experiences are meant only as a stylized overview of the countries analyzed here. The remainder of the study consists of detailed case studies of the five countries in question, which use the analytical tools of modern political economy to shed light on the recent Latin American experience with international financial expansion and collapse.

Part II

FIVE CASE STUDIES

4

Debt, Economic Policy, and Politics in Brazil

BRAZIL IS the economic giant of the Third World. Its economy is larger than the rest of South America's, larger than sub-Saharan Africa's (excluding South Africa). Its industry is the most advanced in the developing world and among the world's top ten producers of such goods as steel, automobiles, and weaponry. Brazilian foreign debt is the Third World's largest.

During Brazil's recent overseas borrowing, from 1967 until 1981, economic and industrial growth were quite impressive. This growth took place with substantial government intervention in the economy under the auspices of an authoritarian military dictatorship. The public sector controlled a large share of national investment, public enterprises dominated the production of many basic industrial inputs, and government regulations influenced every aspect of economic activity.

The financial crisis ushered in a Brazilian industrial depression, and the country exploded in political turmoil. The upheaval led eventually to the "opening" of the political system, as the country's first civilian president in more than twenty years took office in 1985. One of Latin America's longest-lived military regimes left office in ignominy.

This chapter surveys the economic policies and politics of Brazilian borrowing from 1965 until 1985. It argues that the general features of the country's economic and political development can be explained by the political influence of cohesive and concentrated sectors of the economy. In the absence of major labor-capital conflict, Brazil's economic policies and politics were dominated by the activities of influential sectoral actors. Foremost among these were São Paulo's large industrial firms, based in advanced manufacturing with specific assets and generally oligopolistic market structures. The interests of modern industry, finance, and agribusiness were major determinants of economic policy in the financial expansion. By the same token, the regime's inability to meet the policy demands of modern industry once the crisis began propelled the industrial sector toward the movement for democracy after 1980.

Brazil, 1965–1985: An Overview

The principal analytical questions about Brazilian economic and political development after 1964 have to do with explaining government economic policies and the evolution of the country's politics. Understanding why the Brazilian government undertook the economic policies that it did after 1964 takes on special significance because Brazil is widely regarded as having been quite successful. Its borrowing approached the "textbook" ideal in serving primarily to increase capacity to produce exportable (and import-substituting) goods. Especially in regional context, Brazil's foreign borrowing almost exclusively for investment is striking. Industrial production grew rapidly; exports, especially of manufactured products, grew; and there was little capital flight. Brazil is also an important study in politics, as a long-standing military regime was replaced by civilian government in the midst of the crisis. Brazil is a striking case of the triumph of democratic forces over authoritarianism.

My explanations of the economic-policy and political dependent variables center on the role of powerful economic sectors in Brazilian society. Labor-capital conflict in Brazil has normally been overridden by sectoral and regional divisions. The powerful pressures for sector-specific policies explain the general reliance of the government on administrative allocation of resources to favored sectors as opposed to the market mechanism. It also means that political developments were strongly influenced by the interests of powerful sectoral actors.

Because of the generally low salience of labor-capital conflict, sectoral pressures were of primary importance, and the general pattern of Brazilian economic policy was interventionist. The government played a central role in investment, restricted financial markets, often controlled domestic wages and prices, managed foreign borrowing and investment, and imposed major barriers to imports. Throughout, subsidies and incentives to various sectors of the economy were important policy tools.

Changes in the salience of social unrest also help explain the evolution of Brazilian economic policy. The 1964 coup was in large part the result of unprecedented concern over labor strife, and early postcoup policymakers were principally concerned to ensure a favorable investment climate. In the first years after the 1964 military coup, stabilization policy was thus relatively market-oriented by Brazilian standards. As the authoritarian regime and the investment climate became more secure, attention shifted toward sectoral issues and the net of specific policies grew. Government policy activism grew during the "miracle" years (1968–1973). By 1974 concern about political stability had dissipated, and the demand for and supply of sectoral subsidies and incentives had surged. From 1974 until the crisis hit, state intervention grew substantially; the mid and late 1970s were the heyday of the government's "big projects."

The economic sectors favored by the Brazilian state were the country's most politically powerful. Between 1964 and 1980 the biggest beneficiaries of government policy, in general, were large-scale, well-organized economic agents with specific assets. This included consumer durables and capital goods producers, modern export-oriented agriculture; and banking. Most subsidies and incentives went to these sectors, as did most foreign borrowing. Traditional agriculture and industry were not favored by policy. In comparative perspective, then, the low salience of social unrest and threats to property conduced to interventionist economic policies. Over time, the declining salience of such threats pushed policy in an increasingly interventionist direction. Across sectors, those with the most specific assets and cohesive internal organization were most successful at obtaining government support.

Politically, the principal analytical issue has to do with Brazilian democratization. From 1964 until 1985, the country was governed by a military dictatorship; in 1985 an opposition civilian president took office amid political turmoil. To be sure, the level of authoritarianism varied over time. The most repressive period was from 1967 until 1974. In 1974 a new military president began a gradual political liberalization, and in 1979 another military president accelerated the political opening. The actual transition was nonetheless more abrupt and hostile to the military than the dictatorship wanted.

The striking features of Brazilian political democratization flowed, in my analysis, from the country's sectoral conflicts. During the expansion of the late 1960s and 1970s, foreign borrowing helped the regime secure support from politically important economic interest groups. When international financial conditions changed after 1980, substantially reducing the availability of funds, the regime was far less able to satisfy its erstwhile supporters. Modern industry, especially the capital goods producers, was least able to do without government backing, as its assets were closely tied to state subsidies and incentives, and to orders from state enterprises. A solid drumbeat of protest over economic policy thus arose from the modern industrial community centered in São Paulo. As the government was unable to balance pressure from foreign creditors and their domestic allies against the demands of the industrial sector, support grew for the opposition and for a more open political system that would allow the opposition to take power. Eventually the opposition won, with the backing of modern industry for a change in economic policies. Before looking in more detail at Brazilian economic and political development after 1964, I survey the history of the Brazilian political economy and the situation on the eve of its recent borrowing experience.

The Brazilian Political Economy: A Brief History

Modern Brazilian economic growth has been impressive, with economic dynamism and political power concentrated in the developed Southeast. Despite the country's great heterogeneity, economic and political elites maintained substantial unity throughout the nation's recent history, avoiding such traumatic schisms as the Mexican Revolution or Peronism. Instead, a relatively continuous process of economic development and social change was punctuated by transitions that reformulated the political system, gradually changing the ruling coalition without eliminating all of its component parts. Political mobilization, and government policy, reinforced economic trends—the decline of Northeastern sugar and the rise of Southern coffee, the development of an industrial economy, the maturation of domestic industry—without the extreme intra-elite and elite–mass polarization that characterized many Latin American societies.

Modern industrial development dates to the late 1880s, around the time of the abolition of slavery and the Brazilian monarchy. The economy was led by agricultural exports—over two-thirds of agricultural output (by value) was exported—especially by the coffee sector, based in the Southeastern states of Rio de Janeiro and São Paulo. The political system was dominated by coffee interests backed by foreign (primarily British) traders and financiers. The Brazilian equivalent of Germany's marriage of iron and rye, indeed, was the more appetizing *café com leite*—coffee with milk—which tied the coffee sector to traditionalist cattle barons from the interior state of Minas Gerais.

Industrial growth, based in the Southeast, was gradual but impressive, and by 1919 domestic firms supplied over 70 percent of local demand for industrial products—over 95 percent of cotton textiles—and employed 14 percent of the labor force.[1] Manufacturing grew primarily in sectors tied to foreign trade, where transport or raw materials costs made local production competitive, or where growth of the local market made large-scale industry feasible. After the turn of the century, many coffee growers themselves diversified; the persistent decline in international coffee prices drew capital out of the São Paulo countryside and into the city, where it was often invested in industry. Despite the export expansion of the 1920s, the coffee economy's days were numbered by the time of World War I.

With the depression of the 1930s the coffee interests began to lose their grip on economic policy, a loss speeded by the collapse of the world commercial and financial systems upon which the coffee and allied sectors

---

[1] For excellent surveys of early Brazilian economic growth, see Nathaniel Leff's two-volume *Underdevelopment and Development in Brazil* (London: George Allen and Unwin, 1982); Pedro S. Malan, Regis Bonelli, Marcelo de P. Abreu, and José Eduardo de C. Pereira, *Política econômica externa e industrialização no Brasil (1939/52)* (Rio de Janeiro: IPEA/INPES, 1980); Charles C. Mueller, *Das oligarquias agrárias ao predomínio urbano-industrial* (Rio de Janeiro: IPEA/INPES, 1983); Wilson Suzigan, *Indústria brasileira: Origem e desenvolvimento* (São Paulo: Brasiliense, 1986); and Annibal Villela and Wilson Suzigan, *Government Policy and the Economic Growth of Brazil, 1889–1945*, Brazilian Economic Studies no. 3 (Rio de Janeiro: IPEA/INPES, 1977). Figures in this paragraph are calculated from Villela and Suzigan, *Government Policy*, 39, 61, 360.

depended. As the New York price of Brazilian coffee dropped over 60 percent between 1929 and 1931, even concerted government support could not save the sector, and over the course of the 1930s almost half of the country's coffee land was taken out of production. The deterioration of the country's terms of trade and a large depreciation of the *mil-reis* gave a major stimulus to production for the domestic market; for example, the price of imported textiles relative to domestic production nearly doubled between 1929 and 1935.[2]

The depression forced a definitive reorientation of the Brazilian economy away from export agriculture and toward industrial production for the domestic market. The collapse of external demand and eventual supply problems during World War II provided a favorable environment for industrial growth. While imports supplied 42 percent of the Brazilian demand for industrial products during the 1920s, by the late 1930s they were down to 22 percent, and they fell below 15 percent during World War II. Indeed, during the war Brazil exported one-eighth of its cotton textile output. In the 1920s, agricultural production grew by 43 percent and industrial production by 33 percent. Between 1930 and 1945, industrial output grew by 185 percent, while agricultural output grew by only 33 percent. Within industry, the share of intermediate and capital goods production went from 17 percent in 1919 to 31 percent in 1949.[3]

While much of this evolution was driven by market forces, the government reinforced and augmented industrial development. In 1930 Getúlio Vargas seized power; he ruled constitutionally until 1937, when he assumed dictatorial power under the Estado Novo, which lasted until 1945. Vargas had centralizing, modernizing tendencies and a populist appeal to urban nationalism. Especially after the early 1930s, as the protracted nature of the international depression became obvious and the Brazilian economy shifted to domestic industrial growth, Vargas used selective state economic intervention as a tool to speed this shift. Public utilities prices and interest rates were controlled in 1933, the railroad system became a virtual state monopoly, the major shipping line Lloyd Brasileiro was taken over in 1937, and the Banco do Brasil expanded to take on many of the attributes of a central bank and to offer subsidized credit to industry. During World War II, the government founded national steel, mining, automotive, and caustic soda corporations, and began building Latin America's first integrated steel mill.

Industrial development under Vargas had two important sociopolitical features: modern economic elites remained relatively united, and the in-

[2] Mueller, *Das oligarquias agrárias*, 225; Malan et al., *Política econômica externa*, 278.
[3] Villela and Suzigan, *Government Policy*, calculated from pp. 353–60; Malan et al., *Política econômica externa*, 287; Mueller, *Das oligarquias agrárias*, 246.

dustrial labor movement was institutionalized and controlled.[4] Southern Brazil's agrarian and industrializing interests were not fundamentally divided by the depression. To some degree this was because many coffee growers, processors, and traders had begun to diversify as early as before World War I; many São Paulo industrial concerns were tied to coffee fortunes. A government coffee price-support program also cushioned part of the blow of the international crisis for the coffee sector and smoothed the sector's transition to other crops or out of agriculture. This is not to deny the existence of economic, social, and political differences between the coffee sector and industry—as in most of the rest of the region, for example, immigrants were overrepresented among industrial entrepreneurs, while coffee growers tended to be from more traditional rural-elite backgrounds—but the agro-exporting and industrial communities were less antagonistic in Brazil than elsewhere. After all, São Paulo state was the center of both the coffee sector and the country's manufacturing industries.

Industrial development had a contradictory impact on the labor movement, as Vargas pursued a mix of repression and co-optation toward the growing working class. On the one hand, the government removed or disciplined the more oppositional labor leaders, especially those tied to the Communist Party. Labor legislation patterned on that of fascist Italy and Portugal set up unions easily controlled by the government. On the other hand, labor was the beneficiary of a range of social programs, including some aimed specifically at normalizing labor-management relations and some (such as the minimum wage) with more general social purposes. The result, by 1945, was a semi-official labor movement purged of the radical opposition and accorded relatively favorable treatment by the government.

After World War II, as international markets returned to normalcy, Brazil did not revert to pre-1930 patterns of economic policy and politics. The Brazilian social order had changed fundamentally, as economic and political supremacy had shifted from agro-exporting groups to urban industrial centers.[5]

[4] For surveys of the Vargas period, see E. Carone, *A Republica Nova (1930–1937)* (São Paulo: DIFEL, 1976) and *O Estado Novo (1939–1945)* (São Paulo: DIFEL, 1977); John D. Wirth, *The Politics of Brazilian Development, 1930–1954* (Stanford: Stanford University Press, 1970); as well as Warren Dean, *The Industrialization of São Paulo, 1880–1945* (Austin: University of Texas Press, 1969); Peter Flynn, *Brazil: A Political Analysis* (Boulder, Colo.: Westview Press, 1979); and Thomas E. Skidmore, *Politics in Brazil, 1930–1964* (New York: Oxford University Press, 1967). On the role of the business community, see Eli Diniz and Renato Raul Boschi, *Empresariado nacional e estado no Brasil* (Rio de Janeiro: Forense-Universitária, 1978), 21–107.

[5] A fascinating reflection of this was the bitter 1944–1945 debate over economic devel-

Economic policy defended the industrial structure built up during the 1930s and 1940s. In the early postwar years, an improvised combination of multiple exchange rates, tariff protection, and import licenses penalized exporters, protected import-competing manufacturers, and provided cheap capital goods to domestic industry. By the mid-1950s, especially under Juscelino Kubitschek (1956–1961), more concerted policies had been worked out, with similar goals in mind. Tariffs, exchange rates, and quantitative import controls spurred demand for domestic industrial output; incentives for foreign firms stimulated foreign direct investment in manufacturing; and public investment expanded the economic infrastructure.

The economic role of the government expanded continually during this heyday of import-substituting industrialization. During Vargas's second administration, in 1952, the Banco Nacional de Desenvolvimento Econômico e Social (BNDES; the "Social" was added in 1982) was created, originally to channel World Bank loans to the public sector; eventually the development bank became the country's most important source of industrial finance. Vargas also created the national petroleum monopoly Petrobras, along with regional development banks and power companies. The Kubitschek administration established public enterprises in steel, electric power, and transportation. All the while, protectionism remained the rule: by 1963, effective rates of protection for manufacturing averaged 184 percent.[6]

Industrial production quadrupled between World War II and 1962, as industry's share of gross domestic product (GDP) went from 20.6 percent in 1947 to 28.0 percent in 1960.[7] By the early 1960s, Brazil had one of the broadest industrial economies in the developing world. In 1963 the most modern industries—metal products, electrical machinery, transport equipment, and chemicals and allied products—accounted for 44 percent of gross industrial value added, up from 19 percent in 1939. In 1962 domestic production provided 99 percent of the total domestic supply of consumer goods, 91 percent of intermediate goods, and 87 percent of

opment between Roberto Simonsen, a leading São Paulo industrialist and developmentalist, and Eugênio Gudin, an orthodox market-oriented economist with strong ties to foreign enterprises. Much of the debate is reprinted in Eugênio Gudin and Roberto C. Simonsen, *A controvérsia do planejamento na economia brasileira* (Rio de Janeiro: IPEA/INPES, 1978).

[6] Roberto de Rezende Rocha, "Indicadores de Política Comercial," in Paulo Nogueira Batista, Jr. et al., *Ensaios sobre o setor externo da economia brasileira* (Rio de Janeiro: IBRE/FGV, 1981), 177. See also Joel Bergsman, *Brazil: Industrialization and Trade Policies* (London: Oxford University Press, 1970), 51.

[7] For a survey of the period, see Werner Baer, *The Brazilian Economy: Growth and Development*, 2d ed. (New York: Praeger, 1983), 59–91.

capital goods.[8] Rapid growth, along with the systematic protection and subsidization of modern industry, had transformed the economy. It had also created a concentrated industrial structure dependent on government support.

Politics after World War II also reflected the patterns of the 1930s and 1940s. The regimes of the period—from Vargas and Kubitschek to Jânio Quadros (1961) and João Goulart (1961–1964)—relied on variants of the populist coalition of the 1930s and its nationalistic, developmentalist consensus. The modern business community and the urban middle and working classes were crucial electoral support bases; traditional agrarian elites maintained influence through clientelism in backward rural areas; urban and rural "marginals," those outside the modern sector, were powerless. The industrial working class was kept in check by corporatist controls, even as it gained some social and economic benefits. There were few ideological differences among political leaders, which highlighted the personalistic nature of electoral competition and the fluidity of the party structure. The political system was dominated by personal machines based on patronage and government social programs.

The thickening net of government subsidies and incentives for industrial development and the populist coalitions' reliance on government spending for patronage and social purposes put the economy under increasing strain. The anti-export bias of industrial policy, especially chronic currency overvaluation, led to recurring balance of payments crises. As taxation did not meet the needs of the growing government sector, budget deficits grew and inflation accelerated, which exacerbated currency overvaluation and problems in the payments balance. In the early 1960s, crosscutting political pressures made it nearly impossible to manage the external accounts and government finances without alienating one segment or another of the ruling coalition. By 1963 the economy was stagnant, inflation was at unprecedented levels, foreign investment had dried up and foreign lenders had deserted the country. No political actor seemed capable of controlling the situation, and in April 1964 the military overthrew Goulart and took power.

Brazil in 1960 was characterized by an entrenched pattern of sectoral economic policies and a low level of labor-capital conflict. In the early 1960s, as the country crumbled into political turmoil, elite fears about social unrest grew, and they were an important factor in the 1964 military coup. However, even at its high point class struggle in Brazil was relatively tame, and labor hardly represented a serious threat to property rights. As policy and politics evolved after 1964, after a brief stabilization period, sectoral considerations were paramount.

[8] Ibid., 84–86.

Stabilization, 1964–1967

Although the specific causes of the 1964 coup are many and controversial,[9] there is little question that it grew out of generalized elite dissatisfaction with populist political practices, and fear of the turmoil that characterized the last years of democratic government. President Goulart's continual battles with conservatives led him to ally with forces to his left, and in 1963 and 1964 politicians associated with radical nationalism and populism came to the fore. Although real threats to property were few and far between, the memory of the Cuban Revolution was fresh. By Brazilian standards, the months before the coup raised unprecedented questions about the stability of the country's social order. In this context, the business community was, uncharacteristically, more interested in the investment climate broadly defined than in narrower sectoral interests.

Once in power the military government therefore concentrated on ensuring law and order, and its economic policies reflected overriding concern about threats "from below," from an amorphous amalgam of socialism, nationalism, and populism that the military and its business supporters believed was the root of the country's problems.[10] Many also believed that protection from market forces had allowed the growth of artificial industries with inflated wages and that this economic hothouse was a breeding ground for labor militancy and radicalism. The restoration of sociopolitical order thus required building an economy less subject to political manipulation.

In its first few years, the military regime entrusted economic policy to a group of conservative "technocrats" who were quite market-oriented by Brazilian standards. Led by Roberto de Oliveira Campos and Octávio Gouvea de Bulhões, economic policymakers between 1964 and 1967 were general opponents of government intervention in the market. They repressed wages even as the military purged the labor movement. They liberalized the country's commercial and financial relations with the rest of the world. The economic team revamped the financial system to ensure a positive real return on capital. And the government reworked arrangements for the inflow of foreign finance to allow the country to take advantage of international financial markets.

On the wage front, the real minimum wage in Rio de Janeiro was cut by 34 percent between February 1964 and March 1967; in the same

[9] For one survey and point of view, see Michael Wallerstein, "The Collapse of Democracy in Brazil," *Latin American Research Review* 15, no. 3 (1980): 3–40.

[10] Alfred Stepan, *The Military in Politics* (Princeton: Princeton University Press, 1971), is a classic study of the military's views.

period the real national average wage dropped by over 10 percent.[11] There was a substantial deterioration in income distribution during the late 1960s, which did not improve during the subsequent period of rapid economic growth. Between 1960 and 1970 the share of national income going to the bottom 80 percent of the population dropped from 46 percent to 37 percent, while that going to the top 20 percent increased from 54 to 63 percent; while per capita income among the first group grew under 8 percent during the decade, that of the second group grew over 25 percent. Even after the economic boom began, wages in the late 1960s grew more slowly than productivity. One result of these trends in income distribution was dramatic growth of the urban middle classes, who served both as bases of support for the regime and as a market for the consumer durables being produced.

The economic team regarded financial reconstruction as central to the restoration of a vibrant private sector. Indeed, financial intermediation had atrophied under such government policies as usury laws that held nominal interest rates below inflation. Less than 3 percent of national savings were channeled through the financial system, an extraordinarily low figure even for Latin America at the time, where the average was between 10 and 15 percent.[12] Partly as a result, much of the growth of the 1950s was financed by deficit spending, which contributed to the inflation of the early 1960s. The market-oriented team wanted to support a strong private financial market that would allocate resources by economic criteria.

The financial system was overhauled after the 1964 coup in order to strengthen its role in the investment process. Indexing was introduced in a variety of financial instruments, which minimized the possibility of negative real interest rates and regularized government borrowing via index-linked treasury bonds. A modern central bank was created, along with a state-owned housing finance system funded by workers' forced savings and the state-owned savings and loan network. The BNDES expanded long-term industrial lending. A division between commercial and investment banking was introduced, and attempts were made to develop a capital market for corporate stocks and bonds.[13]

[11] André Lara Resende, "A política brasileira de estabilização: 1963/1968," *Pesquisa e Planejamento Econômico* 12, no. 3 (December 1982): 779–80.

[12] André Franco Montoro Filho, *Moeda e sistema financeiro no Brasil* (Rio de Janeiro: IPEA/INPES, 1982), 79.

[13] For details of the financial reforms of the 1960s, and the resulting new financial system, see Montoro Filho, *Moeda e sistema financeiro*, 79–93; Adroaldo Moura da Silva, "Intermediação Financeira" (mimeo, 1981), 9–28; Ernane Galveas, *Evolução do sistema financeiro* (Brasília: Ministério da Fazenda, 1981), 25–68; and Hélio O. Portocarrero de Castro, ed., *Introdução ao mercado de capitais* (Rio de Janeiro: IBMEC, 1979).

Another important set of economic policies taken by the military government facilitated the inflow of foreign capital. In fact, most of the policies adopted toward the domestic financial sector were directly or indirectly tied to ambitious plans to tap the burgeoning Euromarkets. By the same token, restrictions on foreign direct investment were relaxed.

Finally, the new economic team undertook to reduce restrictions on international trade. Many of the measures that had created a severe anti-export bias were revised or eliminated, such as taxes on exports and a consistently overvalued exchange rate. Tariff protection was reduced in the stabilization period. Average rates of effective protection on all goods went from 75 percent in 1963 to 24 percent in 1967, and from 184 percent in 1963 to 63 percent in 1967 on manufactured goods.[14]

The 1964–1967 period was one of structural reform, stabilization, and relative stagnation. The economic team emphasized rebuilding the system of economic incentives itself rather than stimulating economic growth, and the reforms drove many firms into bankruptcy. Despite the travails of businessmen, the regime maintained a market-oriented course until 1967. Between 1964 and 1967, GDP grew at an average annual rate of just 3.5 percent, while per capita GDP growth stagnated at just 0.7 percent a year, compared with average annual growth rates in the 1950s of 6.9 and 3.7 percent respectively. On the positive side, inflation fell from 87 percent in 1964 to 29 percent in 1967.[15]

The stabilization phase in Brazil, then, was the most market-oriented in its recent history. It fits my general analytical expectations, inasmuch as it took place at a time when economic elites were more concerned about the protection of property rights, social order, and the division of national income between wages and profits than they were about specific subsidies and incentives. While memories of the populist turmoil of the early 1960s lingered, until the military had eliminated threats to the existing order, the business community was primarily interested in restoring

---

[14] Rezende Rocha, "Indicadores," 177. For a survey of trade policies in the late 1960s, see Joel Bergsman and Pedro S. Malan, "The Structure of Protection in Brazil," in Bela Balassa and Associates, *The Structure of Protection in Developing Countries* (Baltimore: Johns Hopkins Press, 1971), 103–36.

[15] Figures on Brazilian economic performance used in the remainder of this chapter are derived from a variety of sources. Since the standard general source on the Brazilian economy is Werner Baer, *The Brazilian Economy*, most statistics are drawn from there. Other statistical sources include the Fundação Getúlio Vargas, as published monthly in *Conjuntura Econômica*; the Banco Central do Brasil, as published in its *Boletim Mensal*; and statistical series culled from various sources and divulged by the government think tank IPEA/INPES and by the Instituto de Economia Industrial of the Universidade Federal do Rio de Janeiro in its *Boletim de Conjuntura Industrial*. Unless the data in question are particularly controversial or they are drawn from a source other than those listed above, all basic economic data used here are the consensus figures from the above-mentioned sources.

a favorable investment climate, even if the economic team's market-oriented reforms imposed costs on many businesses. Once the danger had passed, however, the private sector returned to type, and Brazilian economic policy after 1967 became progressively more interventionist.

General Patterns, 1968–1980

The pace of economic, and especially industrial, development from 1967 until 1980 was little short of astounding. Steel production went from under four to over fifteen million tons; the domestic automobile industry's annual output grew from two hundred thousand vehicles to over a million; electrical capacity went from under ten million kilowatts to 135 million. Major portions of the nonindustrial economy—especially construction, finance, telecommunications, and agribusiness—were modernized. Brazilian manufacturers began to export in impressive quantities, becoming important actors in the world steel, auto-parts, footwear, aircraft, and weaponry markets. Of course, industrial prowess coexisted with desperate poverty and depressing socioeconomic marginalism, but the military regime had never pretended that its social goals overrode its developmentalism. In economic terms, the government's policies were successful.

After 1967 Brazilian economic policy relied heavily on sectoral subsidies and incentives to spur growth in favored segments of the economy. Economic policy making rarely involved the formal political system the military had established, and effective political representation tended to circumvent the legislature, relying chiefly upon ties between social groups and segments of the regime. In some instances links were informal, as between certain economic leaders and military factions. In other cases more formal vertical bonds were formed: crucial sectors of organized labor were tied to the Ministry of Labor under the labor legislation originally introduced by Vargas during World War II, while sectoral employers' organizations fed business demands to the regime. The most important business group was the Federação das Indústrias do Estado de São Paulo (FIESP), a stronghold of modern industry founded in the Vargas period by developmentalist industrialist and economist Roberto Simonsen.[16]

[16] Good surveys of the post-coup political system can be found in Flynn, *Brazil*, 308–515; the essays in Alfred Stepan, ed., *Authoritarian Brazil: Origins, Policies, and Future* (New Haven: Yale University Press, 1973); and in Sylvia Ann Hewlett and Richard Weinert, eds., *Brazil and Mexico: Patterns in Late Development* (Philadelphia: ISHI, 1982). On the business community in the 1970s, see Diniz and Boschi, *Empresariado nacional*, 108–200. On labor, see Kenneth Paul Erickson, *The Brazilian Corporative State and Working-Class Politics* (Berkeley: University of California Press, 1977); and Kenneth S. Mericle, "Corporatist Control of the Working Class: Authoritarian Brazil since 1964," in *Authoritarianism and*

A powerful grouping of economic actors was especially important to national development after 1967. The domestic banking system grew institutionally and financially stronger. State firms expanded continually, as their proportion of gross fixed capital formation grew from 13 percent in 1965 to 29 percent in 1979 (the government itself accounted for another 15 percent); this does not take full account of public development banks' financing of investment.[17] The parastatals' ambitious projects brought along with them networks of suppliers, especially in capital goods industries, where parastatals accounted for a large proportion of domestic orders. Consumer durables producers tapped a rapidly growing middle-class market.

Foreign finance was central to the growth process. Domestic banks borrowed abroad and earned virtually ensured profits re-lending dollars to domestic borrowers. State enterprises relied on foreign finance for their investment programs. Domestic suppliers to state enterprises, especially in capital goods, got foreign finance channeled through private Brazilian banks and subsidized credit from the BNDES, often originating on the Euromarkets. Private firms borrowed on the Euromarkets to expand their operations. Large-scale modern agriculture, especially in the Southeast and South, received subsidized credits from public financial institutions.

The "growth coalition" after 1964 was composed of state enterprises, modern industry, domestic finance, and agribusiness. From 1967 until 1980 it succeeded extraordinarily well in using previously installed productive capacity, a reorganized financial system, and foreign finance to obtain impressive rates of growth. The booming international trading and financial systems accelerated the economy's upward trend, and it was not difficult to maintain political agreement among major economic actors so long as the world and local economies were growing.

Table 4.1 is an overview of Brazilian borrowing and economic development from 1964 to 1985. The country's experience can be divided in four periods: stabilization (1964–1967), discussed above; the "miracle" (1968–1973); the "big projects" period (1974–1980); and the crisis (1981–1985). Overseas borrowing began with the "miracle," a period of rapid economic growth amid moderately liberal international financial and commercial relations. During the third period a gradual political opening began, while economic policy turned toward ambitious import-substituting investment projects; overseas borrowing grew rapidly. The

Corporatism in Latin America, ed. James M. Malloy (Pittsburgh: University of Pittsburgh Press, 1977), 303–38.

[17] Philippe Reichstul and Luciano G. Coutinho, "Investimento Estatal 1974–1980," in *Desenvolvimento capitalista no Brasil*, no. 2, ed. Luiz Gonzaga M. Belluzzo and Renata Coutinho (São Paulo: Brasiliense, 1983), 45; Secretaria de Controle de Empresas Estatais, *Empresas estatais no Brasil e o controle da SEST* (Brasília: SEST, 1981), 8–9, 61.

Table 4.1
Brazil: Selected Economic Indicators, 1970–1985
(Billions of current and 1982 U.S. dollars)

	GDP		Current Account 82$s	Medium + Long-Term Debt			S-T[a] Debt 82$s	Total Debt 82$s
	Current Dollars	1982 $s		Public[b] 82$s	Private[c] 82$s	Total 82$s		
1970	51.8	123.3	− 1.4	N.A.	N.A.	12.6	0.5	13.1
1971	61.3	138.1	− 2.9	8.8	6.1	14.9	0.7	15.6
1972	71.3	153.4	− 3.2	N.A.	N.A.	20.4	1.1	21.5
1973	86.5	174.7	− 3.4	13.1	12.3	25.4	2.4	27.8
1974	103.3	191.3	− 13.1	15.7	15.9	31.6	2.4	34.0
1975	119.9	202.2	− 11.3	19.4	16.4	35.8	1.7	37.5
1976	140.0	221.8	− 9.5	23.6	17.6	41.2	4.3	45.5
1977	157.3	233.8	− 5.9	28.7	18.9	47.6	4.2	51.8
1978	176.9	245.0	− 9.7	38.2	22.0	60.2	6.0	66.2
1979	205.7	261.7	− 13.6	43.3	20.2	63.5	5.1	68.6
1980	242.0	282.4	− 15.1	43.5	19.3	62.8	8.2	71.0
1981	261.7	278.4	− 12.4	44.5	20.9	65.4	9.1	74.5
1982	281.0	281.0	− 16.3	47.4	22.8	70.2	13.0	83.2
1983	284.3	273.9	− 6.3	58.1	20.2	78.3	9.9	88.2
1984	312.9	289.5	+ 0.5	66.4	17.9	84.3	8.0	92.3
1985	350.2	313.5	− 1.4	65.4	16.5	81.9	7.3	89.2

Source: Calculated from Jeffry A. Frieden, "The Brazilian Borrowing Experience," Latin American Research Review 22, no. 1 (1987): 103.

Note: Dollar figures are deflated by the U.S. implicit GNP price deflator; N.A. = Not available.

[a] Short term debt, that of less than one year's maturity.
[b] Foreign debt owed or guaranteed by the public sector.
[c] Foreign debt owed by the private sector.

crisis led to a major industrial depression, rampant inflation, and the victory of the civilian opposition.

The height of Brazilian borrowing was between 1968 and 1981, and my analytical expectation for this period is that the political power of different sectors determined the degree which they were favored by policy. In turn, I expect political power to be related to the intensity of the sector's preferences, a function of the specificity of the sector's assets; and to the internal cohesion of each sector. My argument, then, is that government policies that channeled external finance to different sectors were motivated primarily by the political influence of the sectors themselves, and that this influence was a function of the asset specificity and internal cohesion of each sector.[18]

[18] This is far superior to examining sectoral profitability per se, since such factors as con-

The financial expansion after 1967 substantially increased the supply of capital in Brazil, a factor of great importance to private business, since access to external finance was a major determinant of profitability.[19] Yet the government strongly influenced the effects of this increased supply of capital, as virtually the only sources of long-term finance available to the private sector were overseas borrowing and loans from state-owned financial institutions, both of which were regulated by the government. In Brazil, all foreign borrowing had to be approved by the monetary authorities, so that direct external borrowing by the private sector was at the discretion of the government. External borrowing by the public sector similarly allowed the government to channel funds to favored sectors in the form of subsidized credit from public financial institutions. Government support during the borrowing boom thus included easing private-sector access to foreign borrowing, and direct extension of subsidized credit from the public sector to private firms.

Virtually all external borrowing by the private sector was done by financial and industrial firms. Table 4.2 shows private financial institutions' debt to foreigners as a share of their total liabilities (a rough measure of the contribution of foreign borrowing to lending capacity). To use other criteria, by 1981 funds available to private commercial banks under their principal foreign-borrowing category were equivalent to 90 percent of the demand deposits held with them, and to 2.45 times their capital and reserves.[20] The foreign debt of the private banking system increased continually over the period, and foreign funds were a substantial contribution to banks' total resources.

To a certain extent the central role of the financial sector as beneficiary of the inflow of foreign funds was natural. Yet it was not inevitable that domestic private banks should play so important a role in Brazilian borrowing, and government policies strongly encouraged this role. A very important reason for such policies toward the bankers was political.

---

centration may exert a powerful effect on profit rates independent of government policy. In fact, the evidence concerning such an effect is contradictory. Regis Bonelli, "Concentração industrial no Brasil," *Pesquisa e Planejamento Econômico* 10, no. 3 (December 1980): 877, found no significant effect of concentration (measured by Gini coefficient) on profitability, while Helson Braga, *Estrutura de mercado e desempenho da indústria brasileira: 1973/75* (Rio de Janeiro: Editora da Fundação Getulio Vargas, 1980), 76, found a significant positive impact of the eight-firm concentration ratio on profitability. The ambiguity of these results parallels similarly contradictory results of studies elsewhere.

[19] Braga, *Estrutura de mercado*, 95, found that indebtedness had a major and positive impact on profitability.

[20] The category in question is Resolution 63 loans, on which see the appendix to this chapter. Paulo Davidoff Cruz, *Dívida externa e política econômica: A experiência brasileira nos anos setenta* (São Paulo: Brasiliense, 1984), 144. This invaluable study is based on data from the Central Bank's records of loan approvals between 1972 and 1981, and provides more detailed information about overseas borrowing than is available for any other Latin American debtor.

Table 4.2
Brazil: Foreign Borrowing and the Financial Sector
(Brazilian financial institutions' foreign liabilities as a percent of their total
liabilities, 1970–1982)

	Pub. comm. banks[a]	Pvt. comm. banks[b]	Pvt. I. banks[c]	BNDES[d]	State dev. banks[e]
1970	14	10	8	7	7
1971	13	12	11	6	4
1972	12	15	22	7	2
1973	9	16	18	10	13
1974	9	18	18	9	1
1975	8	14	16	9	1
1976	10	20	15	8	1
1977	10	21	13	10	1
1978	13	26	16	12	2
1979	19	32	18	17	3
1980	19	36	34	17	4
1981	18	42	34	15	7

Source: Banco Central do Brasil, Boletim Mensal, various issues.
[a] Public commercial banks, excluding the Banco do Brasil.
[b] Private commercial banks.
[c] Private investment banks.
[d] Banco Nacional de Desenvolvimento Econômico e Social (National Economic and Social Development Bank).
[e] State development banks.

Especially after the reforms of 1964–1967, the financial sector was a powerful social force, and it became increasingly powerful over time.

The Brazilian banking system was strong and cohesive at the start of the recent borrowing experience, and the inflow of funds made it even stronger and more oligopolistic.[21] The rapid growth of the financial sector is illustrated by the increase in its share of national income from 4.3 percent in 1965 to 6.4 percent in 1973 and 9.3 percent in 1978. Financial intermediation grew by a spectacular 18 percent a year in real terms between 1968 and 1979, double the real GDP growth in the period. At the

[21] The financial sector in many ways does not fit the typical picture of an industry with specific assets. Its portfolio is normally quite diversified, so that it would tend to be indifferent among policies to favor different nonfinancial sectors. However, financial institutions themselves have significant firm or sector-specific capital—reputation, experience, networks—associated with their activities of financial intermediation. For examples of the theoretical literature on banking, see Eugene Fama, "What's Different about Banks?" Journal of Monetary Economics 15 (1985): 29–39; and Stephen D. Williamson, "Increasing Returns to Scale in Financial Intermediation and the Non-Neutrality of Government Policy," Review of Economic Studies 53 (1986): 863–75.

same time the financial system as a whole, which financed almost nothing abroad before 1967, had 9 percent of its liabilities in foreign currency by 1970 and 20 percent by 1979.[22] The largest banks had best access to overseas funds, and foreign borrowing quickened the pace of concentration within the banking industry. In 1970 the ten largest private commercial banks accounted for 47 percent of total private commercial-bank lending, and the five largest for 27 percent: by 1980 the respective figures were 78 percent and 56 percent.[23] By the late 1970s the private financial system was dominated by a few conglomerates, generally including a commercial bank, an investment bank, a consumer finance firm and a real estate finance firm, and sometimes leasing and brokerage arms. Before the crisis private financiers were unquestionably the leaders of the private sector; Bradesco, the largest private bank, was the first private firm in Brazilian history with more than one hundred thousand employees. The bankers were also among the government's strongest supporters in the private sector.

In addition to increasing private-sector access to foreign loans, the financial inflow expanded resources available to the public sector. One of the more important uses to which these resources were put was the extension of subsidized credit by public financial institutions to the private sector. The Brazilian public financial sector is very extensive; most of its subsidized loans were made to agriculture, primarily by the Banco do Brasil, and to industry, primarily by the BNDES.

Massive credits were extended by the monetary authorities to Brazilian agriculture, amounts equal to well over half of the country's total agricultural output in the 1970s and early 1980s.[24] The element of subsidy in the agricultural loans varied from year to year but averaged about one-quarter of the total credits. That these credits were a boon to the recipients is indicated by the widespread fraud reported to have gone on in the credit program, with estimates of funds diverted from agriculture ranging up to 30 percent of the total.

Subsidized agricultural credit was concentrated in the advanced areas of the South and Southeast, and in the largest farms. In the backward

[22] Luiz Carlos Bresser Pereira, *Economia brasileira* (São Paulo: Brasiliense, 1982), 123; André Franco Montoro Filho, *Moeda e sistema financiero no Brasil* (Rio de Janeiro: IPEA/INPES, 1982), 100–103, 170–75.

[23] Alvaro Antônio Zini Junior, "Características qualitativas e avaliação do funcionamento do setor financeiro no Brasil" (mimeo, 1982), 6–11.

[24] Information in this section comes primarily from Alexandre Comin and Geraldo Müller, *Crédito, modernização e atraso*, Cadernos CEBRAP 6 (São Paulo: CEBRAP, 1985); World Bank, *Brazil: Financial Systems Review* (Washington, D.C.: World Bank, 1980), 43–66; Mailson Ferreira de Nóbrega, "Taxas de juros e crédito subsidiado," Brasília, 9 April 1981; and Annibal Villela and Werner Baer, *O setor privado nacional: Problemas e políticas para seu fortalecimento* (Rio de Janeiro: IPEA/INPES, 1980), 239–92.

Northeast, where in general farms are small and farmers politically weak, only 11 percent of all farms were beneficiaries of operating credits, while in the state of São Paulo, where in general farms are large and farmers politically strong, 57 percent of all farms received such credits.[25] Nearly three times as much agricultural credit per hectare of farmland was extended to the Southeast as to the Northeast. One striking comparison is between São Paulo state and the Northeastern states of Rio Grande do Norte and Ceará. Together the two backward states have about as many farms as São Paulo, and well over half as much cropped area, but São Paulo received more than eight times the rural credit of the other two states combined. Even within São Paulo, farms over one hundred hectares, large by Brazilian standards, are 16 percent of all farms, but they received 53 percent of all agricultural credit in 1977.[26]

While this evidence about the distribution of subsidized agricultural credit is not systematic, it clearly indicates the political underpinnings of such government programs. It is difficult not to conclude that insofar as lending to agriculture was concerned, the Brazilian public sector's increased access to overseas finance primarily benefited the politically influential, especially larger farmers in the developed South and Southeast.

The BNDES is the most important source of loans for industry in Brazil, accounting for four-fifths of such lending by some accounts.[27] Table 4.3 shows BNDES lending to manufacturing between 1967 and 1981, expressed in constant (1982) dollars; this is the most disaggregated accounting of BNDES loans available. Loans to the steel industry, three-quarters of which is controlled by public enterprises, are shown separately from the largely private remainder of metallurgy. BNDES lending concentrated on modern industries, which generally have very specific assets and are large-scale and well organized.

Much of the inflow of foreign finance benefited private industry. This included short-term loans obtained from private banks for working capital and long-term loans borrowed directly from abroad. Table 4.4 shows direct overseas borrowing by manufacturing firms between 1972 and 1981, a total of $18.7 billion in constant (1982) dollars. Because foreign borrowing was controlled by the government, and because foreign funds were of great assistance to private firms, the distribution of direct foreign borrowing gives a reasonable picture of those sectors favored by government borrowing policies. The table shows each sector's borrowing and its share of total borrowing by the private manufacturing sector. For comparison, it lists each sector's share of 1974 manufacturing output and,

[25] Villela and Baer, O setor privado nacional, 270.

[26] World Bank, Brazil, 56–58.

[27] For an excellent study of the system, see Eliza Willis, "The State as Banker: The Expansion of the Public Sector in Brazil" (Ph.D. diss., University of Texas, Austin, 1986).

Table 4.3

Brazil: Loans Approved by the National Bank for Economic and Social Development System, by Economic Activity, 1964–1981
(Millions of 1982 dollars and percent)

	1964–1973 Loans	As % of Total	1974–1981 Loans	As % of Total	1964–1981 Loans	As % of Total
Mining	$ 79	1.0	$ 1,247	3.3	$ 1,326	2.9
Steel	1,984	24.9	12,657	33.5	14,641	32.0
Metalworking[a]	583	7.3	3,522	9.3	4,105	9.0
Chemicals + fertilizers	957	12.0	5,218	13.8	6,174	13.5
Pulp and paper	504	6.3	2,798	7.4	3,302	7.2
Nonmetallic minerals	420	5.3	2,138	5.7	2,559	5.6
Machinery + electrical equipment	470	5.9	2,596	6.9	3,066	6.7
Transport equipment	494	6.2	805	2.1	1,300	2.8
Textiles + footwear	496	6.2	1,308	3.5	1,804	3.9
Foodstuffs	559	7.0	1,856	4.9	2,416	5.3
Others	1,426	17.9	3,641	9.6	5,067	11.1
Total	7,972	100.0	37,786	100.0	45,758	100.0

Source: Jonas Zoninsein, "Atitudes nacionais e financiamento da indústria: A experiência brasileira," Universidade Federal do Rio de Janeiro, Instituto de Economia Industrial, Texto para Discussão no. 63, December 1984, p. 39.

Note: Totals may not add due to rounding.

[a] Excludes steel.

from a slightly different sample but of more analytical relevance, each sector's share of manufacturing invested capital (patrimônio líquido).[28]

Some industries borrowed significantly more than their invested capital and output would indicate, while others borrowed significantly less. Those which borrowed in excess of their share both of invested capital and output were the electrical material, transport material, chemicals, pharmaceuticals, tobacco, and "other" industries, with 58.39 percent of manufacturing borrowing, 31.35 percent of manufacturing output, and 27.97 percent of manufacturing invested capital. Sectors whose borrowing was near or above their share of one of the two measures were non-

[28] This measure is more valid because we would expect borrowing to be more strongly correlated with the capital stock of the industry than with its output; that is, the former figure controls roughly for differing capital intensities.

Table 4.4
Brazil: Borrowing by Manufacturing Sectors
(Millions of 1982 dollars and percent)

	Borrowing[a]	% Total Borrowing	% Mfg. Output[b]	% Mfg. Capital[c]
Nonmetallic minerals	918	4.91	4.28	5.57
Metallurgy	2,429	12.98	15.03	22.85
Machinery	1,141	6.10	7.74	7.50
Electrical material	1,704	9.11	7.03	6.24
Transport material	3,856	20.61	10.65	8.33
Wood products	68	0.36	3.48	1.74
Furniture	0	0	2.22	0.57
Pulp and paper	623	3.33	4.64	3.55
Rubber products	215	1.15	0.97	2.58
Leather products	0	0	0.63	0.42
Chemicals	4,215	22.53	8.82	9.54
Pharmaceuticals	433	2.31	2.04	1.84
Toiletries	23	0.12	1.52	0.92
Plastic products	0	0	1.47	0.50
Textiles	724	3.87	9.24	6.39
Clothing, footwear	172	0.92	3.80	1.77
Food products	821	4.39	10.31	9.58
Beverages	393	2.10	1.78	3.69
Tobacco	235	1.26	0.77	0.18
Publishing	257	1.37	1.56	1.09
Others	481	2.57	2.04	1.84
Total[d]	18,708	100.00	100.00	100.00

Source: See appendix to this chapter.
[a] 1972–1981.
[b] 1974.
[c] 1975, removing state enterprises from total.
[d] May not add due to rounding.

metallic minerals, metallurgy, machinery, pulp and paper, rubber products, beverages, and publishing, with 31.94 percent of manufacturing borrowing, 36 percent of output, and 46.83 percent of invested capital. Sectors with substantially less than "their share" by both measures were the wood, furniture, leather products, toiletries, plastic, textiles, clothing, and food products industries, with 9.66 percent of manufacturing borrowing, 32.67 percent of output, and 21.89 percent of invested capital.

This division accurately reflects the industries most favored by government policy between 1968 and 1981: modern manufacturing, especially in consumer durables and capital goods, was supported, while more traditional and standardized industries, especially in consumer nondurables, were not. While systematic data are hard to come by, favored industries appear to be associated with asset specificity and concentration, which my approach implies give the incentive and ability to apply political pressure. A few statistical observations along these lines are contained in the appendix to this chapter.

Significant portions of the resources made available to Brazil by international financial markets were allocated to the private sector by the government on the basis of political rather than market criteria. The influence of various sectors was, I argue, largely due to the intensity of their policy preferences (specificity of their assets) and their internal cohesion, in the sense that more oligopolistic sectors received more than "their share" of foreign loans and subsidized credit. Within agriculture, the largest farms received the most support. Within manufacturing, favored sectors were sophisticated large-scale industries. The financial sector was strongly supported.

After 1967 the Brazilian government channeled the bulk of the financial inflow directly or indirectly to the more specific and oligopolistic segments of industry, the financial sector, and modern large-scale agriculture. It is important to note, however, that the pattern of economic policy described in this section dates to 1967. Between 1964 and 1967 the military government pursued more laissez-faire policies. It was only after the populist menace had subsided, after 1967, that economic policy settled into an interventionist pattern. The remainder of this chapter is a chronological analysis of Brazilian borrowing, an explanation of the evolution of economic policy and politics.

The "Miracle," 1968–1973

The political repression and economic austerity of the stabilization period went a long way toward eradicating radical populism from the Brazilian body politic. The labor movement was emasculated, and many precoup politicians were jailed, driven into exile, or denied their political rights. The military suppressed political parties in 1966, then built a tightly controlled political system in which only two parties were permitted, the official Aliança Renovadora Nacional (ARENA) and the official opposition Movimento Democrático Brasileiro (MDB). The economic reforms had, in the meantime, undermined some of the social base of traditional populism, especially by means of the constant pressure the more competitive environment placed on small-scale, labor-intensive, traditional industry.

By 1967 Brazilian elites were more worried about the costs of economic stagnation than about the "threat from below" that had led to the 1964 coup. The result was a shift in economic policy that began when the new government of General Artur da Costa e Silva took office in March 1967 and continued through the successor government of General Emílio Garrastazú Médici. The Campos-Bulhões team of market-oriented technocrats was replaced with Antônio Delfim Netto, who remained finance minister through the two administrations. Delfim had little patience for traditional orthodoxy and far more interest in stimulating industrial growth; he was widely regarded on the Left as the archetypical representative of the "national bourgeoisie."

Economic policy between 1967 and 1973, led by Delfim Netto, maintained many of the reforms of the stabilization period, but it replaced the previous team's macroeconomic orthodoxy with growth-oriented heterodoxy. This was clearly a response to concern about what the new policymakers' manifesto called the "weakening of the private sector;" it regarded "the previous government's efforts to correct distortions in the economy" as "excessive for the economy as a whole." The problems, the new team said, were an overly tight monetary policy, and fiscal and wage policies that excessively restricted growth of aggregate demand.[29]

After 1967, systematically expansionist macroeconomic policies were pursued, while many stabilization-era policies were explicitly rejected. Monetary policy was loosened, even though inflation hovered around 20 percent. A comprehensive scheme of index-linking tied virtually all prices to past inflation and some to expected inflation, abandoning the goal of further reducing inflation.[30] Government investment increased considerably, although the public deficit did not grow. Much of this expansion was made possible by an impressive inflow of capital, primarily in the form of private loans. Between 1967 and 1973 net foreign direct investment averaged $278 million a year, while net foreign lending averaged almost $2.2 billion a year. The country's foreign debt, expressed in constant (1982) dollars, grew from $9.2 billion in 1967 to $27.8 billion in 1973.

The growth-oriented policymakers reaffirmed the regime's commitment to reforms implemented after the coup aimed at strengthening the private sector. The government encouraged the consolidation of private financial institutions, avoided real appreciation of the cruzeiro, encouraged foreign investment in the country, and maintained the moderate trade liberalization put in place by the Campos team. The result was a blend of interventionist heterodoxy and market-oriented orthodoxy.

[29] Ministry of Planning and Economic Coordination, *Diretrizes do governo—Programa Estratégico de Desenvolvimento* (July 1967), 20–21, as cited in Luiz Bresser Pereira, *Development and Crisis in Brazil, 1930–1983* (Boulder, Colo.: Westview Press, 1984), 136–37.

[30] Werner Baer and Paul Beckerman, "Indexing in Brazil," *World Development* 2, nos. 10–12 (October–December 1974): 35–47; and Werner Baer and Paul Beckerman, "The Trouble with Index-Linking," *World Development* 8, no. 9 (September 1980): 677–703.

Between 1968 and 1973, the economy grew very rapidly. Industrial output rose 109 percent, GDP 90 percent, and per capita GDP 62 percent; average annual rates of increase for these indicators were 13.1, 11.3, and 8.4 percent respectively. Growth was led by sophisticated modern industries; the five most prominent—metallurgy, machinery, chemicals, electrical equipment, and transportation equipment—expanded from 47 percent of manufacturing output in 1968 to 55 percent in 1974. Gross domestic investment grew from 19 percent of GDP in 1967 to 26 percent in 1973, while inflation remained around 20 percent.

This remarkable performance took place along with a gradual increase in the country's integration into international trade and payments. Exports grew from $1.7 billion in 1967 to $6.2 billion in 1973, exports and imports combined went from 14 to 20 percent of GDP, and manufactured products went from 12 to 24 percent of total exports. At the same time, as mentioned above, the country experienced a large capital inflow. Indeed, the regime's hospitable attitude toward foreign investors, along with the concentration of local affiliates of multinational corporations in the most dynamic industries, meant that they played a prominent role in the expansion, which gave rise to much political controversy and scholarly attention.[31]

In the political arena, the military tightened its repressive apparatus. During stabilization, the regime had focused on "cleansing" political and economic structures; as the economy grew, the military redoubled the political aspects of its self-styled revolution. Amidst economic success, the Costa e Silva and Médici administrations eliminated all remaining semblances of democracy. In December 1968, Institutional Act No. 5 essentially suspended the constitution and gave total power to the president; Congress was shut down. The remaining pockets of radical resistance—student protests, oppositional priests, and an urban guerrilla movement—were suppressed with overwhelming force. The dictatorship dispelled any residual notions of a connection between growth-oriented economic policies and political openness. The goal was industrial development by whatever means the regime deemed necessary.

There was little mystery to the "miracle." Five years of political uncertainty and economic stagnation, between 1962 and 1967, left room for growth once the situation stabilized. The military built a favorable investment climate in which labor was strictly controlled. Its economic reforms increased the efficiency of financial markets, reduced inflation, and facilitated capital inflows. Once recessionary macroeconomic policies

[31] For an example of the former, see Kurt Rudolf Mirow, *A Ditadura dos Carteis* (Rio de Janeiro: Civilização Brasileira, 1978); for an example of the latter, see Peter Evans, *Dependent Development: The Alliance of Multinational, State, and Local Capital in Brazil* (Princeton: Princeton University Press, 1979).

118   CHAPTER 4

were reversed, the economy expanded rapidly to fill the spaces left by previous stagnation.

Although 1968–1973 growth rates were not miraculous, they were nonetheless impressive by any standard. The relatively interventionist economic policies of the period got most of the credit, especially since Campos-Bulhões orthodoxy had yielded mediocre macroeconomic results. The net of sectoral programs, especially in industry, grew even more rapidly after 1973.

"Big Projects," 1974–1980

The economic policies of the new administration of General Ernesto Geisel that took office in March 1974 reinforced the general pattern established between 1967 and 1973. The government's direct role in the economy indeed increased, along with the sector-specific subsidies and incentives that had been central to the "miracle." Geisel's chief economic policymaker, replacing Delfim Netto, was São Paulo economist and investment banker Mário Henrique Simonsen. Like Delfim, Simonsen was close to the leaders of the São Paulo business community; if anything, he was more interventionist and developmentalist than Delfim.

By 1974 Brazil's circumstances were reinforcing the direction in which the country's political economy had moved after 1967. A blend of prosperity and repression had all but eliminated threats to order. Although the official opposition was active and popular, it was firmly committed to free enterprise and to most of the government's economic program.

The pragmatists who dominated the labor movement agitated only around traditional economic demands, which rapid productivity growth allowed most modern industries to meet easily. The consensus attitude toward labor was probably best expressed by a São Paulo industrialist interviewed in 1972–1973. After insisting on avoiding labor's "political involvement beyond its legal activities," the businessman continued: "The government only intervenes to maintain order when these extraordinary political actions occur, as it already has. Now this is no longer necessary. The unions confine themselves to defending their interests." These opinions were seconded by a Rio de Janeiro industrialist: "No labor problems have arisen, and there has been no deterioration of the harmonious situation between capital and labor. They work in unison, especially in comparison with the situation in other countries of Latin America."[32] In the context of general unconcern about labor relations,

[32] Peter McDonough, *Power and Ideology in Brazil* (Princeton: Princeton University Press, 1981), 286–87. I have retranslated McDonough's "syndicates" as "unions."

the 1973–1974 oil shocks allowed an escalation of support for domestic producers in advanced industrial sectors.[33]

A panoply of economic policies intensified subsidies and incentives to modern industry. At the most general level, after being held more or less stable until 1972 the real exchange rate was allowed to appreciate (that is, the cruzeiro was devalued less than the rate of inflation). By one calculation, the real appreciation of the currency amounted to 23 percent between 1972 and 1978.[34] This represented a subsidy to those using imported intermediate and capital goods; its potential harm to import-competing industries was countered by increased tariff protection. The strong cruzeiro also allowed firms that had borrowed abroad to service their debts with cheap dollars.

The principal components of the 1974–1980 economic policies were contained in the second Plano Nacional de Desenvolvimento (PND). The foremost goal was to strengthen the country's most sophisticated industries producing basic inputs, heavy equipment, and capital goods. At the same time, exports were stimulated, especially of manufactured goods and such nontraditional agribusiness crops as soybeans, while imports were further restricted and a program to develop substitutes for petroleum imports was undertaken.[35]

The government made massive investments in activities that provide basic inputs to modern industry. The investment program was primarily carried out by parastatal enterprises, often in the form of such imposing "big projects" as the Itaipu hydroelectric power plant, the Carajas mineral zone, large petrochemical processing facilities, and integrated steel mills. Public enterprises' share of gross fixed capital formation went from 20 percent in 1970 to 23 percent in 1974 and 29 percent in 1979.[36]

A great deal of this public investment was financed by overseas borrowing: as table 4.1 indicates, the public sector's medium and long-term debt

[33] On this period, in addition to the general works cited above, see Regis Bonelli and Dorothea F. F. Werneck, "Desempenho industrial: Auge e desaceleração nos anos 70," in *Indústria: política, instituções e desenvolvimento*, ed. Wilson Suzigan (Rio de Janeiro: IPEA/INPES, 1978), 167–225; the articles in *Desenvolvimento Capitalista no Brasil*, no. 2, and *Desenvolvimento Capitalista no Brasil*, no. 1, ed. Luis Gonzaga M. Belluzzo and Renata Coutinho (São Paulo: Brasiliense, 1980); Albert Fishlow, "A economia política do ajustamento brasileiro aos choques do petróleo: Uma nota sobre o período 1974/84," *Pesquisa e Planejamento Econômico* 16, no. 3 (December 1986): 507–50; and Celso L. Martone, *Macroeconomic Policies, Debt Accumulation, and Adjustment in Brazil, 1965–84*, World Bank Discussion Paper no. 8 (Washington, D.C.: World Bank, 1987).

[34] Martone, *Macroeconomic Policies*, 15.

[35] On the petroleum-replacement program, see Michael Barzelay, *The Politicized Market Economy: Alcohol in Brazil* (Berkeley: University of California Press, 1986).

[36] For an excellent study of the public enterprises in this period, see Thomas J. Trebat, *Brazil's State-Owned Enterprises: A Case Study of the State as Entrepreneur* (Cambridge: Cambridge University Press, 1983).

grew (expressed in 1982 dollars) from $13.1 billion in 1973 to $43.3 billion in 1979. The public-private mix of the foreign debt indeed changed drastically; while in 1974 the private sector owed more than half the country's medium- and long-term foreign debt, by 1979 it owed less than one-third. Table 4.5 shows how important external borrowing was to the public enterprises: by 1980 foreign-currency liabilities were between one-third and one-half of the leading parastatals' total liabilities. Since on average about half of parastatal investment was debt-financed, it can be inferred that over one-fifth of their expansion was directly paid for by foreign borrowing—and this does not take into account funds borrowed abroad by the central government and public financial institutions and transferred to the public enterprises.

Debt-financed public investment was the principal source of dynamism for important segments of private industry. First, the expansion of basic inputs production by parastatals benefited those who used them, primarily modern private industries. The increased supply of these inputs—reinforced by pricing policies that cheapened public enterprise products (except petrochemicals) in real terms by nearly 20 percent between 1975 and 1979—acted as a major subsidy to their consumers, mostly modern industrial firms.[37] Second, public enterprises were major customers of private firms in the capital goods industry. Such sectors as metallurgy, machinery, electrical equipment, and transport equipment came to rely heavily on the parastatals; in the late 1970s state enterprises absorbed between two-thirds and three-quarters of the domestic output of heavy capital goods.[38]

The second major feature of the "big projects" period was a systematic network of subsidies and incentives to more advanced portions of private industry.[39] Tariffs were substantially increased beginning in 1974, and were supplemented with fiscal exemptions for capital goods producers.[40]

[37] Trebat, *Brazil's State-Owned Enterprises*, 185.

[38] Luiz A. Corrêa do Lago, Fernando Lopes de Almeida, and Beatriz M. F. de Lima, *A indústria brasileira de bens de capital* (Rio de Janeiro: Instituto Brasileiro de Economia/ Editora da Fundação Getúlio Vargas, 1979), 233.

[39] For convenience, we follow the convention of calling the favored sectors "capital goods producers," although some of them (chemicals, metallurgy) fall outside a traditional definition of the capital goods industry. The overlap between the most modern, concentrated industries with specific assets that we have identified as politically powerful and the "capital goods sector" is so great that for our purposes they can be regarded as nearly interchangeable.

[40] On trade policy, see William G. Tyler, "Proteção tarifária efetiva recente do Brasil," *Estudos econômicos* 10, no. 3 (September–December 1980): 47–59. On the capital goods policies more generally, see Corrêa do Lago et al., *A indústria brasileira*; William G. Tyler, *The Brazilian Industrial Economy* (Lexington, Mass.: Lexington Books, 1981), 33–77; and Villela and Baer, *O setor privado nacional*.

Table 4.5
Brazil: Financial Data on Selected Parastatals, 1980
(Millions of dollars and percent)

	Short-Term Foreign Currency Liabilities	As % of All ST Liabilities	Long-Term Foreign Currency Liabilities	As % of All LT Liabilities	Total Foreign Currency Liabilities	As % of All Liabilities
Electric energy						
Eletrobras	$715	15	$10,571	50	$11,286	43
Itaipu	109	44	1,526	73	1,635	34
Nuclebras	33	16	372	57	405	47
Steel						
Siderbras	737	28	4,223	54	4,960	47
Acesita	264	46	337	66	601	55
Petrobras[a]	1,518	21	1,547	59	3,065	31
Telebras[b]	449	35	1,667	51	2,116	47
RFFSA[c]	207	32	934	33	1,141	33
CVRD[d]	73	15	666	68	739	50

Source: Calculated from Presidência da República, Secretaria de Planejamento, Secretaria de Controle de Empresas Estatais—SEST, *Cadastro das Empresas Estatais* (Brasilia: SEST, 1981).

Note: "All liabilities" exclude shareholders' equity; figures converted at end-of-year exchange rate.

[a] National petroleum company.
[b] National telephone company.
[c] Railroad system.
[d] Public mining company.

Public financial institutions, especially the BNDES, concentrated resources on heavy private industry, and the inflow of foreign finance allowed for a major expansion of public lending. At the same time, the subsidy element in BNDES and other public lending to industry was increased, as nominal interest rates were allowed to lag behind inflation. Finally, export subsidies encouraged nontraditional manufacturing exports; by one estimate, total subsidies to manufactured exports rose from 48 percent of the value of such exports in 1970–1973 to 73 percent in 1976–1978.[41]

Modern agricultural enterprises, especially large-scale producers of export crops in the South and Southeast, were also favored by economic policy under the second PND. Efforts to expand production of industrial crops and nontraditional agricultural exports were emphasized. This reinforced the position of the more politically powerful farmers: as I have mentioned, large farms were disproportionate recipients of the generous subsidized credit offered to agriculture. While production of such small-farm crops as beans, manioc, and corn fell or stagnated, production of such large-farm crops as soybeans, oranges, sugar cane, and wheat grew very rapidly.[42]

The investment programs of the 1970s would have been virtually unthinkable without the availability of foreign finance. In the aggregate, foreign savings accounted for 17.5 percent of domestic investment between 1970 and 1981, and more than 90 percent of the capital inflow took the form of foreign loans. At a more disaggregated level, the centers of dynamism of the economy were tied directly or indirectly to overseas borrowing. State-owned industrial corporations, especially in energy, steel, telecommunications, and transportation, were one such growth pole. The rapid development of parastatal industry was of major importance to another growth pole, locally owned private modern industrial firms that grew in tandem with the parastatals, especially those in capital goods and intermediate industrial inputs. The financial system was a third profit center, with government development banks and private financial conglomerates participating. Finally was large-scale, mostly Southern, and export-

[41] Alberto Roque Musalem, "Política de subsídios e exportações de manufaturados no Brasil," *Revista Brasileira de Economia* 35, no. 1 (January–March 1981): 17–41. See also Renato Baumann Neves and Helson C. Braga, *O sistema brasileiro de financiamento às exportações* (Rio de Janeiro: IPEA/INPES, 1986).

[42] On agriculture, see IPEA/INPES, *Perspectivas de longo prazo da economia brasileira* (Rio de Janeiro: IPEA/INPES, 1985), 163–96; figures on the growth of production and farm size are on p. 168 and p. 189. Other surveys include Gervásio Castro de Resende, "Setor externo e agricultura," *Literatura Econômica* 5, no. 3 (May–June 1983): 299–318; Tamás Szmrecsányi, "Análise Crítica das Políticas para o Setor Agropecuário," in *Desenvolvimento Capitalista no Brasil* no. 2, 223–40; and Villela and Baer, *O setor privado nacional*, 239–92. Barzelay includes a fascinating discussion of the political economy of agricultural policies related to the alcohol program.

oriented agribusiness. In all cases, foreign finance was responsible for major portions of the expansion.

Influential segments of the private sector were major beneficiaries of the government's borrowing and investment. With much of its activity financed by foreign borrowing, the private financial sector expanded its lending steadily and became ever more central to the investment process. Meanwhile, the sector became far more concentrated, as the strongest banks strengthened their position even further. By the same token, nearly every aspect of the borrowing model spurred modern private industry between 1967 and 1979, especially the core of large-scale industry—metallurgy, machinery, electrical equipment, transportation equipment, and chemicals. As parastatals grew with foreign finance, they ordered more from local suppliers. To expand, these suppliers borrowed from the BNDES—often funds originating abroad. To cover burgeoning requirements for working capital, local firms borrowed from the local commercial banks, especially in the form of foreign-currency loans.

Brazil's borrowing, then, went first and foremost to pay for major government efforts to finance, subsidize, and otherwise support industrial development. Borrowed funds were used for a flurry of sectoral programs aimed primarily at the most modern and concentrated segments of the industrial sector, the financial sector, and large-scale agribusiness. Government subsidies to investment finance, export credits, and farm loans were made possible in part by foreign loans, as were public investment projects that provided modern private industry with cheap inputs and a guaranteed source of orders.[43]

Economic performance under the second PND was impressive. Between 1974 and 1980, gross domestic product grew 62 percent and industrial production 66 percent; annual rates of growth for both indicators averaged over 7 percent. By 1980 Brazil was producing more steel and automobiles than Great Britain, and it was a major exporter of both. Exports grew dramatically, from $6.2 billion in 1973 to $20.1 billion in 1980, while the share of manufactured products in total exports went from 29 to 52 percent. On the negative side, inflation accelerated throughout the period. After the first oil shock, inflation jumped from its 1970–1973 average of about 20 percent to a 1974–1978 average of nearly 40 percent; after the second oil shock, it went to almost 80 percent in 1979 and 110 percent in 1980.

In the political sphere, the Geisel administration marked the end of the most repressive period of the dictatorship. Geisel pursued a more conciliatory policy widely known as *distensão* or loosening; torture and cen-

---

[43] For a more detailed account, see Jeffry A. Frieden, "The Brazilian Borrowing Experience," *Latin American Research Review* 22, no. 1 (1987): 95–131.

sorship were reduced, and the electoral system was made less fraudulent. The reasons for the loosening are hotly debated, but there is general agreement that three intersecting considerations were important: reduced threats from radical and labor opposition movements, increased elite dissatisfaction with the dictatorship's limited accountability, and a desire to strengthen middle-class support for the regime. The first factor weakened the justification for massive repression; the second and third factors enhanced the pressures on the administration for more political openness.[44]

The loosening of control over the political system revealed widespread discontent, especially among the working and middle classes of the urban centers. This allowed the opposition to make major advances in the 1974 and 1978 national elections. In November 1974, in the first reasonably free elections since the coup, the MDB scored important victories. The official opposition took more than 50 percent of the popular vote in Senate races, winning sixteen of the twenty contested seats (ARENA took 35 percent, and the remainder were null or blank). The MDB did somewhat less well in proportional elections for the Chamber of Deputies (38 percent of the popular vote as against 41 percent for ARENA), but was able to win control of six state assemblies, including those of São Paulo, Rio de Janeiro, and Rio Grande do Sul—the centers of economic and political influence.

In 1978 judicious manipulation of the electoral apparatus avoided further deterioration of the regime's position, but the MDB was able to maintain a significant presence in the legislature. The 1978 vote indicated among other things how restricted the military's electoral base was to less developed areas. ARENA received only 27 percent of the Chamber of Deputies vote in cities with more than a half million people, but three-quarters of the vote in rural areas and towns with less than twenty thousand people; it got 38 percent of the vote in the developed Southeast and 72 percent in the backward Northeast.[45]

Against the backdrop of limited and declining support for the regime in the developed areas of the country, many leaders of the business community, especially São Paulo industry, supported a deepening of the trend

[44] The literature on this period is enormous. One good survey of the literature and events, going through the subsequent *abertura*, is Eli Diniz, "A transição política no Brasil: Uma reavaliação da dinâmica da abertura," *Dados* 28, no. 3 (1985): 329–46. See also Fernando H. Cardoso and Bolivar Lamounier, eds., *Os partidos e as eleições no Brasil* (Rio de Janeiro: Paz e Terra, 1975) and Bolivar Lamounier, ed., *Voto de desconfiança: Eleições e mudança política no Brasil* (Rio de Janeiro: Vozes, 1980). The essays in Luiz Carlos Bresser Pereira, *O colapso de uma aliança de classes: A burguesia e a crise do autoritarismo tecnoburocrático* (São Paulo: Brasiliense, 1978), give a good running commentary on the period.

[45] David Fleischer, "The Brazilian Congress: From *Abertura* to New Republic," in *Political Liberalization in Brazil: Dynamics, Dilemmas, and Future Prospects*, ed. Wayne Selcher (Boulder, Colo.: Westview Press, 1986), 120.

toward political openness. In late 1978, as Geisel was preparing to leave office in favor of a new president, João Baptista Figueiredo, a group of influential businessmen—eight of the "top ten" as defined by the business daily *Gazeta Mercantil*—released a prominent call for a more concerted commitment to democratization. In a document of national political significance, they wrote:

> We believe that economic and social development, as we conceive it, can only be possible within a political framework that permits the broad participation of all. Only democracy is capable of promoting the full expression of interests and opinions, and has sufficient flexibility to absorb tensions without transforming them into an undesirable class conflict.[46]

By 1979, then, leading elements of the business community, especially those in modern industry, supported democratization. Whatever uncertainty about the investment climate existed before the coup was gone, removing some of the justification for authoritarianism. Indeed, insulation of the dictatorship from social pressures sometimes threatened the interests of modern business, since it shielded policymakers from their demands.

The combination of relative unconcern about social order and worries about the regime's general unpopularity and its potential unresponsiveness to elite interests led some of the country's most prominent businessmen to champion political openness. Their position was rarely oppositional and always moderate; it was at most critically supportive of the government. This movement in 1977–1978 on the part of some elements in the business community to distance themselves from the military regime, which one participant called with some exaggeration "the collapse of a class alliance,"[47] set the stage for the more dramatic rift between the military and the industrialists that developed during the economic crisis of the 1980s.

The Crisis, 1981–1985

In 1981 the Brazilian economy began a downward spiral that had dramatic effects on patterns of political activity, as it drove influential social groups into opposition and culminated in the accession to power of a civilian opposition government in March 1985. Economic policymakers' ability to provide a thick net of sectoral subsidies between 1967 and 1980 depended on an inflow of foreign finance. This pattern was hit first

[46] As cited in *Senhor*, 17 August, 1983, p. 25.
[47] Bresser Pereira, *O colapso*.

by a rise in international interest rates that increased payments on the country's variable-rate debt, then by stagnation in world trade and a deterioration in the country's terms of trade, and finally in mid-1982 by a near-total cutoff of new lending. As external resources dried up, sectoral programs were slashed and their erstwhile beneficiaries, especially modern industry, turned to political pressure on the government and, eventually, to support for an opposition that promised to be more favorable to them.

The international financial contours of the crisis can be seen from the net financial resource transfer, the amount lent to Brazil minus the country's repayment of principal and interest. Between 1974 and 1978 the net financial inflow averaged $4.4 billion a year ($9.4 billion in lending minus $3.3 billion in amortization and $1.7 billion in interest payments). From 1979 to 1981, when international interest rates rose while funds were still available, the annual net inflow averaged $1.5 billion ($13 billion in lending minus $5.9 billion in amortization and $6.6 billion in interest payments). In 1982–1983, the net financial flow was strongly *negative*, as debt-service payments outweighed new lending by $7.7 billion a year ($10.8 billion in lending minus $8 billion in amortization and $10.5 in interest payments).[48] A political economy that had come to rely on foreign finance was driven into economic and political crisis by so major a reversal in its international financial position.

The military government's commitment to preserve its creditworthiness in the 1981–1983 international economic environment dictated policies with disastrous consequences for many domestic economic actors.[49] Rising international interest rates and deteriorating terms of trade had predictable implications for a country with an enormous stock of foreign debt—again, assuming priority to maintaining international creditworthiness. The public sector needed to free resources to meet rising debt-service payments: given the difficulty of rapidly raising taxes to the required levels, this implied major cuts in domestic spending by the public sector, along with redoubled borrowing. Increased borrowing and the avoidance of capital flight required interest rates high enough to attract foreign and domestic investors. The debtors' needs for foreign exchange, especially in the context of international recession and declining terms of trade, called for specific measures to reduce imports and increase exports,

[48] Calculated from Paulo Nogueira Batista, Jr., *International Financial Flows to Brazil since the Late 1960s*, World Bank Discussion Paper 7 (Washington, D.C.: World Bank, 1987), 33.

[49] See Carlos Diaz Alejandro, "Some Aspects of the 1982–83 Brazilian Payments Crisis," *Brookings Papers on Economic Activity* 2 (1983): 515–42, for an analytical survey of the events.

such as devaluations and recessionary policies to increase international competitiveness.

The need for domestic resources and foreign exchange to meet rising debt service payments forced a regime committed to its international financial obligations to cut public spending, tighten monetary policy, and devalue. After mid-1982, when foreign borrowing ceased to be an option, the public sector was thrown back upon domestic financial markets to raise funds, driving interest rates still higher and exacerbating pressure on debtors. These policies struck directly at the industrialists who had come to rely on cheap finance and government orders, as financial costs skyrocketed and orders plummeted. By 1982 business discontent was widespread; by 1984 it was nearly universal, and the regime had lost most of its support.[50]

The drama began almost as soon as João Baptista Figueiredo took over the presidency in March 1979. Simonsen was replaced as chief economic policymaker in August by Antônio Delfim Netto, amid widespread acclaim from business, which regarded him as the architect of the "miracle." During what critics called his "Second Coming" or the "Second Delfinate," however, Delfim Netto faced a more hostile international environment. Originally he tried to please all of his business-community constituents, but eventually he was driven to programs that sacrificed most of industry to the maintenance of debt-service payments.

Delfim's plans to ride out the international "malaise" without domestic austerity soon collapsed. Demands for continued growth were constant, especially in the São Paulo business community, but attempts to meet them ran rapidly into external constraints. Efforts to stimulate the economy fueled inflation and drained foreign exchange reserves. The result was a roller coaster of stop-and-go economic policies, as Delfim first tried to maintain high rates of growth, then attempted to reduce inflation and the balance of payments deficit, then once again concentrated on economic growth, and so on. For example, most of the effects of a December

[50] For details on this period, see among others Edmar Bacha, "Choques externos e perspectivas de crescimento: O caso do Brasil—1973/89," *Pesquisa e Planejamento Econômico* 14, no. 3 (December 1984); Antonio Barros de Castro and Francisco Eduardo Pires de Souza, *A economia brasileira em marcha forçada* (Rio de Janeiro: Paz e Terra, 1985); Paulo Nogueira Batista, Jr., *Mito e realidade na dívida externa brasileira* (Rio de Janeiro: Paz e Terra, 1983); Luciano Coutinho and Luiz Gonzaga de Mello Belluzzo, "Política econômica: Infleções e crise, 1974–1981," in *Desenvolvimento capitalista no Brasil*, no. 1; Persio Arida, ed., *Dívida Externa, Recessão, e Ajuste Estrutural* (Rio de Janeiro: Paz e Terra, 1982); Fishlow, "A economia política"; Rogério L. Furquim Werneck, "Poupança estatal, dívida externa e crise financeira do setor público," *Pesquisa e Planejamento Econômico* 16, no. 3 (December 1986): 551–74; Ernane Galveas, *A política econômico-financeira do Brasil* (Brasília: Banco Central do Brasil, 1982); IPEA/INPES, *Perspectivas*; and Antônio Carlos Lemgruber, "Política Cambial," in Nogueira Batista, Jr. et al., *Ensaios*, 91–103.

1979 anti-inflation package, including a 30 percent devaluation, were washed out during 1980 by policies intended to counteract the contractionary aspects of the package.

As Delfim tried to meet demands for economic growth, balance-of-payments constraints became tighter and tighter. One set of constraints was financial: real interest rates charged to Brazil (that is, discounting for inflation) went from their 1968–1978 average of 2.5 percent to 4 percent in 1979, 6 percent in 1980, 9 percent in 1981, and 14 percent in 1982. Another set was commercial: the countries' exports faced the general stagnation of world trade after 1980 and a 45 percent deterioration in Brazil's terms of trade between 1977 and 1981. The two factors combined to make the country's debt burden unsustainable: by 1982 debt-service payments were equivalent to 91 percent of Brazil's merchandise exports, up from 51 percent in 1977.[51]

A variety of policies was implemented to keep foreign finance coming into the country and to avoid an outflow of domestic "flight capital." Most important was a tightening of monetary policy, which drove interest rates to astronomical levels—200 percent *in real terms* for consumer credit, and nearly 50 percent for bank credit to industry. As Finance Minister Ernane Galveas told the Superior War College, "High interest rates in the free segment of the financial market are the price that Brazilian society is paying in order to increase exports and sustain the process of balance of payments adjustment."[52]

Domestic credit was controlled, while foreign borrowing was exempt from quantitative limits. Interest subsidies were offered to agricultural, energy-related, and export activities. Other private firms, encouraged by policy and soaring domestic interest rates, borrowed heavily in foreign currencies. Between end-1979 and end-1982, the foreign liabilities of Brazilian banks under the on-lending program went from $7.7 billion to $16.1 billion.[53]

The government also tried to avoid capital flight by allowing firms with foreign debt to hold dollar deposits with the central bank, and to hedge against any eventual devaluation. By 1981 the central bank was holding $11.4 billion in such deposits, a figure equal to 123 percent of the country's monetary base. The government also offered treasury bonds (ORTNs) linked to devaluation rather than inflation indices. Treasury securities, in other words, were tied to the U.S. dollar, for otherwise the government would have found it difficult to borrow domestically. By 1983, an estimated 90 percent of outstanding long-term government domestic debt

[51] Nogueira Batista, Jr., *International Financial Flows.*
[52] Galveas, 30.
[53] This refers only to Resolution 63 loans (see appendix).

was linked to the dollar. Efforts to keep capital at home had "dollarized" the economy.[54]

As external conditions deteriorated, the government kept reducing public investment, raising interest rates and generally trying to overcome the widening balance-of-payments gap regardless of recessionary domestic consequences. Industrialists were furious. Capital goods producers were used to ample increasing orders from the state sector, financed with subsidized credit from the BNDES and other quarters. All at once, state orders were drying up. So was subsidized credit, and the only alternative to bankruptcy for many was to contract short-term loans at usurious interest rates.

By 1981 the industrial sector was in a tailspin, and the descent, like the previous ascent, was led by the country's modern industries. After averaging 7 percent annual growth between 1978 and 1980, in 1981 manufacturing production dropped 10 percent, stagnated in 1982, and dropped another 8 percent in 1983. The capital goods sector's output fell 17 percent in 1981, 13 percent in 1982, and another 20 percent in 1983, putting 1984 production levels 43 percent below those of 1980. Corresponding 1981–1983 output declines were 13 percent in the intermediate goods industries, 21 percent in the consumer durables industries, and 4 percent in the consumer nondurables industries.[55] For the first time in years, there were massive layoffs of factory workers and urban violence reached an unprecedented scale. Perversely, the financial sector remained very profitable, charging enormous spreads on foreign-currency lending.

The political fallout of the crisis was almost immediate. The political liberalization begun during the Geisel government had continued, now renamed *abertura* (opening). The party structure was reformed, and a host of new parties sprang up. Most of ARENA went to the Partido Democrático Social (PDS); most of the MDB went to the Partido Movimento Democrático Brasileiro (PMDB), and a number of smaller parties also formed. The electoral process culminated in the general legislative elections of 15 November 1982.

In the meantime the country's political coalitions were shifting rapidly. The influential São Paulo industrialists, disenchanted with the government, swung toward the opposition. The opposition parties made interest-rate policy a central target in order to tap growing business and middle-class discontent. Indeed, the program of the PMDB stated categorically

---

[54] Confidential interview by the author, Banco Central do Brasil, Diretoria da Dívida Pública, 12 August 1983. For background, see Banco Central do Brasil, Demob, *Relatorio de Atividades—1981* (Rio de Janeiro: Demob, 1982), 16–22; and Adroaldo Moura da Silva and Rudiger Dornbusch, "Taxa de juros e depósitos em moeda estrangeira no Brasil," *Revista Brasileira de Economia* 38, no. 1 (January–March 1984): 39–52.

[55] IPEA/INPES, *Perspectivas*, 202.

that "it is impossible to carry out any economic recovery without reducing the current extraordinarily high level of domestic interest rates. . . . For this, it is indispensable to cut the existing tie between monetary policy and obtaining the foreign loans necessary to close the balance of payments deficit."[56]

The opposition parties swept the elections, winning a combined 52 percent of the gubernatorial popular vote and 48 percent of the Chamber of Deputies popular vote (against 37 percent for the PDS in both). Perhaps more significant, the opposition swept São Paulo state, with 21 percent of Brazil's population but nearly 60 percent of its industrial output—the PDS won only 27 percent of the Chamber vote in the state. The country's three largest industrial states—São Paulo, Minas Gerais, and Rio de Janeiro, with 42 percent of national population and two-thirds of GDP—all got opposition governors. The only industrial state in which the PDS won was Rio Grande do Sul, where two opposition candidates split the vote and where, even so, the PDS governor became a major critic of government economic policy.[57]

As the crisis deepened, indeed, member after member of the "growth coalition" defected to the opposition as their interests were sacrificed to financial stabilization. By 1983 it was difficult to find a progovernment businessman outside the financial sector. After about a year of Figueiredo's administration, in early 1980, a survey of businessmen found that 41 percent considered the government either "excellent" or "good," while only 10 percent considered it "bad" or "awful" (the remainder opted for "O.K."); the corresponding percentages were 69 percent positive and 5 percent negative for chief economic policymaker Delfim Netto. By July 1983, 43 percent of the businessmen held negative opinions of the government, while only 13 percent were positively inclined; for Delfim Netto the decline was even more precipitous as 12 percent of the businessmen still liked him while 60 percent now found him "bad" or "awful."[58]

In the wake of its November 1982 electoral humiliation the government went to the International Monetary Fund (IMF). The country strug-

[56] *Senhor,* 17 August 1982, p. 28.

[57] On political developments in this period, see, among innumerable others, Scott Mainwaring, "The Transition to Democracy in Brazil," *Journal of Interamerican Studies and World Affairs* 28, no. 2 (Spring 1986): 149–79; Bolivar Lamounier and Rachel Meneguello, *Partidos políticos e consolidação democrática* (São Paulo: Brasiliense, 1986); Bolivar Lamounier and Alkimar Moura, "Economic Policy and Political Opening in Brazil," in *Latin American Political Economy: Financial Crisis and Political Change,* ed. Jonathan Hartlyn and Samuel Morley (Boulder, Colo.: Westview Press, 1986), 165–96; William C. Smith, "The Political Transition in Brazil," in *Comparing New Democracies,* ed. Enrique Baloyra (Boulder: Westview Press, 1987); and the articles by Candido Mendes, Marcilio Marques Moreira, and Bolivar Lamounier in *Government and Opposition* 19, no. 2 (1984).

[58] *Exame,* 10 August 1983, pp. 18–21.

gled through rounds of IMF agreements, debt renegotiations, and financial austerity. Private industry's bitterness, as the winds of austerity got colder, grew apace. One leading capital goods producer said in late 1982: "Today civil society has no influence. On the economic side we have closure, even while there is a political opening. There was more freedom for the private sector under Geisel than there is today." Along with the government, he blamed domestic banks, which continued to support austerity. "The private financial sector has taken advantage of government policy with little sensitivity to the problems of private industry. . . . The problem is that the banks have gone from being simple intermediaries to the determiners of economic trends."[59]

The industrialists' resentment of the military's policies grew as the crisis continued, especially after another 30 percent devaluation in February 1983. Antônio Ermírio de Moraes, director of the nation's largest private firm Votorantim, called the devaluation "a betrayal of the Brazilian business community that was induced to borrow overseas." An ex-president of FIESP was dramatic: "We are living a nightmare. I pray to God to illuminate our rulers, if not we are lost."[60] Others, less willing to rely on divine intervention, called for resignation of the economic team and, more generally, for access to power.

The president of one major group of firms inveighed bitterly against the military regime's monopoly of power. "Brazil's main problem is not economic but political. Less errors would be committed with the alternation of power at all levels."[61] A major firm that failed in mid-1983 went out with a flourish, charging the regime and its financial-sector supporters with leading the country to "a pre-Marxist state." The firm's directors declared bitterly: "All that remains of capitalism is the pale image of a capital market, where unproductive capital is rewarded in a financial orgy stupefied by the State itself and its securities. . . . The unproductive market is managed so as to eliminate any possibility of survival for production."[62]

On 11 July 1983 an illustrious group of business leaders—led by the eight who had issued the influential 1978 call for democracy—put out

[59] Interview, Bardella—Industria Mecanica, São Paulo, 22 September 1982. On the interest-rate problem see Nogueira Batista, Jr., *Mitos e realidades*, 172–79, and Luiz Corrêa do Lago, "Taxa de juros: Características e opções," *Conjuntura Econômica* 36, no. 2 (February 1982): 219–25.

[60] *Exame*, 9 March 1983, pp. 16–20.

[61] Ibid.

[62] *Jornal do Brasil*, 19 July 1983, p. 15. See also *Veja*, 27 July 1983, pp. 68–74. The firm involved, Matarazzo, was a veritable symbol of Brazilian industrialization; its founding family had much the same aura as the Rockefellers in the United States.

another position paper calling for a radical renegotiation of the foreign debt and an end to the government's austerity programs:

> Our creditors and the governments of fraternal countries must understand that it is reckless to subject Brazil to a recessive adjustment of uncertain duration. . . . The prolonged shrinkage of productive activity will inevitably lead to the destruction of Brazilian private industry and could even threaten the continuance of the free enterprise system. National firms will be swallowed by a whirlwind of bankruptcies and failures.[63]

The industrialists' willingness to confront the military head-on was undoubtedly strengthened by the relative cooperation they received from industrial labor leaders, who were generally happy to join forces with management against an unpopular regime.[64]

Even some domestic bankers were convinced that government policies had to change. Originally bankers appreciated the windfall profits brought by higher interest rates, but by the end of 1983 many were alarmed by spreading bankruptcies and the prospect that their swollen loan portfolios might be worthless. Especially for bankers with close ties to industry, such as those based in São Paulo, government policy had outlived its usefulness. The chairman of the board of the country's largest private bank, Bradesco, called on the government to reduce interest rates and lashed out at his colleagues: "Truly, the bankers are the bandits of the story, since they are keeping interest rates excessively high."[65] Olavo Setúbal, one of the country's most respected businessmen, former mayor of São Paulo and head of Itaú, Brazil's second-largest private bank, also became a vocal opponent of government policy. He endorsed the PMDB economic platform late in 1983 and led a campaign to bring down domestic interest rates. For Setúbal: "Delfim made a fundamental error of international economic strategy when he signed an agreement with the IMF. All the bankers want is a balance of trade surplus and they forget all else. This is a profound error and has led Brazil to an impasse."[66]

In great measure because of the broad social influence of the industrial

---

[63] *Senhor*, 17 August 1983.

[64] It should be noted in this regard that the 1978–1980 São Paulo strike wave did not present a *political* threat to capital comparable to the labor unrest of the early 1960s; although hard-fought, the strikes were almost purely economic and did not lead the industrialists of FIESP to shy away from political alliance with the labor-based opposition. On the strikes, see John Humphrey, *Capitalist Control and Workers' Struggle in the Brazilian Auto Industry* (Princeton: Princeton University Press, 1982), 160–207; for a more general survey of recent developments, see José Pastore and Thomas E. Skidmore, "Brazilian Labor Relations: A New Era?" in *Industrial Relations in a Decade of Economic Change* (Madison, Wis.: Industrial Relations Research Association, 1985), 75–113.

[65] *Veja*, 13 July 1983.

[66] Interview, Banco Itaú, São Paulo, 4 August 1983.

sector, the military government's position became increasingly untenable. Despite a gradual economic recovery and continued attempts to manipulate the electoral system, an antigovernment coalition of domestic businessmen, organized labor, and the urban middle classes prevailed. In late 1984 and early 1985 segments of the PDS, including Figueiredo's vice-president, left the party and established a Partido Frente Liberal (PFL) that allied itself with the PMDB to elect an opposition president, Tancredo Neves. In March 1985 the opposition took office, with wide backing from São Paulo industrialists, and the military and its allies were swept from power. The new government took a firmer negotiating stance with creditors and focused on promoting industrial growth.[67]

The change in regimes and policies was not without drama. On the eve of his planned 15 March swearing-in, President-elect Tancredo Neves was hospitalized, and he eventually died without taking office. His place was taken by José Sarney, one of the defectors to the opposition from the PDS, whose selection as vice-president had originally been little more than a sop to skittish former progovernment politicians. Once Sarney became president, cynics were quick to point out that the opposition had only succeeded in bringing to power the former head of the PDS. Nonetheless, after some uncertainty, Sarney moved away from the previous regime's international and domestic conservatism.[68] The extraordinary predominance of Paulistas (those from São Paulo) in the government's higher reaches—in late 1985 they included the ministers of foreign affairs, finance, industry and commerce, labor, and planning, along with the president of the Central Bank—was an indicator of the industrial base of the opposition coalition that drove the military back to the barracks.

After 1967 foreign finance helped cement a growth coalition that included the state, domestic banks, the most modern industries, and large-scale agribusiness. When the financial glue that held this alliance together

---

[67] The post-1985 vicissitudes of the Brazilian political economy are beyond our scope here. Two preliminary surveys are William C. Smith, "The Travail of Brazilian Democracy in the 'New Republic,' " *Journal of Interamerican Studies and World Affairs* 28, no. 4 (Winter 1986–1987): 39–73; Werner Baer and Paul Beckerman, "The Rise and Fall of Brazil's Cruzado Plan" (mimeo, 1987); Robert Kaufman, *The Politics of Debt in Argentina, Brazil, and Mexico* (Berkeley: Institute of International Studies, 1988); and Eul-Soo Pang, "Debt, Adjustment, and Democratic Cacophony in Brazil," in *Debt and Democracy in Latin America*, ed. Barbara Stallings and Robert Kaufman (Boulder, Colo.: Westview Press, 1989), 127–42.

[68] It is sometimes asserted that had Neves lived he would have been a more conservative president than Sarney, since Neves had a strong personal and party-machine base and fundamentally conservative political tendencies. Sarney's lack of any personal political strength forced him to be especially responsive to the opposition's bases of support. Although there may be some truth to this, it is hard to believe that Neves would not also have eventually distanced himself from the previous regime's international and domestic economic policies.

began to dissolve, the alliance went with it. On one side of the economic policy debates stood those whose fortunes were inextricably linked to Brazil's international economic ties. Most of the domestic financial sector closed ranks behind the military government, as did export-oriented agriculture; for them, continued access to overseas markets was paramount. On the other side of the debates, ever-broader opposition forces coalesced. Both capitalists and laborers in modern industry, especially around São Paulo, demanded relief from austerity. So too did much of the urban middle classes, including government functionaries whose livelihood was imperiled by attacks on public spending.

Discontent over economic policy accelerated and reinforced Brazilian democratization. The military regime's gradual loosening of its authoritarian grip, begun in 1974, was rapidly overtaken by the economic crisis; as austerity took its toll, opposition to the government mounted. While the military and its domestic allies pushed on with financial adjustment, economic elites harmed by the process turned to the opposition and demanded greater access to power. The deepening crisis increased opposition until the military and its supporters were forced from office disheartened and discredited.

After 1980, in other words, the Brazilian government's response to changes in the international environment struck directly at the interests of Brazil's most modern industrial sectors. These groups pressed for policies to insulate them from external trends, while such sectors as finance and export agriculture, whose overseas ties gave them an incentive to maintain Brazilian economic policies congenial to the country's creditors, resisted a change in course. Eventually the depth and length of the crisis, and the overwhelming influence of the industrial economy, led to changes in both regime and policy that are still working their way through Brazil's political economy.

Summary and Evaluation of the Brazilian Experience

Between 1967 and 1981 international financial markets lent heavily to Brazilian borrowers, and funds went overwhelmingly to finance industrial investment. About half of Brazilian foreign borrowing was done by parastatal firms to expand production of such intermediate industrial inputs as steel, petrochemicals, and electric energy. Much of the rest was borrowed by public or private financial institutions, which re-lent the funds domestically, primarily to the dynamic modern industries that grew along with the parastatals. Some of the country's foreign borrowing went directly to industrial firms themselves. The pattern was one of deep government involvement in the economy and a thick net of subsidies and incentives to favored sectors.

When international financial conditions changed after 1980, the Brazilian government was quite incapable of meeting the demands of all of its erstwhile beneficiaries. In 1980 international interest rates began to rise, which put pressure on the government to mobilize more domestic resources and foreign currency for debt service. In 1982 the supply of external finance was drastically curtailed. The government attempted to maintain debt-service payments, and even though these attempts were hardly successful they did entail a domestic depression that hit formerly favored industrial sectors hardest. As a result, both labor and capital in the country's industrial centers turned definitively against the government, in favor of an opposition that promised less contractionary policies at home and less concern with financial obligations abroad.

I return to my analytical framework to summarize the development of the Brazilian political economy. I am first concerned with explaining Brazil's patterns of economic policy, both as compared with other countries, as they evolved over time, and as they affected different segments of the economy.

Cross-National Comparison

Brazilian economic policy was interventionist by virtually any standard. Overall the country experienced rapid economic growth in the context of state control or regulation of wages, prices, interest rates, international goods and capital movements. My explanation of this is that class conflict in Brazil was in general insignificant, and sectoral pressures on policymakers came to the fore.

Evolution over Time

Brazilian economic policy was not of course static. At the start of the period, in the aftermath of the military coup, concerns about the investment climate and even about property rights were at their highest point in recent Brazilian history. In the aftermath of the unprecedented social conflicts of the early 1960s, the military gave priority to restoring order, especially getting control of the labor movement and other supporters of radical populism. Virtually all the country's economic elite supported this campaign, and subordinated many sectoral demands to the goal of restoring a stable investment climate. This lasted until 1967; with social order secure, sectoral pressures resurfaced and came increasingly to dominate economic policy. In other words, labor-capital conflict was relatively salient (by Brazilian standards) at the outset of the experience, but it became less important over time; policy was relatively market-oriented between 1964 and 1967, then became more interventionist over time.

Cross-Sectional Variation

Once economic policy settled into a clearly interventionist pattern, the beneficiaries of government policy were, as expected, the most politically powerful sectors of the economy. Favored groups included the most modern industries, especially sophisticated capital goods and consumer durables producers; finance; and Southern large-scale agribusiness. This does not mean that only these groups profited from the country's economic policies, but they were systematically favored over others by the government at virtually every turn, and systematically overrepresented in their access to foreign finance, subsidized credit, cheap parastatal-produced industrial inputs, and lucrative government orders for their output. When the crisis hit, previously favored industries were hit hard by fiscal retrenchment and monetary stringency, while finance and agribusiness were relatively unscathed.

The Brazilian experience with foreign borrowing fits the framework of this study: labor-capital conflict was negatively correlated with interventionist economic policies, and sectoral policies benefited those with the most specific assets and the most political cohesion. One puzzle, however, is why the government responded so slowly to the pleas of modern industries once the crisis began. Some reduction in public subsidies to industry was inevitable, but the government's reaction was probably less flexible than it could have been. One possibility is that the crisis made the preferences of previous supporters of the government incompatible. The financial and export agricultural sectors required little in the way of government support to prosper in the context of high international interest rates and devaluation-assisted expansion in demand for agricultural exports, and therefore it was easy for the government to maintain their support. The financial and agribusiness sectors, however, tended to regard more systematic government support for industry as incompatible with the maintenance of their access to overseas financial and goods markets. In other words, as long as modern industry benefited from financial openness, it was conciliatory toward foreign lenders and its preferences were congruent with those of other groups; once the debt crisis drove modern industry toward positions more hostile to foreign creditors, the coalition broke up. Although interviews and impressionistic evidence tend to support this view, there is far too little information available at this point to decide the issue conclusively.

Our second concern, as we summarize the Brazilian case, is to explain political patterns, especially during the financial crisis. The dynamics of democratization after 1980 were crucially affected by the growing dissatisfaction of modern industry with government economic policies. This dissatisfaction led to powerful protests from both unions and management in modern industry. As it became clear between 1981 and 1984 that the government would not be responsive to demands for more confrontation with foreign creditors and less austerity at home, major portions of the economic elite turned away from the military and threw their support to the PMDB-PFL opposition coalition. The dissatisfaction of the modern industrial sector with government economic management, and the low salience of threats to property rights, led to a multiclass opposition alliance based in the country's industrial centers.

Although such broad issues are beyond the scope of this study, we can also make several general observations about the interaction of economic growth and political repression. First, rapid economic growth in the Brazilian context did not mitigate authoritarian rule. In fact, political repression was at its peak during the period of most rapid economic growth. Second, economic crisis did not lead to a tightening of the military's grip on society, but rather speeded its return to the barracks. These points are evidence against any rigid positive or negative correlation between economic growth and democracy. Brazil since 1964 has experienced periods of authoritarianism and stagnation (1964–1967), authoritarianism and rapid growth (1968–1973), and democratization and stagnation (1981–1985). The one combination with which it has not been blessed is democracy and rapid growth, yet nothing presented here indicates that such an outcome can be excluded. Rather, recent Brazilian history reinforces the notion that trends toward or away from democracy are largely a function of political actors' evaluation of which institutional arrangement will best serve their interests, not of structural characteristics of developing societies.

Brazil, then, is a prototype of a country that used access to foreign finance to pursue sectoral economic policies in the absence of major class conflict. The beneficiaries of these policies were the most politically powerful groups in society: large-scale modern industries, finance, and agribusiness. When external financial conditions changed, and the capital inflow stopped and then was reversed, one set of these powerful groups, modern industry, was extremely hard hit. Both management and labor in the country's modern industrial centers pressed for a change in government policies, but the military regime was unresponsive. It was this lack of response that drove the country's influential industrialists, former supporters of the regime, into the arms of the opposition and that eventually brought the civilian opposition to power.

Appendix

THIS appendix discusses in detail some of the statistics used in chapter 4 and some of their implications. The purpose is to push available data as far as possible and to indicate how future work might investigate causal arguments more rigorously.

My explanation of Brazilian economic policy during the financial expansion is that policy responded to the political influence of various sectors of "civil society." The quality and quantity of information on Latin American economics and politics seriously limit the possibilities for statistical appraisal of my approach. However, the cross-sectional data presented in table 4.4 allow for some observations about my arguments.

Brazil's overseas borrowing was carried out under two statutes, Law 4131 and Resolution 63. Law 4131, originally enacted in 1962 and reinforced after the coup, permitted firms to borrow directly from foreign banks, and (along with a short-lived allied measure, Central Bank Instruction No. 289) was the single most important form of foreign borrowing for Brazil.[1] Resolution 63, introduced in 1967, permitted Brazilian banks to borrow abroad at medium or long term and "re-pass," or on-lend, the *cruzeiro* equivalent of the foreign currency to domestic borrowers at relatively short term (generally six months). Resolution 63 loans were attractive to Brazilian banks, since the foreign exchange risk was borne by the ultimate borrower and the spread between the rate at which the banks borrowed overseas funds and domestic lending rates was high; they were attractive to domestic businessmen unwilling or unable to borrow directly abroad.[2] By 1982, the Brazilian private sector's medium and long-term debt to foreign creditors was $22.8 billion, about half under Law 4131 and half under Resolution 63.

Private financial institutions took out a few loans under Law 4131, $1.4 billion in gross borrowing between 1972 and 1981, but the vast

---

[1] On Law 4131 see SUMOC minutes, 1043ᵃ Ata, 24 October, 1962, pp. 4–6; 1095ᵃ Ata, 11 October 1963, pp. 57–150; and 1170ᵃ Ata, 8 February 1965, pp. 22–36.

[2] See Conselho Monetario Nacional minutes, 81ᵃ Ata, 17 August 1967, pp. 7–8. For a good summary of the basic legislation, see José Eduardo de Carvalho Pereira, *Financiamento externo e crescimento econômico no Brasil: 1966/73* (Rio de Janeiro: IPEA/INPES, 1974), and Eduardo A. Guimarães and Pedro Malan, "A opção entre capital de empréstimo e capital de risco," IPEA Working Paper no. 46 (March 1982), 54–74. Mônica Baer, *A internacionalização financeira no Brasil* (Petrópolis: Vozes, 1986), is an exhaustive and definitive work on various aspects of Brazil's financial internationalization: Part IV focuses on foreign borrowing.

majority of its overseas funds came by way of Resolution 63 loans, $15.4 billion in gross borrowing between 1972 and 1981 (figures are in current dollars).[3] For industry, Resolution 63 loans became a common source of working capital. However, many private firms borrowed directly from overseas banks under Law 4131. These are the data presented in table 4.4.

I expect access to foreign funds to be correlated with political strength, and political strength to be correlated with asset specificity and organizational cohesion. Although there are no unproblematic quantitative measures for such variables, the four-firm concentration ratio (the percentage of output accounted for by the largest four firms in the industry) probably picks up asset specificity (inasmuch as it is related to entry barriers), as well as a rough sense of cohesion (inasmuch as more concentrated sectors are easier to organize). This measure is presented in table A4.1.[4] These concentration ratios refer to a weighted average of four-firm concentration ratios in the subsectors that make up the broader aggregations.

There appears to be a general correlation between access to borrowing and concentration. To use relatively broad categories, the sectors that borrowed more than "their share" (see pp. 113–14) had an average concentration ratio of 51.1 percent; that is, on average the largest four firms of these sectors accounted for 51.1 percent of the sector's output. Intermediate sectors had an average concentration ratio of 42.1 percent. Industries with less than expected borrowing had an average concentration ratio of 28.5 percent.

A simple bivariate regression to test the relationship between concentration and access to overseas finance gives a strongly positive coefficient and an adjusted r-squared of 0.41; the results are significant at the 1 percent level. However, the results exhibit heteroskedasticity, and dropping two outliers reduces the coefficient, the adjusted r-squared (to 0.14), and the statistical significance of the results (although they remain significant at the 5 percent level). In any case, the small numbers involved and the parlous nature of the data do not warrant much reliance on more powerful statistical techniques.

[3] Paulo Davidoff Cruz, *Dívida externa e política econômica: A experiência brasileira nos anos setenta* (São Paulo: Brasiliense, 1984), 103, 127.

[4] It is important to note that concentration ratios are primarily a function of characteristics of the industries themselves, and not of political, cultural, or other unique national features. Sergio Buarque de Holanda Filho, *Estrutura industrial no Brasil: Concentração e diversificação* (Rio de Janeiro: IPEA/INPES, 1983), 100, for example, shows that highly concentrated industries in Brazil are also highly concentrated in the United States, West Germany, France, and Italy. The ultimate cause of the outcomes noted here is thus to be searched for in industrial organization rather than other noneconomic factors.

Table A4.1

Brazil: Concentration Ratios of Manufacturing Sectors

	Four-firm Concentration Ratio
Nonmetallic minerals	45.4%
Metallurgy	33.1%
Machinery	28.0%
Electrical material	50.2%
Transport material	62.0%
Wood products	13.7%
Furniture	17.0%
Pulp and paper	31.2%
Rubber products	73.6%
Leather products	23.8%
Chemicals	38.1%
Pharmaceuticals	16.7%
Toiletries	55.6%
Plastic products	26.2%
Textiles	22.5%
Clothing and footwear	20.7%
Food products	48.7%
Beverages	52.1%
Tobacco	95.9%
Publishing	31.4%
Others	43.9%
Average	38.0%

Note: For sources and explanation of data, see text in the appendix.

One obvious potential problem with the argument that concentration is related to overseas borrowing by way of its effect on asset specificity and political cohesion is that concentration might simply be picking up differences in firm size across sector, and foreign bankers might be more likely to extend loans to large firms than to small firms. It is plausible that oligopolistic sectors are likely to have more large firms than competitive sectors. This possibility was assessed using data in Sergio Buarque de Holanda Filho, *Estrutura industrial no Brasil: Concentração e diversificação* (Rio de Janeiro: IPEA/INPES, 1983) on the relative importance of large firms, with large firms defined as those with output of more than approximately $34 million; there were 163 such firms. No correlation was found between the prevalence of large firms in each sector and the sector's external borrowing. The number of large firms was primarily a function of the size of the sector rather than its concentration. Many other potential independent variables—participation of foreign corporations, capital-output ratios, export orientation—were also tested, with no statistically significant results.

Data reported in tables 4.4 and A4.1 come from a variety of sources. The information on private-firm borrowing under Law 4131 is from Paulo Davidoff Cruz, *Dívida externa e política econômica* (São Paulo: Brasiliense, 1984), p. 104, and is based on information obtained by the author from Central Bank records. This is first compared to each sector's share of manufacturing output, obtained from Buarque de Holanda Filho, p. 106, which is based on a survey of about ninety thousand manufacturing firms in 1974.

Sectoral share of invested capital, rather than of manufacturing output, is a better benchmark for our purposes: concentration may be related to capital-to-output ratios, and more capital-intensive firms may be more likely to borrow abroad. Unfortunately, exactly comparable data on sectoral shares of invested capital are not available. The closest thing is Andrea Calabi et al., *Geração de poupanças e estrutura de capital das empresas no Brasil* (São Paulo: Instituto de Pesquisas Econômicas, 1981), a study based on a sample of about thirty-two hundred manufacturing firms in 1975. This study does have figures for *patrimônio líquido*, a measure of invested capital, and these data are used in table 4.4 under "Percent of manufacturing capital." Although coverage of the Calabi et al. study is less complete than the Buarque de Holanda Filho study, it includes firms accounting for 82.2 percent of all operating earnings of the sample used by Buarque de Holanda Filho, and the two samples are similar in other regards. Because measures of invested capital are more accurate for our purposes, we use the Calabi et al. figures.

Information about industrial concentration presented in table A4.1 comes from the study by Buarque de Holanda Filho. Sectoral four-firm concentration ratios are a weighted average of the four-firm concentration ratios of the subsectors within each industry. Buarque de Holanda Filho's excellent study has several drawbacks from our perspective, primarily having to do with the concentration ratios and the sectoral breakdown used.

First, the concentration ratio of interest to us is probably larger than four: we could reasonably expect there to be significant entry barriers and intrafirm political cooperation in sectors dominated by as many as eight, or even twenty, leading firms. Second, sectoral concentration ratios derived from subsectoral concentration ratios on the basis of a weighted average of their output may be misleading about features of political significance. Within an unconcentrated sector, highly concentrated sub-sectors may have far greater political influence than their share of sectoral output might indicate. For example, while most firms in the metallurgy sector may be too atomistic to organize as such, the steel subsector may be highly concentrated and thus dominate the political action of the metallurgy sector. In the Brazilian case, for instance, while the machinery sector (no. 12) is not concentrated (four-firm concentration ratio of 28 percent), the important office machinery (no. 1253) and consumer appliances (no. 1254) subsectors are extremely concentrated (four-firm concentration ratios of 67 and 65 percent, and eight-firm concentration ratios of 85 and 82 percent, respectively). In this case, at least two relevant possibilities may not be captured in sectoral figures aggregated on the basis of output: office machinery and consumer appliance producers may be well-organized, and politically influential in and of themselves, while the rest of the machinery sector as a whole is not; or the two sectors may dominate the whole machinery industry's political action. Both problems are insurmountable with available data.

It should be stressed that the data are limited at best. The coverage, time periods, and levels of aggregation differ from measure to measure, and the primary sources themselves may be suspect. Nonetheless, they are the best available, and they appear to support my argument. In any case, it is to be hoped that future research will allow for the more systematic evaluation of this and other analyses, perhaps by extending such tests as the one described above.

5

Debt, Economic Policy, and Politics in Chile

CHILE'S experience with foreign borrowing is quite unique in recent Latin American history. The country ran up a substantial foreign debt between 1976 and 1982, but this debt was contracted almost entirely by the private sector. Bucking the borrowing-country tide, the Chilean military regime carried out a sweeping liberalization of the economy: it privatized public enterprises, eliminated the government budget deficit, and removed most barriers to international trade and payments. The economy grew rapidly as it borrowed, but the crisis that began in 1982 was more severe in Chile than in any other Latin American country.

The crisis of the early 1980s, however, did not lead to the kind of dramatic political change observed in other authoritarian debtors. Despite mass protests, the military regime held onto power with little difficulty. A gradual democratization began in the late 1980s, but it was unrelated to the debt crisis, and indeed the Chilean economy had recovered and was growing rapidly at the time of democratization.

Perhaps the most striking characteristic of the Chilean political economy, and one which is central to my explanation of its experience in borrowing and financial crisis, is the centrality of labor-capital conflict in recent Chilean political history. Over the course of the postwar period, Chilean politics became increasingly polarized, culminating in the socialist-led Popular Unity administration of Salvador Allende. The strength of the Chilean left drove the country's business community to a level of concern over property rights unmatched elsewhere in Latin America, and set the stage for the military coup of September 1973 and for the authoritarian regime's turn to market-oriented policies once its power was consolidated.

Throughout the borrowing period and the ensuing financial crisis, continuing worries about the socialist threat dampened the business community's willingness to oppose the military regime's policies, even when these policies were detrimental to the specific interests of groups of capitalists. Although some sectors expressed concern about the military's policies, and the regime responded to some of these concerns, in general factoral (class) pressures dominated sectoral pressures, and this had substantial effects both on economic policies and on politics.

Chilean developments in the 1970s and 1980s are the subject of bitter debate. This makes analysis difficult, as most interpretations of Chilean economic and political events are colored by the political position of the interpreter. Seemingly innocuous macroeconomic data are subject to challenge and counterchallenge.[1] At the same time, the extreme authoritarianism of the dictatorship made most economic policy making opaque to observers. At best I can attempt to reconstruct the broad trend of economic policy and outcomes and of political activity with the information at hand.

Chile, 1973–1985: An Overview

Much of the intellectual interest in recent Chilean economic development is due to the military's implementation of policies as liberal (that is, free-market) as have been seen in the developing countries in fifty years. Observers are fascinated with how this experiment affected economic performance, and indeed the experience is rich in potential economic lessons.

My interest in the Chilean economic-policy experiment is primarily in *explaining* the country's turn toward the market, rather than in evaluating it. In fact, the Chilean government's reduction of the public sector's economic role, and wholesale commercial and financial liberalization, put Chile on a policy course diametrically opposed to that of most of the world's borrowing countries. Argentina and Uruguay followed Chile's example, so that the phenomenon might be regarded as more Southern Cone than Chilean, but the Chilean regime's policies were by far the most consistently and radically market-oriented.

The principal analytical issue concerning Chilean economic policy, then, is why the government did not take advantage of plentiful external finance to expand its role in the economy; why, indeed, it went in quite the opposite direction. On this dimension the Chilean experience confounds prior expectations of the effects of foreign borrowing. Chilean economic management was characterized by great "orthodoxy" (a term which has come to be associated in Latin America with a market orientation) both in such structural reforms as privatization and commercial liberalization, and in macroeconomic policy.

My explanation for Chile's unusual pattern of economic policy rests, as detailed below, on the salience of labor-capital conflict in the country. Chapter 3 noted that where class conflict threatens the division of na-

[1] For example, Patricio Meller and his associates at the Christian Democratic think tank CIEPLAN have, in a series of articles, attempted to correct and reconstruct Chilean national accounts. One summary is Mario Marcel and Patricio Meller, "Empalme de las cuentas nacionales de Chile 1960–1985: Metodos alternativos y resultados," *Colección Estudios CIEPLAN* 20 (December 1986): 121–46.

tional income between profits and wages, and even private property rights, I expect the common interests of capitalists to outweigh their specific sectoral interests. Where class conflict is especially prominent, general factoral (class) pressures to maintain or restore a favorable investment climate will dominate particularistic pressures for public subsidies and incentives.

Chilean politics has indeed been, since the 1960s at least, the most class-based and among the most conflictual in all of Latin America. Battles between labor and capital peaked during the 1970–1973 Allende government, and the business community's policy preferences and pressures have been dominated ever since by fear of a return of the left to political power.

If developments before the debt crisis raise interesting questions about why Chile took so different an economic-policy path from other borrowers, developments after the debt crisis raise equally important questions about the relationship between the state of the economy and the stability of the political regime. The 1982–1983 crisis was more severe in Chile than anywhere else in Latin America. Between 1981 and 1983 real per capita GNP dropped 20 percent, unemployment went over 30 percent, and virtually the entire private sector was bankrupted.[2]

Despite the deep economic crisis and widespread political discontent, the dictatorship emerged from the crisis virtually unscathed. Mass protests did sweep the country, and the military regime appeared briefly to respond to these protests with a moderate political opening. However, by the end of 1984 the opening had ended, with the military firmly in power. Five years later, on a timetable established by the military, elections were held and a civilian government was elected—but this was a far cry from the crisis-era democratizations experienced in other countries in the region. In other words, and unlike elsewhere, desperate economic conditions did not lead to striking political changes. Protests were repressed, and the military stayed in power until long after the economic crisis passed.

My explanation of the unusual character of the Chilean political experience during the debt crisis relies, once again, on the centrality of class conflict in Chilean politics. The crisis, as elsewhere, had a devastating effect on many segments of the Chilean population, including important portions of business. Mass protests were in fact large and vociferous from the onset of the crisis. However, very few in the business community

---

[2] As mentioned above, even macroeconomic data on the Chilean economy are controversial. These are from José Pablo Arellano and René Cortázar, "Inflación, conflictos macroeconómicos y democratización en Chile," *Colección Estudios CIEPLAN* 19 (June 1986): 61. Other figures vary by a few percentage points. Those working in the government's make-work programs are counted as unemployed.

joined in the chorus of discontent with the regime. In part this was because the government met some of the needs of Chilean businessmen, especially in providing relief to Chilean private debtors. However, the private sector was devastated, and government action was limited. In other societies, such as Brazil, a similar level of inaction brought forth a storm of business protest, but in Chile the private sector's concern about government economic policy was overshadowed by its continued apprehension about the strength of the Left. The mass protests that erupted with the crisis did nothing to dispel business fears, and an incipient armed opposition fueled them. Crisis or no, class concerns continued to override sectoral discomfort and drive businesses to temper their demands on the government.

What follows is a more detailed description of the Chilean political economy during the financial expansion of the 1970s and the crisis of the 1980s, with a more detailed explanation of the patterns of economic policy and politics in the two periods. Through it all we insist on the cardinal importance of class conflict in affecting the confluence of factoral and sectoral pressures brought to bear in the political arena.

The Chilean Political Economy: A Brief History

Perhaps the best-known characteristic of pre-1973 Chile was its long-standing democratic tradition. For whatever reasons—and the reasons are controversial—Chile had the closest thing in Latin America to a European democratic political system, with parties of the right, center, and left.

Another constant of Chilean history was the importance of natural resources to the economy. Silver, copper, and nitrates dominated the economy from the 1870s until 1930, accounting for one-quarter to one-third of GDP and as much as half of government revenue throughout this period. Indeed, it may be that the availability to the government of these resource rents, and the fact that exploitation of the resources was primarily in foreign hands, contributed to the democratic nature of Chilean politics. The government was able to extract a share of the resource rents from foreign investors and to meet sociopolitical demands by distributing this share among a relatively wide portion of the population.[3]

Given Chilean reliance on primary exports, the Great Depression hit the country especially hard. Between 1929 and 1932 Chile's terms of

---

[3] Background on Chilean economic history can be found in Markos Mamalakis and Clark Reynolds, eds., *Essays on the Chilean Economy* (Homewood, Illinois: Irwin, 1965); and Markos Mamalakis, *The Growth and Structure of the Chilean Economy: From Independence to Allende* (New Haven: Yale University Press, 1976).

trade dropped 45 percent, export volume 71 percent; the value of exports fell from $283 million in 1929 to $20 million in 1931. The 1932 purchasing power of Chilean exports was 15 percent of 1929 levels, and GDP had dropped 27 percent.[4]

After several years of turmoil, Liberal party candidate Arturo Alessandri, a moderate conservative, was elected president. The Alessandri administration (1932–1938) oversaw gradual recovery from the depression with relatively orthodox economic policies. It was succeeded by a series of leftist Popular Front and Radical administrations that ruled until 1952. These governments stimulated industrial development and moderate income redistribution, especially to the urban population. Among the more lasting effects of the reformist governments' policies was the systematic increase in public-sector support for industry, led by the Corporación de Fomento (CORFO). Founded in 1939, CORFO was an umbrella parastatal agency to subsidize and encourage industrial growth, and it came to play a central role in the economy. Trade policy was protectionist in the extreme, and the exchange rate was consistently overvalued. Per capita income grew by about 2 percent a year from 1937 to 1950, but reformist governments had a high tolerance for inflation, which increased throughout the period.[5] Through this era, Chile also developed a relatively broad network of social programs.

In 1952, with inflation and the payments deficit growing dangerously, the candidate of the center-right won the presidency. The relatively apolitical General Carlos Ibáñez had been an important political figure in the 1920s, but he had few new economic ideas to offer. As inflation soared past 50 percent in 1954 and past 75 percent in 1955,[6] Ibáñez turned to an American consulting firm for a stabilization plan (the so-called Klein-Saks Mission). The plan involved restrictive fiscal and monetary policies

[4] Figures are from Angus Maddison, *Two Crises: Latin America and Asia, 1929–38 and 1973–83* (Paris: OECD, 1985), 84–87. Gabriel Palma, "From an Export-Led to an Import-Substituting Economy: Chile 1914–1939," in *Latin America in the 1930s*, ed. Rosemary Thorp (New York: St. Martin's Press, 1984), 50–80, is an excellent survey of the period.

[5] Information in the following paragraphs on modern Chilean economic development is drawn from Mamalakis, *Growth and Structure*; Jere R. Behrman, *Macroeconomic Policy in a Developing Country: The Chilean Experience* (Amsterdam: North-Holland, 1977), 15–77; Jere R. Behrman, *Foreign Trade Regimes and Economic Development: Chile* (New York: Columbia University Press, 1976); Ricardo Ffrench-Davis, *Políticas Económicas en Chile 1952–1970* (Santiago: Ediciones Nueva Universidad, 1973); and Oscar Muñoz Gomá, *Chile y su industrialización* (Santiago: CIEPLAN, 1986). On the politics of the period, see Barbara Stallings, *Class Conflict and Economic Development in Chile, 1958–1973* (Stanford: Stanford University Press, 1978); on the political economy of the country's copper industry, see Theodore Moran, *Multinational Corporations and the Politics of Dependence: Copper in Chile* (Princeton: Princeton University Press, 1974).

[6] These are Ffrench-Davis's *Políticas económicas* corrected measures of consumer price inflation (p. 246); official figures are different.

that helped reduce inflation but drove the economy into recession. At the end of Ibáñez' term, the Right ran Jorge Alessandri, son of Arturo, who won the presidency and continued restrictive policies. Inflation was finally reduced below 8 percent in 1961, but the cost was economic stagnation during the two conservative administrations: between 1953 and 1960 per capita income dropped by 6 percent. To make matters worse, the administration's economic program collapsed in December 1961, and inflation rose back to 47 percent in 1963.

Meanwhile, the political system settled into a tripartite pattern that would persist until 1973. In simplistic terms, landowners and many businessmen favored a conservative right supportive of anti-inflation policies; the working class backed a socialist left in favor of redistribution; and the middle classes (including some business groups) championed a center-left Partido Democrático Cristiano (PDC) that advocated both redistributive reforms and a capitalist economy.[7] There was little constituency for trade liberalization: with some exceptions, Chile's protectionism was taken as a given. Electoral support for the three groupings was roughly equal: in the 1958 presidential elections, Alessandri won with 32 percent of the vote against 29 percent for the socialist Allende and 21 percent for the Christian Democrat Eduardo Frei. Over the next fifteen years, jockeying among these three coalitions tended to make economic policy making difficult and to polarize the political system.

The failure of the Alessandri administration's anti-inflation policies, and their impact on economic growth, real wages, and income distribution, made it clear that the right could not win the 1964 presidential election. Conservatives thus threw their support to Christian Democrat Eduardo Frei, seen as the only hope against the leftist alliance led by Allende. Conservative backing for Frei was reluctant at best, as the PDC promised a "Revolution in Liberty;" its economic platform was strongly influenced by the structuralist critique of orthodoxy.

After an easy victory, the Frei administration pursued expansionary policies and implemented substantial reforms. The government took a leading role in the ownership and management of the copper industry, and a land reform was carried out. The economy grew quite rapidly, and inflation was reduced. Despite an expressed desire for more openness to the world economy, trade barriers remained extremely high: in 1967 effective protection was above 250 percent for many important manufacturing sectors (food products, textiles, rubber products, petroleum and coal products, electrical machinery, transport equipment).

[7] This ignores the continued importance of the Radicals, who maintained a substantial base in some areas. During the 1960s, however, most of their supporters went over to the Christian Democrats or the right.

After the Frei administration's initial successes, economic growth slowed and inflation began to rise again. The reformism of the Christian Democrats seemed incapable of satisfying both the redistributive desires of the lower classes and the anti-inflationary demands of the private sector. One result was a radicalization of segments of Christian Democracy who saw a market economy as incompatible with their social-welfare goals.

Conservative dissatisfaction with the Christian Democrats, and increasing leftist pressures within the PDC itself, broke up Frei's center-right coalition before the 1970 elections. The Right ran Jorge Alessandri again, the Unidad Popular (UP) coalition ran Allende, and the Christian Democrats put forth a member of their left wing, Radomiro Tomic. This time, for the first time, the three-way split fell toward the left—but just barely. Allende received 36 percent of the vote, Alessandri 35 percent, and Tomic 28 percent. After some delay, Congress confirmed Allende as president.

The economic policies of the Allende administration, despite the socialist rhetoric of members of the government, were of a piece with those of other Latin American populist experiments—although more extreme.[8] Expansionary fiscal and monetary policies brought unemployment down and income up; redistributive measures favored some of the poorer segments of the population. More far-reaching structural reforms were also undertaken, including land reform and the full nationalization of large copper mines, most banks, and some other private firms.

Two interrelated problems came to plague the Allende government: the collapse of its macroeconomic policies and the rise of groups of the radical right and left. Initial growth proved unsustainable, as investment and output dropped in 1972 and 1973. Faced with insistent demands for income growth and social programs, public spending expanded while revenues fell. In 1973 the government deficit reached 25 percent of GDP and, despite price controls, inflation roared over 600 percent.

In the midst of these macroeconomic problems, the UP administration faced growing opposition on its right and left flanks. Labor militancy grew by leaps and bounds, while radical groups occupied farms and factories, often forcing the government to nationalize properties abandoned by their owners. Businessmen and the middle classes mobilized to try to block both UP policies and radical activism, often by means of political

[8] The UP years are of course extremely controversial. Among the hundreds of books on the subject are Federico Gil, Ricardo Lagos, and H. A. Landsberger, eds., *Chile at the Turning Point* (Philadelphia: ISHI, 1979); Paul Sigmund, *The Overthrow of Allende and the Politics of Chile* (Pittsburgh: University of Pittsburgh Press, 1977); Arturo Valenzuela, *The Breakdown of Democratic Regimes: Chile* (Baltimore: Johns Hopkins University Press, 1978). The interpretation of a leading Chilean analyst is in Manuel Antonio Garretón, *El proceso político chileno* (Santiago: FLACSO, 1983), 23–63.

confrontation and economic sabotage. During 1973 the economy deteriorated, politics became increasingly polarized, and the ruling coalition began to splinter. On 11 September 1973, with the support of the right and most of the Christian Democrats, the armed forces staged a coup in which President Allende died.

A stylized picture of the Chilean political economy since the 1930s would show three well-organized, sociopolitical groupings with different policy preferences: conservative landowners and businessmen, moderate middle classes, and socialist workers. These groupings have alternated in power, often in loose coalition with one another. The existence of three such groups, of course, can create chronic problems, in which no combination is stable over time. Something along these lines happened in Chile in the forty years before 1973. The right came to power with some moderate votes, then proceeded to alienate moderate supporters. In the next round, a center-left coalition took office, but proceeded to lose much of its leftist support. The right came back, but eventually lost the moderates. The center stepped in with rightist support, which it soon alienated. The left got its turn in office, but was thrown out of office by a coup backed by both the center and the right.

To make matters worse, political alternation and uncertainty shortened the time horizons of economic policymakers, and each new episode in the succession of policy failures tended to make the various positions more extreme. Chilean politics and economic policies exhibited something of a downward spiral, with continual alternation of increasingly conflictual positions.

By the early 1970s, Chile was a highly polarized polity dominated by class conflict and fundamental questions about whether capitalism would be preserved. Although the Allende administration itself may not have had immediate socialist transformation in mind, some of its policies appeared to place private property rights in jeopardy, and groups to the left of the UP (and sometimes within it) seemed set on an anticapitalist revolution. In this context, the previously largely apolitical Chilean armed forces engineered a coup and some of the bloodiest repression in recent Latin American history.

Stabilization, 1973–1976

There is little question that class conflict dominated Chilean politics at the time of the military coup, and this fact set the tenor of the experience that followed. The business community and wide sections of the middle classes had been traumatized by their brush with socialism and were adamant about the overriding need to avoid a return to mass labor militancy and threats to property. Class fear eclipsed sectoral concerns; class fear drove business to support a ruthless military regime. In the words of a leading observer, "The persistence of fear within the upper bourgeoisie was an important element in the bourgeoisie's willingness to accept individual policies that hurt the upper class . . . but were seen to be the necessary cost of protecting its overall interests. It is impossible to understand the passivity of the industrial fraction of the bourgeoisie in Chile . . . outside of the context of fear."[9]

In 1973, then, the Chilean private sector essentially subordinated its specific interests to a military dictatorship that promised to restore favorable conditions for private investment. Of course, as time went on many businessmen were harmed by the regime's policies, but the ever-present threat of a return to the early 1970s made it difficult to rally business opinion to challenge the government. In other words, sectoral dissatisfaction with the government's economic programs was counteracted by class support for the government's general attempts to restore an investment climate favorable to private capital. And over time, the military's market-oriented policies created new economic interests that did very well in the new Chilean environment and owed their success to the dictatorship.

The military junta that took power in September 1973, which army general Augusto Pinochet rapidly came to dominate, had two interrelated goals, which Manuel Antonio Garretón has aptly called the "reactive" and "foundational" dimensions of the regime.[10] The former dimension consisted of eliminating the left to overcome the immediate political crisis. The latter involved the reconstruction of society to remove the structural socioeconomic and political bases of the left and make unlikely the resurgence of a powerful anticapitalist movement.

Many of the regime's actions were purely political, including massive and brutal repression in the short run and wholesale attempts to revamp the country's political order in the long run. Almost immediately after the coup, the central labor federation and the UP parties were outlawed. Over time, the dictatorship dissolved all political parties, severely restricted labor union activities, and purged other social institutions, including the military, of potential opponents. Pinochet eventually set forth a program for a new quasi-democratic constitutional order, to be established very gradually, and to exclude large portions of the pre-1973 political spectrum.

[9] Alfred Stepan, "State Power and the Strength of Civil Society in the Southern Cone of Latin America," in *Bringing the State Back In*, ed. Peter Evans, Dietrich Rueschemeyer, and Theda Skocpol (Cambridge: Cambridge University Press, 1985), 321.

[10] Garretón, *El proceso político chileno*, 125–29; see also Manuel Antonio Garretón, "Political Processes in an Authoritarian Regime: The Dynamics of Institutionalization and Opposition in Chile, 1973–1980," in *Military Rule in Chile*, ed. J. Samuel Valenzuela and Arturo Valenzuela (Baltimore: Johns Hopkins University Press, 1986), 144–83.

Major elements of the military's dual goals, however, were economic. On the reactive dimension, the military was faced with enormous imbalances: runaway inflation, huge budget and payments deficits. One important task was macroeconomic stabilization. On the foundational dimension, leading groups within the military came to believe that a "healthy" Chilean social structure required a significant reduction of the role of the government in the economy, and of barriers to international trade and payments.

While the need for macroeconomic stabilization is not hard to see, the longer-term structural program of the military government requires elaboration.[11] The military's mandate from the private sector, so to speak, was to restore and safeguard a functioning market economy—even if this meant contravening specific sectoral demands. The view that motivated many of the reforms was in fact hostile to sectoral policies.

The underlying idea was that many years of government intervention in the economy had created an artificial social structure that stifled private initiative, stunted the private sector, and swelled the size and importance of interest groups hostile to a market economy. For example, high levels of trade protection inflated profits and wages in the manufacturing sector. As a result, businessmen had more incentive to be lobbyists than entrepreneurs, since their success depended first and foremost on government support. In addition, rents from protection and government-backed oligopolies allowed employers to pay high wages, unjustified by productivity, to industrial workers, and this gave workers more incentive to mobilize politically than to work productively. Similar arguments were made for other forms of government intervention in the economy, and the solution was straightforward: eliminate the subsidies and incentives, and force Chileans to earn their way.

The regime's long-term economic policies were thus strongly market-oriented and included the privatization of public enterprises, elimination of the government budget deficit, and movement toward the free flow of goods and capital across borders. The plans aimed at building or rebuilding a vibrant private sector that would not rely on government favors and could not be manipulated or held hostage by anticapitalist interest groups. The political subtext to the reform program has been summarized

[11] The analysis is reproduced in Alvaro Bardón, Camilo Carrasco, and Alvaro Vial, *Una década de cambios económicos: La experiencia chilena 1973–1983* (Santiago: Editorial Andrés Bello, 1985), 1–31. Other official statements are gathered in Juan Carlos Méndez, ed., *Chilean Economic Policy* (Santiago: Budget Directorate, 1979). More general discussions of the Southern Cone experiences are in Alejandro Foxley, *Latin American Experiments in Neo-Conservative Economics* (Berkeley: University of California Press, 1983), and Joseph Ramos, *Neoconservative Economics in the Southern Cone of Latin America, 1973–1983* (Baltimore: Johns Hopkins University Press, 1986).

by a sympathetic Chilean economist: "It assumed that public-sector growth was incompatible with an eventual return to democracy, in the sense that it would increase the possibility of a socialist regime. A strong private sector would reduce the possibility of a return to power of the Socialists; even if they came to power, they would face a large and thriving private sector, unlike between 1970 and 1973."[12]

Chilean economic policy after 1973 ran on two tracks: macroeconomic measures to reduce inflation, and structural reforms to curtail government intervention in the market.[13] The two were often hard to disentangle—reducing public spending and the fiscal deficit served both—but can be traced separately.

On the macroeconomic front, during the first three years the regime concentrated on overcoming the immediate crisis and stabilizing the economy.[14] The first phase, from the coup until April 1975, consisted of gradual reductions in the fiscal deficit and monetary growth. Prices were decontrolled, the currency was devalued and multiple rates simplified, wage readjustments were reduced, government spending was cut back and revenue increased, and monetary policy was tightened. The result was a serious depression with a moderate reduction in inflation. As table 5.1 shows, between 1973 and 1975 the fiscal deficit was brought down from 24.6 to 2.6 percent of GDP and inflation came down from 606 to 343 percent a year; real GDP dropped by 12 percent, unemployment went from 5 to 18 percent of the labor force, and real blue-collar wages fell by 29 percent (putting them 37 percent below 1970 levels).[15] The authorities did have the misfortune to be trying to stabilize the economy in the midst

[12] Confidential interview by the author, Santiago, 7 August 1985.

[13] The single best source on Chilean economic development from 1973 to 1985 is Sebastian Edwards and Alejandra Cox Edwards, *Monetarism and Liberalization: The Chilean Experiment* (Cambridge, Mass.: Ballinger, 1987). Other general surveys are in Vittorio Corbo, "Reforms and Macroeconomic Adjustments in Chile during 1974–1984," *World Development* 13, no. 8 (1985): 893–916; and Ricardo Ffrench-Davis, "The Monetarist Experiment in Chile: A Critical Survey," *World Development* 11, no. 11 (1983): 905–26. Except where noted, statistics used here are from Edwards and Edwards, *Monetarism and Liberalization*.

[14] Tomás Moulián and Pilar Vergara, "Estado, ideología y políticas económicas en Chile: 1973–1978," *Colección Estudios CIEPLAN* 3 (June 1980): 65–120, is an outstanding analysis of the first years of the military regime's economic policies. The analysis is expanded and continued through 1983 in Pilar Vergara, *Auge y caída del neoliberalismo en Chile* (Santiago: Facultad Latinoamericana de Ciencias Sociales, 1985).

[15] Real wage data vary widely, partly because of major monthly variations immediately after the coup and because of the inherent difficulties of measuring real wages in conditions of hyperinflation. The figures used here are from Edwards and Edwards, *Monetarism and Liberalization*, 158. Similar magnitudes are in Ramos, *Neoconservative Economics*, 14–15, who has real wages dropping by 22 percent between pre-coup 1973 and 1975.

Table 5.1
Chile: Macroeconomic Data, 1970–1985

	GDP[a]	CPI[b]	Def/GDP[c]	REER[d]	Wages[e]	Unemp.[f]
1970	3.6	35	2.9	100	100	6
1971	8.0	35	11.2	N.A.	129	5
1972	−0.1	217	13.5	N.A.	115	4
1973	−4.0	606	24.6	N.A.	64	5
1974	5.5	369	10.5	131	60	9
1975	−16.6	343	2.6	179	64	18
1976	4.2	198	2.3	145	77	22
1977	8.5	84	1.9	121	81	19
1978	6.3	37	0.9	134	83	18
1979	7.7	38	−1.7	131	84	17
1980	5.9	31	−0.6	114	96	17
1981	5.1	10	−3.0	97	110	15
1982	−13.8	21	−2.3	113	108	26
1983	−0.4	23	3.8	136	96	31
1984	8.3	23	1.4	140	96	25
1985	1.1	31	−0.9	175	92	22

Sources: More than for other Latin American countries, most of the data on Chilean macroeconomic performance are controversial. Data on GDP growth and unemployment are from careful reworking and corrections of official data. Other figures were taken, where possible, from Sebastian Edwards and Alejandro Cox Edwards, *Monetarism and Liberalization: The Chilean Experiment* (Cambridge, Mass.: Ballinger, 1987), widely regarded as a neutral source. Specific sources and explanations follow.

[a] GDP is the annual rate of change of GDP, from Mario Marcel and Patricio Meller, "Empalme de las cuentas nacionales de Chile 1960–1985," *Colección Estudios CIEPLAN* 20 (December 1986): 125, using the rate of change method.

[b] CPI is annual rate of change in the Consumer Price Index, from Edwards and Edwards, *Monetarism and Liberalization*, 28, through 1984; for 1985, from José Pablo Arellano, "Crisis y recuperación económica en Chile en los años 80," *Colección Estudios CIEPLAN* 24 (June 1988): 72.

[c] Def/GDP is the public deficit as a percentage of GDP. A minus sign is a budget surplus. From Edwards and Edwards, 32, through 1983; for 1984 and 1985, from Inter-American Development Bank, *Economic and Social Progress in Latin America*, various issues.

[d] REER is real effective exchange rate, defined as the exchange rate deflated by the consumer price index and inflated by the trade-weighted index of external inflation; 1970 is set at 100. A rise in the index indicates a depreciation, a fall an appreciation. From Ricardo Ffrench-Davis, "The Foreign Debt Crisis and Adjustment in Chile, 1976–1986" (mimeo, 1987), 35. N.A. = not available.

[e] Wages is real wages, corrected by the GDP deflator; 1970 is set at 100. From Sebastian Edwards, "Stabilization and Liberalization: An Evaluation of Ten Years of Chile's Experiment with Free-Market Policies, 1973–1983," *Economic Development and Cultural Change* 33, no. 2 (January 1985): 228, through 1982; since 1982, Inter-American Development Bank, *Economic and Social Progress in Latin America*, various issues.

[f] Unemp. is percent of the labor force unemployed, defined as total open unemployment plus those in "make-work" public programs (PEM and POJH). From Esteban Jadresic, "Evolución del empleo y desempleo en Chile, 1970–85," *Colección Estudios CIEPLAN* 20 (December 1986): 151.

of world recession; the 30 percent drop in Chile's terms of trade from 1973 to 1975 exacerbated the effects of contractionary policies.

As time went on, economic policy became dominated by a group of orthodox economists known as the "Chicago boys" due to the ties many of them had to the University of Chicago's Department of Economics. The appointment of Jorge Cauas as finance minister in July 1974 was an early signal of the rise of the Chicago boys, and in April 1975 he announced an orthodox shock plan to bring inflation down to more manageable levels. Government spending was cut further, money growth was controlled more, and the pace of devaluations increased. By 1976 inflation was down to 198 percent and declining (it reached 84 percent in 1977 and 37 percent in 1978). The economy resumed growth, albeit from depressed levels, and registered an unusual balance of payments surplus. Unemployment remained extremely high, but the initial crisis atmosphere had been overcome.

Although macroeconomic policy was important, especially in the initial postcoup period, the regime's structural reforms were of more long-lasting significance.[16] The first step was to turn most public enterprises over to the private sector. This included the devolution of firms that the UP government had seized, virtually all of which were given back to their former proprietors in 1974 and 1975. Many of the lands distributed during the reforms of the 1960s and early 1970s were similarly returned to their original owners. Privatization also involved the sale of public enterprises (often of long standing) to the highest bidder. Between 1974 and 1976 CORFO sold off ninety-nine firms for $130 million, and thirteen packages of bank stocks for $177 million.[17] Privatization of the commercial banks went along with freeing the capital markets; by 1976 credit to the private sector in real terms was more than double its 1970 level.[18]

Barriers to international trade began to be reduced almost immediately after the military coup. The government announced its firm intention to reverse fifty years of import substitution. Between 1974 and the end of 1976, average nominal tariffs dropped from 94 percent to 27 percent, while average rates of effective protection came down from 151 to 51

[16] Useful time-lines of the regime's structural reforms are in Corbo, "Reforms and Macroeconomic Adjustments," 911–16; and Donald Mathieson, "Estimating Models of Financial Market Behavior During Periods of Extensive Structural Reform: The Experience of Chile," IMF Staff Papers 30, no. 2 (June 1983): 352–60.

[17] Daniel Wisecarver, "Economic Regulation and Deregulation in Chile 1973–1983," in The National Economic Policies of Chile, ed. Gary Walton (Greenwich, Conn.: JAI Press, 1985), 151.

[18] José Pablo Arellano, "De la liberalización a la intervención: El mercado de capitales en Chile 1974–1983," Colección Estudios CIEPLAN 11 (December 1983): 9–11; Edwards and Edwards, Monetarism and Liberalization, 54–62.

percent.[19] Regulations on foreign investment in the country were substantially relaxed, as were restrictions on foreign financial inflows. Chile's liberalization policies put it at odds with its partners in the Andean Pact, and in October 1976 the country officially withdrew.

All in all, between September 1973 and the end of 1976, the Chilean military government began a sweeping restructuring of the economy. The reasons for the radical market-oriented reformism of the Chilean military dictatorship, I argue, are to be found in the backdrop of class conflict against which policies were devised and implemented. This led economic actors with sectoral interests to mute their demands in favor of factoral (class) considerations; from the standpoint of businessmen, the reconstruction of a functioning capitalist economy was more important than specific subsidies and incentives.

Alternative explanations are not convincing. One might be that policies were determined by international economic pressures. However, in the middle 1970s, external conditions—especially the plentiful supply of offshore loans—would have been expected to lead the public sector to expand its economic activities, as indeed happened in almost all other borrowing countries. Instead, the Chilean regime undertook the most sweeping set of market-oriented reforms in recent Latin American history. It is true that Chile did little foreign borrowing until 1976. However, this was largely due to unsettled domestic economic conditions, and in 1976 the country started to tap the offshore markets. The authorities indeed began their liberalization and stabilization programs with full expectations that the nation would have access to foreign finance. The decision to drastically reduce the role of the public sector in the economy (by privatizing public firms, reducing government spending, and eliminating many controls on economic activity) cannot be ascribed to a shortage of external funds—especially since these policies accelerated as the country borrowed.

Another potential explanation based on the ideology of the Chilean military is not tenable: modern-day Latin American generals have been more often interventionist and nationalistic than market-oriented and free-trade, and the Chilean military had no tradition of economic liber-

---

[19] The subject of trade liberalization has generated an enormous literature. See Edwards and Edwards, *Monetarism and Liberalization*, chap. 5; Roberto Zahler, "Recent Southern Cone Liberalization Reforms and Stabilization Policies: The Chilean Case, 1974–1982," *Journal of Interamerican Studies and World Affairs* 25, no. 4 (November 1983): 509–62; Pilar Vergara, "Apertura externa y desarrollo industrial en Chile: 1973–1978," *Desarrollo Económico* 20, no. 80 (January–March 1981): 453–89; Ricardo Ffrench-Davis, "Exports and Industrialization in an Orthodox Model: Chile, 1973–1978," *CEPAL Review* 9 (December 1979): 95–113; and the articles in the special issue of *Cuadernos de Economía*, nos. 54–55 (August–December 1981).

alism. Indeed, almost nothing in the pre-1970 positions of the Chilean right foreshadowed the military's program.[20] Nor does the seriousness of the macroeconomic imbalances explain the radical market reforms: resolute inflation-fighting can be, and usually is, carried out without wholesale privatization and commercial liberalization.

One other possible explanation of Chilean economic policy might be that the military regime was responding to particularistic interest-group pressures. This, too, seems untenable. Although there were, of course, both winners and losers within the private sector (of which more is said below), the traditional leaders of the business community were hard hit by the stabilization and liberalization policies, which reversed fifty years of Chilean development. Manufacturing output was especially devastated, dropping 26 percent in 1975. Indeed, the serious economic distress of the first postcoup years, due both to contractionary macroeconomic policies and to structural reforms, led many businessmen who supported the coup to press for relaxation or reversal of the relevant policies.

However, despite the early presence in government of businessmen sympathetic to specific private-sector demands, the general thrust of the regime was in a very different direction. The triumph of the Chicago boys implied the defeat of those who wanted to mitigate the effects of the stabilization program on particular sectors.[21] The bulk of business opinion supported the reforms, and under the orthodox team, economic policy was made by economists who ignored sectoral demands and concentrated on restoring an investment climate favorable to the private sector.

The April 1975 shock plan was striking evidence of the predominance of the orthodox position, with which General Pinochet, by then president, identified himself openly. The 1976 appointment of Sergio de Castro to succeed Jorge Cauas as minister of finance cemented orthodox command of economic policy. From then on it was clear that reconstruction of a market economy took precedence over specific problems faced by traditional businessmen. Indeed, in 1976 the central bank president invoked the model's unpopularity as evidence of its interest-group–free origins: "The fact that more than 90 percent of the people are against our policies is proof that the model is working, that it has affected everybody and that it has privileged nobody."[22]

Despite widespread distress, some economic actors did well as a result of the military regime's policies. The most prominent were a cluster of conglomerates, the "economic groups" or *grupos* who concentrated their activities in finance, trade, real estate, natural resources, and resource-

[20] Vergara, *Auge y caída*, 22–27.
[21] Moulián and Vergara, "Estado, ideología, y políticas económicas," 93–98.
[22] Quoted in Karen Remmer, "Public Policy and Regime Consolidation: The First Five Years of the Chilean Junta," *Journal of Developing Areas* 13, no. 4 (July 1979): 453.

based manufacturing. It would be too much to say that these prosperous entrepreneurs, and less successful businessmen, had no influence over policy making. However, especially before the "Chilean model" began to show signs of strain in 1981, there is little evidence that policy was made with sector-specific targets in mind. The goal of policy was to reinforce the role of the market in allocating resources. Of course this was bound to harm those who could not compete and help those who could, but all indications are that this was secondary to the broader target of creating a socioeconomic structure that would not permit a leftist resurgence.

Borrowing and Liberalization, 1976–1981

Foreign finance flowed into Chile in large quantities from 1976 until 1982, during which time the country's foreign debt went from $4.7 billion to $16.8 billion. Meanwhile, Chilean economic policy continued along the lines established in the two years after the coup. Although the threat of hyperinflation was past, macroeconomic policy centered on reducing the still-high rate of inflation, culminating in a "global monetarist" attempt to use a fixed nominal exchange rate to eliminate inflationary expectations. The reforms went even faster than originally planned, leading to a budget surplus, virtual free trade, and relatively free capital movements by 1979.

Macroeconomic policy was dominated by continuing concern about inflation.[23] Traditional measures seemed unable to reduce inflation to acceptable levels—in 1977 it remained 84 percent, despite tight money and a fiscal deficit of just 1.9 percent of GDP. The economic team thus began to experiment with tools informed by the monetary approach to the balance of payments, sometimes known as "global monetarism." This approach argues, to simplify, that international goods and/or capital movements tend to eliminate imbalances between the supply and demand for money. If, for example, excess supply of money leads domestic producers to raise prices, foreign goods will flow in and force prices back down; paying for the imports will also reduce the domestic supply of funds. More pragmatically, the Chilean authorities believed that much of the country's inflation was due to expectations of future price rises. Since currency devaluations were widely watched by economic agents as signals of probable future inflation, the authorities felt that the best way to break

---

[23] For surveys of this phase of the stabilization experience, see Edwards and Edwards, *Monetarism and Liberalization*, 30–52; Ramos, *Neoconservative Economics*, 70–108; Vergara, *Auge y caída*, 175–92; and Hernán Cortés Douglas, "Stabilization Policies in Chile: Inflation, Unemployment, and Depression, 1975–1982," in *The National Economic Policies of Chile*, 47–78.

inflationary expectations was to manipulate the peso's nominal exchange rate to imply that Chilean inflation would fall rapidly.

Whether for doctrinal or more pragmatic reasons, beginning in 1976 the Chilean authorities increasingly used the exchange rate to fight inflation. The first steps, taken in June 1976 and again in March 1977, were to interrupt temporarily the continual (crawling peg) devaluations of the peso in line with past inflation and *revalue* the currency to signal that inflation would be reduced. This of course put substantial pressure on domestic producers of traded goods: as tariffs were slashed, the currency was revalued to make them even less able to compete with foreign products. The fact that protests against the revaluation were scattered and ineffectual indicated both the relative lack of influence of previously powerful sectors, especially manufacturing, and the general belief within the business community that the regime's policies were a necessary evil.

In 1978 and 1979 the exchange rate took center stage in Chilean anti-inflation policy. In Febuary 1978, with inflation still above 40 percent, the authorities unveiled a pre-announced devaluation schedule. The *tablita*, as it was called, was meant to signal a declining rate of inflation and thus to overcome the expectational component of price rises. By mid-1979, inflation was still above 30 percent, and in June the government fixed the peso at thirty-nine to the dollar; shortly thereafter, the regime committed itself to maintain this exchange rate indefinitely. The result was a continual, eventually extreme, real appreciation of the peso against other currencies. This appreciation was exacerbated by the concurrent rise of the U.S. dollar on the foreign exchanges. The downward pressure on domestic prices for traded goods exerted by continual real appreciation of the peso did bring inflation down substantially, below 10 percent (close to U.S. inflation) by 1981. However, the appreciation was only made possible by a massive inflow of foreign funds.

Meanwhile, the military government's structural reform program continued. Trade protection was reduced steadily: average nominal tariffs went from 27 percent at end-1976 to 15.7 percent at end-1977. By June 1979 the government had established uniform tariffs of 10 percent (except for automobiles, due to prior commitments to local producers). Effective protection dropped from an average of 51 percent for manufactured products in 1976 to 13.6 percent in 1979.

The commercial liberalization dramatically increased the importance of foreign trade in the Chilean economy: exports and imports of goods and services went from 35 to 54 percent of GDP between 1970 and 1981. However, most of this growth was on the import side, reflecting both the effects of the real appreciation of the peso and the relatively slower adjustment of production than consumption to the new trade regime. Between 1976 and 1981 exports grew by 20 percent in real terms, while imports grew by 287 percent in real terms.[24] Some export sectors did well: foreign sales of agricultural products and resource-based manufactures (fish meal, timber and paper products, basic metals) went from $293 million in 1975, 19 percent of all exports, to $1.22 billion in 1981, 31 percent of all exports.[25]

The import surge, much of which reflected the use of foreign loans for current consumption, was remarkable. By one measure, nonfood consumer goods imports grew from $101 million in 1976 to $1.9 billion in 1981; expressed in 1985 constant dollars, the rise was from $171 million to $2.0 billion.[26] A critical study charged that from 1977 to 1982 the regime's policies led to "excess imports" of around $6 billion, which with interest accounted for three-quarters of the country's debt accumulation in this period.[27] Whether the critical perspectives are accepted or not— defenders of the regime argue that the overall effect was a more efficient allocation of Chilean resources—there is little doubt that the experience helped shift the economy away from the production of traded goods. From 1977 to 1981, Chilean output of tradables rose by 31 percent, while output of nontradables rose by 52 percent.

Other elements of the reform program proceeded. Privatization continued as CORFO sold off $585 million in assets between 1977 and 1981.[28] The domestic financial market was progressively deregulated, and financial intermediaries proliferated. The ability of financial institutions to borrow abroad was limited at first. Over time, however, the authorities removed many restrictions on international capital movements. Apart from the general desire to rely on market forces, the government was motivated by a desire to bring down the very high level of domestic real interest rates. By 1979 capital inflows by way of the banking sector were quite free.[29] The result was an extraordinary surge in foreign borrowing by Chilean banks. As table 5.2 shows, foreign private borrowing grew rapidly after 1977, while the foreign debt of the central government dropped and that of parastatal enterprises rose gradually.

Trade and financial liberalization, privatization, deregulation, and (af-

[24] Calculated from Ricardo Ffrench-Davis, "Import Liberalization: The Chilean Experience, 1973–1982," in *Military Rule in Chile*, 71.

[25] Edwards and Edwards, *Monetarism and Liberalization*, 123.

[26] Patricio Meller, "Un enfoque analítico-empírico de las causas del actual endeudamiento externo chileno," *Colección Estudios CIEPLAN* 20 (December 1986): 33.

[27] Ricardo Ffrench-Davis and José De Gregorio, "Orígenes y efectos del endeudamiento externo en Chile," *Nota Técnica CIEPLAN* 99 (August 1987): 33–40.

[28] Wisecarver, "Economic Regulation," 151.

[29] Wisecarver, "Economic Regulation," 190–96; Ricardo Ffrench-Davis and José Pablo Arellano, "Apertura financiera externa: La experiencia chilena en 1973–1980," in *Las relaciones financieras externas*, ed. Ricardo Ffrench-Davis (Mexico City: Fondo de Cultura Económica, 1983), 300–41.

Table 5.2
Chile: External Debt, 1973–1985
(Billions of dollars)

	Total Debt[a]	Central Govt.[b]	Public Firms[c]	Pvt. Fin.[d]	Prvt. Nonfin.[e]
1973	3.7	——— 3.2 ———		——— 0.4 ———	
1974	4.4	——— 4.0 ———		——— 0.5 ———	
1975	4.9	3.2	0.9	0.2	0.6
1976	4.7	2.5	1.3	0.2	0.8
1977	5.2	2.6	1.4	0.3	1.0
1978	6.7	2.7	2.0	0.7	1.3
1979	8.5	2.7	2.3	1.5	2.0
1980	11.1	2.5	2.5	3.5	2.5
1981	15.6	2.7	2.7	6.5	3.6
1982[f]	16.8	2.8	2.9	7.0	4.0
1983	18.1	——— 9.1 ———		——— 9.0 ———	
1984	19.7	——— 13.2 ———		——— 6.5 ———	
1985	20.5	——— 15.3 ———		——— 5.2 ———	

Source: Sebastian Edwards and Alejandro Cox Edwards, *Monetarism and Liberalization: The Chilean Experiment* (Cambridge, Mass.: Ballinger, 1987), 71 for 1973 and 1974; Patricio Apiolaza, "Evolución Reciente del Endeudamiento Externo de Chile," Banco Central de Chile (mimeo, 1982), 42, for 1975–1982; for 1983–1985, José Pablo Arellano, "Crisis y recuperación económica en Chile en los años 80," *Colección Estudios CIEPLAN* 24 (June 1988): 84.

Note: Totals may not add up due to rounding.
[a] Total short, medium, and long-term external debt.
[b] External debt owed by the central government and the central bank; includes all public short-term debt.
[c] External debt owed or guaranteed by autonomous government agencies; most important are CORFO and affiliates.
[d] External debt owed by private financial institutions.
[e] External debt owed by private nonfinancial firms.
[f] Figures are for 30 June 1982.

ter 1979) currency appreciation had striking effects on different segments of Chilean society. Among the losers was labor, harmed by government restrictions on union activities, labor-market trends, and the reduction in government social spending. Also hard-hit were owners and workers in previously protected industries and some traditional farm sectors, newly exposed to foreign competition that was exacerbated by the peso's real appreciation after 1979. Among the beneficiaries of government policy up to 1981 were three overlapping sets of actors. First, investors who took advantage of the government's rapid sale of public enterprises were able to purchase these assets at prices that were probably lower than would have prevailed if the government had been in less of a hurry to privatize.[30] Second, sectors that had traditionally faced negative effective protection (especially primary production and some traditional manufacturing industries) were aided by the commercial liberalization. Third, financial intermediaries were given a major boost by the freeing of domestic financial markets from many regulations. To a large extent, these three sectors came together in the economic groups, or *grupos*, that prospered during the financial expansion.

The labor movement was decimated, and the working class in general did relatively poorly. Open unemployment averaged 13.2 percent between 1976 and 1981, while the government's make-work programs employed on average another 4.8 percent of the labor force. Even at the height of the boom in 1981, open unemployment was over 10 percent, and "workfare" programs employed another 5 percent of the labor force.[31] Real wages remained low by historical standards: by one measure, even in 1981 they were three percent below 1970 levels, while by another measure (see table 5.2) they only regained 1970 levels in 1981.[32] These dire labor-market trends were accompanied by a dramatic decline in unionization, from 28 percent of all nonagricultural workers in 1973 to 11 percent in 1983.[33] Overall, income distribution became more unequal over time, while government social spending per person stayed well below 1970 levels.[34]

Apart from the general upward redistribution of income, the regime's reversal of previous import substitution and regulation had a negative impact on economic sectors that had come to rely on such programs. Table 5.3 shows the evolution of key segments of the Chilean economy as the structural reforms were implemented and, after 1979, as the real exchange rate appreciated. The manufacturing sector did especially poorly, and previously heavily protected industries were particularly affected. In 1980 manufacturing output was 11 percent above 1970 levels, but output of leather products was down 56 percent; textiles, 37 percent; rubber

[30] Pilar Vergara, "Changes in the Economic Functions of the Chilean State under the Military Regime," in *Military Rule in Chile*, 90; Fernando Dahse, *Mapa de la extrema riqueza* (Santiago: Editorial Aconcagua, 1979), 175–87.

[31] Esteban Jadresic, "Evolución del empleo y desempleo en Chile, 1970–1985," *Colección Estudios CIEPLAN* 20 (December 1986): 151. These figures are somewhat controversial, but even the more optimistic official numbers indicate a persistently high rate of unemployment.

[32] René Cortázar, "Distributive Results in Chile, 1973–1982," in *The National Economic Policies of Chile*, 82.

[33] Guillermo Campero and René Cortázar, "Lógicas de acción sindical en Chile," *Colección Estudios CIEPLAN* 18 (December 1985): 8.

[34] Luis Riveros, "Desempleo, distribución del ingreso y política social," *Estudios Públicos* 20 (Spring 1985): 315–47.

Table 5.3

Chile: Sectoral Economic Trends, 1974–1982

(Sectoral output and employment as percent of total)

	1974	1979	1982
Primary[a]			
Output	17.7	17.1	13.3
Employment	25.6	24.0	23.5
Manufacturing			
Output	29.5	21.2	18.9
Employment	19.5	16.7	14.1
Commerce			
Output	14.1	16.7	15.6
Employment	11.6	15.6	16.8
Financial services			
Output	5.3	8.1	11.2
Employment	1.9	2.7	3.6

Sources: Sebastian Edwards and Alejandra Cox Edwards, *Monetarism and Liberalization: The Chilean Experiment* (Cambridge, Mass.: Ballinger, 1987), 119, for output; for employment Esteban Jadresic, "Evolución del empleo y desempleo en Chile, 1970–85," *Colección Estudios CIEPLAN* 20 (December 1986): 152.

Note: Figures are for the sector's output as a share of total output, and employment as a share of the labor force (not including those employed in government make-work programs).

[a] Primary is agriculture, forestry, fishing, and mining.

products, 23 percent; footwear, 19 percent.[35] Many export-oriented farmers and manufacturers prospered during the commercial liberalization, but even they had difficulties as the peso appreciated.

Those harmed by the evolution of the economic environment were not completely silent. The labor movement was, of course, either disorganized, repressed, or ignored by a regime that regarded it as a principal cause of the country's problems. But many businessmen suffered as the stabilization and reform policies were put into effect, and some were alarmed by the turn the dictatorship's economic policies were taking. Orlando Sáenz, a leading industrialist and former president of the Sociedad de Fomento Fabril (SOFOFA), early on charged that the regime's reform program "encourages economic concentration and financial speculation instead of productive investment."[36] In 1977, in the midst of trade liber-

[35] Edwards and Edwards, *Monetarism and Liberalization*, 120.

[36] Guillermo Campero, *Los gremios empresariales en el período 1970–1983: Comportamiento sociopolítico y orientaciones ideológicos* (Santiago: Instituto Latinoamericano de

alization and currency revaluation, the head of the owners' organization in the formerly highly protected metal-working sector declared that his members were "profoundly disconcerted. . . . The tariff rate, along with exchange-rate policy, will mean a greater deterioration of national industry."[37]

However, the discontent of those in the business community hurt by government policy was muted by three factors. First and foremost, even critical businessmen continued to regard the military regime as their saviour from the threat of socialism; criticisms were almost always made in the context of support for the government's overall social purpose. Second, new lucrative investments were becoming available to businessmen whose previous lines had become unprofitable. Over time many capitalists in declining sectors diversified into better-paying assets. Although this alone would not have been enough, the fact that financial liberalization and boom allowed many investors to diversify out of unprofitable activities cushioned some of the sectoral impact of policy trends. Finally, while many sectors of the economy did poorly due to the reforms, others experienced a lucrative expansion, and their support for the distributional effects of the military regime's policies helped counteract whatever business opposition there was to them.

Indeed, nontradables sectors in general, especially financial services and real estate, did extremely well over the period. Part of this was simply due to the "liberation" of heavily controlled markets, such as for financial services. Another part was due to the reversal of the prior import-substituting bias; the new policy regime, among other things, allowed middle- and upper-income consumers to divert some of their expenditures from manufactured goods (which could now be bought more cheaply, often from abroad) to such other uses as housing construction. Some portion may have been the result of policies, such as the hurried privatizations, that contributed to a speculative bubble in asset markets. Indeed, the real price of urban land in 1981 was nearly nine times its 1970 level, and real stock prices in 1980 were more than ten times their 1970 levels.[38]

Financial regulation allowed banks to reap great profits by arbitraging between overseas and Chilean financial markets.[39] For reasons that are

---

Estudios Transnacionales, 1984), 120. This is an excellent study of trends in business-community sentiment; its analysis is largely the same as that presented here.

[37] Ibid, 162–63.

[38] Arellano, "De la liberalización a la intervención," p. 14.

[39] Roberto Zahler, "The Monetary and Real Effects of the Financial Opening Up of National Economies to the Exterior: The Chilean Case, 1974–1978," *CEPAL Review* 10 (April 1980): 127–54; and, more generally, Roberto Zahler, "Estrategias financieras latinoamericanas: La experiencia del Cono Sur," *Colección Estudios CIEPLAN* 23 (March 1988): 117–43.

controversial, interest rates in Chile were very high throughout the period: the real cost of peso-denominated credits averaged 28 percent between 1977 and 1981, while over the same period the real domestic-currency cost of foreign-currency credits averaged less than 1 percent.[40] Controls on foreign borrowing gave well-positioned banks an opportunity to profit on the basis of this differential.

The "boom" in the nontradables sectors was accentuated by the real appreciation of the peso that took place between 1979 and 1982. In fact, the sectoral effects of the 1976–1982 period might be interpreted as a special instance of "Dutch disease" (see chapter 3). In this view, deregulation, privatization, and foreign borrowing made financial services a typical booming sector experiencing a resource inflow from abroad. Much of this inflow was used for the consumption of traded goods, leading to a surge in imports; another portion "leaked" into increased local demand for such nontraded goods and services as housing. As increased demand for nontradables raised their price, foreign goods became ever cheaper and the import surge accelerated.[41] Whatever the explanation, the undeniable fact is that the most striking characteristic of the borrowing-period Chilean economy was the euphoria of the financial and real estate asset markets.

The economic "model" did not of course project reliance on an expansion of production of nontradables to pull the economy forward; it anticipated rapid growth in the production of goods in line with Chile's comparative advantage. In fact, there was movement in this direction. Output grew rapidly in manufacturing industries that had been relatively unprotected, and therefore presumably were able to compete internationally even before the reforms. Manufacturing based on the processing of natural resources with which Chile is well endowed also did well. By 1980 output of beverages was up by 68 percent over 1970 levels; paper products, 60 percent; tobacco products, 59 percent; in the basic metal industries, 48 percent; electrical products, 32 percent; food products, 16 percent.[42] However, even manufacturers that did well in the late 1970s began

[40] Arellano, "De la liberalización a la intervención," 36. For other evaluations of the issues see Edwards and Edwards, *Monetarism and Liberalization*, chap. 3; and Arnold Harberger, "Observations on the Chilean Economy, 1973–1983," *Economic Development and Cultural Change* 33, no. 3 (April 1985): 451–62.

[41] See, for example Vittorio Corbo, "Chilean Economic Policy and International Economic Relations since 1970," in *The National Economic Policies of Chile*, especially 121–39. Two other approaches are Rudiger Dornbusch, "External Debt, Budget Deficits, and Disequilibrium Exchange Rates," especially 220–24, and Arnold Harberger, "Lessons for Debtor Country Managers and Policymakers," especially 239–49, both in *International Debt and the Developing Countries*, ed. Gordon Smith and John Cuddington (Washington, D.C.: World Bank, 1985).

[42] Edwards and Edwards, *Monetarism and Liberalization*, 120.

to experience difficulties as the peso appreciated after 1979 and they were priced out of home and export markets.

One interesting result of the Chilean experience, which largely subsumes the intersectoral distributional effects of Chilean policies, was the rise of a series of conglomerates, the *grupos*. Chile had a long-standing tradition of related firms connected by ties of family or friendship, but such horizontally integrated conglomerates proliferated under the military.[43] By the end of 1978, before the process had culminated, the three largest groups—Cruzat-Larraín, Vial, and Matte—included firms with 46 percent of the capital of the 250 largest companies in the country (another 31 percent was in firms associated with other groups, 13 percent in foreign-owned firms, and 10 percent in firms owned by individual entrepreneurs).[44]

The typical *grupo* was centered around a financial institution. The Cruzat-Larraín group, for example, controlled three of Chile's ten largest private banks (Banco de Santiago, Banco Hipotecario de Fomento Nacional, and Banco Colocadora Nacional de Valores) with 17.1 percent of total financial-system loans by 1982. The Vial/BHC group was organized around Banco de Chile (Chile's largest bank) and included two other major financial institutions (Banco BHC and Morgan-Finansa) with a 1982 total of 24.9 percent of total loans.[45] *Grupo* banks did much of their lending to *grupo* firms—nearly half of the Banco de Santiago's loans were to firms related to the group. Groups also owned such smaller financial institutions as insurance companies.

Most *grupo* activities were in nontraded goods and services, natural resources, and export-oriented manufacturing. They were typically active in real estate and construction, wholesale and retail trade, large-scale agriculture and forestry, and selected manufacturing. The Cruzat-Larraín group in 1978, for example, had thirty-three firms in real estate, construction, and investment companies; six in financial services; ten in commerce; sixteen in agriculture, forest products, and mining; and thirty-four in industry, especially wood products, pulp and paper, copper products, seafood, food products, and beverages. The group's assets were $1 billion; its debt was $739 million. In the same year, respective numbers for the Vial/BHC group were twenty, nine, three, nine, and fifteen firms; manufacturing affiliates were primarily in metal-working, appliances, and

---

[43] One possible interpretation of the development is that as lobbying for government protection was eliminated as an option for firms, they were driven to diversify their asset portfolios. This is another indication of the general (imperfect) substitutability between political markets and capital markets for the diversification of risk.

[44] Dahse, *Mapa*, 147.

[45] Arellano, "De la liberalización a la intervención," 24.

food products. The Vial/BHC group's total assets were $520 million and its debts $437 million.[46]

The *grupos* were a concentrated expression of the most successful portions of the Chilean business community. They had important activities in nontraded services, and in the production of traded goods in which Chile had a clear comparative advantage.[47] Management of the *grupos* tended to be modern and technically sophisticated, and their ties with the economic team became very good. Cruzat-Larraín, especially, had many directors with government experience and contacts. It is not surprising, of course, that such successful enterprises would be favorably disposed toward the regime, nor that the regime would look kindly on success stories that seemed to be fulfilling the best expectations of the economic team.

Over time, in fact, the *grupos* came to exert some influence on economic policy. The financial liberalization of the late 1970s, which made foreign borrowing by Chilean banks easier, may in part have been encouraged by the *grupos*' desire to gain access to cheap foreign funds and to the arbitrage opportunities made possible by the interest-rate differential between domestic and overseas financial markets. However, *grupo* political influence should not be exaggerated. For one thing, the *grupos* were diversified enough that losses in one sector could easily be counteracted by gains in another: they had few explicitly sectoral concerns. It is more accurate to regard the *grupos* as a logical *response* to government policies. If sectoral policies were to be avoided and the market allowed to operate, well-placed investors wanted a diversified portfolio in activities in which the country had a natural comparative advantage.

It is nonetheless ironic that the Chilean military government, whose economic policies were the closest thing to laissez faire that Latin America had seen in fifty years, presided over a major concentration of assets. By 1981 an enormous proportion of economic activity was in the hands of a few oligopolistic entities with a very anticompetitive bent in their patterns of financing and management. Such developments were due in large part to the great importance of access to financial resources, and to the fact that these resources (especially from abroad) were concentrated in a few hands; there may also have been scale economies in the implementation of modern management techniques. Whatever the reason, the regime's market-oriented policies gave rise to more powerful conglomerates than Chile had ever seen. Afficionados of the model could, of course, take

[46] Dahse, *Mapa*, 27–46.

[47] For the perspective of the Vial/BHC group, see the comments by Rolf Lüders in Nicolás Ardito Barletta, Mario Blejer, and Luis Landau, eds., *Economic Liberalization and Stabilization Policies in Argentina, Chile, and Uruguay* (Washington, D.C.: World Bank, 1983), 66–69.

heart in the fact that conglomerate affiliates were generally in activities that reflected Chile's comparative advantage.

A detailed study of the effects of the economic environment on a sample of 177 firms confirms general impressions about the winners and losers during the borrowing period.[48] The least successful firms were those in import-competing sectors that had previously had high rates of protection. Firms in export-oriented activities did only a little better, especially with the adverse effects of the peso appreciation after 1979. Import-competing companies that had not previously been protected from foreign competition did well, as did firms producing nontradable goods. Affiliation with a *grupo* improved performance, whether for management or financial reasons. Industrial firms came to rely very heavily on external sources of finance, which eventually contributed to the depth of the crash after 1981.

Chilean borrowing and liberalization are of interest for both economic and political-economy reasons. Economically, there are both positive and negative sides to the experience. On the positive side, inflation was reduced dramatically, consumer choice was increased and many inefficiencies were eliminated. There was substantial investment in some export production and in previously underprovided goods and services: Chile's production structure more closely reflected its comparative advantage. On the negative side, unemployment was extremely high and real wages depressed, and income distribution deteriorated. Domestic savings and investment remained low, and the economy skewed toward speculation in financial assets and real estate. Large portions of the economy were concentrated in oligopolistic groups, and excessive borrowing left the balance sheets of many firms precarious. The reforms made the economy more efficient, but at great social cost; whether the increased efficiency was worth the cost is hard to measure. Macroeconomic policy was probably more failure than success, especially the extremism of 1979–1982: the benefits of reduced inflation were outweighed by the costs of the exchange rate's contribution to the financial bubble and crash.

Leaving the interesting economic issues aside, the borrowing period had important effects on the Chilean political economy. Organized labor was substantially weakened, as was formerly import-substituting manufacturing. Middle- and upper-class consumers and investors in real estate

[48] Julio Galvez and James Tybout, "Microeconomic Adjustments in Chile during 1977–1981: The Importance of Being a *Grupo*," *World Development* 13, no. 8 (1985): 969–94. Complementary discussions are in Vittorio Corbo and Jose Miguel Sanchez, "Adjustments by Industrial Firms in Chile during 1974–1982," 83–117, and Pedro Arriagada, "Adjustments by Agricultural Exporters in Chile during 1974–1982," 119–52, both in *Scrambling for Survival: How Firms Adjusted to the Recent Reforms in Argentina, Chile, and Uruguay*, ed. Vittorio Corbo and Jaime de Melo (Washington: World Bank, 1985).

and financial assets did well. So too did firms and individuals associated with the *grupos*, concentrated as they were in the nontradables sectors and export-oriented manufacturing. In other words, those successful in the freewheeling atmosphere of 1976–1982 included those whose activities matched Chile's comparative advantage, and those able to take advantage of such policy-created opportunities as cheap imports and cheap foreign-currency loans. The crisis that began late in 1981 tested the economic and political fabric woven during the borrowing period.

The Crash and Its Aftermath, 1982–1985

In 1982 the Chilean economy deteriorated with startling ferocity. In the space of a few months, the peso collapsed, capital inflows stopped, most of the private sector was bankrupted, and the financial system fell apart. Per capita GDP declined 16 percent and manufacturing output 21 percent; open unemployment went to 20 percent, with an additional 6 percent in public make-work programs. In 1983 per capita GDP fell another 2 percent; open unemployment was 19 percent, and another 12 percent of the labor force was in public programs, so that nearly one-third of the laboring population lacked normal employment.

Although the economic crisis was similar to but far more serious than those of other Latin American authoritarian debtor nations, the political fallout was quite different. To be sure, many segments of the working and middle classes protested bitterly over the crisis, leading to mass demonstrations and a renascent armed opposition. Indeed, there seemed little doubt that only a small minority of the population continued to support the government. However, the regime was able to stay in power without much difficulty. Of course, Pinochet's personal control over the military played a role in this, but I argue that the crucial difference from other Latin American dictatorships was that the private sector would have little to do with the opposition. Continued fear of the labor-based opposition drove business to moderate its criticisms of the military; moderation was encouraged by selective government support for debtors.

The first signs of the crisis came amidst the euphoria of 1981, when in April a major sugar firm with *grupo* connections went bankrupt. By the end of the year it was clear that a large number of firms were facing severe financial difficulties. Total banking-system loans had by 1981 reached 55 percent of GDP, after a meteoric rise from 8 percent in 1970 to 15 percent in 1977 and 28 percent in 1979. Danger signals abounded, especially concerning the proliferation of *grupo*-bank loans to struggling *grupo* firms. In November 1981 six small financial institutions had to be taken over by the government due to insolvency. (The Spanish term used to describe

the government's action is *intervención*, intervention, in the banks.) Increasing signs of financial instability led Pinochet to criticize the *grupos'*
activities in December 1981. Eventually open feuds developed between
the government and Javier Vial, of the Vial/BHC group, over links between *grupo* banks and nonfinancial firms.[49]

By the end of 1981 and the beginning of 1982, evidence of imminent
catastrophe was everywhere. SOFOFA's industrial production index for
the fourth quarter of 1981 was down over 10 percent from the third quarter, and it dropped another 10 percent in the following six months.[50] Although most private-sector groups continued to hope, along with the government, that the crisis would pass, dissent grew. Many representatives
of small and medium-sized businesses stepped up their criticisms of the
model's effects on them. Even within the normally supportive SOFOFA,
for the first time since the coup an alternate list critical of the government
ran for the society's board. Although progovernment candidates won, the
open division was significant.

In April 1982, in clear recognition that the economy was in serious
trouble, Finance Minister de Castro was replaced with another Chicago
boy, Sergio de la Cuadra. In June the government announced that the
peso, whose exchange rate it had fixed "forever," would be devalued, and
the peso was soon floating downward. The government recognized that
financial crisis was threatening, as nonperforming loans reached 39 percent of Chilean banks' capital and reserves.[51] The response of the economic team was to encourage the *grupos* to loosen ties with financial
institutions, but this was not enough.

As the depression worsened, de la Cuadra was replaced in August 1982
by Rolf Lüders, a former executive of the Vial group. Although Lüders
tended toward pragmatic positions, supporters of orthodoxy continued

[49] For summaries of the events of the period, see, in addition to sources already cited, José
Pablo Arellano, "Crisis y recuperación económica en Chile en los años 80," *Colección Es-
tudios CIEPLAN* 24 (June 1988): 63–84; Edgardo Barandiarán, "Nuestra crisis finan-
ciera," *Estudios Públicos* 12 (Spring 1983): 89–107; Nicolás Eyzaguirre, "La deuda interna
chilena, 1975–1985," in *Deuda interna y estabilidad financiera*, ed. Carlos Massad and
Roberto Zahler (Buenos Aires: Grupo Editor Latinoamericano, 1988), 2:341–85; Oscar
Muñoz, "Chile: El colapso de un experimento económico y sus efectos políticos," *Colección
Estudios CIEPLAN* 16 (June 1985): 101–22; Barbara Stallings, "Political Economy of
Democratic Transition: Chile in the 1980s," in *Debt and Democracy in Latin America*, ed.
Barbara Stallings and Robert Kaufman (Boulder, Colo.: Westview Press, 1989), 181–99;
and Laurence Whitehead, "The Adjustment Process in Chile: A Comparative Perspective,"
in *Latin American Debt and the Adjustment Crisis*, ed. Rosemary Thorp and Laurence
Whitehead (London: Macmillan Press, 1987), 117–61. Campero, *Los gremios empresariales*, 231–88, is an excellent review of the business community's response to the economic
crisis.
[50] Foxley, "The Neoconservative Economic Experiment," 22.
[51] Ibid., 27.

to wield power within the economic team. On 10 January 1983 Lüders announced an agreement with the IMF for a standby credit. Three days later the government intervened in five banks, including the country's two largest, liquidated three others, and began supervising two more directly. The government now controlled banks responsible for 80 percent of the financial sector. Since the banks were at the center of conglomerates that dominated the economy, the state was for all intents and purposes running the economy to a degree unseen even under Allende: critics spoke of a new, military, road to socialism.

The impact of the crisis was not the same on all economic activities, of course. While in 1982–1983 output dropped, depending on the measure used, by 15 to 18 percent, the cessation of financial inflows caused aggregate spending to drop by almost 28 percent. Output in the financial-services sector fell by 34 percent; construction, 28 percent; manufacturing, 23 percent; commerce, 20 percent. Other activities, especially in primary production, were less hard hit: agricultural output fell by just 6 percent, while output in the mining and fishing sectors rose 4 and 19 percent respectively. Within manufacturing, the depression had varied effects, hitting the export-oriented sectors least hard. The combined output of the food, beverages, tobacco, paper and paper products, and basic metals industries fell by less than 5 percent between 1981 and 1983; the combined output of the textiles, clothing, leather, wood-products, metal-products, machinery, and equipment industries dropped by over 41 percent.[52]

The concern of the business community deepened as the crisis dragged on, reaching a high point during the last few months of 1982 and the first few months of 1983.[53] For the first time since the Allende period, business leaders called for important changes in economic policy. A typical appeal came from the business federation of the southern city of Valdivia in October 1982 which saw "with profound alarm the destruction of the entire productive agricultural and industrial apparatus" and called on "the national authorities to develop urgent measures to halt and lessen the effects of the paralysis of productive and commercial activity."[54] Demands were for greater trade protection, reflation, and subsidies to debtors. As one manufacturer put it, "We knew this government was repressive. When the economy was good, it was easy to ignore all that. Now that the good times are over, the veil is off and we want Pinochet out."[55]

As the economy continued to stagnate, protest broadened and became more explicitly political. In March 1983, the civilian opposition began organizing. Almost immediately, the political forces prominent in pre-

---

[52] Calculated from Edwards and Edwards, *Monetarism and Liberalization*, 197–200.

[53] Campero, *Los gremios empresariales*, 260–72, is an excellent summary.

[54] Ibid., 264.

[55] *Wall Street Journal*, 11 February 1985, p. 22.

1973 Chile jumped to the fore, confounding the hopes of regime supporters that its policies had fundamentally transformed the country's body
politic. Two broad opposition alliances coalesced. The Alianza Democrática (AD) was centered around the Christian Democrats but included
other parties and factions of the center-right, center, and center-left, most
prominently moderate elements of the conservative National party and of
the Socialist party. The Movimiento Democrático Popular (MDP) included the Communist party, harder-line segments of the Socialist party,
and other left-wing organizations. The former alliance was based in the
middle classes and segments of the labor movement, along with some
businessmen; the latter found its principal support among other segments
of the working class and residents of shantytowns on the urban periph-
eries.[56]

Beginning in May 1983, the new civilian opposition launched a series
of monthly days of protests. Despite often-brutal repression, the protests
were extremely successful, and continued with one five-month interrup-
tion through November 1984. Although tension among the coalition
partners was great—elements of the Communist Party were stepping up
armed opposition even as the centrists called for constitutional reform—
there was general unity on the need for democratization and revision of
the economic model. This was not surprising, for the regime had become
overwhelmingly unpopular. A September 1983 public opinion poll
showed that 66 percent of the population thought its standard of living
was lower than in 1973; the figure was 73 percent among upper-class
Chileans. Virtually all respondents, regardless of social class, explicitly
blamed the government for the crisis, rejecting regime claims that the depression was caused by external factors.[57]

As 1983 wore on, it seemed Chile might accompany other Latin American debt-ridden dictatorships toward democratization and economic-
policy heterodoxy. In March 1983 tariffs were doubled to 20 percent. In
April "productive debtors" were given public debt relief, and foreign exchange was made available at a preferential rate to those with foreign-
currency liabilities.[58]

[56] Good summaries of the opposition are Silvia Borzutzky, "The Pinochet Regime: Crisis
and Consolidation," in *Authoritarians and Democrats: Regime Transition in Latin America*, ed. James Malloy and Mitchell Seligson (Pittsburgh: University of Pittsburgh Press,
1987), 67–89; and Guillermo Campero and René Cortázar, "Actores sociales y la transición
a la democracia en Chile," *Colección Estudios CIEPLAN* 25 (December 1988): 115–58.

[57] Carlos Huneeus, "From Diarchy to Polyarchy: Prospects for Democracy in Chile," in
*Comparing New Democracies: Transition and Consolidation in Mediterranean Europe and
the Southern Cone*, ed. Enrique Baloyra (Boulder, Colo.: Westview Press, 1987), 128, 138.

[58] Eyzaguirre, "La deuda interna chilena," 378–81, and José Pablo Arellano and Manuel
Marfán, "Ahorro-inversión y relaciones financieras en la actual crisis económica chilena,"
Colección Estudios CIEPLAN 20 (December 1986): especially 80–90, summarize the sup-

To some extent the government rescue of troubled private debtors was driven by the spectre of financial disaster. By May 1983, according to one estimate, Chilean banks' nonperforming loans were 113 percent of their capital and reserves, while the country's two largest banks, the Banco de Chile and Banco de Santiago, had end-1983 bad debts equal to nearly three and more than four times their capital and reserves, respectively.[59] Faced with financial collapse, the several billion dollars spent on bailing out debtors may have seemed a small price to pay.[60] Another, ironic reason for the authorities' socialization of privately incurred debts was that foreign creditors insisted that the Chilean government take responsibility for the Chilean private sector's overseas debts. The confluence of political pressure from domestic debtors and foreign creditors, and concern over financial panic, led the government to take over most of the nation's foreign debt: as shown in table 5.2, the share of Chile's overseas debt owed or guaranteed by the public sector went from just 35 percent in 1981 to 75 percent in 1985.[61]

Meanwhile, politics seemed to be moving in a more democratic direction. In August 1983 Pinochet appointed a new cabinet headed by a civilian politician of the far right, who began negotiations with the leadership of AD and promised political reforms in 1984. Although repression of the protests continued, political debate became more open. In April 1984, the relative pragmatist Luis Escóbar, with close ties to the business community, replaced the more orthodox Carlos Cáceres as minister of finance. Over the following months further concessions were granted to debtors, and tariffs were raised again to 35 percent.

Although it seemed the military might lose its grip on a discontented society, the private sector gradually moderated its dissatisfaction, which played a major role in allowing the dictatorship to hold onto power. The first reason was the modest compromises with economic pragmatism made in 1983 and 1984—especially tariff increases and debt relief—which helped keep business relatively satisfied. In fact, many firms were loath to endanger the support they received. As one economist said, "The enterpreneurs' firms are concessions held with the banks at the sufferance of government debt-rollover policy. The firms belong to the banks and

---

port measures implemented. A more general perspective is in Carlos Diaz Alejandro, "Good-bye Financial Repression, Hello Financial Crash," *Journal of Development Economics* 19 (1985): 1–24.

[59] Diaz-Alejandro, "Good-bye Financial Repression," 11; Arellano and Marfán, "Ahorro-inversión," 82.

[60] For estimates of the cost of the bailout, see Arellano and Marfán, "Ahorro-inversión," 87–89.

[61] On Chile's debt negotiations and their domestic impact, see Jaime Estévez, "La negociación financiera externa en Chile, 1983–1987," in *Entre la heterodoxia y el ajuste*, ed. Roberto Bouzas (Buenos Aires: Grupo Editor Latinoamericano, 1988), 181–204.

the banks belong to the government."[62] An indication of the dangers of private-sector dissent was provided when the highly critical Vial group was smashed by the government, and Vial and Lüders (who had lost his government post in February 1983) were jailed for alleged fraud. The Cruzat-Larraín group was conciliatory toward the regime and was rewarded by being allowed to maintain control of its empire.[63]

A second reason for the private sector's unwillingness to join the opposition, which increased in importance over time, was renewed concern about threats to property. As the leftist MDP launched large and militant protest demonstrations, fears of the anticapitalist opposition were rekindled. Despite assurances from AD that *its* members would respect private property, the spectacle of hundreds of thousands of Chileans following the Communists and their allies, even after a decade of dictatorship, convinced businessmen that a firm hand was still needed. One leading opposition politician lamented: "Businessmen might think that we are more likely to reactivate the economy, and that democratization would increase Chile's bargaining power with foreign creditors. Unfortunately, what worries Chilean businessmen is not specific policies on debt or trade, but the security of property. We offer them full assurances of private property rights, but businessmen worry about the social demands that would arise from civil society with democracy."[64]

As more pragmatic economic policies and misgivings about the character of the opposition dampened business discontent, the regime moved swiftly to put down the protest movements. In November 1984 a state of siege was declared, press censorship was tightened, and in the following months tens of thousands of activists were arrested. The dictatorship had successfully contained massive dissatisfaction.

In 1985, as the crisis eased, the economic model was restored. Social dissatisfaction remained rife—only in 1989 did per capita income and real wages regain their 1981 levels—but the military regime was largely able to contain it. Loss of a 1988 plebiscite and victory for the opposition candidate in 1989 elections indicated the depth of opposition to the regime, but unlike elsewhere in the region, this opposition was forced to abide by rules devised and enforced by the military.

Summary and Evaluation of the Chilean Experience

Between 1976 and 1982 Chile was one of the developing world's largest borrowers from the international banking system, especially relative to

[62] Interview by the author with Joseph Ramos, Santiago, 5 August 1985.

[63] Andrés Sanfuentes, "Los grupos económicos: Control y políticas," *Colección Estudios CIEPLAN* 15 (December 1984): especially 144–47.

[64] Interview by the author with Sergio Molina, Santiago, 8 August 1985.

the size of the country's population and economy. Unlike in other LDC debtors, however, foreign loans went almost entirely to private firms. Most of the new borrowing was in fact done by major private banks, which generally were at the center of diversified conglomerates. The capital inflow served to dramatically increase imports, including many imports of consumer goods; large portions of it helped fuel a boom in real-estate and financial markets; it also financed investment in export-oriented activities encouraged by the military government's economic policies. As with so much else in Chile, the exact proportions involved are controversial.

The Chilean government did not use the country's access to foreign resources to do what almost all other LDCs did—expand the role of the public sector in the economy. A turn toward the market was relatively common in the 1980s, as external finance dried up and LDC governments were forced to rely on their own scarce domestic resources. However, Chile undertook the most radical experiment in economic liberalism in recent Latin American history at a time when external resources to go in the opposite direction were abundant. Tariffs were virtually eliminated, markets deregulated, state firms privatized, and the public deficit eliminated. The financial inflow strengthened the economic position of the beneficiaries of liberalization, especially the nontradables sectors (trade and finance) and competitive producers. Many of these were concentrated in large conglomerates, the *grupos*. Some of the distributional consequences of the Chilean experiment were due to macroeconomic policy, especially the real appreciation of the peso after 1979.

When the financial crisis hit in 1982, it caused enormous destruction. Popular dissatisfaction was nearly universal, and even after a decade of repression mass protests sprang up almost immediately. Business began, after ten years of support for the regime's policies, to question the economic model. However, private-sector opposition to the government was restrained by two factors: the government rescued some of the country's more troubled firms, and the opposition rekindled memories of the socialist threat. For both reasons, business criticism of the regime dwindled rapidly, the opposition was isolated, and Pinochet was able to hold onto power with little difficulty.

The first puzzle we face is to explain Chilean economic policy in comparative perspective, over time, and across sectors.

Cross-National Comparison

Chilean economic policy was as close to orthodox liberalism as has been seen in a developing country since World War II. My explanation of this anomalous case rests on the extreme salience of labor-capital conflict in

Chile, culminating in the overthrow of the Allende government in 1973. Sectoral issues were subordinate, for both capital and labor, to broader class issues that were, unlike in almost all countries almost all of the time, on the immediate political agenda. In these circumstances, the military dictatorship concentrated on restoring favorable investment conditions in general, rather than supporting specific groups of investors.

Evolution over Time

Once the model was in place, of course, new interests developed and new issues came to the fore. As structural reforms were implemented and the economy grew rapidly, sectoral pressures began to rise. The *grupos*, for example, lobbied successfully for opening the capital account to give them access to cheap foreign finance. However, although sectoral demands grew somewhat over time, they never became particularly strong; and the military regime ignored most of them. The principal evolution of policy was on the macroeconomic front, where the impact of sector-specific demands was minimal.

Cross-Sectional Variation

Of course, liberalization had major distributional consequences, with especially negative effects on formerly protected traded-goods producers. By the same token, those able to take advantage of market opportunities opened up by the liberalization did very well; this included those in the nontraded goods and services sectors, export-competers, and previously unprotected manufacturers. However, policy was extremely market-oriented, and policymakers often expressed and acted upon a general opposition to sectoral subsidies and incentives. There was probably some relationship between size and concentration and political influence—the *grupos* had relatively close ties with policymakers. But even sectoral pressures from the *grupos* were quite limited. Apart from continued fear of socialism, financial-market liberalization had allowed investors to diversify their portfolios. The *grupos'* interests could not be easily connected to any set of sectors; they, along the lines of the incentives put in place by the model, did not depend on sector-specific subsidies and incentives. Although the military regime's policies had differential sectoral effects, this was a second-order consequence of the market orientation that infused the economic model. Even after the crisis hit, there is no obvious pattern of specific support: many debtors were rescued, but executives of the country's second largest *grupo* (Vial/BHC) were jailed, probably for having feuded openly with the regime.

The second set of analytical questions about the Chilean experience has to do with political patterns once the crisis hit. Unlike in other Latin American dictatorships, the Chilean military held onto power with little difficulty. After an initial relaxation of economic orthodoxy, modified versions of past repression and the past economic model were reinstated. After several years, a plebiscite held by the regime resulted in defeat and the election of a civilian government in 1989, but this process took place on the military's schedule and terms.

Despite the great economic distress of the early 1980s, the business community in general eschewed open criticism of the government and avoided alliances with the opposition. Military repression may have played a role—although it does not seem to have in Argentina or Brazil, and although elements of the military were sympathetic to business complaints. In addition, selected government programs did cushion the crisis for many firms. However, my argument is that the most important factor in staving off a society-wide movement for democratization was the private sector's unwillingness to support it, and that this unwillingness was, once again, a result of continuing fear of labor. Indeed, renewed political protests once the crisis hit reinforced business apprehension about the opposition.

The Chilean experience is a fascinating one on many accounts. Economists and others will long debate the effects of the liberalization undertaken after the 1973 coup. It is fascinating for my purposes, too, occupying an extreme position on the continuum of labor-capital conflict. I argue that the bitterness of this conflict had a great impact both on economic policy and politics in Chile between 1973 and 1985.

6

Debt, Economic Policy, and Politics in Mexico, Venezuela, and Argentina

IF BRAZIL and Chile are two poles of an economic-policy continuum stretching from high levels of government intervention in the economy to laissez faire, the next three cases are arrayed between the two poles. Mexico and Venezuela were more like Brazil, with public sectors that expanded aggressively during the borrowing period. Government policy aimed principally at spurring industrialization, especially in such basic industries as steel and petrochemicals and in such sophisticated modern manufacturing as consumer durables and capital goods. Argentina was more like Chile, with a regime dedicated to reducing both the size of the public sector and its level of intervention in the market. However, Argentina's government was less extreme and less successful than Chile's in its market orientation.

Politically, the three countries varied in their response to the financial crisis of the 1980s. The Mexican political system did not change dramatically, but it did evolve away from its single-party tradition and toward multiparty democracy. The ruling party splintered and politics became competitive for the first time: radical populists left the ruling party to form their own group, while conservatives both inside and outside the ruling party gained strength and cohesion. In Venezuela, the pre-existing electoral system remained in place unaltered. Normal electoral competition led to a change in government, turning out a relative conservative in favor of a moderate populist. Chronically troubled Argentine politics continued to lurch from side to side. The military dictatorship that presided over borrowing slunk back to the barracks after the collapse of its economic program was followed by military defeat. Non-Peronists won their first free election victory since Perón, but further economic decay brought the Peronists back to power again. In all three cases, austerity tended to call forth a populist and nationalist response, but this response varied in form, in success, and in effect on the political system.

My explanations of the patterns of economic policy during the borrowing period are those outlined in the discussions of Brazil and Chile. Mexico and Venezuela had long been characterized by semicorporatist political systems in which labor-capital conflict was dampened by populism, patronage, and multiclass alliances. Argentina, which for thirty years was led or haunted by Peronist nationalist populism, had in the middle 1970s collapsed into violent and virulent labor conflict. In the first two instances, sectoral pressures dominated. The most favored groups were large-scale and concentrated segments of advanced modern industry, along with some agribusinesses and the financial communities. Some popular groups also tapped into the financial resources (and oil rents) flowing into Mexico and Venezuela. In Argentina, social strife brought to power a dictatorship dedicated to breaking organized labor and organized Peronism and intent, during most of the borrowing period (1976–1982), on using the market to do this work for it.

The political developments that hit Mexico, Venezuela, and Argentina after the financial crisis also follow from my discussion of the Brazilian and Chilean cases. Those whose specific physical- and human-capital assets were threatened by the payments crisis mobilized to defend them: organized labor, government employees, and protected industries banded together to support political movements based on a rejection of austerity. Those whose assets were liquid enough to be safe, or otherwise placed to benefit from the crisis, for their part pressured for more liberal economic policies and cooperation with external creditors: they formed the backbone of conservative movements whose strength varied from country to country and over time.

This chapter presents the Mexican, Venezuelan, and Argentine cases in telegraphic form. The purpose is not to replicate the detailed discussion of Brazil and Chile, only to signal the outlines of an explanation of the three national experiences.

Background to Borrowing

One striking similarity among the three countries is the importance of natural resource exports. Venezuelan oil, Mexican oil and minerals, and Argentine beef and wheat all bring in major foreign currency earnings; in varied ways, they have been crucial to the respective political economies. The countries vary as to how central the resource-based sector is; whether the resource is in private or public hands; and the uses to which resource rents have been put.

The modern economic history of all three began with a dramatic expansion of raw materials exports. During this early period—before World War I in Mexico and Argentina, before World War II in Venezuela—the political economy was dominated by producers of the export commodity and their allies.

In all three, opposition to the centrality of the export economy eventually arose, based in such urban groups as industrialists, workers, and the middle class (and, in Mexico and Venezuela, the traditional peasantry). In one way or another, these forces gave rise to nationalist and populist movements and to some form of import-substituting industrialization with strong state support. Conflict between more nationalistic and more internationally oriented groups remains important in all three countries. In Mexico and Venezuela, the inward-oriented forces tapped into the oil sector rather easily, allowing for social programs and the political incorporation of the working class in quasi-corporatist systems. In Argentina, however, resource-based producers remain private and hostile to the populist agenda, and labor-capital relations have been more conflictual.

Mexico

The Mexican Revolution of 1910–1920 and its aftermath created a semicorporatist system with strong nationalist, developmentalist, and populist orientations. The administration of Lázaro Cárdenas (1934–1940) made the definitive break with an economy dominated by primary exports, assisted by the effects of the depression on export markets and later by the wartime cutoff of manufactured imports. The government also came to play a central role in the economy. Cárdenas nationalized the petroleum industry and railroads, created the Comisión Federal de Electricidad (CFE), and founded state financial institutions—especially a development bank, Nacional Financiera or Nafinsa—to complement the central bank (Banco de México) established in 1925.

After the natural import substitution of the 1930s and 1940s, postwar governments embarked on import-substituting industrialization and considerable state involvement in the economy. Tariffs and quantitative restrictions practically eliminated imports of consumer nondurables and reduced them in other sectors. Between 1941 and 1946 nearly 60 percent of all investment was public, and 40 percent in the 1950s.[1]

In the political realm, from Cárdenas on the regime drew its support primarily from national businessmen, workers in modern industry, and segments of the peasantry. The political system institutionalized under Cárdenas remained intact for fifty years, representing one of the most

---

[1] Timothy King, *Mexico: Industrialization and Trade Policies since 1940* (London: Oxford University Press, 1970), 48; Dwight Brothers, "El financiamento de la formación de capital en México, 1950–1961," *Comercio Exterior* (December 1963): 903; Jorge Tamayo, "El papel del sector público en el proceso de acumulación de capital," *Investigación Económica* 23, no. 92 (October–December 1963): 709–47. The best single source on Mexican economic development, which is used extensively in this discussion, is Leopoldo Solís, *La realidad económica mexicana: Retrovisión y perspectivas*, 16th ed. (Mexico City: Siglo Veintiuno, 1987).

distinctive examples of political integration in the Third World.[2] The only party that counted was the Partido Revolucionario Institucional (PRI), which has ruled under a variety of names since the revolution. The PRI gave formal representation to labor, the peasantry, and the middle class, specifically excluding economic elites. Businessmen influenced decisions informally, while the working class and peasantry were politically integrated into the party. The polity was responsive to the requirements of major investors, while it managed to combine co-optation, government spending, and repression to maintain the support of small businessmen, workers, and peasants.

Although the government protected and subsidized national industry and targeted social spending at politically important popular groups, politics and policies did not go to the extremes found in some other Latin American societies. The incorporation of important popular groups into the regime gave them a stake in the system and led them toward relative moderation. At the same time, businesses with ties to the U.S. market, especially bankers and Northern entrepreneurs, tended to moderate private-sector demands for protection.[3]

Postwar economic policy passed through a number of stages. The first, known as "inflationary growth," ran approximately from 1940 to 1956 and was characterized by vigorous import substitution, especially in consumer nondurables, and massive public investment. The unavailability of foreign capital and the government's limited tax base led it to inflationary finance. This forced successive devaluations of the peso from over twenty cents in 1948 to eight cents in 1954.[4]

The devaluations ushered in a period of "stabilizing growth," lasting roughly until 1970 and based on four pillars: public investment, foreign direct investment, import substitution, and conservative macroeconomic management. The public sector accounted for nearly 40 percent of in-

[2] Among the innumerable studies of the Mexican political system, two classic sources are Roger D. Hansen, *The Politics of Mexican Development* (Baltimore: Johns Hopkins University Press, 1971); and the articles in José Luis Reyna and Richard S. Weinert, eds., *Authoritarianism in Mexico* (Philadelphia: ISHI, 1977).

[3] On the role of bankers in the Mexican political economy see the excellent study by Sylvia Maxfield, *Governing Capital: International Finance and Mexican Politics* (Ithaca: Cornell University Press, 1990). The work also contains a good summary of Mexican political and economic trends in the 1970s and 1980s.

[4] On this period see, for example René Villarreal, "The Policy of Import-Substituting Industrialization," in *Authoritarianism in Mexico*, 67–107; Clark Reynolds, *The Mexican Economy: Twentieth Century Structure and Growth* (New Haven: Yale University Press, 1970); Guillermo Ortiz and Leopoldo Solís, "Financial Structure and Exchange Rate Experience: Mexico 1954–1977," *Journal of Development Economics* 6, no. 3 (September 1979): 515–48; and Rogelio Ramirez de la O, "Industrialización y sustitución de importaciones en México," *Comercio Exterior* 30, no. 1 (January 1980): 32.

vestment, Nafinsa for one-third of all industrial lending.[5] The government made a big effort to attract foreign firms, and multinationals accounted for 28 percent of manufacturing sales by 1970.[6]

Import-substituting policies were redoubled. Effective protection increased for manufacturing, while primary producers suffered from negative effective protection. In 1960, by one measure, effective protection was 22 percent for nondurable consumer goods, 13 percent for intermediate goods, and 65 percent for durable consumer and capital goods.[7] Macroeconomic policy gave priority to avoiding inflation and fixing the exchange rate at 12.5 pesos to the dollar. This implied relatively conservative monetary policies, especially high domestic interest rates, to keep inflation low and capital at home.[8]

All of this combined to provide an extended period of noninflationary growth. Industrial production grew by 8.4 percent a year between 1957 and 1970, while wholesale and consumer prices grew by only 2.6 and 3.5 percent a year respectively.[9]

"Stabilizing development" eventually proved unstable. Trade barriers and government pricing policies created relative price distortions. The structure of effective protection made imported capital equipment cheap to manufacturers and raised the prices of the finished goods they produced, so imports of inputs rose while manufactured exports lagged. Agricultural exports stagnated, largely because the government underpriced food products and undersupplied economic infrastructure to traditional rural areas. The current account deficit grew continually from 1.5 percent of GDP between 1954 and 1966 to 2.5 percent between 1967 and 1972, despite government efforts to reverse the trend.[10]

[5] Rosa Olivia Villa M., *National Financiera* (Mexico City: Nacional Financiera, 1976), 41.

[6] Ernesto Zedillo Ponce de Leon, "External Public Indebtedness in Mexico" (Ph.D. thesis, Yale University, 1981), 40; U.N. Centre on Transnational Corporations, *Transnational Corporations in World Development: A Re-Examination* (New York: United Nations, 1978), 269.

[7] Adriaan ten Kate and Robert Bruce Wallace, *Protection and Economic Development in Mexico* (New York: St. Martin's Press, 1981), 135. See also Gerardo Bueno, "The Structure of Protection in Mexico," in Bela Belassa et al., *The Structure of Protection in Developing Countries* (Baltimore: Johns Hopkins University Press, 1971), and Roberto Apodaca Ramirez, "Protección efectiva y asignación de recursos en las manufacturas mexicanas," *Comercio Exterior* 31, no. 10 (October 1981): 1104. The ten Kate and Wallace figures are used here throughout, as theirs reflect the most careful elaboration of the data.

[8] Brothers, "El financiamento," 904–7; Tamayo, "El papel," 744–45; E. V. K. Fitzgerald, "The State and Capital Accumulation in Mexico," *Journal of Latin American Studies* 10, no. 2 (November 1978): 263–82.

[9] Ramirez de la O, "Industrialización," 32.

[10] The period is controversial; for some good summaries, see Leopoldo Solís, *Economic Policy Reform in Mexico: A Case Study for Developing Countries* (New York: Pergamon

By the late 1960s, Mexican economic policy was at an impasse. Import substitution seemed at a dead end, but sheltered industries resisted attempts to reduce protection. The cities swelled with rural migrants, but opposition to fiscal reform ruled out social programs to meet new needs. Traditional PRI patronage seemed unequal to the task of satisfying such important new urban groups as students and urban professionals. Mexican access to international financial markets, however, opened new possibilities for industrial development and social policy.

Venezuela

Since the 1920s the Venezuelan political economy has been dominated by oil. Early exploitation of petroleum resources was presided over by military dictator Juan Vicente Gómez (1908–1935), then by more moderate military dictators Eleazar López Contreras (1935–1941) and Isaías Medina Angarita (1941–1945). The foreign oil companies kept government coffers full, and petroleum exports kept the national currency, the bolívar, strong—during the depression, it actually appreciated.

The boom, as predicted by the literature on Dutch disease, helped the oil sector and producers of nontraded goods and services, and harmed producers of traded goods other than oil. There was predictable conflict on two dimensions. First, the oil and nontradables sectors were militant free-traders, while tradables producers were protectionist. Second, there were battles over how petroleum rents would be distributed. In the early decades, politics were dominated by traditional elites, who had moved out of export agriculture and into trade, finance, and services. They, and the military rulers they supported, remained closely allied to the oilmen and committed to relatively free trade, encoded in the U.S.-Venezuelan trade treaty of 1939.

Economic growth gave rise to or strengthened groups that wanted a share of the country's oil rents, and manufacturers and farmers that could not prosper with traditional free trade.[11] Over the course of the 1930s

Press, 1981), 1–38; Francisco Gil Díaz, "Mexico's Path from Stability to Inflation," in World Economic Growth, ed. Arnold Harberger (San Francisco: ICS Press, 1984), 333–76; and Clark W. Reynolds, "Why Mexico's 'Stabilizing Development' Was Actually Destabilizing (with Some Implications for the Future)," World Development 6, no. 7/8 (July–August 1978): 1005–18.

[11] The most complete survey of modern Venezuelan politics is Ramón J. Velásquez, "Aspectos de la evolución política de Venezuela en el último medio siglo," in Ramón J. Velásquez et al., Venezuela moderna: Medio siglo de historia 1926–1976, 2d ed. (Caracas: Editorial Ariel, 1979), 11–433. Somewhat more analytical surveys include David Eugene Blank, Politics in Venezuela (Boston: Little, Brown and Company, 1973); Judith Ewell, Venezuela: A Century of Change (London: C. Hurst and Company, 1984); and Daniel H.

and early 1940s, many of the discontented groups in the middle class, business, and labor came together as Acción Democrática (AD) under the leadership of Rómulo Betancourt. In 1945 a military uprising by young officers brought AD to power; its rule was sanctioned by landslide victories in elections in 1946 and 1947.

The AD government raised trade barriers to protect domestic producers and pushed through a wide range of social reforms. Trade protection was not popular with the commercial, financial, and oil-related sectors; some of the social measures threatened the business community generally. AD became isolated, and in 1948 a military coup installed Marcos Pérez Jiménez as dictator. Pérez Jiménez outlawed AD and the Communist party and stole the 1952 elections. Growing world petroleum demand led to rapid economic growth, but eventually the regime's corruption and mismanagement alienated even its business supporters.

In January 1958 a broad opposition coalition came together to bring the Pérez Jiménez dictatorship down. The civilian opposition was bent on avoiding the fate of the 1945–1948 regime. Before the coup, leaders of AD, the Social Christian Comité de Organización Política Electoral Independiente (COPEI), another opposition party, and the private sector worked out a joint agreement to stabilize democratic rule; a parallel cooperative commitment was reached by business and labor.[12] These agreements largely created the modern Venezuelan political system.

Over time Venezuelan politics came to be dominated by AD and COPEI, and the political system became a hybrid of electoral competition and populist corporatism. The search for the median voter drove both major parties toward the center. Over the course of the 1960s AD shed its left wing and became a more moderate populist party with control of the labor movement and a PRI-like structure. AD dominated national politics: it won six of eight presidential elections between 1947 and 1988, losing (in 1968 and 1978) only when weakened by internal divisions. In pursuit of electoral success COPEI, despite its original conservative base, adopted more populist policies. The leftist Movimiento al Socialismo (MAS) got about a sixth of the vote; the country was often described as having two and a sixth parties. Other parties were of solely historical or nuisance interest.[13]

Levine, *Conflict and Political Change in Venezuela* (Princeton: Princeton University Press, 1973).

    [12] On the socioeconomic and political developments leading to the establishment and stabilization of Venezuelan democracy, see Terry Lynn Karl, "Petroleum and Political Pacts: The Transition to Democracy in Venezuela," *Latin American Research Review* 22, no. 1 (1987): 63–94.

    [13] On the rise and evolution of AD and COPEI see, in addition to works cited above, Robert J. Alexander, *Rómulo Betancourt and the Transformation of Venezuela* (New Brunswick:

The sectoral characteristics of the Venezuelan economy were reflected in policy debates. The oil sector was economically important and shared interests with such nontraded sectors as finance, commerce, and real estate. This alliance was a force for free trade and capital movements, and conservative fiscal and monetary management. COPEI tended to be more sympathetic to these factions of the business community. On the other side, industry and allied traded-goods producers strongly favored trade protection and subsidies to domestic industrial production. AD, both directly and through its labor base, was more traditionally associated with these elements of business, especially import-substituting enterpreneurs. In the background were demands for social programs and consumption subsidies. Despite their differences, all post-1958 governments used oil rents and trade protection to subsidize industry, agriculture, and social services while trying to keep more internationally oriented groups satisfied with free capital movements and conservative macroeconomic management. COPEI tended toward liberalism and AD toward developmentalism, but the variations were not extreme.[14]

Venezuela was thus characterized by a political system that incorporated labor and by an economy divided into relatively more and less internationally oriented sectors. These sectors clashed on import substitution, membership in the Andean Pact, and abrogation of the U.S.-Venezuelan trade treaty. The business community as a whole and the middle classes opposed a tax reform in 1966, with modest success.[15]

Transaction Books, 1982); Donald L. Herman, *Christian Democracy in Venezuela* (Chapel Hill: University of North Carolina Press, 1980); and David Blank, *Venezuela: Politics in a Petroleum Republic* (New York: Praeger, 1984), especially 45–95. Specific features of the political system are analyzed in Jennifer McCoy, "Labor and the State in a Party-Mediated Democracy: Institutional Change in Venezuela," *Latin American Research Review* 24, no. 2 (1989): 35–67; Humberto Njaim, "El sistema venezolano de partidos y grupos de influencia," *Politeia* 7 (1978): 181–213; Enrique Baloyra and John Martz, *Political Attitudes in Venezuela* (Austin: University of Texas Press, 1979); and the relevant articles in Donald L. Herman, ed., *Democracy in Latin America: Colombia and Venezuela* (New York: Praeger, 1988), especially those by Abente and Martz.

[14] Surveys of modern Venezuelan economic development are in Oscar Echevarría, *La economía venezolana 1944–1984* (Caracas: FEDECAMARAS, 1984); Carlos Rafael Silva, "Bosquejo histórico del desenvolvimiento de la economía venezolana en el siglo XX," in *Venezuela moderna*, 763–861; Sergio Bitar and Eduardo Troncoso, *El desafío industrial de Venezuela* (Buenos Aires: Editorial Pomaire, 1983); Loring Allen, *Venezuelan Economic Development* (Greenwich, Conn.: JAI Press, 1977); Asdrúbal Baptista, "Más allá del optimismo y del pesimismo: Las transformaciones fundamentales del país," 20–40, and Gustavo Escobar, "El laberinto de la economía," 74–101, both in *El caso Venezuela: Una ilusión de armonía*, ed. Moisés Naím and Ramón Piñango (Caracas: Ediciones IESA, 1984).

[15] On the business community see José Antonio Gil, "Entrepreneurs and Regime Consolidation," in *Venezuela: The Democratic Experience*, ed. John Martz and David Myers (New York: Prager Publishers, 1977), 134–57; and José Antonio Gil Yepes, *The Challenge of Venezuelan Democracy* (New Brunswick: Transaction Books, 1981), 179–224.

Generally, however, petroleum—which typically provided 90 percent of exports, two-thirds of government revenue, and one-fifth of GDP—allowed government to meet the demands of the various segments of the private sector, as well as of popular groups. New economic opportunities opened up in 1973, as oil price hikes and increased access to the Euromarkets brought the country substantial new resources.

Argentina

The Argentine political economy has been more divided and conflictual than those of Mexico and Venezuela. The country earns major rents from its extraordinarily fertile agricultural land. As in Venezuela, the rent-earning sector and the nontraded services sectors were free-trade and conservative, while the other tradeables sectors (especially import-competing industry) were protectionist and developmentalist. However, while in Venezuela the government had easy access to the natural resource that was so important a component of the country's income, in Argentina this resource-based income accrued to private farmers, and government attempts to appropriate it met with less success.[16] Partly as a result, Argentina's two broadly defined coalitions followed a highly contentious course.

Pampean agricultural interests and their agro-industrial, financial, and commercial supporters dominated Argentine politics until around World War I.[17] By then urban business and middle-class interests had made their political presence felt, and in 1916 their Unión Cívica Radical (UCR) won

[16] The government could, of course, tax agricultural rents, but politics and economics have limited this. Direct taxes on land were militantly opposed by landowners. As for indirect taxes, especially on exports, the incentive effects on Pampean farming impose important constraints: exportable output declines rapidly when exorbitant taxation is imposed. Private oil producers also reduce output in response to increased taxation, but the constraints are different. Oilfields, unlike wheat fields, cannot be reseeded for nonexport crops, and the government can far more easily nationalize oil production than it can medium-sized family farming.

[17] The classic economic history of modern Argentina is Carlos Diaz Alejandro, *Essays in the Economic History of the Argentine Republic* (New Haven: Yale University Press, 1970). Other surveys include Juan Corradi, *The Fitful Republic: Economy, Society, and Politics in Argentina* (Boulder, Colo.: Westview Press, 1985); Richard Mallon and Juan Sourrouille, *Economic Policymaking in a Conflict Society: The Argentine Case* (Cambridge: Harvard University Press, 1975); Laura Randall, *An Economic History of Argentina in the Twentieth Century* (New York: Columbia University Press, 1978); David Rock, *Argentina, 1516–1982: From Spanish Colonization to the Falklands War* (Berkeley: University of California Press, 1985); Carlos Waisman, *Reversal of Development in Argentina* (Princeton: Princeton University Press, 1987); and Gary Wynia, *Argentina in the Postwar Era* (Albuquerque: University of New Mexico Press, 1978).

the presidency. The power of urban groups grew during the 1920s, but when the depression hit, rural interests fomented a military coup that brought conservative politicians to power. They maintained control by fraud and repression and alienated urban interests, especially industrial entrepreneurs and workers and the middle classes. Economic policy during the depression tended to favor agrarian interests and foreign trade more than in the rest of Latin America, although manufacturing was encouraged.[18]

Conservative control of the political system eventually collapsed under the press of the disenfranchised sociopolitical forces. The labor movement especially, always relatively strong in labor-scarce Argentina, grew as migrants came to work in growing urban industries. In 1943 nationalistic military officers overthrew the government, and three years later one of the officers, Juan Domingo Perón, won election as president.[19]

After 1946 Argentine politics was dominated by conflict between Peronism and its opponents. A stylized version of the division is tripartite. Peronism was supported by organized labor, small businessmen, and some industrialists, especially in import-substituting sectors; its policies were populist and proindustrial. The agro-exporters and their allies supported the right, which was free-trade and conservative. The middle classes backed the Radicals, who pursued moderate developmentalism. The electoral base of the right was small despite its great economic importance, and this generally led it to have recourse to military intervention to achieve its purposes.[20]

Perón first ruled from 1946 until 1955. At the outset he pursued policies that heavily protected national industry, taxed agriculture, and raised real wages by 44 percent between 1946 and 1948.[21] Such measures were not sustainable, and eventually Perón was forced toward austerity. Mean-

[18] On the depression, in addition to sources cited above, see Arturo O'Connell, "Argentina into the Depression: Problems of an Open Economy," in *Latin America in the 1930s*, ed. Rosemary Thorp (New York: St. Martin's Press, 1984), 188–221. Central to the period is the Anglo-Argentine trade agreement of 1933; this, along with other aspects of Argentine foreign economic policy, is dealt with in Marcelo de Paiva Abreu, "Argentina and Brazil in the 1930s: The Impact of British and American International Economic Policies," in Thorp, ed., *Latin America in the 1930s*, 144–62.

[19] On the rise of labor-based Peronism, see Torcuato Di Tella, "Working-Class Organization and Politics in Argentina," *Latin American Research Review* 16, no. 2 (1981): 33–56.

[20] For the classic analysis of postwar Argentine politics, see Guillermo O'Donnell, "State and Alliances in Argentina, 1956–1976," *Journal of Development Studies* 15 (1978–1979): 3–33. My description of Argentine political cleavages is drastically oversimplified; the real divisions are far more intricate, intersecting, and less clearly defined.

[21] Except where otherwise noted, figures throughout are from the statistical appendix to Guido di Tella and Rudiger Dornbusch, eds., *The Political Economy of Argentina, 1946–83* (London: Macmillan Press, 1989), 325–338.

while, escalating sociopolitical tension went beyond what the military was willing to accept, and in 1955 it overthrew the elected Perón government and outlawed Peronist participation in politics.

From 1955 to 1966 the Radicals and the military rotated through government.[22] The military and its conservative allies had too narrow a base to rule alone, while the Radicals could not rule without making concessions to the Peronists that the military conservatives would not countenance. The triangular stand-off was inherently unstable. The first anti-Peronist military regime was succeeded in 1958 by the elected government of Radical Arturo Frondizi. Frondizi promised to legalize the Peronists in return for their backing, and for four years he struggled to implement moderate developmentalist economic policies while trying to win support away from the Peronist social bases. The balancing act proved impossible, and when in March 1962 the Peronists swept midterm elections the military stepped in and removed Frondizi. After a military interregnum, Radical Arturo Illia tried again in 1963, only to run up against the same intractable problem of irreconcilable Peronists and conservative military men. Illia was overthrown in 1966.

The military dictatorship that took power in 1966 under Juan Carlos Onganía was determined to overcome the political stalemate of the 1950s and 1960s, but eventually fell victim to it with a vengeance. The Onganía regime undertook repressive measures and implemented a major stabilization plan that met with some success. However, labor and student radicals reacted virulently to the dictatorship. The result was a spiral of urban violence and a decline in the ability of the military to govern. Onganía ceded to two short-lived military administrations that cleared the way for new presidential elections in 1973, in which the Peronists were allowed to take part. Predictably, Peronist candidate Héctor Cámpora won easily; after a few weeks, he resigned to allow Perón himself to take office. As in Chile, for twenty years the political system had swung from side to side, with positions ever more extreme as time went on. Polarization reached its height under the new Peronist administration.

Despite the political instability of the 1955–1973 period, and substantial variation on some policy dimensions, the central aspects of government economic policies were quite stable. All of the regimes of the period supported import-substitution policies to protect the country's large industrial plant. Some were more favorable to agriculture, others more hostile, but economic policy always combined a commitment to industrial

---

[22] The classic studies of Argentine politics after 1955 are those of Guillermo O'Donnell. See, for example, "Permanent Crisis and the Failure to Create a Democratic Regime: Argentina, 1955–66," in *The Breakdown of Democratic Regimes: Latin America*, ed. Juan J. Linz and Alfred Stepan (Baltimore: Johns Hopkins University Press, 1978), 138–77; and *El estado burocrático autoritario, 1966–1973* (Buenos Aires: Editorial de Belgrano, 1982).

protection with some level of support for agro-export production. By 1973 effective protection for manufacturing was 84 percent: manufactured exportables (primarily processed food) suffered negative effective protection (− 2.6 percent) while import-competing manufactures received effective protection of 130 percent.[23] Economic-policy variation was related to chronic balance of payments problems: pro-industrial policies were pursued until a payments crisis hit and forced the adoption of austerity measures. Postwar conflict revolved around how strongly (not whether) to tax agriculture, and how seriously (not whether) to safeguard agricultural production for export—around, in other words, how many of the agro-export goose's golden eggs the urban majority could get without killing the goose itself.

Perón stood for radical redistribution from countryside to city, and in his second coming he acted true to form.[24] In 1974 real wages rose 18 percent, even as Perón attacked the growing left wing of his movement. However, in July 1974 Perón died and left the government to his politically weak wife. As the economy stagnated and inflation jumped from 24 percent in 1974 to 183 percent in 1975, the government was immobilized by organized labor's vehement opposition to austerity. Battles over economic policy became ever more bitter, while urban violence escalated. In 1976 the economy stagnated, the fiscal deficit reached 15.1 percent of GDP, and wholesale price inflation was 499 percent. The business community became increasingly horrified by sociopolitical and economic disorder: agricultural producers struck twice in late 1975, and urban employers led a lockout in February 1976. As the country collapsed into crisis and violence, the military took power again in March 1976.

Borrowing to 1980: Cheap and Plentiful Finance

As the three countries gained access to offshore financial markets, their governments were faced with the choice of what to do with this access. In Mexico and Venezuela, as in Brazil, the government used foreign finance to support favored segments of the business community, especially those in concentrated and technologically sophisticated import-substituting industries. The populist base of the two regimes also led them to use some

[23] Julio Nogués, "Distorsiones en mercados de factores, empleo y ventajas comparativas en el sector manufacturero argentino," Ensayos económicos 20 (December 1981): 51.

[24] On the second Peronist administration see Guido di Tella, Argentina under Peron, 1973–6 (London: Macmillan, 1983); Guido di Tella, "Argentina's Economy under a Labour-Based Government, 1973–6," in The Political Economy of Argentina, 213–46; and Edward Epstein, "Inflation and Public Policy in Argentina," paper presented at the 1985 Annual Meeting of the American Political Science Association, New Orleans, 3–15.

of their borrowed funds for social programs. Argentina was more of a hybrid. In principle the regime intended to pursue the Chilean model, reducing state economic intervention and leaving most borrowing to the private sector. Some of this took place, but sectoral pressures were too strong for the Argentine dictatorship to ignore. This led both to business opposition to the regime's neoliberal programs and to borrowing by state enterprises to satisfy the demands of their politically powerful networks of managers, employees, suppliers, and consumers.

Mexico

In the mid-1960s, Mexico became the first LDC to borrow regularly from postwar international financial markets. Between 1965 and 1970 private financiers loaned Mexico $2.3 billion, public agencies $1.5 billion, and suppliers and others $675 million. By 1973, 65 percent of Mexico's external public debt was owed to banks and bondholders, 6 percent to suppliers, and 29 percent to official institutions.[25] Through the 1970s and until 1982, Mexico alternated with Brazil as the developing world's largest borrower on international financial markets.

About three-quarters of Mexico's foreign borrowing was done by the public sector; the principal borrowers are shown in table 6.1. Most loans to the country went to parastatal enterprises, among which three stand out. Petróleos Mexicanos (Pemex) is the government's petroleum monopoly, controlling oil exploration and development, the sale of petroleum products, and an array of petrochemical industries. The electric energy sector, dominated by the CFE, runs power generation facilities along with the distribution and sale of electric energy. Nafinsa, the development bank, provides loans and equity for private and public investment, especially in industry. The figures in the table understate Nafinsa's foreign activities; for every dollar the development bank borrowed directly, it borrowed two dollars on behalf of other Mexican firms and guaranteed another fifty cents in foreign borrowing by Mexican companies.[26]

The uses to which overseas finance was put between 1965 and 1982 can be summarized in descending order of rough importance:[27]

[25] Rosario Green, *El endeudamiento público externo de México 1940–1973* (Guanajuato: El Colegio de México, 1976), 154; and Zedillo, "External Public Indebtedness," 65.

[26] On Nacional Financiera, see Miguel D. Ramirez, *Development Banking in Mexico: The Case of the Nacional Financiera, S.A* (New York: Praeger, 1986).

[27] For more details on the sources and uses of Mexican foreign borrowing, see Jeffry A. Frieden, "Studies in International Finance" (Ph.D. diss., Columbia University, 1984), chap. 7. An interesting decomposition of the uses to which Mexican borrowing was put is in Ernesto Zedillo Ponce de Leon, "External Public Indebtedness in Mexico" (Ph.D. thesis,

Table 6.1
Mexican External Debt Outstanding, End-1981
(Millions of dollars and percent)

	Amount	Percent of Total
MEDIUM- AND LONG-TERM DEBT	$49,569	68.7
Public sector	42,217	58.5
Central government	7,646	10.6
Petróleos Mexicanos	11,414	15.8
Electric energy sector	8,225	11.4
Telephone system	730	1.0
Iron and steel sector	527	0.7
Railroads	407	0.6
Other non-financial parastatals	2,358	3.3
Nafinsa	2,642	3.7
Banobras	1,906	2.6
Banrural	1,616	2.2
Other financial parastatals	4,746	6.6
Private sector	7,352	10.2
Mexican-owned firms	3,958	5.5
Foreign affiliates	3,394	4.7
SHORT-TERM DEBT	$22,567	31.3
Public sector	10,754	14.9
Petróleos Mexicanos	4,063	5.6
Nafinsa	2,002	2.8
Banrural	790	1.1
Banobras	727	1.0
Others	3,172	4.4
Private sector	11,813	16.4
Mexican-owned firms	9,264	12.9
Foreign affiliates	2,549	3.5
GRAND TOTAL	$72,136	100.0

Source: Banco de México; Secretaría de Hacienda y Crédito Público; and José Manuel Quijano et al., *La banca: Pasado y presente* (Mexico City: CIDE, 1983), 247–54.

1. Parastatal investment projects to increase production of intermediate industrial inputs (including petroleum).

2. Private investment in target import-substituting industries, especially basic inputs, capital goods, and consumer durables production.

3. Expansion of the resource base of the private financial system.

4. Expansion of the provision of certain social services by federal government agencies, especially subsidies to urban consumers of food and housing.

In the first three instances, several mechanisms were used. Parastatals and private banks and corporations borrowed abroad directly. Nonfinancial enterprises borrowed from Mexican financial institutions whose resources in turn came from foreign loans. Parastatals got transfers from the central government, which borrowed abroad to cover its costs.

The result was very rapid growth of the parastatals, public and private financial institutions, and large private firms in favored modern industries. Public spending grew from an average of 21 percent of GDP in the late 1960s to 33 percent in the late 1970s; over this period the public-sector deficit grew from 1.7 to 5.8 percent of GDP.[28] Much of this was invested: public investment as a share of GDP went from 5 percent in 1970 to a 1978–1980 average of 10.4 percent.[29] Most of this investment was concentrated in parastatal enterprises supplying intermediate inputs: public enterprise sales went from 12 to 18 percent of GDP between 1970 and 1980, and the share of public-enterprise investment accounted for by goods-producing firms went from 23 to 70 percent in the same period.[30] Public financial institutions also grew very rapidly, funding over half of their resources overseas: by 1982 Nafinsa had over $13 billion in loans outstanding, $2.5 billion in loan guarantees, and holdings of $1.2 billion in shares of Mexican firms.[31]

As the public sector grew, the private sector grew along with it. One

Yale University, 1981), and is updated in Leopoldo Solís and Ernesto Zedillo, "The Foreign Debt of Mexico," in *International Debt and the Developing Countries*, ed. Gordon Smith and John Cuddington (Washington, D.C.: World Bank, 1985), 258–88.

[28] Calculated from Francisco Gil Díaz, "Mexico's Path from Stability to Inflation," in *World Economic Growth*, ed. Arnold Harberger (San Francisco: ICS Press, 1984), 372.

[29] Leopoldo Solís, *Alternativas para el desarrollo* (Mexico City: Joaquín Mortiz, 1980), 128; Leopoldo Solís and Ernesto Zedillo, "The Foreign Debt of Mexico," in *International Debt and the Developing Countries*, ed. Gordon Smith and John Cuddington (Washington, D.C.: World Bank, 1985), 260.

[30] Alejandro Carrillo Castro and Sergio Garcia Ramírez, *Las empresas públicas en México* (Mexico City: Miguel Angel Porrúa, 1983), 150, and Octavio Gómez, "Las empresas públicas en México: Desempeño reciente y relaciones con la política económica," *El Trimestre Económico* 49, no. 2 (April–June 1982), 459.

[31] Figures on overseas liabilities are in Banco de México, *Indicadores de moneda y banca*, various issues; on Nafinsa, in Nacional Financiera, *Informe Anual*, various issues, and *El Mercado de Valores*, various issues.

important connection was between public enterprises and their suppliers. Pemex and CFE were required to buy most supplies at home and purchased much locally produced capital equipment. Another connection was between public enterprises and private consumers of their goods and services. In 1975, Pemex and CFE price subsidies transferred $1.3 billion and $810 million to the private sector respectively.[32] Public transfers and subsidies—the result of spending, pricing, and financial policies—grew from 3.6 percent of GDP in 1970 to 11.7 percent of GDP in 1980, averaging 7.2 percent of GDP for the decade.[33]

The foremost private beneficiaries of government policy during the borrowing period were large firms in modern industry and banking. These sectors had most access to foreign finance, government subsidies, subsidized development finance, parastatal orders, and (if relevant) trade protection.

Modern private industry was favored with a wide range of incentives. Parastatal purchases and subsidized credits were especially important to the capital goods producers, the principal private recipients of Nafinsa support in the 1970s. Trade policy also targeted more modern and concentrated industries. Effective protection in 1970 averaged 1.7 percent for such traditional industries as food products, textiles, clothing, footwear, wood products, and leather goods, but 23.2 percent on average for such modern sectors as chemicals, machinery, and transport equipment. Looked at another way, effective protection was 7.4 percent for nondurable consumer goods and 34.6 percent for durable consumer and capital goods. Intermediate goods, largely inputs supplied by public corporations to private industry, received *negative* effective protection, − 0.8 percent.[34] Those favored were the country's more oligopolistic industries: four-firm concentration ratios in "traditional" industries averaged 32.9 percent in 1970, while in "modern" industries they averaged 53.9 percent.[35]

Large private industrial firms also benefited from direct access to overseas finance. According to one government survey, by 1981 "giant" firms' foreign currency liabilities were 52 percent of total liabilities; correspond-

[32] Rolando Cordera Campos, "Estado y economía: Apuntes para un marco de referencia," in *Panorama y perspectivas de la economía mexicana*, ed. Nora Lustig (Mexico City: El Colegio de México, 1980), 376–78. For background on the important petrochemical expansion, see Luis Angeles, "La industria petroquímica mexicana en la dinámica internacional," in Carlos Rozo et al., *Mexico en la división internacional del trabajo* (Mexico City: CIDE, 1984), 165–221.

[33] Gerardo Dávila Jiménez, "La política de precios y subsidios," in *El sistema económico mexicano* (Puebla: Premia Editora, 1982), 243.

[34] Ten Kate and Wallace, *Protection and Economic Development*, 120–21.

[35] Calculated from José de Jesús Martínez and Eduardo Jacobs, "Competencia y concentración: El caso del sector manufacturero, 1970–1975," *Economía Mexicana* 2 (1980): 158.

ing figures were 34 percent for large, 12 percent for medium-sized, and 3 percent for small firms.[36] Borrowing was concentrated by industry as well as by size. Between 1975 and 1979 over three-quarters of all long-term external borrowing by publicly traded companies went to the metal-working, chemicals, mining, and nonmetallic minerals sectors, while firms in traditional industries accounted for less than 2 percent of foreign bank borrowing in the period.[37]

Growth during the 1970s reflected the policy bias in favor of oligopolistic modern industries. Between 1970 and 1981 the share of traditional sectors with standardized products (food, beverages, tobacco, textiles, leather, wood, paper and printing) in manufacturing output dropped from 53.8 percent to 46.1 percent, while the most modern sectors (chemicals, rubber, plastic, machinery and equipment, automotive) grew from 32.5 percent to 40.2 percent of total manufacturing production.

The country's largest industrial firms gained substantially during the 1970s. The share of industrial production accounted for by the country's top hundred went from 16.6 to 25.7 percent between 1973 and 1979. Within this, the share of the top hundred's output produced by private Mexican firms rose from 30 to 36 percent, that of public-sector firms went from 38 to 39 percent, and that of foreign firms fell from 33 to 25 percent.[38]

Many large private firms were organized in groups under family control. The twenty-three largest such groups accounted for about a third of the sales and assets of Mexico's five hundred largest firms in 1980; the most prominent set of conglomerates was the "Monterrey Group," which divided into four segments in 1974. The component parts of the former Monterrey Group—Alfa, VISA, Vitro, and Cydsa—accounted in 1980 for 14.2 percent of the assets of the country's five hundred largest corporations. By 1980, Alfa alone had assets of nearly $4 billion, comprised an empire of 157 firms and fifty thousand employees, and was the largest private firm in Latin America. It accelerated its expansion by borrowing $2 billion abroad, some 70 percent of the group's total liabilities.[39]

Mexico's principal private banks were major overseas borrowers, and they too grew rapidly as a result of the country's access to foreign finance in the 1970s. By 1980 their foreign liabilities were more than $8 billion

[36] María Elena Cardero and José Manuel Quijano, "Expansión y estrangulamiento financiero, 1978–1981," *La banca: Pasado y presente*, ed. José Manuel Quijano (Mexico City: CIDE, 1983), 269.

[37] Isabel Molina Warner, "El endeudamiento externo del sector privado y sus efectos en la economía mexicana," *Comercio Exterior* 31, no. 10 (October 1981): 1140–47.

[38] Eduardo Jacobs, "La evolución reciente de los grupos de capital privado nacional," *Economía Mexicana* 3 (1981): 23–44; Eduardo Jacobs and Wilson Perez Nuñez, "Las grandes empresas y el crecimiento acelerado," *Economía Mexicana* 4 (1982): 99–113.

[39] Cardero y Quijano, "Expansión y estrangulamiento," 265. On Alfa, see José Luiz Manzo, "El caso del Grupo Alfa," in *La banca*, 286–304.

and were funding 15 percent of all operations; domestic dollar lending was one-third of all domestic credit.[40] Of course, the largest private banks were best able to take advantage of external borrowing, both because of their greater attractiveness to foreign lenders and because the government permitted them to establish overseas branches and subsidiaries. This contributed to the greater profitability of the largest banks, whose profit margins by 1980 were more than 75 percent higher than those of the smallest banks. As a result, the financial system became more concentrated. In 1970 there were 240 banks in the country, and eighteen of them controlled 75 percent of the system's resources; by 1979 the number of banks was one hundred, and just six controlled 75 percent of total resources.[41]

The pattern of government policy in Mexico's financial expansion certainly fits my analytical expectations. Mexico was a society with little labor-capital conflict: such strife had been subsumed, co-opted, mediated, or repressed by the PRI. Policy was dominated by sectoral considerations, and favored the concentrated, sectorally specific, modern portions of industry, finance, and agriculture.[42] Policy benefited some politically important popular constituencies, especially in the urban working class. Although there are few rigorous studies of how links between business and government have affected economic policy, the evidence seems to indicate that the relationship had a significant impact on policy outcomes.[43] A survey of the course of policy over time helps illustrate the connection.[44]

[40] Banco de México, *Indicadores de moneda y banca*, no. 46 (August 1982): 47–51.

[41] Tomás Peñaloza Webb, "La productividad de la banca en México, 1980–1983," *El Trimestre Económico* 52, no. 206 (April–June 1985): 471, 484. A good survey is María Elena Cardero, José Manuel Quijano, and José Luis Manzo, "Cambios recientes en la organización bancaria y el caso de México," in *La Banca*, 161–219.

[42] Here we have ignored the interesting agricultural developments of the period. Suffice it to say that, as in Brazil, agricultural policy tended to concentrate on the large modern commercial farmers (agribusinessmen often tied to the U.S. market), and to ignore the traditional rural sector, much of which is organized in quasi-cooperative *ejidos*. For details, see the surveys in Cynthia Hewitt de Alcantara, *Modernizing Mexican Agriculture* (Geneva: United Nations, 1976); David Mares, *Penetrating the International Market: Theoretical Considerations and a Mexican Case Study* (New York: Columbia University Press, 1987); and Leopoldo Solís, *La realidad económica mexicana*, 16th ed. (Mexico City: Siglo Veintiuno Editores, 1987), 108–68.

[43] Three recent volumes stand out: Maxfield, *Governing Capital*; Sylvia Maxfield and Ricardo Anzaldúa Montoya, eds., *Government and Private Sector in Contemporary Mexico* (San Diego: Center for U.S.-Mexican Studies, 1987); and Dale Story, *Industry, the State, and Public Policy in Mexico* (Austin: University of Texas Press, 1986). See also Sergio Zermeño, "Los empresarios frente al estado," *La Jornada Semanal*, 6 and 13 July 1986. Useful background information is available in Flavia Derossi, *The Mexican Entrepreneur* (Paris: OECD, 1971); Mario Ramírez Rancaño, *La burguesía industrial: Revelaciones de una encuesta* (Mexico City: Editorial Nuestro Tiempo, 1974); and Menno Vellinga, *Economic Development and the Dynamics of Class: Industrialization, Power and Control in Monterrey, Mexico* (Assen, Holland: Van Gorcum, 1979).

[44] For surveys of the course of policy and economic outcome, see, in addition to works

When Luis Echeverría took office as president in 1970, the consensus was that "stabilizing development" had played itself out. Echeverría tried a series of initiatives to overcome the impasse, all of which faced major political opposition. Commercial policy was essentially off limits. There had been debates since the mid-1960s over whether to liberalize ("rationalize protection") or increase trade barriers ("deepen import substitution"), but entrenched interests on both sides of the issue prevented change. The business community, to simplify, was divided between "nationalistic" sectors based in traditional import-substituting activities and "internationalist" sectors tied to foreign markets. This division affected debates about policy toward foreign trade, investment, and other issues, and meant that few policies received broad business support.[45]

Unable to unfreeze the political stalemate over trade and investment policy, Echeverría attempted a tax reform that would have increased government revenues and removed some of the pressure on public finances. The proposed reform was, however, vetoed by the principal business organizations in a series of private meetings with chief policymakers.[46]

Echeverría's frustration with the standoff over economic policy led him in two directions. First, he turned to external financial markets to fund public investments aimed at reducing dependence on imports and increasing exports. Growth of the foreign debt from $6 billion in 1970 to $21 billion in 1976 allowed government spending to rise from 22 to 33 percent of GDP, transfers and subsidies from 3.6 to 7.4 percent of GDP, and

---

already cited, Eliana Cardoso and Santiago Levy, "Mexico," in *The Open Economy*, ed. Rudiger Dornbusch and F. Leslie C. H. Helmers (New York: Oxford University Press, 1988), 348–69; and Rudiger Dornbusch, "Mexico: Stabilization, Debt and Growth," *Economic Policy* 7 (October 1988): 233–83.

[45] The precise contours of the division are controversial. Most analysts would place the Cámara Nacional de la Industria de Transformación (CANACINTRA) at the head of the nationalists, with the Confederación de Cámaras Industriales (CONCAMIN) paramount among the internationalists. The Confederación Patronal de la República Mexicana (COPARMEX), along with organizations of bankers and exporters, tended to side with CONCAMIN. By the 1980s, as discussed below, many of the differences among the various business groups faded beside their fundamental antagonism to interventionist government policies. For details, see Maxfield and Anzaldúa Montoya, eds. *Government and Private Sector in Contemporary Mexico*, and Story, *Industry, The State, and Public Policy*; the issues are also discussed in Leopoldo Solís, *Controversias sobre el crecimiento y la distribución* (Mexico City: Fondo de Cultura Económica, 1972), 45–62; and Miguel Basáñez, *La lucha por la hegemonía en México, 1968–1980* (Mexico City: Siglo Veintiuno Editores, 1981), 81–111, 183–201. The early debates go back to Sanford Most, *Industrial Revolution in Mexico* (Berkeley: University of California Press, 1950); see also Robert Jones Shafer, *Mexican Business Organizations: History and Analysis* (Syracuse: Syracuse University Press, 1973).

[46] An excellent survey of the period is Leopoldo Solis, *Economic Policy Reform in Mexico: A Case Study for Developing Countries* (New York: Pergamon Press, 1981); the tax reform episode is described on 72–76.

the public deficit from 2.2 to 7.6 percent of GDP. Public investment doubled while private investment increased 16 percent.[47]

Second, after 1973 Echeverría appealed to nationalistic elements of the PRI for support in his dealings with recalcitrant groups in the private sector. With political rhetoric and public spending, he curried favor with organized labor and the peasantry. He also issued a series of decrees limiting foreign investment, in a play for the support of domestic businessmen.

Echeverría's attempts to use massive public spending and redoubled government intervention in the economy to build a base among popular constituencies and nationalist businessmen proved economically and politically untenable. The foreign debt grew rapidly, inflation accelerated, the peso appreciated, flight into the dollar grew, and the current account deficit ballooned. At the same time, many in the business community worried about Echeverría's turn toward radical populism. In 1976 Echeverría was forced to devalue the peso, implement austerity measures, and enter into a three-year Extended Fund Facility agreement with the IMF.[48] The attempt to avoid conflict among sectors with different policy preferences had failed, and the issues—whether to open the economy more to trade, how to meet the crisis in public finances, what to do about the parastatals—remained.

The succeeding administration of José López Portillo was, however, saved from hard policy choices by the major expansion of petroleum exports that began in 1977. Exploitation of petroleum reserves increased foreign exchange earnings and raised the country's credit rating, allowing for redoubled borrowing. After an austere 1977, from 1978 until 1981 the economy boomed. GDP grew 36 percent, the petroleum sector more than doubled in size, and manufacturing production grew by 38 percent. Within this, the consumer durables and capital goods sectors were especially dynamic: their output rose 69 and 79 percent respectively. The spur was a combination of oil rents and new foreign borrowing, which was $3.2 billion in 1978, $5.5 billion in 1979, and $9.7 billion in 1980.[49] The

[47] Gil Díaz, "Mexico's Path," p. 372; Dávila Jiménez, "La política de precios," p. 243; Wilson Pérez Nuñez, "La estructura de la industria estatal," *Economía Mexicana* 4 (1982): pp. 118–22. On the period, see also C. Gribomont and M. Rimez, "La política económica del gobierno de Luis Echeverría (1971–1976): Un primer ensayo de interpretación," *El Trimestre Económico* 44, no. 4 (October–December 1977): 771–835.

[48] On the stabilization experience see Sidney Weintraub, "Case Study of Economic Stabilization: Mexico," in *Economic Stabilization in Developing Countries,* ed. William Cline and Sidney Weintraub (Washington, D.C.: Brookings Institution, 1981), 271–92.

[49] On this period, see Cardero and Quijano, "Expansión y estrangulamiento"; Leopoldo Solís and Sócrates Rizzo, "Excedentes petroleros y apertura externa: El caso de México," in *Relaciones financieras externas y su efecto en la economía latinoamericana,* ed. Ricardo Ffrench-Davis (Mexico City: Fondo de Cultura Económica, 1983), 354–92; Banamex, *Ex-*

resources made available from petroleum and petroleum-backed borrowing were used to expand public investment and subsidies to the private sector: public spending grew from 31 percent of GDP in 1977 to 44 percent of GDP in 1981.[50]

In 1981, however, the joint shock of dramatically increased interest rates and unexpected declines in oil prices demonstrated the unsustainability of the Mexican boom. Financial costs burgeoned, spending continued to accelerate, and the public deficit reached 15.2 percent of GDP in 1981 and 17.9 percent in 1982. The current account deficit soared to $11.7 billion in 1981, and in that year the country borrowed an astounding $23.3 billion, nearly half of it at less than one year's maturity. The peso had meanwhile appreciated by 27 percent in real terms over 1977 levels, and devaluation expectations gave rise to capital flight estimated at $9.7 billion in 1981 and $8.2 billion in 1982. Large portions of the borrowed funds, indeed, went to support the exchange rate and were rapidly channeled abroad by private investors taking the "one-way bet" that devaluation was imminent.[51] After a significant devaluation in February 1982 and a modest stabilization program in March failed to calm the economy, in August the government suspended debt service payments, went to the IMF for a stabilization loan, and enacted a broad package of economic policies (about which more is said below).

The character of public spending and other policies was a good indication of the kinds of sectoral demands made on the Mexican government. The large-scale modern industrial, financial, and agricultural sectors were the period's principal beneficiaries, along with politically strategic portions of the working and middle classes. At the same time, the course of policy from the late 1960s until 1980 indicates the delicate sectoral balancing act in which the Mexican government was engaged. Internationally oriented businesses received unrestricted access to foreign financial markets and dollars. Large uncompetitive businesses were protected by trade barriers and subsidized by credit, purchasing, and parastatal pricing policies. Major banking conglomerates were permitted to make enormous profits by intermediating between external and domestic financial markets. Portions of the working class and peasantry got subsidized food, housing, and other services, and government workers received generous wages in the burgeoning public sector. This spectrum of

amen de la situación económica de México, various issues; and Judith Teichman, *Policymaking in Mexico: From Boom to Crisis* (Boston: Allen and Unwin, 1988), 63–126.

[50] Gil Diaz, "Mexico's Path," 372.

[51] Ernesto Zedillo, "Mexico," in *Capital Flight and Third World Debt*, ed. Donald Lessard and John Williamson (Washington, D.C.: Institute for International Economics, 1987), 177; Cardero and Quijano, "Expansión y estrangulamiento"; Gil Diaz, "Mexico's Path," 370–72.

public policies was too broad for the fiscal capacity of the Mexican government, and portions of it were internally contradictory; the temporary solution was found with recourse to massive external borrowing.

Venezuela

Since 1958 Venezuela has been characterized by low levels of labor-capital conflict. This is due both to spending made possible by oil rents, and to the incorporation of labor into Acción Democrática. I expect sectoral government intervention in the economy, and expect it to benefit primarily groups with political influence, especially those with specific assets in concentrated sectors.

The political influence of organized labor and of different private-sector groups varied to some extent with the party in power. Indeed, AD and COPEI had somewhat different bases of support: the former got strongest backing from labor and import-substituting entrepreneurs, the latter from the middle class and more economically liberal sectors (finance, commerce). AD controls organized labor: during AD governments from 1960 to 1983 an annual average of four hundred thousand worker-hours was lost to strikes, while during COPEI governments the annual average was more than four times greater, 1.8 million.[52] I thus expect AD to favor import-substituting sectors, and COPEI to be more market-oriented and to favor more "internationalist" groups.

Venezuelan government policy during the financial expansion was in fact highly sectoral, resembling a hybrid of Mexican and Brazilian policies. The public sector invested in infrastructure, intermediate inputs, and petroleum-related industries, along with massive programs to open the Amazon frontier and expand the output of hydroelectric power and of such raw materials as iron ore and bauxite.[53] The government also gave major subsidies to private industry, especially in import-substituting lines. Social programs grew significantly, targeting especially AD's popular base. There was the expected variation in the policies of the two parties: AD aggressively intervened in favor of domestic entrepreneurs and labor, while COPEI tended toward more liberal policies favoring its supporters in the financial and commercial sectors and the middle classes.

Three points need to be made in discussing Venezuelan debt. First, Venezuela's borrowing was tied to its fortunes as an oil exporter. Fortunately for analysis, borrowing more or less coincided with oil price in-

[52] Calculated from McCoy, "Labor and the State," 48–49.

[53] It might be noted that, given the country's oil wealth, hydroelectric power is something of an indirectly traded good: increased electric energy production allows for less domestic use of petroleum and a higher level of exports.

creases, and the financial crisis with oil price declines, so both variables moved in the same direction. Nevertheless, the oil market is of great independent importance to understanding Venezuela's political economy.

Second, despite its large foreign debt, Venezuela as a nation is a net international creditor. From 1973 to 1983 the public sector was a net borrower from abroad, while the Venezuelan private sector was a net investor in the rest of the world.

Third, until 1981 Venezuelan borrowing was not closely monitored. Private actors were free to borrow and invest abroad, and the government had little knowledge of these transactions. Medium- and long-term public external borrowing needed central government approval, but government agencies could circumvent this requirement by short-term borrowing. Not until the debt crisis hit and the authorities consulted with creditor banks did the government get a clear sense of how much it and its citizens owed to foreigners. Among other things, this allowed some decentralized government agencies to continue to float loans after the central government attempted to slow such borrowing.

With these points in mind, we can look at the structure of Venezuela's external debt as of end-1982. Table 6.2 indicates that 80.6 percent of the external debt was owed by the public sector; over half of this was unregistered, incurred without central government supervision. Another source indicates that 29 percent of end-1982 public external debt was owed or guaranteed by the central government, 32 percent by state enterprises, 24 percent by public financial institutions (including 14 percent by the Banco Industrial de Venezuela, the industrial-development bank), and 16 percent by a variety of general, regional, and sectoral development corporations and autonomous agencies.[54]

The pattern of use of borrowed funds is relatively well known.[55] Among public firms, most of the borrowing was done by enterprises car-

[54] Calculated from Janet Kelly de Escobar, "Las empresas del estado: Del lugar común al sentido común," in *El caso Venezuela*, 142. Figures do not add up to 100 percent due to rounding.

[55] For general surveys of the Venezuelan debt problem, see Luis Zambrano, Matías Riutort, Charlotte de Vainrub, Chi-Yi Chen, "La deuda externa de Venezuela," *Resumen*, no. 508, 31 July 1983, 19–41; Fernando Porta, Miguel Lacabana, and Víctor Fajardo, *La internacionalización financiera en Venezuela* (Buenos Aires: Centro de Economía Transnacional, 1983); Pedro Palma, "Venezuela's Foreign Public Debt," 163–68, and Henry Gomez-Samper, "The Management of Venezuela's External Debt," 57–63, both in *Foreign Debt and Latin American Economic Development*, ed. Antonio Jorge, Jorge Salazar-Carillo, and Rene Higonnet (New York: Pergamon Press, 1983); Robert Bottome, "Public Debt: Where Did It Come From?" *VenEconomy Monthly*, November 1983, 12–14; and Ramón Escovar Salom, "Venezuela: The Oil Boom and the Debt Crisis," in *Latin America and the World Recession*, ed. Esperanza Durán (Cambridge: Cambridge University Press, 1985), 120–29. More specific information is available from sources cited further on.

Table 6.2
Venezuelan External Debt Outstanding, End-1982
(Millions of dollars and percent)

	Amount	Percent of Total
MEDIUM- AND LONG-TERM DEBT	$18,843	56.9
Public sector	15,865	47.9
Central govt., registered	8,446	25.5
Parastatals, registered	3,712	11.2
Nonfinancial, unregistered	1,834	5.5
Financial, unregistered	1,873	5.7
Nonfinancial private sector	2,978	9.0
SHORT-TERM DEBT (ALL UNREGISTERED)	14,262	43.1
Public sector	10,825	32.7
Nonfinancial	6,610	20.0
Financial	4,215	12.7
Private sector	3,437	10.4
Nonfinancial	814	2.5
Financial	2,623	7.9
GRAND TOTAL	$33,105	100.0

Source: Luis Zambrano et al., "La Deuda Externa de Venezuela," Resumen, no. 508, 31 July 1983, pp. 26–27.

rying out large-scale investments. Especially prominent were projects in the frontier Guayana region, including the Guri hydroelectric power plant, bauxite mines and processing facilities, iron mines, and steel mills. Parastatals also made major investments in the transportation and communications infrastructure. Public financial institutions made substantial subsidized loans, especially to import substituting industry. Petroleum earnings and borrowing combined to allow a massive government drive to industrialize. At the height of the process, between 1976 and 1978, public current spending averaged 32.3 percent, and public investment 16.7 percent, of GDP.[56]

[56] Calculated from Miguel A. Rodriguez F., "Public Sector Behavior in Venezuela: 1970–

The beneficiaries of these public investments included employees of parastatal firms, private suppliers to the parastatals, and private consumers of the parastatals' subsidized output. Import-substituting businesses, especially, gained from the resource inflows through public subsidies, loans, and orders. Firms in internationally oriented and service sectors such as finance, real estate, and construction expanded on the basis of general economic growth and cheap foreign credit.

Venezuelan external public borrowing also served to finance overseas investment by Venezuelan citizens. Especially after 1979, the currency's real value appreciated; the government also briefly imposed interest-rate controls. The result was devaluation expectations and an interest-rate differential in favor of foreign deposits. With free convertibility and capital movements, this gave Venezuelans with access to foreign assets, primarily those in the upper and middle classes, the opportunity to evade controls on deposit interest rates even as they bet against the bolívar. Meanwhile, the public sector borrowed the dollars necessary to provide investors these arbitrage opportunities. Estimates vary, but Venezuelans probably invested $30 billion abroad between 1974 and 1984—an amount roughly equal to the country's new borrowing in this period.[57]

A survey of Venezuelan developments between 1973 and 1983 sheds light on the general pattern of government economic policy, and on the differences between AD and COPEI administrations.[58] Before 1973 Venezuela had had little recourse to overseas borrowing, and total external debt was just $2 billion as that year opened. At the end of that year, however, OPEC massively raised oil prices and AD candidate Carlos Andrés Pérez (often known as CAP) swept Venezuela's presidential elections.

Pérez immediately committed himself to redoubling traditional AD policies of "sowing petroleum," using oil rents for development programs. The Pérez administration (1974–1979) undertook major public invest-

---

1985" (Caracas: mimeo, 1987), Table 13. This paper is a detailed and comprehensive survey of government revenue and expenditures, and except where noted figures on these matters are drawn from this source.

[57] For various estimates and interpretations, see the articles in Lessard and Williamson, eds., *Capital Flight and Third World Debt*.

[58] Information on this period is taken, in addition to general sources cited above, from Rodriguez, "Public Sector Behavior"; Ewell, *Venezuela*, 193–227; Gil Yepes, *Challenge*, 205–17; Miguel Rodríguez F., "Auge petrolero, estancamiento y políticas de ajuste en Venezuela," *Coyuntura Económica* (Bogotá), December 1985, 201–27; Ricardo Hausmann and G. Márquez, "La crisis económica venezolana: Origen, mecanismos, y encadenamientos," *Investigación Económica* 165 (July–September 1983), 117–54; Ricardo Hausmann and Gustavo Márquez, "Venezuela: Política de estabilización y mercado de trabajo en 1984," *Economía de América Latina* 13 (1985): 145–57; and Felipe Pazos, "Efectos de un aumento subito en los ingresos externos: La economía de Venezuela en el quinquenio 1974–1978" (Caracas: mimeo, 1979).

ment projects, established a network of subsidies to domestic entrepreneurs, and expanded public services. Funds came from both oil revenues and external public borrowing. Specifically, the nonoil state enterprises ran large deficits, which they financed out of borrowing and capital transfers from the central government; the central government and oil sector ran large surpluses, some of which were transferred to the parastatals, and some of which went into overseas assets. By one estimate, external public debt increased by $10.5 billion between 1974 and 1978, while external public assets increased by $9.6 billion.[59] The public sector therefore used offshore markets to intermediate between its oil-based savings and its developmentalist investments. The reasons for this are not clear: it may have been a conscious attempt to dampen the effects of the resource boom, or an unplanned result of uncoordinated behavior by decentralized public agencies, or a result of domestic financial-market inefficiencies.

Early on, the Pérez government nationalized the iron-ore and oil industries. Nationalization with full compensation had the support of virtually all political and economic groups.[60] Pérez also began large-scale public undertakings to round out the industrial structure: hydroelectric power stations, steel mills, petrochemical plants. National purchasing requirements and subsidized credit gave a massive stimulus to suppliers of inputs to the parastatals. As a result, intermediate and capital goods industries grew rapidly: from 1974 to 1978, while traditional manufacturing output rose 25 percent, intermediate and mechanical manufacturing output rose 49 percent. By 1978 the share of the latter two groups in total manufacturing output was 49 percent, up from 39 percent in 1968.[61]

Pérez built strong ties with businessmen in nontraditional import-substituting sectors. In the words of one leading AD politician: "Pérez put the state enterprises, and great capital resources, in the hands of the private sector. It was not the traditional private sector, but men of medium capital in industry and construction. CAP made them multimillionaires."[62]

---

[59] Rodriguez, "Public Sector Behavior," table 15.

[60] On oil, see Gustavo Coronel, *The Nationalization of the Venezuelan Oil Industry* (Lexington, Mass.: Lexington Books, 1983), which also surveys the management of the petroleum industry once it was nationalized.

[61] Calculated from Bitar and Troncoso, *El desafío industrial*, 259, 268; figures do not include petroleum refining and derivatives. On the relationship between the oil companies and private suppliers, see Laura Randall, *The Political Economy of Venezuelan Oil* (New York: Praeger, 1987), chap. 7. Other discussions are Ricardo Hausmann, "El patrón de inversiones en las empresas del estado," 107–18, and Nelson Segarra, "¿Cómo evaluar la gestión de las empresas públicas venezolanas?" 131–54, both in *Empresas del estado en América Latina*, ed. Janet Kelly de Escobar (Caracas: Ediciones IESA, 1985).

[62] Confidential interview by author, Caracas, 21 June 1985. For a more systematic treatment of business-state relations in the CAP government, see Blank, *Venezuela*, 123–27; and,

The administration also secured AD's labor base with mandated wage increases, expanded government employment and social programs. The economy grew 6 percent a year, while inflation was kept near international levels. Sectoral investment programs and wage policies primarily helped AD's business and labor supporters, while free convertibility and macroeconomic restraint staved off open discontent in the commercial and financial sectors.

The 1978 presidential elections were won narrowly by COPEI candidate Luis Herrera Campins, largely because of internecine warfare within AD. The Herrera administration (1979–1983) oversaw a remarkable phase in Venezuelan economic history: despite a second oil price hike, the economy collapsed into depression. GDP, which rose 33 percent under Pérez, dropped by 5 percent under Herrera; industrial production rose 55 percent under AD but 4 percent under COPEI. Unemployment went from 4.7 percent in 1978 to 11.9 percent in 1983, as real wages dropped 22 percent (after a 39 percent rise under Pérez). Herrera justified many of his policies as necessary to cool an overheated economy and did bring inflation down from 13.4 percent in 1979 to 6.3 percent in 1983, but on average inflation was higher under COPEI (13.4 percent a year) than under AD (8.4 percent a year).[63]

Under Herrera Campins, Venezuela's international financial position changed dramatically. From 1978 to 1983 the external public debt grew from $12 billion to $27 billion, while external public assets stagnated at about $11.5 billion; meanwhile, external private debt grew from $3.2 billion to $8.0 billion, and external private assets grew by $29.2 billion. An approximately $20 billion increase in the foreign debt, three-quarters of it public, was offset by nearly $30 billion in private capital flight.[64]

The COPEI administration's failure was largely the result of inability to resist conflicting pressures, a problem exacerbated by its lack of a majority in Congress. The commercial and financial communities wanted conservative fiscal and monetary policies, which Herrera tried to implement. However, demands for fiscal stringency were counteracted by pressures from businessmen, workers, and others who were dependent upon public spending, and the decentralized parastatals continued to expand by borrowing abroad. Despite a large real appreciation of the bolívar, Herrera refused to devalue, ostensibly in the interests of monetary stability. This

---

a critical view, Fernando Coronil and Julie Skurski, "Reproducing Dependency: Auto Industry Policy and Petrodollar Circulation in Venezuela," *International Organization* 36, no. 1 (Winter 1982): 61–94.

[63] Figures on GDP and industrial production are from Echevarría, *La economía venezolana*, 50, 54, 76, 80; on real wages, unemployment, and inflation (which is the rate of change in the consumer price index), from Hausmann and Márquez, "Venezuela," 149.

[64] Rodriguez, "Public Sector Behavior," tables 25 and 26.

encouraged an outflow of private savings, subsidized by government support for the bolívar. The result was a downward spiral, as uncontrolled parastatal spending contravened central government austerity and capital flight undermined the fixed exchange rate.

Herrera Campins took office claiming that Pérez had mortgaged the country to foreigners and dissipated the country's oil wealth in ill-conceived public investments. The new government moved to slow or halt many of the parastatal projects, reduce food subsidies, and tighten monetary policy. Herrera also freed prices of 150 previously controlled products, and reduced tariffs. The unexpected oil price increase of 1979, which drove exports from $9.2 billion in 1978 to $19.3 billion in 1980, did not lead to a reevaluation of government policies.[65]

Reaction to the government's contractionary policies took various forms. The austerity and antisubsidy programs were especially menacing to organized labor. The labor movement threatened a general strike, and mounted a legislative campaign that led the opposition-controlled Congress to mandate wage increases. Plans to cut public investment threatened the parastatals and their networks of private-sector supporters. These responded largely by evading central government policy, maintaining previous levels of spending by borrowing abroad. Total spending by nonoil, nonfinancial state enterprises stayed at previous levels of about 20 percent of GDP through 1982, but capital transfers from the central government went from nearly all of the parastatals' deficit financing under Pérez to about half under Herrera; the remainder was borrowed overseas.[66]

The government's policies induced an economic downturn in 1980 and 1981, but inflation stayed high. In yet another contradictory effort to shore up his popularity, Herrera tried to moderate his contractionary policies by freezing domestic interest rates. The result of recession, inflation, and below-market domestic interest rates was to make offshore investment irresistible. Depending on the estimate, between $8 billion and $13 billion fled the country in 1980 and 1981.[67] Finally, in August 1981 Herrera freed interest rates. At much the same time the administration moved to get control of all external borrowing, including that by the parastatals.

[65] On this period, see Echevarría, *La economía venezolana*, 75–113; Rodriguez, "Public Sector Behavior," 33–52; Rodriguez, "Auge Petrolero"; Hausmann and Márquez, "Venezuela," 148–51; Hausmann and Márquez, "La crisis económica," 149–53; Jennifer L. McCoy, "The Politics of Adjustment: Labor and the Venezuelan Debt Crisis," *Journal of Interamerican Studies and World Affairs* 28, no. 4 (Winter 1986–1987): 112–22; and Tim Anderson, "Venezuela's Great Clean-up Disappoints the Banks," *Euromoney*, November 1981, 108–18.

[66] Calculated from Rodriguez, "Public Sector Behavior," tables 10, 19, 30.

[67] Capital flight estimates in this paragraph are from Lessard and Williamson, ed., *Capital Flight*.

By mid-1981, however, the bolívar had appreciated enough in real terms (by 16 percent between 1979 and 1982, by one measure)[68] that devaluation expectations were widespread. Eight to fifteen billion dollars fled Venezuela in 1982 and 1983; in the first six weeks of 1983, capital flight averaged $500 million a week. Government efforts to support the bolívar were extremely expensive. The public petroleum firm was ordered to transfer $8 billion in overseas assets to the central bank, which sold them to defend the parity. Billions more in borrowed funds went to stave off a devaluation. Finally, in mid-February 1983, the Herrera Campins government admitted defeat, devalued the bolívar, imposed exchange controls, and began negotiations for debt rescheduling.

The overall pattern of public spending and the evolution of economic policies under AD and COPEI illustrate the general characteristics of the Venezuelan political economy and the differences among the nation's economic interests. Labor-capital conflict has been muted, especially because of AD's quasi-corporatist inclusion of labor; Venezuelan economic policy has been highly interventionist with strong sectoral components. AD is closely tied to labor and import-substituting entrepreneurs: the economic policies of Pérez supported domestic industry and organized labor. COPEI has weak ties to labor and is associated more with the nontradables sectors and the middle classes: the policies of Herrera Campins attempted to manage the economy in ways most appealing to these groups. Herrera's policies foundered because of their inconsistency; the deeper reason was that economic interests opposed to them used their powerful positions in the political economy, with Congress or the parastatals, to contravene or circumvent Herrera's policies. The foreign debt thus grew out of the political and economic system's attempts to meet a myriad of private-sector demands.

Argentina

At the time of the military coup of March 1976, Argentina had broken into camps that roughly tracked the labor-capital divide. The Peronists had alienated business, which was eager to see the labor-based movement defeated. Argentine positions were not so polarized as in Chile, partly because Peronism was never anticapitalist and partly because disagreements between import-substituting and export-competing producers remained great. Economic policy reflected these crosscutting pressures: market-oriented liberalization with an anti-labor bias, along with the maintenance of much sectoral intervention. This contradiction in Argen-

---

[68] Rodriguez, "Auge Petrolero," 218.

tine economic policy under the military was responsible for one of the least successful borrowing experiences in Latin America. On the one hand, the liberalizing thrust freed domestic banking and cross-border capital movements, dramatically increasing the opportunities for financial speculation. On the other hand, sectoral policies kept the fiscal deficit large and confounded many of the liberalization and stabilization measures, making speculation against the government very attractive. As the currency appreciated, traded goods producers came under serious competitive pressure, investment stagnated, capital fled, the financial sector collapsed, and by 1982 the country's per capita GDP was below 1970 levels.

Domestic turmoil meant that Argentina became a major Euromarket borrower relatively late. Despite some access to international financial markets in the late 1960s and early 1970s, the country's debt was nearly stagnant until 1976. The military governments that reigned from the 1970 overthrow of Onganía until 1973 were unsteady caretakers; after the Peronists took office in March 1973, political unrest made Argentina unattractive to potential lenders. By end-1975 the country's foreign debt was under $8 billion (see table 6.3).

Once the military took power in March 1976, Argentine borrowing grew rapidly. As table 6.3 shows, through 1980 most borrowing was done by the private sector and public enterprises. Unfortunately, a detailed breakdown of public enterprise debt is not available. However, most observers believe that the public firms that did most borrowing were those involved in investment projects in industries the military favored (especially steel and armaments) and in the energy and transportation infrastructure. Most private borrowing was done by large firms: ten large banks and ten large nonfinancial corporations combined accounted for one-third of total foreign private borrowing. Borrowing was heaviest by firms producing nontraded goods and services and those competing with imports. In the context of financial liberalization and large interest-rate differentials between Argentina and the rest of the world, banks were also major borrowers.[69]

The general contours of Argentine economic experience between 1976

[69] Jorge Schvarzer, *Martínez de Hoz: La lógica política de la política económica* (Buenos Aires: CISEA, 1983), 153–54. Data on the sectoral paths under the military are in A. Humberto Petrei and James Tybout, "Microeconomic Adjustments in Argentina during 1976–1981: The Importance of Changing Levels of Financial Subsidies," *World Development* 13, no. 8 (1985): 964–65; and Domingo Cavallo and A. Humberto Petrei, "Financing Private Business in an Inflationary Context: The Experience of Argentina between 1967 and 1980," in *Financial Policies and the World Capital Market: The Problem of Latin American Countries*, ed. Pedro Aspe Armella, Rudiger Dornbusch, and Maurice Obstfeld (Chicago: University of Chicago Press, 1983), 171–75.

208   CHAPTER 6

Table 6.3
Argentine External Debt Outstanding, 1975–1982
(Millions of dollars and percent)

	1975	1980	1982
PUBLIC SECTOR	4,021	14,459	28,616
(*Percent*)	(51.1)	(53.2)	(65.6)
Monetary authorities	1,053	459	4,949
(*Percent*)	(13.4)	(1.7)	(11.3)
General government	826	5,007	9,453
(*Percent*)	(10.5)	(18.4)	(21.7)
Public enterprises[a]	2,142	8,993	14,214
(*Percent*)	(27.2)	(33.1)	(32.6)
PRIVATE SECTOR	3,854	12,703	15,018
(*Percent*)	(48.9)	(46.8)	(34.4)
Guaranteed by govt.[b]	1,897	0	9,475
(*Percent*)	(24.1)		(21.7)
Unguaranteed	1,957	12,703	5,543
(*Percent*)	(24.9)	(46.8)	(12.7)
GRAND TOTAL	$7,875	$27,162	$43,634
(*Percent*)	(100.0)	(100.0)	(100.0)

Source: Ricardo Arriazu, Alfredo Leone, and Ricardo López Murphy, "Políticas macro-económicas y endeudamiento privado," in *Deuda interna y estabilidad financiera*, vol. 2, ed. Carlos Massad and Roberto Zahler (Buenos Aires: Grupo Editor Latinoamericano, 1988), 214, 306.

Note: Percentage totals may not add due to rounding.

[a] Includes binational enterprises and official banks.

[b] With government guarantee as to exchange rate.

and 1982 reflected crosscutting political and economic pressures. Economic policy after 1976 was dominated by a market orientation that included financial deregulation, commercial liberalization, and an antilabor bias. At the same time many sectoral policies were maintained, including public investment programs and tariff protection for some industries. Inflation resisted a series of stabilization programs, and in 1978 the orthodox team adopted a pre-announced devaluation plan similar to that being tried in Chile. As in Chile, the resulting real appreciation put major pressure on traded goods producers. Unlike in Chile, however, in Argentina businessmen protested government policy, their complaints untempered by lingering concern over threats to private property. In 1981 a new military administration bowed to pressure and changed policies, but this reversal was itself reversed by an orthodox counterreformation in 1982. Amidst great political and economic discontent and a disastrous war, civilian government was restored in 1983.

The principal beneficiaries of government policy between 1976 and 1981 were a mixture of those helped by liberalization and those who received continued subsidies and incentives. The financial sector expanded very rapidly once it was deregulated, from 3.4 percent of GDP in 1977 to 9.0 percent in 1981. Financial investors also did quite well including, of course, those who took their savings abroad to bet against the peso. Early in the dictatorship, as the peso depreciated and trade was liberalized, export-oriented producers profited. The portion of manufacturing with continued high levels of protection grew, although not rapidly: output in these sectors (iron and steel, transport equipment, nonferrous metals, nonmetallic minerals, rubber products, and a few consumer lines) grew 13 percent between 1977 and 1980, although employment fell 9 percent.

Among the losers under the military were, first and foremost, organized labor. Unions were disbanded or tightly controlled, and real wages between 1976 and 1981 averaged 15 percent below their position in the early 1970s; they dropped 36 percent in 1976, then gradually recovered, although even at the height of the boom in 1980 they remained well below precoup levels. Between 1970 and 1974 an average of over 49 percent of GDP accrued to wage-earners; between 1976 and 1981 the average was under 39 percent.[70] Along with the general attack on labor, industrial producers in the (mostly labor-intensive) import-competing sectors whose protection was reduced did very poorly: output in these sectors (food and beverages, textiles and clothing, leather goods, metal products, machinery and a few other lines) dropped 10 percent between 1977 and 1980 while employment fell 19 percent.[71] As the peso appreciated, traded goods producers who had done well early in the program faced increased import competition or were priced out of export markets, and by 1980–1981 even agriculture and resource-based manufacturing were hit by the strong peso. Growing political pressure from agriculture and industry, indeed, led to the military's brief reversal in its economic policies.

The military junta that seized power in March 1976, headed by General Jorge Rafael Videla as president, almost immediately chose José Alfredo Martínez de Hoz as minister of economics and a Martínez de Hoz

[70] Figures on real wages and wage-earners share of GDP are from *The Political Economy of Argentina*, 329.

[71] Figures on the sectoral trends in these two paragraphs are from Humberto Petrei and Jaime de Melo, "Adjustment by Industrial Firms in Argentina during 1976–81," in *Scrambling for Survival: How Firms Adjusted to the Recent Reforms in Argentina, Chile, and Uruguay*, ed. Vittorio Corbo and Jaime de Melo (Washington, D.C.: World Bank, 1985), 46.

supporter as president of the Central Bank.[72] This reflected military support for the market-oriented program that Martínez de Hoz had formulated in the waning months of the Perón administration. As in Chile, the armed forces had come to believe, in the words of Adolfo Canitrot, "that the politico-institutional structure that they sought to replace was closely tied in with a supporting economic order. . . . The economic plan found its justification not so much in the economic objectives it pursued as in its relevance to the political objectives of the Armed Forces' transformation project."[73] Import substitution and subsidies to manufacturing had, in this view, created swollen industries and artificially powerful unions where Peronism found its base. To attack Peronism labor's power base had to be attacked, and this meant exposing industry to competition.

Business was willing to countenance some disregard for specific interests in pursuit of social and political order. In the words of an informed student of military-business relations: "The crisis was so deep that sectoral economic interests were in the background, and pro-systemic pur-

---

[72] The literature on the Argentine 1976–1981 experience is enormous. The most important sources include, in addition to works already cited, L. Beccaria and R. Carciofi, "The Recent Experience of Stabilising and Opening Up the Argentinian Economy," *Cambridge Journal of Economics* 6, no. 2 (June 1982): 145–65; Guillermo Calvo, "Fractured Liberalism: Argentina under Martínez de Hoz," *Economic Development and Cultural Change* 34, no. 3 (April 1986): 511–33; Guillermo Calvo, "Trying to Stabilize: Some Theoretical Reflections Based on the Case of Argentina," in *Financial Policies and the World Capital Market*, 199–216; Adolfo Canitrot, "Teoría y práctica del liberalismo: Política antiinflacionaria y apertura económica en la Argentina, 1976–1981," *Desarrollo Económico* 21, no. 82 (July–September 1981): 131–89; Rudiger Dornbusch and Juan Carlos de Pablo, *Deuda externa e inestabilidad macroeconómica en la Argentina* (Buenos Aires: Sudamericana, 1988); Roque Fernandez, "The Expectations Management Approach to Stabilization in Argentina during 1976–82," *World Development* 13, no. 8 (1985): 871–92; Roque Fernandez and Carlos Rodriguez, eds., *Inflación y estabilidad* (Buenos Aires: Ediciones Macchi, 1982); Roberto Frenkel, "La apertura financiera externa: El caso argentino," in *Las relaciones financieras externas: Su efecto en la economía latinoamericana*, ed. Ricardo Ffrench-Davis (Mexico City: Fondo de Cultura Económica, 1983), 146–91; Bernardo Kosacoff and Daniel Azpiazu, *La industria argentina: Desarrollo y cambios estructurales* (Buenos Aires: Centro Editor de América Latina, 1989); Julio Nogués, *The Nature of Argentina's Policy Reforms during 1976–81* (Washington, D.C.: World Bank, 1986); David Pion-Berlin, "The Fall of Military Rule in Argentina: 1976–1983," *Journal of Interamerican Studies and World Affairs* 27, no. 2 (Summer 1985): 55–76; Larry Sjaastad, "Argentine Economic Policy, 1976–81," in *The Political Economy of Argentina*, 254–85; Juan Sourrouille, Bernardo Kosacoff, and Jorge Lucangeli, *Transnacionalización y política económica en la Argentina* (Buenos Aires: Centro Editor de América Latina, 1985), especially 63–129; and Guido di Tella, "Argentina's Most Recent Inflationary Cycle, 1975–85," in *Latin American Debt and the Adjustment Crisis*, ed. Rosemary Thorp and Laurence Whitehead (London: Macmillan, 1987), 162–207.

[73] Adolfo Canitrot, "Discipline as the Central Objective of Economic Policy: An Essay on the Economy Programme of the Argentine Government since 1976," *World Development* 8 (1980): 918. See also Epstein, "Inflation and Public Policy," 15–21.

poses were in the foreground. The ruling class was willing to deny some sectoral interests in favor of economic reorganization—to overcome the decomposition of authority relations."[74]

However, several features of the political economy tempered the commitment to laissez faire on the part of the military and business. First, although powerful private-sector groups supported the military's restoration of order, they were not nearly so willing as those in Chile to abandon all sector-specific policies. The threat to property was never strong enough to swamp sectoral demands, and many sectors had strong supporters within the military. Indeed, the Argentine military had a tradition of involvement in import-substituting industries deemed important to national security, such as steel and armaments. Martínez de Hoz never had the blanket permission of the military to override sectoral demands, and the economic cabinet included key representatives of agriculture and industry. Second, the military believed that armed opposition found its principal base in the urban unemployed, and made clear to Martínez de Hoz that while wage-slashing was permissible mass unemployment was politically unsustainable. Therefore, from the start the economic team had less room to maneuver free from societal pressures than did the like-minded team in Chile.

Nonetheless, Martínez de Hoz moved rapidly to implement liberalizing economic reforms. In the first nine months after the coup prices were freed, multiple exchange rates were unified and the peso was devalued in real terms, export taxes were reduced, some import controls were removed, and import financing was made easier. All of these measures aimed to increase incentives to export and to remove the most extreme protectionist barriers. In March 1977 a three-month "price truce" was imposed to try to bring inflation down, and in June 1977 a financial reform took effect. These measures freed interest rates, facilitated the entry of new financial institutions, reduced reserve requirements, and extended deposit insurance. The result was a financial system with positive real interest rates for practically the first time since World War II, and rapid financial deepening.[75] At much the same time public finances were reorganized to eliminate monetization of the budget deficit. The government also adopted liberalizing changes in legislation concerning industrial promotion and technology transfer.

[74] Interview by the author with Andrés Fontana, 31 July 1985, Buenos Aires.

[75] On the origins of the reform see the account by then–Central Bank President Adolfo Diz in Juan Carlos de Pablo, *La economía que yo hice* (Buenos Aires: Ediciones El Cronista Comercial, 1986), 113–23. Evaluations of its effects are in the Calvo articles cited above; Schvarzer, *Martínez de Hoz*, 49–63; and Donald Mathieson, "Inflation, Interest Rates, and the Balance of Payments during a Financial Reform: The Case of Argentina," *World Development* 10, no. 9 (1982): 813–27.

In 1977 the economy grew, the trade balance was strongly positive, the budget deficit had been cut, and inflation came down. However, although wholesale price growth was reduced from 499 percent in 1976 to 149 percent in 1977 and 146 percent in 1978, it stayed stubbornly high. Worse, in 1978 the economy slowed substantially. On a different front, the threat of military conflict over a border dispute with Chile was growing.

Over the course of 1978 the regime's economic policies moved in a firmly neoliberal direction, despite the fact that many business leaders were unenthusiastic about this course. Part of the reason was regime frustration with continued inflation, much of which was blamed on the "social irresponsibility" of protected entrepreneurs. Another part of the reason was the consolidation of the position of Videla, whom the military voted in mid-1978 to give three more years in office. Finally, border tension with Chile and the nationalism it bred may have encouraged the regime to ignore the business community, while the conflict's resolution by papal intervention in late 1978 appeared to strengthen the military further. However, there were clear signs of business opposition to orthodoxy. In late 1977 the Secretary of Foreign Trade resigned, followed in August 1978 by the Under-Secretary for Agriculture. The military reshuffle that confirmed Videla also added General Roberto Eduardo Viola to the junta, and Viola was known to have major reservations about the Martínez de Hoz orthodoxy. Between 1978 and 1982 these contradictory tendencies played themselves out, with supporters of orthodoxy and more traditional business supporters in constant battle.

In the middle of 1978 the economic team began consciously to allow the devaluation of the exchange rate to lag behind the rate of inflation. The rationale was as in Chile: first, real appreciation would force down the price of tradables, and second, lagged devaluations would dampen inflationary expectations.

At the end of 1978 the team announced a major plan to fight inflation and liberalize foreign trade. The anti-inflation program represented a full-fledged commitment to the monetary approach to the balance of payments ("global monetarism"). As in Chile, the Argentine authorities published a *tablita* of pre-announced devaluations based on a declining rate of inflation. The announcement covered the following eight months; every few months thereafter the authorities extended the *tablita* a few more months, always in ways predicated on substantial declines in inflation. The concurrently announced tariff reform was also drastic. Trade liberalization would proceed in steps until 1984, by which time nominal tariffs would average about 15 percent.[76]

---

[76] On the plan in general, see Schvarzer, *Martínez de Hoz*, 64–85; and Sourrouille et al.,

The 20 December 1978 Plan, as it was known, met with some success on the inflation-fighting front. Wholesale prices had been rising at an average rate of about 8 percent a month in 1978; after the *tablita* went into effect, wholesale price inflation declined gradually until in the last half of 1980 it was averaging less than 3 percent a month. Consumer price inflation dropped from 176 percent for 1978 to 101 percent in 1980; wholesale price inflation for 1980 was 75 percent.

However, the reduction in inflation was too slow to avoid real exchange rate appreciation. The process was similar to that in Chile. Financial liberalization and high real interest rates in Argentina led to a great inflow of funds: the foreign debt of the private sector went from $4.1 billion at end-1978 to $12.7 billion at end-1980, while that of the public sector went from $8.4 to $14.5 billion. The increased spending this allowed went partly to imports, which soared from $3.9 to $10.5 billion; this was encouraged by continuing tariff reductions. But much of the spending was on nontradeable goods and services, including industrial products that maintained high levels of protection. The result was a very substantial real appreciation. According to one measure the peso appreciated 26 percent in real terms over the course of 1978, and a further 31 percent between the end of 1978 and the end of 1980.[77] By 1979 the Argentine currency was clearly overvalued, and by 1980 it was dramatically so.

The new monetary policies, financial reforms, and tariff reductions had varied effects. First, commercial liberalization and real appreciation put substantial competitive pressure on import-competing manufacturers, and even on export-oriented producers of primary products and resource-based manufactured goods. By one measure, in October 1980 effective protection for the machinery sector would have been 67 percent at a

Transnacionalización, 100–124. On monetary policy see Juan Carlos de Pablo, "El enfoque monetario de la balanza de pagos en la Argentina: Análisis del programa del 20 de diciembre de 1978," *El Trimestre Económico* 50, no. 198 (April–June 1983): 641–69; Carlos Alfredo Rodriguez, "The Argentine Stabilization Plan of December 20th," *World Development* 10, no. 9 (1982): 801–11; and Carlos Alfredo Rodriguez, "Políticas de estabilización en la economía argentina, 1978–1982," *Cuadernos de economía* 20, no. 59 (April 1983): 21–42. On the tariff reform see Julio Berlinski, "Dismantling Foreign Trade Restrictions: Some Evidence and Issues on the Argentine Case," in *Trade, Stability, Technology, and Equity in Latin America*, ed. Moshe Syrquin and Simon Teitel (New York: Academic Press, 1982), 57–68; Juan Medina, "Resultados y Perspectivas del Plan de Apertura de la Economía Argentina," in *Inflación y estabilidad*, 99–108; and Julio Nogués, "Protección nominal y efectiva: Impacto de las reformas arancelarias durante 1976–1977," *Ensayos Económicos* 8 (December 1978): 147–212.

[77] Calvo, "Fractured Liberalism," 513; this is his RER2 measure. Most other indexes show less real appreciation in 1978 and more between 1978 and 1980; the results depend, of course, on how the indexes are constructed. A catalog of alternative indexes is Juan Llach, "Los precios de una década," *Estudios* 24 (October–December 1982): 139–94.

realistic exchange rate; with a 30 percent overvaluation (near most estimates), effective protection for the sector was − 11 percent.[78] Second, firms
borrowed heavily, especially in foreign currencies. For one sample of private companies, total debt went from 68 percent of net worth in 1976 to
106 percent in 1980, foreign-currency debt from 25 to 35 percent.[79] Some
of this borrowing was in response to competitive pressures, as import-
competing firms modernized; some of it was distress borrowing by firms
on the brink of collapse; and some of it was induced by the extraordinary
cheapness of dollar credits in an atmosphere of currency overvaluation
and high domestic interest rates.[80] Third, the combination of easy credit
and a strong peso fueled a boom in consumption and imports: imports of
consumer electronics, which were $7 million a year in the early 1970s,
averaged $370 million in 1980–1981.[81] There was a widespread percep-
tion of prosperity that helped bolster the military regime's flagging legit-
imacy, especially in the middle classes.

The military regime clearly needed whatever support it could gather,
for its economic policies were alienating important segments of the business community. As the peso appreciated and tariff reductions advanced,
businessmen became hostile to the Martínez de Hoz policies. In December 1978 the Under-Secretary of Stockraising resigned, and in March and
April 1979 the secretaries of industrial development and of agriculture
and stockraising followed. Peso appreciation was having disastrous effects on import-competing industries and agricultural exporters; industrial producers also resisted tariff reductions. Cabinet ministers close to
affected constituents began trying to contravene the Martínez de Hoz policies. The antiliberalization front was evidently joined by what one observer has called the Argentine military-industrial complex, companies
run by the armed forces that produce goods deemed important to the
national security: well-placed military men apparently halted planned
tariff reductions in such strategic industries.[82]

In the words of a leading Argentine observer and policymaker: "Originally, the rural sector supported the dictatorship for its liberalism, indus-

[78] Roque Fernandez, "Consideraciones ex-post sobre el Plan Económico de Martínez de Hoz," in *Inflación y estabilidad*, 266.

[79] Cavallo and Petrei, "Financing Private Business," 167.

[80] Petrei and Tybout try to separate the different motives for indebtedness in their sample of private firms.

[81] Daniel Azpiazu, Eduardo Basualdo, and Hugo Nochteff, "La industria electrónica argentina: Apertura comercial y desindustrialización," *Comercio Exterior* 37, no. 7 (July 1987): 545.

[82] Nogués, *The Nature of Argentina's Policy Reforms*, 39–45. On business-community and other political pressures see Sourrouille et al., *Transnacionalización*, 110–11; Pion-Berlin, "The Fall of Military Rule," 58–60; Epstein, "Inflation and Public Policy," 21–30; Schvarzer, *Martínez de Hoz*, 65–66, 75–76.

try for its promises to reduce wages. After 1978, however, it became increasingly divorced from its social bases. At the same time, the liberals lost control of public spending to the armed forces on the one hand, and to state enterprises important to the private sector on the other. What happened was a fatal delinking from society."[83]

The confrontation between the Martínez de Hoz economic team and business became increasingly bitter. In 1979, with inflation still high, the team used the threat of tariff reductions to try to force individual entrepreneurs not to raise prices. Businessmen in turn used their influence with segments of the military, with other ministries, and with the media to protect themselves. While investors whose assets were affected by policy protested, those with liquid assets got them out of the country: depending on the estimate, between 1979 and 1982 from $14.5 to $22.4 billion fled Argentina. From 1979 to early 1981 capital flight was motivated primarily by the strong peso; in late 1981 and 1982 it was driven largely by political instability.[84]

In early 1980 the contradictory economic policies began to unravel. The free-wheeling financial markets collapsed first: in March 1980 the country's largest bank was closed by the government, and in the next couple of months four more of Argentina's largest banks were also "intervened." Between 1980 and 1982 the government took over 71 financial institutions and spent billions of dollars to prop up the financial system.[85] While those with access to dollars enjoyed an orgy of foreign travel, imports, and capital flight, the economy as a whole teetered on the verge of collapse.

As Martínez de Hoz's successor in the Economics Ministry put it several years later:

> There was a political sense to the management of Martínez de Hoz. He had his base of support in liberal sectors and those with an anti-Peronist bias, and his policy was to destroy Peronism's labor base. The labor base was attacked directly, by cutting social projects and suspending labor contracts, and indirectly, by affecting the industrial sector. But the partners of Martínez de Hoz began to desert him as his policies began to hurt them. Industry left, then agriculture, and finally in April 1980 even his closest associates in the financial sector were in terrible crisis. By the end of 1980 Martínez de Hoz was playing alone.[86]

[83] Interview by the author with Adolfo Canitrot, 30 July 1985, Buenos Aires. At the time Canitrot was Secretary of Economic Coordination for the Ministry of Economics in the Alfonsín government.

[84] For the various estimates, see Lessard and Williamson, eds., Capital Flight, 52–53.

[85] Roque Fernandez, "La crisis financiera argentina, 1980–1982," Desarrollo Económico 23, no. 89 (April–June 1983): 79–97, and following comments by Ernesto Feldman, 449–55; the figures are at 454.

[86] Interview by the author with Lorenzo Sigaut, Buenos Aires, 31 July 1985.

The Politics of Economic Crisis after 1982

The financial crisis that began in 1982 had a major impact on economic activity in all three countries. Its impact, of course, was differential: some were harder hit than others, and some prospered through the crisis. So severe an economic downturn, with such varied distributional consequences, was bound to give rise to major political conflicts.

As elsewhere, capital flows reversed course abruptly from the net new borrowing (net inflow) before 1982 to the servicing of outstanding debt (net outflow) that began in that year. The financial shocks had direct effects on the supply of foreign exchange, capital, and government finance: exchange rates dropped, interest rates soared, and governments faced severe constraints on expenditures (which often led to inflationary finance). In the short run, this set of price changes had very detrimental effects on economic agents who had come to depend on cheap foreign exchange, cheap loans, and plentiful government spending; the immediate effect of the shock was that these sectors made major demands for government support.

In the longer run, the reduction in foreign loan supply and the ensuing relative price changes affected patterns of economic activity. At lower real exchange rates, exporting was far more lucrative. The unavailability of external sources of government finance and the need to service existing debt made obtaining government favors more difficult—indeed, on net governments *demanded* private resources, instead of supplying them. Over time, private-sector interests changed along with the economic environment, with more attraction to foreign markets, and to reducing the burden of government demands on the private sector.

When the crisis hit, then, all three governments faced insistent demands from those whose assets were threatened by these relative price changes. The Mexican government responded with most alacrity to pleas for support from the very adversely affected industrial sectors. Venezuela's COPEI administration was far less successful at satisfying such demands and was quickly voted out of office. In Argentina, initial support for the private sector was reversed by a quick return to neoliberal policies. The new team's unwillingness to meet demands from the private sector and labor gave rise to massive opposition, fueled by the regime's military defeat in the South Atlantic. The result was the replacement of the dictatorship with civilian governments more sympathetic to business and labor.

After this original response to the crisis, governments confronted both dramatic reductions in available resources and the gradual increases in private-sector support for more internationally oriented policies (especially at new, much lower, real exchange rates). The Mexican government moved toward reducing intervention in the economy and liberalizing foreign trade and payments; in the process, it alienated much of its labor base. Successive AD administrations in Venezuela moved in a similar direction, albeit with many concessions to labor. In Argentina too, there was a gradual evolution toward reduction in public spending and liberalization, but resurgent sectoral strife made this evolution halting and uncertain.

Mexico

The Mexican political economy on the eve of the crisis was dominated by the largest private firms in modern industry and finance, whose exceptional dynamism was due to the economy's pattern of growth, access to external finance, and government support. This was especially true of the financial conglomerates and major enterprises in modern industry: capital goods, consumer durables, and intermediate inputs. Many of these firms had substantial foreign-currency debts. Despite peso appreciation, trade barriers had virtually eliminated import competition in finished goods. At the same time, many investors had diversified out of Mexican assets, taking tens of billions of dollars out of the country. Real wages in modern industry were advancing, although inflation was a threat to wage-earners.

Politically, over the course of the 1970s the business community had changed somewhat. Echeverría's populist turn convinced many businessmen that radical elements in the PRI were dangerous. Almost all business organizations agreed on the need for the government to block a return to radical populism.

Despite increased agreement within the private sector on the desirability of more probusiness policies, divisions persisted, especially concerning international economic relations. These divisions were highlighted in a 1979–1980 debate over plans for the country to join the General Agreement on Tariffs and Trade (GATT): domestically oriented businesses opposed to commercial liberalization defeated exporters, bankers, and large internationally oriented firms to block planned Mexican accession to the GATT.[87] Despite the defeat of the more internationally oriented groups and

[87] On the decade as a whole, see Basañez, *La lucha por la hegemonía*, 185–201; the various articles in Maxwell and Anzaldúa Montoya, eds., *Government and Private Sector in Contemporary Mexico*; and Salvador Cordero, "Estado y burguesía en México en la década de 1970," in *El Estado Mexicano*, ed. Jorge Alonso (Mexico City: Editorial Nueva Imagen, 1982). On the GATT debates, see Saúl Escobar Toledo, "Rifts in the Mexican Power Elite, 1976–1986," in *Government and Private Sector in Contemporary Mexico*, 65–88; the articles in Instituto Mexicano de Comercio Exterior, *El comercio exterior de México* (Mexico City: Siglo Veintiuno Editores, 1982), 2:287–471; and Story, 127–49.

regions in the GATT debate, their numbers and influence were clearly growing.

Both of these trends—the increased business-community concern about radical populist tendencies in the PRI, and the growth of groups and regions with more international economic interests—improved the political fortunes of the conservative opposition party, the Partido Acción Nacional (PAN). The PAN was especially strong in the North, where economic links with the U.S. market were most important. Even where businessmen and middle-class voters did not defect to the PAN, they increasingly threw their support behind moderate currents within the PRI.

In Mexico, as elsewhere, the crisis bankrupted heavily indebted private firms and those who relied on government largess. The Mexican government met most of the demands of the country's important modern sectors, providing exchange-rate and interest-rate subsidies to the most affected firms. The longer-run relative price changes also led economic agents to alter their activities and their policy preferences. Once the immediate crisis was over, the Mexican government gradually shifted its policy emphasis in line with changes in the private sector, now more interested in access to foreign markets.

The principal losers in the Mexican government's response to the crisis were the PRI's historic working-class and peasant supporters, along with some traditional small and medium businesses. The political result was a groundswell of popular opposition to the government that eventually split the ruling party. In other words, the crisis finally forced the Mexican government to choose between populism and orthodoxy, and between economic nationalism and liberalization; it eventually chose moderate orthodoxy and moderate liberalization, and supporters of populism and nationalism defected from the ruling coalition.

The immediate impact of the crisis was felt through the exchange rate.[88] The peso went from 27 to 150 per dollar in less than a year, and firms with foreign obligations were bankrupted. As the peso value of outstanding dollar obligations soared, the liabilities of the Alfa group, for example, went from 63 percent of its assets in December 1981 to 157 percent of its assets in August 1982.[89] The banking system had generally passed the exchange risk to ultimate borrowers, but waves of insolvencies by some of the banks' best customers shook the financial community.

---

[88] Jaime Ros, "Mexico from the Oil Boom to the Debt Crisis: An Analysis of Policy Responses to External Shocks, 1978–1985," in *Latin American Debt and the Adjustment Crisis*, ed. Rosemary Thorp and Laurence Whitehead (London: Macmillian, 1987), 68–116; and Robert Kaufman, *The Politics of Debt in Argentina, Brazil, and Mexico* (Berkeley: Institute of International Studies, 1988), 78–104, survey the crisis period.

[89] Cardero and Quijano, "Expansión y estrangulamiento," 281.

Those with overseas assets denominated in foreign currencies, of course, were protected from the devaluations.

The second major shock was to public finances. The public sector found its recourse to foreign funds to meet its financing needs cut off, even as overspending, the recession, and spiraling interest payments drove the fiscal deficit to 17.9 percent of GDP in 1982. As noninterest public spending dropped, the parastatals wound down their orders from the private sector, and government subsidies and transfers were cut drastically.

All of this implied substantial downward pressure on real wages, especially in the modern industrial sector and among public employees. By one measure real manufacturing wages dropped nearly 20 percent between 1980 and 1983.[90]

The initial government reaction was to bail out the hardest-hit firms, but in a most unexpected manner. In August and September 1982 López Portillo replaced his economic team with left-leaning nationalists whose policies veered into uncharted waters. For the first time in fifty years, exchange controls were imposed. The official exchange rate was kept well above market-clearing levels to lessen the impact of the devaluation on debtors. For similar reasons, real interest rates were held strongly negative, and administrative means were used to allocate credit. Most startling was the 1 September nationalization of the private banking system.[91] López Portillo, like Echeverría before him, seemed set on playing upon nationalist sentiment to defuse popular dissatisfaction.

Just as Mexico seemed headed for a new bout of economic radicalism, Miguel de la Madrid Hurtado took office in December 1982 and implemented more traditional austerity measures. The government continued to act to limit damage to the country's most important firms. Trade barriers were raised substantially to stanch the trade deficit and protect domestic producers. Domestic interest rates were kept negative in real terms, and a series of measures to rescue heavily indebted private firms was introduced. Most of the schemes involved the government absorbing some of the cost of the devaluation, and in some instances assuming some of the private-sector debt itself.[92]

Despite attempts to cushion major private firms, the financial crisis drove the economy into a depression from which recovery was extremely slow. Some spending was available to smooth the transition for crucial

[90] Bela Balassa et al., *Toward Renewed Economic Growth in Latin America* (Mexico City: El Colegio de México, 1986), 72.

[91] Carlos Tello, *La nacionalización de la banca en México* (Mexico City: Siglo Veintiuno Editores, 1984), is the report of a participant.

[92] Roberto Gutiérrez r., "El endeudamiento externo del sector privado de México: Expansión y renegociación," *Comercio Exterior* 36, no. 4 (April 1986): 337–43.

sectors, but aid to private firms was limited by the squeeze on public finances. Little was done to support real wages, and social spending dropped.

Initial postcrisis economic policy gave rise to varied political reactions. Those supported by the government were appreciative. However, many saw the bank nationalization as a dangerous concession to populist proclivities. Discontent was especially great among more internationalist and market-oriented groups, especially in the North, who were also concerned by exchange controls and redoubled trade protection. This led to an unprecedented strengthening of the PAN, which won control of the Northern state of Chihuahua's ten largest cities in 1983 elections. Despite the decline in real wages, historic ties between the PRI and organized labor served to dampen labor opposition in the hopes that the crisis would soon pass.[93]

The PRI responded to business concern about economic nationalism in two ways. First, it gradually moderated its rhetoric, reduced trade barriers, relaxed exchange controls, and freed financial markets. In 1985 and 1986 elections in the North, in fact, the PRI presented conservative candidates closely aligned with the private sector, which, in one observer's words, "effectively 'bought off' the local business community."[94] Second, for good measure, elections in the North were rigged to avoid further losses by the PRI.

As time went on, private-sector support for more market-oriented economic policies grew. Financial investors, including the holders of tens of billions of dollars in flight capital abroad, demanded a market return. Real peso depreciation made exporting attractive, and many manufacturers developed stronger interest in foreign markets than they had ever had. By the same token, the government bailout of seriously affected firms at the outset of the crisis reduced the most insistent demands for support. In 1986 the government brought the country into the GATT and reduced trade barriers.[95] Portions of the public sector were privatized, both to re-

[93] Barry Carr, "The Mexican Economic Debacle and the Labor Movement," in *Mexico's Economic Crisis*, ed. Donald L. Wyman (San Diego: Center for U.S.-Mexican Studies, 1983), 91–116.

[94] Wayne Cornelius, *The Political Economy of Mexico under De la Madrid: The Crisis Deepens, 1985–1986*, Research Report Series no. 43 (San Diego: Center for U.S.-Mexican Studies, 1986), 39.

[95] Enrique Fernandez and Sergio Nava, "México-GATT: Historia de una reconciliación," *La Jornada Semanal*, 25 July 1987; Fernando de Mateo, "La política comercial de México y el GATT," *El Trimestre Económico* 55, no. 217 (January–March 1988): 175–216; Adriaan ten Kate and Fernando de Mateo Venturini, "Apertura comercial y estructura de la protección en México," *Comercio Exterior* 39, no. 4 (April 1989): 312–29. For an example of the private-sector turnaround, see David Gardner, "Grupo Industrial Alfa: Now that the Burden of Debt Has Gone," *Financial Times*, 13 July 1988.

duce government economic intervention and to raise funds for the treasury.[96] The pattern of interventionist policies was gradually reversed.

While the weight of interest and influence in the private sector shifted toward more internationalist and market-oriented positions, and government policy followed suit, the traditional popular base of the PRI was left behind. In the run-up to the 1988 presidential elections, Cuauhtémoc Cárdenas led a left-wing split from the PRI, whose Frente Democrático Nacional mounted the first real challenge to the ruling party in its history.[97] Only fraud allowed the PRI to carry a majority of the popular vote.

The administration of Carlos Salinas de Gortari, which took office in 1988, accelerated the previous tendency in economic policy and politics—Salinas is from Monterrey and is close to the city's internationalist business community. Economic liberalization proceeded apace, and Salinas launched a frontal attack on some of the country's traditional labor leaders. In the aftermath of the election, Cárdenas and his supporters formed a new party of the Partido de la Revolución Democrática or (PRD). Suddenly Mexico appeared to have genuine parties of the right (PAN), center (PRI), and left (PRD).

To summarize the political economy of the Mexican crisis and its aftermath, the Mexican government quite successfully balanced various demands from business, but was less successful at maintaining its popular base. In the first period, the government largely met demands to rescue the most seriously affected modern business sectors, especially firms the return to whose assets had come to depend on government orders, cheap foreign exchange, and cheap loans. This response was not particularly popular with internationally oriented firms and holders of more liquid assets, especially since it involved controls on trade, capital movements, and interest rates. These last sectors reacted by throwing support to the PAN.

Over time demands from the most affected firms subsided, as the public rescue and economic conditions allowed them to adjust. At this point, around 1985–1986, the government moved toward more market-oriented policies, which pleased both PAN supporters in the business community and those with new interests in external markets. The movement toward freer trade and less government involvement in the economy also caused defection of major portions of the PRI's traditional popular base to the new PRD.

Two potential conclusions are at odds with conventional wisdom about the PRI. First, the party responded with alacrity to powerful ele-

[96] José Gasca Zamora, "Fuentes para el estudio de las empresas paraestatales de México y su privatización, 1983–1988," *Comercio Exterior* 39, no. 2 (February 1989): 151–75.
[97] For useful economic, political, and social background to the 1988 elections, see Abraham Nuncio, ed., *La sucesión presidencial en 1988* (Mexico City: Grijalbo, 1987).

ments in the private sector, both as they demanded specific subsidies and as they came to support economic openness. Second, the PRI seemed willing to jettison much of its popular base; this apparent lack of concern may indicate the end of Mexico's semicorporatist political system.

Venezuela

Conditions at the outset of the debt crisis in Venezuela were different from those in Mexico, since 1982 was Venezuela's fourth year of economic stagnation. However, just as elsewhere in the region the loan cutoff of 1982–1983 forced the Venezuelan government to adjust its policies. The result was a round of devaluation and fiscal austerity, hitting firms with dollar debts, those dependent on public investment, and workers' real wages. In the first phase of the crisis, the COPEI government was generally unresponsive to business and labor demands, and lost the 1983 election. The new AD administration met many private-sector demands, especially on bailing out the hardest-hit firms. Over time economic actors adjusted to the new environment, and policy shifted toward commercial liberalization.

The debt crisis hit Venezuela in earnest in the last year of the COPEI administration of Luis Herrera Campins.[98] COPEI faced conflicting pressures. On the one hand, its principal base was in the commercial and financial sectors and the middle class, which tended to favor monetary and fiscal orthodoxy. On the other hand, 1983 was a presidential election year and austerity would hardly play well to the electorate. Herrera was eventually forced to devalue, but he tried to reduce the impact of the bolívar's decline by limiting the devaluation to about 20 percent (too little, according to most analysts), and by promising private firms access to dollars at the previous exchange rate for amortization of their foreign debts. Monetary policy remained tight and public investment was slashed, although some import controls were imposed. The overall result was a 5.6 percent drop in GDP and a 7.2 percent drop in real wages; imports dropped from $12.8 billion in 1982 to $6.4 billion in 1983. The electoral

[98] On this period in Venezuelan economic developments, see Rodriguez, "Auge Petrolero," 220–27; Rodriguez, "Public Sector Behavior," 53–62; Hausmann and Márquez, "Venezuela"; McCoy, "The Politics of Adjustment," 122–29; Eduardo Mayobre, "The Renegotiation of Venezuela's Foreign Debt during 1982 and 1983," in *Politics and Economics of External Debt Crisis*, ed. Miguel S. Wionczek (Boulder, Colo.: Westview Press, 1985), 325–47; and Miguel Rodriguez Mendoza, "Venezuela y la renegociación de la deuda externa," in *Entre la heterodoxía y el ajuste*, ed. Roberto Bouzas (Buenos Aires: Grupo Editor Latinoamericano, 1988), 273–98. Figures are drawn from Inter-american Development Bank, *Economic and Social Progress in Latin America*, various issues.

outcome was a foregone conclusion: AD candidate Jaime Lusinchi won by a landslide.

The new government, as would be expected given AD's base in industry and labor, moved to stimulate the economy and assist troubled firms. Monetary policy was loosened. Lusinchi systematized the multiple exchange rate system, which allowed private firms with overseas debts to purchase foreign currency at the predevaluation rate for principal payments and a low, controlled rate for interest payments. The program involved a massive subsidy to indebted firms, although the government did scrutinize the debts carefully and ended up providing subsidized foreign exchange for only about half of the private foreign debt.[99] General austerity measures were maintained, given the fiscal and foreign exchange pressures on the government, but Lusinchi tried to ensure labor cooperation by mandating small wage increases and some public employment programs.

The AD government's stimulative measures were too modest to forestall a 1.2 percent decline in GDP, and a 7.6 percent decline in real wages, in 1984. As protests from the labor movement and AD supporters in the business community accelerated, the Lusinchi administration cautiously increased attempts to aid its backers. The bolívar was allowed to depreciate significantly, which provided protection to domestic producers without harming private debtors with access to subsidized foreign exchange. Despite a dramatic decline in oil prices in 1986, which drove exports from $14.7 billion to $9.1 billion in a year, government spending levels were maintained and monetary policy was loosened further; reserves were drawn down substantially. The result was a modest recovery, with average annual GDP growth of 3.8 percent in 1985–1988 and comparable rates of growth of real wages. Inflation, however, accelerated to around 30 percent in 1987 and 1988. Meanwhile, in the context of debt negotiations, public and private debtors repaid principal to foreign creditors, which reduced the foreign debt from $37.4 billion in 1983 to $34.8 billion in 1988—the only Latin American country to effect a nominal reduction over this five-year period.[100]

As the economy recovered and the debt burden was reduced, economic activity adjusted to the new environment. The bolívar depreciation stim-

[99] René Salgado, "Economic Pressure Groups and Policy-Making in Venzuela: The Case of FEDECAMARAS Reconsidered," *Latin American Research Review* 22, no. 3 (1987): 91–105 (with comments on 107–21), discusses the controversy over the preferential rate. Salgado argues that the foreign exchange subsidy was insignificant and not due to private-sector pressure. However, both the evidence he cites and the comments (especially those by Kelly de Escobar and Abente) make it clear that his conclusions are untenable.

[100] Figures are from Inter-american Development Bank, *Economic and Social Progress*, various issues; Rodriguez Mendoza, "Venezuela," 294, reports a much greater nominal reduction.

ulated manufacturing and agriculture. Nontraditional exports grew, although oil continued to dominate. Fiscal pressures restrained public spending and forced businesses to find new suppliers and customers. Liberal elements of the business community stepped up demands for freer trade and macroeconomic conservatism.[101]

The 1988 presidential race was won easily by Carlos Andrés Pérez (Venezuelan presidents cannot succeed themselves but can serve more than once). Pérez played all his populist cards, attempting to capitalize on sentiment in organized labor and the business community that he would be able to put the country back on the track of rapid growth he had overseen in the 1970s. However, with changed international conditions Pérez had more limited options, and immediately after taking office in 1989 he removed most price and exchange controls, adopted austerity measures, liberalized trade, and moved to privatize some state enterprises. The intent was to bring inflation down, restructure public spending, and set the stage for renewed growth and revitalized social programs.

The immediate result of the crisis, then, was insistent demands from heavily affected groups, especially dollar debtors, firms reliant on public spending, and organized labor. The COPEI administration was half-hearted in its attempts to meet these demands, pulled as it was in more orthodox directions by its financial and commercial-community constituency; COPEI paid for its hesitation by losing the presidency. The new AD government responded to calls for public support by devaluing, bailing out debtors, increasing public spending, and cautiously reflating. Eventually demands subsided, and another AD administration undertook an ambitious reformulation of economic policy.

Argentina

The course of economic and political events in the Argentine crisis was dramatic. As the economy spiralled downward, the discontented business community sought and obtained a brief reversal of economic policy and measures to alleviate its plight. At the end of 1981, however, a counter-coup by hard-line elements in the military brought back an economic team that tried to return to orthodox policies with a vengeance. The great unpopularity of these new economic measures may have contributed to the hard-liners' decision to launch a military adventure in the South Atlantic, but the combined failure of the war and of the economy forced the

---

[101] The leadership of this pressure came from the Roraima Group, made up primarily of business leaders from outside the manufacturing sector. For one of the organization's programmatic statements, see Grupo Roraima, *A Proposal to the Nation: The Roraima Project* (Caracas: Roraima Institute, 1985).

military back to the barracks. As democratization proceeded, sectoral interests asserted themselves with a vengeance, leading eventually to hyperinflation. Despite a series of attempts, neither the first (Radical) nor the second (Peronist) civilian administrations overcame the conflicts that have bedevilled the Argentine political economy since the 1950s.

The crisis began with the economy already in difficulty. The real exchange rate appreciation, tariff reductions, and high real interest rates had driven most of the country's industrial and agricultural leaders into open opposition to the Martínez de Hoz policies. In October 1980, in apparent recognition of the depth of opposition to the neoliberal program, the military junta announced that General Roberto Eduardo Viola would succeed Videla as President in March 1981. Viola was known to be critical of the Martínez de Hoz team, and before his inauguration Viola made it clear that he would involve the business community in policy making, and that he was not committed to a continuation of orthodoxy. The expectation of policy change, which clearly would include an abandonment of the *tablita*, fueled further speculation against the peso. In February 1981 Martínez de Hoz was forced to announce an unplanned 10 percent additional devaluation, insufficient to correct the real overvaluation but enough to effectively admit the failure of the *tablita*.

In March 1981 Viola took office and appointed Lorenzo Sigaut minister of economics.[102] Sigaut moved immediately to satisfy the demands of the business community. A dual exchange rate was established, and the peso was devalued continually: by one measure it depreciated 36 percent in real terms from March to June 1981.[103] Firms with foreign-currency debts had the exchange risk assumed by the government. Domestic interest rates were controlled. The devaluation restored the competitive position of industry and agriculture, while financial and exchange-rate subsidies cushioned the impact of the crisis on heavily indebted firms.[104] In the words of a leading political commentator, "The Viola government brought the lobbies back to power—not with a general program but for specific problems and interests."[105]

[102] On the transition from Videla to civilian rule, see Pion-Berlin, "The Fall of Military Rule," 62–73; di Tella, "Argentina's Most Recent Inflationary Cycle," 175–81; Rudiger Dornbusch, "Argentina after Martínez de Hoz, 1981–3," in *The Political Economy of Argentina*, 286–320; Andrés Fontana, *Fuerzas armadas, partidos políticos y transición a la democracia en Argentina* (Buenos Aires: CEDES, 1984); Oscar Oszlak, ed., *"Proceso," crisis y transición democrática/2* (Buenos Aires: Centro Editor de América Latina, 1984); Marcelo Cavarozzi, "Peronismo and Radicalismo: Argentina's Transitions in Perspective" (Buenos Aires: mimeo, 1985).

[103] Adalbert Krieger Vasena and Enrique Szewach, "Inflation and Indexation: Argentina," in *Inflation and Indexation*, ed. John Williamson (Washington, D.C.: Institute for International Economics, 1985), 21.

[104] Petrei and Tybout, "Microeconomic Adjustments," 957–958.

[105] Interview by the author with Juan Carlos de Pablo, 30 July 1985, Buenos Aires.

Along with the revision of economic policies, Viola also presided over a political opening. Peronists, Radicals, and other civilian groups came together in the *Multipartidaria* to press for an accelerated transition to democracy.

Opposition from business to orthodox economic policies had led to a reversal of these policies, but hard-liners in the military were not reconciled to their defeat. In December 1981, General Leopoldo Galtieri carried out a "coup within a coup" and installed himself as president at the head of an instransigent team.[106] His minister of economics, Roberto Alemann, was if anything more committed to orthodoxy than Martínez de Hoz, and he reversed the policies of the Sigaut period. Societal opposition to the reversal was strong and immediate. The business community renewed its protests, and now labor joined in. At the end of March a leading labor federation held a massive antigovernment rally, the first since the dictatorship had taken power in 1976. Against the backdrop of economic disaster, swelling discontent, and divisions within the armed forces, the regime launched an invasion of the Falkland (Malvinas) Islands in April 1982.

The country's defeat at the hands of the British completely discredited the government of the armed forces. Of course, the economic shambles contributed to the general sense that the military was unfit to rule. General Reynaldo Bignone succeeded the disgraced Galtieri in a caretaker capacity, to clear the way for civilian rule. Bignone's first economic team, led by José María Dagnino Pastore at the Economics Ministry and Domingo Cavallo at the Central Bank, aggressively reversed course. Real interest rates were held negative, and private debts were restructured and massively reduced at public expense. Government access to external sources of finance had by now come to an end, and these major subsidies could only be financed by inflationary means. Dagnino Pastore resigned over policy disputes after less than two months in office, but his replacement Jorge Wehbe continued most of his policies. Wehbe also presided over an increase in real wages of almost 25 percent during 1983.

The transitional military governments appeased virtually all of the major sectoral pressures exerted on them. They bailed out heavily indebted private firms. They devalued continually to help traded goods producers. They encouraged significant real wage increases. All of this was politically expedient, especially given the disdain in which the military had come to be held, but it left the incoming civilian administration with an economy in disarray. GDP dropped by 8 percent between 1981 and 1983, while investment dropped over 40 percent. The fiscal deficit went from 13 per-

---

[106] The details of this period are especially murky, connected as they are to the Falklands (Malvinas) War. It is not entirely clear why hard-liners were able to prevail, or why they felt so attached to the orthodox economic program. Firmer conclusions will have to await the availability of more information.

cent in 1980 to 20 percent in 1983, by which time consumer price inflation was 343 percent.

The October 1983 elections led to a surprising victory for Radical candidate Raúl Alfonsín—the first time the Peronists had lost a presidential
election. Alfonsín picked up most of the right's votes, along with some of
the Peronists', apparently in the hope that he would overcome the political stalemate.[107] During his first year in office in 1984, Alfonsín tempo-
rized while trying to continue to satisfy all relevant interest groups. Real
wages were increased, the budget deficit stayed high, and the annualized
inflation rate passed 1,000 percent.

In early 1985, Alfonsín replaced his politically well-connected economics minister with a team of technocrats, who in June 1985 introduced the
Austral Plan, the first of the Latin American heterodox attempts to control inflation without economic contraction. The plan included a wage-
price freeze, de-indexation of the economy, a new currency, a tough
stance with creditors, and commitments to a realistic exchange rate, a
reduced budget deficit, and no inflationary financing.

The Austral Plan collapsed under the pressure of affected interest
groups. For a year and a half the plan nearly held together. The budget
deficit was significantly reduced, and 1986 inflation dropped below 100
percent for the first time in years. However, economic stagnation in 1985
and a decline in real wages led to insistent demands for relief, and eventually the Radical administration was unable to hold the line. By late
1987 the budget deficit was rising, inflation was surging past 300 percent,
and the Radicals were soundly defeated in midterm elections. Presidential
elections in October 1988 were won by Peronist Carlos Saúl Meném, who
took office early in December. Once in office Meném, like Pérez in Venezuela, confounded his populist past and rhetoric to introduce a series of
relatively orthodox stabilization and reform policies.

[107] On the election, see Torcuato Di Tella, "The October 1983 Elections in Argentina,"
Government and Opposition 19, no. 2 (1984): 188–92. On the Alfonsín admininstration,
see Roberto Bouzas and Saúl Keifman, "Las negociaciones financieras externas de la Argentina en el período 1982–1987," in *Entre la heterodoxia y el ajuste*, ed. Roberto Bouzas
(Buenos Aires: Grupo Editor Latinoamericano, 1988), 27–83; Roberto Frenkel and José
María Fanelli, "El Plan Austral: Un año y medio después," *El Trimestre Económico* 54
(September 1987): 55–117; Pablo Gerchunoff and Carlos Bozzalla, "Posibilidades y límites
de un programa de estabilización heterodoxo: El caso argentino," *El Trimestre Económico*
54 (September 1987): 119–54; Robert Kaufman, *The Politics of Debt in Argentina, Brazil,
and Mexico* (Berkeley: Institute of International Studies, 1988), 26–58; José Luis Machinea
and José María Fanelli, "El control de la hiperinflación: El caso del Plan Austral, 1985–
1987," and Alfredo Canavese and Guido Di Tella, "Estabilizar la inflación o evitar la hiperinflación? El caso del Plan Austral: 1985–1987," with following comments, in *Inflación
y estabilización: La experiencia de Israel, Argentina, Brasil, Bolivia y México*, ed. M. Bruno,
G. Di Tella, R. Dornbusch, and S. Fischer (Mexico City: Fondo de Cultura Económica,
1988), 141–256.

Summary and Evaluation of the Three Countries' Experiences

The responses of economic policy and political participation to financial expansion and crisis in Mexico, Venezuela, and Argentina share some similarities. In all three, to different degrees, borrowing helped fuel an increase in public investment programs, although Argentina also went through a major attempt at financial and commercial liberalization. All three experienced a substantial real appreciation of the exchange rate; all three saw massive capital flight. The crisis caused great economic distress in the three nations, to which their governments reacted with varying degrees of solicitude for the most heavily affected private firms. In Mexico, the government met most of the demands of the private sector but ignored most of those raised by labor; it staved off political opposition from the business community but drove much of the working class and peasantry into a populist opposition alliance. In Venezuela, COPEI failed to satisfy social demands and was voted out of power; subsequent AD governments cautiously mediated the demands of their supporters in business and labor. In Argentina, a neoliberal military administration (that had pushed aside a more pragmatic one) ignored a broad-based clamor for support and was swept aside in favor of elected civilian governments. The three countries can be compared more systematically on the two dependent-variable dimensions. First are patterns of economic policy during the borrowing period.

Cross-National Comparison

The degree of sectoral pressure on policymakers was, as expected, roughly correlated with the level of labor-management conflict. Argentina was characterized by the most class strife, and its policies were the most militantly neoliberal of the three, albeit not as militant as in Chile, where class conflict was much more bitter. Venezuela and Mexico had relatively cooperative labor-capital relations, and most economic-policy pressure was for subsidies and incentives to specific economic actors and sectors.

Evolution over Time

Mexican economic policy changed little during the borrowing period, except for the brief bout of macroeconomic instability and stabilization in 1975–1977. Throughout it maintained its heavily interventionist orientation. In Venezuela, policy shifted somewhat with the entry of the COPEI administration in 1979, which reduced the level of support for import-substituting industrialists and workers that were the principal AD base. Nonetheless, here too policy remained quite interventionist. In Argentina, the regime's market-oriented and liberalizing policies eventually gave rise to great business opposition, and this opposition gradually swamped the support the military's antilabor bias had garnered from the private sector. As class issues faded, sectoral pressures reasserted themselves.

Cross-Sectional Variation

In all three countries, the demand for and the supply of policy support was greatest from and to sectors characterized by large-scale, well-organized firms in sophisticated modern industries. This fits my expectation that firms with specific assets care most about sector-specific policies and that such firms are best able to exert pressure for preferred policies. Most support was provided by or through parastatals; some consisted of direct transfers from the central government. The sectors in question in Venezuela and Mexico were quite similar: import-substituting producers of capital goods, consumer durables, and some intermediate inputs; and large-scale agribusiness. In both nations the well-organized labor movement based in the modern industrial sectors also received support out of borrowed funds. In Argentina, the neoliberal team attempted largely to ignore sectoral pressures. Although it was not fully successful, divisions in the bureaucracy made access to government support less predictable: generally, firms and sectors with privileged ties with segments of the armed forces were best able to achieve their goals. Here too, however, the firms favored by policy did tend to be those in modern large-scale industry. In all three countries, policy was least favorable to small-scale producers of standardized products.

A second set of analytical issues concerns the political activities observed once the financial crisis began. There was a clear pattern of support for, and opposition to, existing governments on the basis of how successfully they met demands from major groups in the private sector. Those whose assets were endangered by the relative price changes brought on by the crisis mobilized to defend themselves. In Mexico the government responded favorably to the mobilization of affected private firms, but not to the labor movement: it lost labor backing to the new PRD, but maintained its private-sector support. In Venezuela the COPEI administration was incapable of satisfying both its liberally minded traditional supporters and the affected firms and labor, and lost the 1983 elections; AD successfully if only partially met the demands of *its* traditional labor and industry supporters. In Argentina, although the military under Viola responded favorably to private-sector pleas for support, when a hard-line countercoup brought in a team that ignored these pleas it was swept from office in favor of governments more sympathetic to both business and labor.

This chapter is not a full-fledged analysis of the Mexican, Venezuelan, and Argentine political economies in the 1970s and 1980s. It is merely an attempt to show that the analysis presented in more detailed fashion in my discussions of Brazil and Chile is applicable elsewhere and can help shed light on complex patterns of economic and political behavior.

Part III

IMPLICATIONS

7

Observations and Implications

THE CASES presented here and the framework within which they were presented give rise to observations of broader significance and implications for analysis and policy. What follows is a summary of the case studies, a review of how my approach compares with competitors and how it might be extended by including additional variables, and some theoretical and policy implications.

Summary of the Case Studies

The previous three chapters presented five national experiences with international financial markets. It would be redundant, perhaps impossible, to recapitulate the analysis of the chapters; here I simply refresh the reader's memory of the broad arguments and their application to the case studies.

The first argument concerns economic policies during the borrowing period. I argue that policies were a function of pressures from economic interest groups, and that these pressures increased with the preference intensity of the group, which followed from the specificity of the assets held by its members. The ability of the group to achieve its policy goals increased with its cohesiveness. High levels of class conflict tended to reduce the strength and impact of demands from sectoral groups. In "normal" times—the absence of major class-based conflict over the division of national income between wages and profits—policy benefited cohesive sectors with more specific assets. Class conflict overrode sectoral pressures, and in the Latin American context were associated with liberal economic policies.

The second argument concerns political patterns. It begins with the above notions of economic-policy pressures brought to bear on governments, and goes on to discuss their political implications. The argument is that economic interest groups exerted political pressure on government in line with their material interests; if these pressures did not meet with success, the groups attempted to change the government; if these attempts were unsuccessful, the groups attempted to change the regime.

The five cases illustrate these points and the analytical approach. In

Brazil, Mexico, and Venezuela, in the absence of significant class conflict, the principal beneficiaries of policy during borrowing were large-scale industries with very specific assets: capital goods, consumer durables, and similar sectors. Small-scale competitive sectors benefited little or not at all. In Chile and Argentina, class conflict tended to override sectoral demands, more in the former than in the latter. The result was a market orientation that largely eschewed sectoral subsidies and incentives. The reforms were carried through in Chile, but in Argentina (where class conflict was less severe) they were eventually swamped by resurgent sectoral pressures.

As for politics, as expected, the principal protests arose from those whose assets were most endangered by relative price changes after 1981. This included heavily indebted firms, those dependent on public subsidies and incentives or parastatal orders, government employees, and organized labor.

The political outcome was a function of the character of private-sector demands and the private-sector reaction to the government's response to these demands. In Chile, business protest was muted by fear about labor, and although some business demands were met the regime largely ignored them with little difficulty; demands by the labor movement were dismissed or repressed. In Mexico, business protests were strong and insistent, and the government met most of them. However, labor demands were largely disregarded, and much of labor defected to a new party. In Venezuela, COPEI's inability to satisfy industrial and labor constituencies lost it the 1983 elections; successive AD administrations were more responsive to these demands. The Brazilian and Argentine military regimes tried to ignore sectoral pressures; this led business groups to defect to the opposition, and ultimately to support regime change (democratization).

The analysis presented here does not, of course, do justice to the complexity of the experiences presented in the case studies. However, it does help organize the material in ways amenable to systematic discussion and evaluation. It also suggests general theoretical, analytical, and policy conclusions drawn from the political economy of the international financial experience of Latin American in the 1970s and 1980s.

Competing Explanations

There was no pretense here of presenting a comprehensive confrontation between my analytical framework and that of other schools of thought, for reasons spelled out in the introduction. However, it is worth discussing whether other approaches appear to out-perform my argument. The following is a sketch of how contending explanations of Latin American economics and politics rise to the test of the 1970s and 1980s. It must be reiterated that this evaluation is my own extrapolation from the existing theoretical positions, as I am unaware of systematic attempts by partisans of the positions to explain Latin American economic policies and politics in the period in question.

One set of competing explanations, "structural" in nature, appear disconfirmed almost from the start. The two best-known such approaches posit a direct relationship between the socioeconomic structure of, or faced by, a developing country and its subsequent development path. One, modernization theory, focuses on domestic LDC social structure; another, dependency theory, focuses on the structure of international capitalism. Inasmuch as the five countries examined here began with similar domestic structures and positions in the international economy, but took very different economic and political paths, these two approaches are unsatisfactory explanations of their recent histories.[1]

In the modernization view, prevalent in the 1950s, economic and political development grow out of broader changes in the domestic social structure. Proponents emphasized that economic growth depended on the population adopting modern attitudes toward economic activity. W. W. Rostow wrote of "propensities" to seek material advance, consume, or have children, which expressed "the extent to which the actual economic decisions of a society deviate from those which would obtain if 'economic' motives alone were operative" and which largely determined the ability of society to accumulate capital and grow.[2] Where the prerequisites were lacking, the demonstration effect of foreign success might help dissolve premodern attitudes, and foreign aid, technology, and capital might point societies in the direction of modernization. But the focus was on the preexisting domestic social order; what economic success it experienced was due to its own adaptability to the demands of modernization.

Just as economic development required a modern mind-set, so did political democracy. The obstacles to democratic rule were hierarchical authority relations based on family, clan, or tribe that infused premodern societies. Here, much of the impetus for change came from the modernizing impact of economic growth. Economic growth drew peasants out of

---

[1] Rather than refer the reader to the enormous literature from the two schools, a couple of good surveys can be recommended: Richard A. Higgott, *Political Development Theory: The Contemporary Debate* (London: Croom Helm, 1983); J. Samuel Valenzuela and Arturo Valenzuela, "Modernization and Dependency: Alternative Perspectives on the Study of Latin American Underdevelopment," *Comparative Politics* 10, no. 4 (July 1978): 535–57.

[2] W. W. Rostow, *The Process of Economic Growth* (New York: W. W. Norton and Company, 1952), 36. Other important statements of the approach were Simon Kuznets, *Economic Growth and Structure* (New York: Norton, 1965), and W. W. Rostow, *The Stages of Economic Growth* (Cambridge: Cambridge University Press, 1960).

dependent relationships with landed elites, brought people together in urban settings, introduced them to modern technologies, and created a crucial force for democracy, the middle class. Industrialization, education, urbanization, and agricultural modernization would lay the bases for modern political systems and liberal democracy.[3]

It is difficult to provide a convincing modernization-based explanation of the Latin American experience between 1965 and 1985. Despite similar social structures, the five countries examined here went in strikingly different political and economic directions. Indeed, the predictive and explanatory weaknesses of modernization theories were noted almost immediately: some very modern social systems, such as Argentina, were not doing well economically or politically.

Dependency theory emerged in the 1960s largely as an alternative to modernization. Dependency, whose simpler variants eventually folded into "world systems theory," argued that both economic underdevelopment and political authoritarianism were a function of the subordinate position of developing countries in world capitalism. The pattern of integration of Africa, Asia, and Latin America into the world economy did not allow them to accumulate the capital necessary for development. At the same time, the stranglehold exercised on their political systems by foreign and domestic elites precluded democracy.

The economic arguments of dependency theory ascribed the difficulties of development to structural characteristics of international capitalism.[4] Dependency theorists claimed that the developed "core" exploited the underdeveloped "periphery." In this view, international markets were structurally biased against developing countries, generally by way of declining terms of trade for their products. External dependency interacted with domestic barriers to development, especially local classes allied with foreign capitalists. In this way, the country's dependent position in the international division of labor was replicated within its borders, in ways that reinforced this position.

Dependency implied that the international position of developing countries made democracy nearly impossible.[5] The most common view

[3] Higgott summarizes the argument well. One particularly influential statement was Seymour Martin Lipset, "Some Social Requisites of Democracy," *American Political Science Review* 52, no. 1 (March 1959): 69–105. See also Harry Eckstein's appendix to his *Division and Cohesion in Democracy* (Princeton: Princeton University Press, 1966), 225–88.

[4] A seminal statement was Paul Baran, *The Political Economy of Growth* (New York: Monthly Review Press, 1957); an application to Latin America was André Gunder Frank, *Capitalism and Underdevelopment in Latin America* (New York: Monthly Review Press, 1967). Samir Amin, *Unequal Development* (New York: Monthly Review Press, 1976), was also influential.

[5] Perhaps the most extreme view along these lines was Rui Mauro Marini, *Subdesarrollo y revolución* (Mexico City: Siglo Veintiuno Editores, 1969). See also, for example, Rodolfo Stavenhagen, "The Future of Latin America: Between Underdevelopment and Revolution,"

was that structural dependence of LDCs on external capital and markets meant that capital accumulation required low wages, which precluded inclusion of the working class in politics. Authoritarianism enforced the position of subordinate classes within the subordinate country, and maintained the rule of local groups who supported the country's dependent position.

The wide variety of economic and political trajectories described in this book give no support to the simple dependency view. Since the 1960s, rates of economic growth in Latin America have diverged tremendously, as have national experiences with political democracy. If the net is cast wider, especially to East Asia, variation in both economic development and democracy becomes even greater, and it seems eminently possible that many LDCs may "graduate" to development.[6]

Two prominent theories grew out of dissatisfaction with simple modernization and dependency views. One, advanced by Guillermo O'Donnell, is generally known as the bureaucratic authoritarian approach.[7] O'Donnell contended that dependent societies undergoing import-substituting industrialization reached a point at which working-class demands conflicted with the needs of the developmental model. Specifically, continued development demanded a "deepening" of import substitution, and this deepening was not compatible with a democratic system in which labor might obstruct the requirements of capital accumulation. At this point, when the contradictions of import substitution caused balance of payments crises that could not be surmounted without repressing labor, technocratic authoritarian regimes would be called upon to set the development model back on course. This was perhaps the most explicit challenge to modernization, for O'Donnell argued that economic growth, far from conducing to LDC democracy, made democracy untenable.[8]

Latin American Perspectives 1, no. 1 (Spring 1974): 124–49; and James Petras, *Politics and Social Forces in Chilean Development* (Berkeley: University of California Press, 1969). Fernando Henrique Cardoso and Enzo Faletto, *Dependency and Development in Latin America* (Berkeley: University of California Press, 1978), summarizes both economic and political analyses; although their position is less extreme and deterministic than that of many others, it is unclear whether they are left with any systematic causal explanations.

[6] On East Asia and for a comparative perspective, see Stephan Haggard, *Pathways from the Periphery: The Politics of Growth in the Newly Industrializing Countries* (Ithaca: Cornell University Press, 1990).

[7] Guillermo O'Donnell, *Modernization and Bureaucratic Authoritarianism* (Berkeley: Institute of International Studies, 1973). More recent evaluations and discussions of the approach are in David Collier, ed., *The New Authoritarianism in Latin America* (Princeton: Princeton University Press, 1979); William Canak, "The Peripheral State Debate," *Latin American Research Review* 19, no. 1 (1984): 3–36; and Karen Remmer and Gilbert Merkx, "Bureaucratic-Authoritarianism Revisited," *Latin America Research Review* 22, no. 2 (1987): 3–40, with the subsequent reply by O'Donnell, 41–50.

[8] In this sense there was a clear connection between the work of O'Donnell and that of

The bureaucratic authoritarian approach implied that in the context of Latin America's semi-industrial societies, balance-of-payments crises led to a collapse of democracy and its replacement by authoritarian regimes that deepened import substitution. These expectations are confounded by the cases examined here[9] at every turn. The authoritarian regimes in Chile and Argentina—both often identified as the result of the "crisis of easy import substitution"—pursued policies resolutely opposed to deepening import substitution. Of the three countries in our sample that did try deepening, only one could uncontroversially be categorized as bureaucratic authoritarian.[10] And the severe balance of payments crisis of the 1980s did not lead to a collapse of democracy in Mexico and Venezuela, but rather to a collapse of authoritarianism in Brazil and Argentina.

Another second-generation school is "dependent development." This view accepts the possibility of economic development in some of the Third World and ascribes such successes to autonomous local elites and, most important, a state able to counter the power of international capitalism.[11] A summary by Peter Evans asserts that even where industrial development is well under way, "an active state apparatus [is] still required to counteract the tendency of international capital to centralize newer, higher-return kinds of industrial activity in the core. . . . a more active and entrepreneurial state [is] essential for successful capital accumulation at the local level." As for politics, Evans cautioned that dependent development implied "neither political democracy nor economic equality, but instead authoritarian rule and the highest levels of income inequality in the world."[12] This perspective borrows from dependency, from bureaucratic authoritarianism, and from the state-centered view of politics.[13]

Samuel Huntington, *Political Order in Changing Societies* (New Haven: Yale University Press, 1968).

[9] Not to speak of those examined elsewhere. See especially José Serra, "Three Mistaken Theses Regarding the Connection Between Industrialization and Authoritarian Regimes," in *The New Authoritarianism in Latin America*, 99–163.

[10] Many analysts argue that Mexico was authoritarian in the period; see José Luis Reyna and Richard S. Weinert, eds., *Authoritarianism in Mexico* (Philadelphia: ISHI, 1977).

[11] Two seminal statements were Fernando Henrique Cardoso, "Associated-Dependent Development: Theoretical and Practical Implications," in *Authoritarian Brazil*, ed. Alfred Stepan (New Haven: Yale University Press, 1973); and Peter Evans, *Dependent Development: The Alliance of Multinational, State, and Local Capital in Brazil* (Princeton: Princeton University Press, 1979).

[12] Peter Evans, "Class, State, and Dependence in East Asia: Lessons for Latin Americanists," in *The Political Economy of the New Asian Industrialism*, ed. Frederic Deyo (Ithaca: Cornell University Press, 1987), 205, 221.

[13] On the last, see Eric Nordlinger, "Taking the State Seriously," in *Understanding Political Development*, ed. Myron Weiner and Samuel P. Huntington (Boston: Little, Brown and Company, 1987), 353–90. It might be noted that many in the dependent development tra-

The core dependent-development notion is that economic growth demands autonomous state intervention to break the domination of foreign capital. This study challenges the central tenets of dependent development on two fronts. First, economic success does not appear related to state intervention in the economy—Chile grew rapidly with the most laissez-faire government in the region, and much of the economic intervention in Mexico, Brazil, and Venezuela produced questionable results. Second, state intervention in the economy was closely related to domestic political pressures. In other words, growth does not appear correlated with state intervention in the economy, nor does state intervention appear particularly autonomous.

These approaches share several intellectual characteristics. They assert a simple relationship between starting level of development and subsequent economic and political outcomes. They rely for the explanation on structural characteristics of the domestic and/or international orders. And they do not have explicit microfoundations for their causal arguments. Inasmuch as they expect similar results from countries at similar levels of development, they fail the recent Latin American test, where results diverged greatly. And expectations that can be extrapolated from their broad structural arguments and applied to the period discussed in this book appear not to be born out by the facts. Of course, adepts of these schools, and others, will undoubtedly be able to present more convincing defenses, but I conclude that these approaches underperform my own.[14]

Potentially Complementary Variables

This book makes three principal analytical claims, in descending order of generality. First, I claim that analytical tools associated with modern po-

dition regard the approach to be a heuristic device. If it does not give rise to causal propositions, it is not in competition with modern political economy. However, practitioners clearly have more direct cause-and-effect notions in their minds, even if they are not clearly stated in their studies.

[14] Some structuralists might aver that the time period in question is too short to serve as a true test of broad trends. Yet a quick look at a longer sweep seems to help little, and in any case it is hard to see how a causal argument could be always wrong in the short run but right in the long run.

There are other schools of thought, but they do not appear to present clear causal arguments. One interesting view is what Richard Sklar calls postimperialism, which analyzes the process of transnational class formation in the developing world. Yet the approach does not include predictive propositions about the economic and political outcomes of interest here. A collection of essays on the theme is in David Becker et al., *Postimperialism: International Capitalism and Development in the Late Twentieth Century* (Boulder, Colo.: Lynne Rienner Publishers, 1987).

litical economy, developed and applied in very different settings, can usefully be applied to the study of Latin America. Second, I claim that within this approach the role of economic interest groups is central. Third, I claim that the level of influence on policies and politics of an economic actor is primarily a function of the specificity of the actor's assets, the measure I use to subsume preference intensities associated with high entry barriers, costly exit, and little diversification. It is certainly possible to accept only some of these claims. Many analysts may well agree with the first, but not with the second and third; they may, in other words, question the explanatory power of economic interests or of the types of economic interests described here.

Chapter 1, indeed, made clear that my analytical framework did not attempt to include all factors of explanatory importance, and I presented a few variables that might be incorporated into a more complete explanation. It is worth returning to these variables to see what the cases suggest. In my view, these factors may well be complementary to my approach, in that they could be—and often are—incorporated into a modern political economy analysis in which economic interest remained central.

International Economic Conditions

Although the five-country comparison came close to holding external financial factors constant, nonfinancial conditions varied. The most obvious was the evolution of the countries' terms of trade. Mexico and Venezuela are oil exporters; Brazil and Chile are dependent on oil imports; Chile is heavily reliant on copper exports. The oil shocks of 1974 and 1979 had different effects on the importers than on the exporters. Both oil exporters exhibited classic Dutch disease symptoms after 1979; Brazil and Chile had to adjust sharply to both oil price increases.

There are other differences among the international position of the five countries. Mexico's geographical proximity to the United States affected its policy options, both in economic terms and inasmuch as geopolitical considerations influenced U.S. government attitudes toward Mexican debt relief. As a paragon of liberalism, Chile may have been favored by multilateral lending institutions in the 1980s, thus expanding its options. Allowance must certainly be made for variation in the relative price changes and policy options confronting different countries. Nothing in modern political economy requires that countries be economically identical for analytical predictions to hold.

Institutions

A great deal of work within modern political economy has been devoted to understanding the effects of institutions on economic and political outcomes. My model was essentially free of institutions, but a full explanation of Latin American policy and politics requires their incorporation.

The first obvious comment is that institutions mediated economic interest group pressures on policymakers. The military dictatorships tended to be less open to group demands than the two electoral democracies, Mexico and Venezuela. This was especially true in Chile and Argentina, and many observers believe that the regimes' divorce from their societies made possible some of their economic policy mistakes.

The second observation has to do with the effects of political institutions during the financial crisis. The authoritarian regimes appeared less able to respond flexibly to changed international and domestic conditions than the two democratic regimes. Although the dictatorships fulfilled some groups' wishes—especially with the bailout of foreign-currency debtors—segments of the elites, along with most of the working and middle classes, remained fundamentally dissatisfied. In Chile, mass protest had limited impact on the ability of the dictatorship to rule, in large part because the business community did not join in; in the long run, however, Pinochet's unresponsiveness to protest undoubtedly contributed to his defeat at the polls long after the crisis had passed.

In Argentina and Brazil, military regimes seemed incapable of managing the plethora of demands brought down upon them by the crisis; halting initial attempts in Argentina were reversed by retrograde military groups, and the Brazilian regime fumbled from one set of unpopular policies to another. Eventually, the unresponsiveness of both dictatorships to demands engendered by crisis contributed decisively to their unpopularity with both elites and masses, and to their replacement by civilian rule. The military governments seemed singularly rigid in handling the political fallout of the crisis, and this rigidity drove major social groups to demand the removal of the military from power.

The existence of established channels for social pressures in Mexico and Venezuela appears to have increased the efficiency with which demands were addressed, and to have avoided much political instability. In Venezuela, an organized political party was available to serve as conduit for dissatisfaction and an established democracy provided the opportunity for peaceful change via the ballot box. The result was an electoral landslide for the opposition and a new government that changed policy rapidly. In Mexico, where the PRI dominated a quasi-democratic system, the target of dissatisfaction was the dominant party itself. Some protests were addressed satisfactorily by the PRI; others were not, and protestors left the ruling party to take advantage of the (imperfect) electoral opportunities afforded by the system. In other words, where institutionalized means existed for groups to defend their interests, these means were used; in electoral systems, popular and elite dissatisfaction was channeled through existing or newly formed parties.

Whatever the implications for the relative efficiency of democracy and dictatorship, it seems clear that political institutions matter for both policy and politics. This conclusion is mirrored in a wealth of studies in the modern political economy of institutions.[15] The application of this work to the study of developing societies can only be applauded.

Bureaucratic and Political Interests

Apart from the influence of political institutions on other social groups, the inhabitants of these institutions have interests of their own. Countries vary as to the importance of independent bureaucratic interests, and this variation was observed in the five cases. For example, Chile's military was quite cohesive, while Argentina's had a history of factionalism and penetration by society. My analysis looked primarily at differences among the socioeconomic groups that exerted political pressure on the military. However, some of the response may have had to do with the structure of the two military establishments themselves, their historically evolved position in bureaucratic hierarchies, or the interests of the generals involved.

The same can be said about other political or bureaucratic interests. Venezuela and Mexico had large political classes with support networks in the population based on government patronage. Some government spending in these countries undoubtedly went to what in the United States would be considered "pork barrel" projects, motivated in part by the desire of politicians to ensure reelection. Similar processes affected Brazilian policy as well, probably less strongly. While my interpretation focused on pressures from outside the bureaucracy, a full explanation would take into account the interests of bureaucrats, politicians, and military officials themselves.

[15] A general statement is Douglass North, *Institutions, Institutional Change and Economic Performance* (Cambridge: Cambridge University Press, 1990). A more specific application, relevant to the issues addressed in this study, has to do with the effects of policy institutions on the making of economic policy, especially monetary policy. One survey is Keith Blackburn and Michael Christensen, "Monetary Policy and Policy Credibility: Theories and Evidence," *Journal of Economic Literature* 27, no. 1 (March 1990): 1–45; an application is Francesco Giavazzi and Marco Pagano, "The Advantage of Tying One's Hands: EMS Discipline and Central Bank Credibility," *European Economic Review* 32, no. 5 (June 1988): 1055–82.

Ideology

In the countries examined, the strongest case for the independent explanatory effect of ideas on policy is the role of the monetary approach to the balance of payments ("global monetarism") in Chile and Argentina. The popularity of the monetary approach in conservative circles in the United States, and the American training of many economists from these countries (viz., the Chicago boys), probably predisposed the regimes toward "global monetarist" policies. Of course, ideological variables alone do not explain why the dictatorships were so enthralled by the monetary approach, but they may provide part of the explanation for specifics of conservative economic management under the Chilean and Argentine dictatorships.[16]

Strategic Interaction

Fascinating analytical questions are raised by the introduction of strategic interaction into politics.[17] Perhaps the most striking example from the cases is the very different evolution of the Venezuelan and Argentine political systems. Since at least the 1920s, both countries have had important primary export sectors whose interests clashed with those of urban and industrial sectors. In Venezuela, this conflict played itself out with the two camps tending to migrate toward a median position, while in Argentina the two camps tended to become more and more polarized over time. A number of hypotheses to explain this variation might be advanced, including the nonstrategic one that the difference is due to the nature of the exportable resource,[18] but one important set of potential explanations would look at the strategic interaction of the parties to the disputes.

Omnipotence

My interpretation of Latin American politics and economic policies took the starting point as given by history, without trying to explain it. The

[16] For an ideas-based interpretation of North American economic policies, see Judith Goldstein, "Ideas, Institutions, and American Trade," *International Organization* 42, no. 1 (Winter 1988): 179–217, and Judith Goldstein, *Ideas, Interests, and American Trade Policy* (Ithaca: Cornell University Press, forthcoming).

[17] Interesting applications to comparative politics are in George Tsebelis, *Nested Games* (Berkeley: University of California Press, 1990).

[18] The idea here might be that where, as in Venezuela, the resource rents can easily be appropriated by the government, the resource sector is forced to compromise; while where, as in Argentina, the resource rents can more readily be protected from government appropriation, the resource sector can afford to be more intransigent.

types and characteristics of the economic interests I examined were not explained, only described. Any theory that explained asset specificity and internal organization, along with policy demands and supplies, would be superior to the approach presented here. So too would any theory that explained *both* the level of class conflict *and* the market orientation of policy.

There is no question that my analysis did not capture the full complexity of the social phenomena it examined. The five societies have long histories; they are intricate combinations of socioeconomic, political, cultural, and other institutions. To understand why Latin America had the industrial structure it had at the onset of foreign borrowing requires an understanding of economic policies adopted after World War II. To understand these policies requires a look at the experiences of the 1930s and 1940s, as well as the predepression character of the countries' political economies. The predepression political economies themselves grew out of historically specific patterns of interaction with the international economy; and so on back to the European conquest and beyond. By the same token, isolated analysis of the political economy of borrowing cannot capture the role of color and region in Brazil, of immigrants in Argentina, of indigenous populations in Mexico. History matters, and societies are more complicated than my simple model.

On all these dimensions, I can only welcome contributions that incorporate the variables omitted here. I hope that these variables are included in the spirit of modern political economy, that is with systematic regard for microfoundations, and with logical deduction of their implications. Nevertheless, the necessarily incomplete nature of this study is no reason to ignore its implications for theory and policy.

Implications

The attempt to integrate political and economic factors to explain political and economic outcomes provides insights that a strictly political, or strictly economic, study might not. Similarly, the detailed comparison of five nations provides more breadth than a study of a single country and more depth than a multicountry statistical survey. Most of the insights have to do with the interrelation of politics, policies, and economics; some have to do with the simple effects of one on the other.

Sources of Economic Outcomes

Perhaps the single clearest message of the five cases is that economic policy matters deeply as a determinant of the general contours and specific details of economic performance. Certainly international market conditions were of great importance to all five countries, both during the financial upswing and the crisis. However, the national economic outcomes that grew out of these conditions varied widely, and this variation was largely due to patterns of economic policy.

The economic response to capital flows diverged enormously, due primarily to divergent policies. During the borrowing period, overall economic performance ranged from abysmal in Argentina to excellent in Brazil, while less aggregate measures were just as varied. Industry grew rapidly in Brazil, Mexico, and Venezuela, but stagnated in Argentina and Chile. Public spending patterns ranged from exorbitant in Venezuela to conservative in Chile. The cases highlighted how economic policies affected outcomes.

Sources of Economic Policies

Because policy had a major impact on performance, the next challenge is to explain economic policy. Many analysts ascribe policies to the state of technical doctrine or knowledge; to ideology; or to inertia. These may play a part, but the case studies show that political pressures were ubiquitous and extremely important constraints on policy.

In most instances, socioeconomic actors were aware of their interests and strove to defend and promote them, and policymakers took account of these efforts. Even where issues seemed arcane, such as the nominal exchange rate or debt guarantees, groups mobilized to affect policy. Even where rulers attempted explicitly to eliminate or ignore self-interested lobbying, as in Chile, such lobbying continued and could affect policy.

The existence of interest-group pressures on policymakers did not mean that all such pressures were successful, and a full explanation of policy would include the variables discussed above. However, the cases indicate that the demand-side factors discussed in chapter 1—asset specificity, concentration, intrasectoral cooperation—were good predictors of which sectors would be favored by policy, and of whether policy would favor sectoral subsidies and incentives over a market orientation.

The Sources of Political Pressures

A related issue has to do with the determinants of the sorts and strengths of political pressures brought to bear on economic policymakers. The cases tend to support my contention that most such pressures were distributional in character, whatever rhetoric was used to market them. Calls to defend the currency, presented as defense of national honor, often came from firms with dollar liabilities. Appeals for the government to stave off financial collapse, put forth as protection for depositors, were often motivated by the desire of bankers or debtors to get the public sector to assume their obligations. Even so general a position as support for more market-oriented policies, in the context of Latin America, often masked a desire to eviscerate the labor movement.

The political pressures on economic policymakers reflected attempts by owners of human or physical capital to protect their assets—factories, skills, financial networks. The desire to mobilize to protect these assets was largely a function of how specific they were, how difficult movement was into or out of the sector; the ability to mobilize was largely a function of their organization and concentration.

Inasmuch as at least some assets will be specific and some sectors organized for the foreseeable future and in foreseeable circumstances, distributional pressures on economic policy will continue. Even where policy attempted to discourage rent-seeking interests, as in Chile, such interests developed in the form of enormous and entrenched *grupos*. Such patterns involve enduring characteristics of even the most freewheeling of economies.

Theories of Economic Development

The different patterns of development in the five cases reinforce the view that these patterns are primarily due to domestic characteristics of the countries in question. They also reinforce the view that political economy, rather than just politics or economics, is crucial to understanding the development process.

Approaches that posit a relationship between position in the "international division of labor" and potential for economic growth are resoundingly rejected by the five-country comparison. After the 1970s and 1980s, it will be difficult to argue that "peripheral" countries cannot develop economically, or that a strong state is a necessary condition for growth. Simplistic views that look only at factor endowments to explain different patterns of growth also jibe poorly with the cases. Latin American countries' modern production structures have rarely been in line with comparative advantage; only post-1975 Chile may come close. For whatever reason, other nations (and perhaps Chile as well) are far away from the optimal production structure in neoclassical terms. Like international position, endowments of land, labor, capital, and other factors of production affect, but do not determine, patterns of economic development.

Since international position and natural endowments cannot explain intercountry variation in economic outcomes, theory must turn to the domestic level and include economic and political variables. The cases underline the need for a domestic political economy of development; for analysis that looks at the interaction of external conditions with national sociopolitical and economic factors. Certainly international economic trends affect the real or potential return to domestic factors of production, but these factors largely belong to private owners who act in politics as well as the market to increase their returns. In this context, interest groups have a powerful impact on the use to which each nation puts its resource endowments.

An example of contemporary interest is the process of liberalization in many developing countries. This study implies political-economy reasons for the trend, in contradistinction to the commonly held idea that liberalization is either the result of external political pressure or domestic technocratic ascendancy. My approach suggests that several interactive elements encouraged trade liberalization, privatization, and other market-oriented trends in LDC economic policy.

The first consideration is the reduction in external resources available to LDC public sectors. Just as increased loan supply gave governments an incentive to expand their role in the economy, the drying up of foreign loans constrained them to reduce their economic activities. In this sense the reduction of budget deficits throughout the developing world is a predictable response to the disappearance of inexpensive foreign finance.

Another potential factor that modern political economy implies may have led toward economic liberalization is sectoral political demands from firms and individuals that stood to gain from more liberal policies. Real currency depreciation and domestic stagnation drove many Latin American producers to search for overseas markets. The resulting exporting interests tended to exert antiprotectionist pressures on policy, in the developing world as elsewhere; the same was true of the accumulation of overseas assets by LDC nationals.[19]

A final factor in liberalization is a decline in sectoral demands. In the Latin American cases, class conflict tended to reduce sectoral pressures on policymakers in favor of demands for a hospitable investment climate more generally. Similar factors elsewhere might have exerted a similar influence. Class conflict might not be the only such consideration; whatever served to reduce sectoral demands could tend to reduce sectoral government intervention in the economy.

My application of modern political economy thus suggests at least three causes of economic liberalization. A reduction in the supply of re-

[19] Helen Milner, *Resisting Protection: Global Industries and the Politics of International Trade* (Princeton: Princeton University Press, 1988), and I. M. Destler and John S. Odell, *Anti-Protection: Changing Forces in United States Trade Politics* (Washington, D.C.: Institute for International Economics, 1987), discuss such factors in a developed-country context.

sources to the government made intervention more difficult and liberalization more desirable. A reduction in the demand for sectoral policies made them less politically appealing. An increase in the preference intensity or political influence of proliberalization groups made liberalization more politically attractive to policymakers. These hypotheses, and others, could easily be put to the test with evidence from the wave of liberalizations sweeping the developing world.

Economic development, then, is not the simple outgrowth of position in the international economy, resource endowments, or technocratic commitment to the "right" policies. The complex interaction of domestic socioeconomic and political trends determines how each nation will respond to the international economic environment, and how successful that response will be.

Implications for Economic Policy

Just as the cases highlight the importance of integrating economic and political analysis to understand outcomes, they reinforce the view that effective policy can only be designed and implemented if such factors are considered. The failure to recognize the potential political sources of, or responses to, economic policies can lead to perverse results.

For example, purely economic analysis would be hard put to understand why in the early 1980s Venezuelan and Argentine private agents simultaneously borrowed and deposited dollars abroad, and policymakers might be forgiven for discounting this possibility. However, a rounded analysis would point to the political importance of these private actors, and their ability to force their respective governments to subsidize debt-service payments in the event of a crisis. In other words, Venezuelan and Argentine investors were not just betting that their currencies would be devalued, they were also betting that they would be politically able to force the government to assume or subsidize whatever debts they incurred. They were right; after the peso and bolívar were devalued, dollar debtors were able to purchase dollars at subsidized rates, even though many of them had used their borrowings to open bank accounts abroad.

Prospective policymakers ignore at their peril the possibility that powerful socioeconomic actors will use political means to circumvent or profit from policies intended to be distributionally neutral. An example is infant-industry tariffs, in which new industries are given protection which may be justified on broad national grounds. Once protection is in place, the industries lobby to ensure that it is never removed, even when it serves only to enrich the protected firms. It is not commonly appreciated how wide is the range of policies that appear to be general but whose effects are subject to self-seeking political manipulation, from the exchange rate to deposit insurance. Naive as policy analysts or advisers may be, the people of Latin America are well aware that the experiences of the 1970s and 1980s had major distributional consequences.

The many examples presented in this study of the effects of political pressure on economic policy, and the effects of policy on income distribution, should sound a cautionary note to those with uncomplicated ideas about the relationship between "correct" policies and desired outcomes. Policies that appear appropriate to observers may have unobserved implications or effects, and if the policies are cover for plunder they are unlikely to have the effect observers anticipate. Put another way, in both economic and political realms there is great potential for powerful interests to write or bend the rules to their advantage.

Neither simple laissez faire nor undifferentiated state intervention are, therefore, likely to achieve the goals of their academic supporters. No matter how thoroughly market-oriented policies attempt to "level the playing field," the political and economic system has not been devised that can keep powerful interests from getting at least some of what they want. As in Chile, even a very level playing field allowed powerful groups to divert resources to themselves, to the detriment of others, on grounds other than social efficiency or welfare. By the same token, even a developmental state can be penetrated by self-seeking groups and used to channel subsidies from the politically weak toward the politically strong. Laissez-faire and statist prescriptions alike are informed by a naive belief in the separability of economics and politics; neither theory nor evidence supports such notions.

These considerations can be extended to evaluate policy proposals. For example, while increasing exports would help Latin America, export-promoting policies can be distorted by self-seeking groups. Export credits can degenerate into credit subsidies to powerful firms; preferential exchange rates for exports can be manipulated by transfer pricing or misinvoicing. Political economy is not only of value as an analytical tool; it also has something to say to the policymaker.

While the cases speak eloquently to the damage bad policies can wreak, they also indicate how destructive policy uncertainty can be in and of itself. Instability forces economic agents to shorten their time horizons, for example, to forego investments that might be swamped by a policy shift and to look instead for liquid short-term assets that do not contribute to society's productive capacity—especially if they are held abroad. Almost any set of consistent policies would have been an improvement over the unpredictability of Argentine economic policy after 1960. This instability has been a major contributor to the low savings rate, low investment coefficient, and great financial insecurity that have helped reduce Argentina from one of the world's wealthiest nations to just another LDC. By the same token, while economists are quick to point out inefficiencies in the economic policies pursued by Mexico in the 1960s and 1970s, social stability and policy predictability allowed Mexican economic agents to take the long view.

No magic formulas for economic development emerge from the cases, although several tensions can be identified. One such tension is between policies to encourage the efficient use of the economic structure in place, and policies that encourage a shift of resources out of activities for which the country as a whole is ill-suited. Certainly it is good to have policies that reward the efficient use of existing productive capacity, but the efficient use of resources at the level of the firm or industry may not represent the best use of the resources of society as a whole. For example, a proliferation of efficiently run capital-intensive manufacturing firms can still lead to an enormous waste of human resources in the form of involuntarily unemployed or underemployed labor. On the other hand, radical reforms to the economy can cause dislocations that themselves involve lost income—as the vagaries of the Chilean reform program illustrate.

Along similar lines, there may be conflict between short-term political stability, on the one hand, and policies to promote efficiency, on the other. Trade liberalization, for example, may increase economic efficiency, but if it leads to sociopolitical unrest that makes it impossible to conduct economic policy, the costs may outweigh the benefits. Inasmuch as policy and political predictability are important to development, and inasmuch as structural reforms lead to unrest, there may be tension between the two.

Two sets of trade-offs suggest themselves: between using the existing production structure more efficiently and encouraging the development of a more socially efficient production structure; and between increasing efficiency and pursuing redistributive policies necessary to maintain political and policy stability. Both of these involve sacrifices by private actors that presumably will be counterbalanced by eventual rewards, but short time horizons can make this trade-off politically very difficult. Managing potential conflicts between social stability and improved policies may depend on a mechanism with which bargains can be struck and enforced among groups that will be harmed or helped by such policies, in which winners can be taxed and losers compensated without contravening the policies but without causing social turmoil. Such a mechanism depends fundamentally on political behavior, to which we now turn.

The Sources of Political Activity

Shifting to political analysis, the cases speak eloquently of the effects of economic conditions, socioeconomic interests, and political institutions, on political outcomes ranging from election results to democratization. The crisis had a uniformly unsettling impact on political activity in the region but, contrary to the expectation of many theoretical currents, economic and political crisis did not necessarily lead to or exacerbate authoritarian tendencies.

Virtually everywhere, higher interest rates and reduced loan supply limited governments' abilities to respond to social demands, and drove major groups into oppositional activity. The content of political behavior was a function of the interests in question: workers denounced real wage cuts, government employees opposed public austerity, subsidized sectors protested reduced subsidies, firms with foreign-currency debts demanded cheap foreign exchange. The massive relative price changes wrought by the crisis provoked massive political response.

How political reaction to the debt crisis worked its way through various political systems was in important measures a function of the political institutions—parties, coalitions, bureaucracies, leaderships—faced by sociopolitical actors. The discussion above has already indicated some potential implications for the study of politics in the developing world.

The cases suggest no determinate relationship between economics and politics. They do nonetheless suggest that economic conditions have powerful effects on political activity; and that socioeconomic actors weigh their political options as they seek to protect their interests. Specifically, Latin American social groups, both elite and popular, looked first to the existing institutional structures for alternatives to the suffering born of crisis; if the institutions were unresponsive they weighed the possibilities of institutional change.

Theories of Political Development

This study provides mostly negative inputs for theories of LDC politics. It rejects structural hypotheses about democracy and authoritarianism, but does not suggest equally uncomplicated alternatives.

No simple relationship existed between economic growth and political openness, between position in the international political hierarchy and domestic repression, or between economic crisis and bureaucratic authoritarianism. Where democratization took place it was largely because dissatisfaction with the economic situation—especially business dissatisfaction—was not addressed satisfactorily by military regimes, causing demands to escalate from calls for policy change to calls for regime change. Democracy did not grow out of structural conditions faced by nations or groups, but rather out of the contingent interaction of groups in a political arena in which contention over policies came to affect debates over regime type.

The cases do indicate, even if only tentatively, that more or less free bargaining among social interest groups or their representatives was likely to preserve social stability. If important interest groups were left out of negotiations, they disrupted the implementation of whatever decisions were made. Whether directly or indirectly, then, policymakers had to take into account the varied interests of sociopolitical groups; doing so indirectly, by presumption, was likely to lead to less accurate representation of the interests at stake and less satisfactory response to their demands. Intelligent policymaking was assisted by an environment of freely accessible information about the preferences of social groups.

An encouraging inference that can be drawn from this, and from the five experiences in the 1980s, is that more democratic governments than military dictatorships dealt with the crisis well. This is true on both economic-policy and political dimensions. By most measures Mexican and Venezuelan economic policies after the crisis hit were more coherent and successful than policies in Argentina and Brazil. Similarly, Mexican and Venezuelan politics weathered the crisis reasonably well—and perhaps even became more democratic during the process. Although Argentina and Brazil democratized in the 1980s, few believe that their political systems are sturdy. The Chilean example is different, of course; the consensus would probably be that both Chilean economic policies and Chilean politics entered the 1990s in good shape, despite the authoritarian circumstances of their evolution. The five experiences nonetheless suggest that the relative susceptibility of democratic regimes in Mexico and Venezuela to social demands, compared to the relative policy and political inflexibility of the military dictatorships, contributed (somewhat counterintuitively, perhaps) to greater regime stability in the former than in the latter.[20]

The five-country comparison also provides evidence of vicious and virtuous circles in the political economy. Mexican and Venezuelan political stability allowed policymakers and groups to take a relatively long view; even in Chile, political stability bred policy stability, albeit under the aegis of a dictatorship. Meanwhile, Argentine and Brazilian instability encouraged short-term thinking by politicians and constituents alike. The more instability, the more short-sighted economic and political actors were,

---

[20] This point is controversial, and a large literature exists on the relative ability of authoritarian and democratic political systems to deal with economic crises. For two exemplary explorations see Robert Kaufman, "Democratic and Authoritarian Responses to the Debt Issue," *International Organization* 39, no. 3 (Summer 1985): 473–503; and Karen Remmer, "Democracy and Economic Crisis: The Latin American Experience," *World Politics* 52, no. 3 (1990): 315–35.

and the more unsustainable the outcomes—leading to even greater instability.

Unfortunately, my analysis of the five experiences offers no simple formula for breaking out of (or into) this vicious (or virtuous) circle, or for avoiding undesirable economic or political outcomes more generally. It might in fact be read as suggesting that there is no hope for improvement other than some exogenous force, inasmuch as policy and political results are determined by economic factors that are quite stable, at least in the short run. This is far too pessimistic and misunderstands the purpose of the exercise. There is no question that considerations other than brute, immutable economic interest matter to society's development. However, the challenge confronted here is to specify as carefully as possible how such economic forces constrain results. Another challenge—not confronted here—is to learn how to work within or around the objective constraints imposed by economic factors in order to improve the social order. An analytically accurate modern political economy of development may be a first step toward determining the reasons for developmental success or failure and for doing something about them, but it is still only a first step.

Conclusions

This study does not claim to provide an all-encompassing explanation of every aspect of Latin American politics and economics. Nor does it claim to explain every detail of the events within its purview. It does nonetheless highlight several relationships that have been inadequately studied in the past. The study stresses the importance of economic policy to economic outcomes. It insists on the centrality of political pressures in the determination of economic policies. And finally, to close the circle, it argues for the crucial importance of economic interests to political behavior. These assertions and other analytical assertions made along the way are not "proved" by the five cases presented here, and skeptics will undoubtedly remain unconvinced. I do nonetheless hope that this study prompts others to carry out further analyses of the relationships examined here, both to provide a more accurate picture of them and to hone the analytical tools brought to bear on them.

8

Conclusions

EVERY CASE is a case; every nation's economic development and political trajectory is different. These differences reflect the diversity of social, economic, and political histories found in the world. The nuances of national politics and economics cannot fully be captured without detailed attention to national specifics. Studies illuminating the path taken by an individual country are invaluable, and without them broader generalizations would not be possible.

Social science, however, is only justified if it arrives at such broader generalizations. For this we need to identify regularities in socioeconomic and political behavior and outcomes, and to explain the causal connections among these regularities. Logical deduction gives us the tools to construct theories to explain and predict these regularities; detailed analysis of specific experiences allows us to test our theories.

The purpose of this book has been to propose and analyze a series of generalizations about Latin American economic and political developments. Its theoretical basis is modern political economy, with a focus on how economic interest groups operate to maximize the income of their members in the economic and political arenas. Its empirical method has been to compare five Latin American countries, each with a different history and a different socioeconomic and political order, as they confronted similar international financial conditions. By observing the different responses of these five, I illustrated the applicability of modern political economy to problems of development and set forth an interpretation of these problems.

The five countries were very different from one another in their economic response to the availability of external finance and in their political response to the financial crisis of the early 1980s. In Brazil, Mexico, and Venezuela, governments used much of the money borrowed by these countries to build major public investment projects aimed at spurring industrialization; in Chile and Argentina, the governments tended to reduce their economic roles, leaving most borrowing and investment to the private sector. In Brazil and Argentina, the crisis led to the democratization of military dictatorships; in Mexico the political system was opened gradually; Venezuela experienced a simple electoral alternation of power; in

Chile the military regime held onto power until long after the crisis passed.

My explanation for these different national patterns is based on the role of organized economic interests. Well-organized economic sectors with intense preferences about economic policies (growing from highly specific assets) were expected to have more success in obtaining favorable policies. This, I argue, explains the pattern of government policy in Brazil, Mexico, and Venezuela, and at times in Chile and Argentina. However, in the latter two cases, conflict between labor and capital led the relevant economic interests to relegate sectoral concerns to the background and pushed policymakers to focus on protecting or restoring a favorable general investment climate. In the Latin American context, this drove policy in a less interventionist, more market-oriented direction.

By the same token, I argue that the differential distributional consequences of the financial crisis led severely affected economic interests to demand relief. Where this relief was not forthcoming, these interests moved on to demand a change in political leadership or institutions. The inability of dictatorships in Brazil and Argentina to meet demands from powerful groups in the business community, especially, was a crucial catalyst to their downfall. In Venezuela the elected government's similar inability led to a similar (electoral) downfall. The Mexican ruling party was better able to respond to business-community demands, although in the process it forced major supporters in the working class and peasantry out of the ruling coalition. The Chilean dictatorship withstood popular pressure for change because the country's business community remained primarily concerned about the investment climate and the threat of socialism and was willing to forego some specific support in favor of the more general protection of property and profits.

None of these explanations is all-encompassing. There are thousands of details in the five country cases that cannot be analyzed without much more careful attention to national and local particularities than these short treatments allow. Further work would undoubtedly reveal information and trends that would not comfortably fit the analysis presented here. However, the present study is of a broad sweep across a wide range of countries. It is not intended to be definitive, but rather to highlight the issues at stake and the methods that modern political economy can bring to bear upon them.

The analysis in this study differs from that presented by other scholars in a number of ways. It does not give much explanatory weight to the independent role of the state, or of the military, or of the policy bureaucracy, or of culture; that is, it argues that I can explain the outcomes in question without placing these factors at the center of our analysis. It does not, of course, argue that these factors are unimportant, only that they do not hold explanatory primacy. I ascribe this pride of place to economic interest.

The Latin American experience with borrowing and financial crisis in the 1970s and 1980s is rich with potential lessons. The experience highlights the extraordinary importance of economic policy to understanding economic outcomes in the development process, and in turn the centrality of political pressures to understanding economic policies. Similarly, the experience underscores the importance of economic developments and economic interests to understanding political behavior and political outcomes in the developing world.

The analysis presented here and the framework within which it is presented connect directly to the questions with which I began: how to explain underdevelopment and authoritarianism, or more optimistically development and democracy. This study suggests no sweeping generalizations to counter or reinforce those who believe that international capitalism inevitably causes or retards development and democracy. It does, however, suggest that development and democracy can be analyzed fruitfully by focusing on the economic interests of groups in developing societies. Along these lines, it presents a logically consistent approach to the effects of economic interests on economic policies and political behavior, and an analysis of five societies using this approach. The challenge to other scholars and observers is to demonstrate the logical or analytical flaws of modern political economy as applied here, if they find the approach wanting, or to extend it if they find it attractive.

Select Bibliography

NOTE: This is not a complete list of all works cited; it includes only those deemed most significant.

Alexander, Robert J. *Rómulo Betancourt and the Transformation of Venezuela.* New Brunswick: Transaction Books, 1982.

Allen, Loring. *Venezuelan Economic Development.* Greenwich, Conn.: JAI Press, 1977.

Alonso, Jorge, ed. *El Estado Mexicano.* Mexico City: Editorial Nueva Imagen, 1982.

Ames, Barry. *Political Survival.* Berkeley: University of California Press, 1987.

Apodaca Ramirez, Roberto. "Protección efectiva y asignación de recursos en las manufacturas mexicanas." *Comercio Exterior* 31, no. 10 (October 1981): 1099–1106.

Ardito Barletta, Nicolás, Mario Blejer, and Luis Landau, eds., *Economic Liberalization and Stabilization Policies in Argentina, Chile, and Uruguay.* Washington, D.C.: World Bank, 1983.

Arellano, José Pablo. "Crisis y recuperación económica en Chile en los años 80." *Colección Estudios CIEPLAN* 24 (June 1988): 63–84.

———. "De la liberalización a la intervención: El mercado de capitales en Chile 1974–1983." *Colección Estudios CIEPLAN* 11 (December 1983): 5–49.

Arellano, José Pablo, and René Cortázar. "Inflación, conflictos macroeconómicos y democratización en Chile." *Colección Estudios CIEPLAN* 19 (June 1986).

Arellano, José Pablo, and Manuel Marfán. "Ahorro-inversión y relaciones financieras en la actual crisis económica chilena." *Colección Estudios CIEPLAN* 20 (December 1986): 61–93.

Arida, Persio, ed. *Dívida Externa, Recessão, e Ajuste Estrutural.* Rio de Janeiro: Paz e Terra, 1982.

Aspe Armella, Pedro, Rudiger Dornbusch, and Maurice Obstfeld, eds., *Financial Policies and the World Capital Market: The Problem of Latin American Countries.* Chicago: University of Chicago Press, 1983.

Azpiazu, Daniel, Eduardo Basualdo, and Hugo Nochteff. "La industria electrónica argentina: Apertura comercial y desindustrialización." *Comercio Exterior* 37, no. 7 (July 1987): 542–54.

Bacha, Edmar. "Choques externos e perspectivas de crescimento: O caso do Brasil—1973/89." *Pesquisa e Planejamento Econômico* 14, no. 3 (December 1984): 583–622.

Bacha, Edmar Lisboa, and Carlos Diaz Alejandro. *International Financial Intermediation: A Long and Tropical View.* Princeton Essay in International Finance no. 147. Princeton: International Finance Section, 1982.

Baer, Mônica. *A internacionalização financeira no Brasil.* Petrópolis: Vozes, 1986.

Baer, Werner. *The Brazilian Economy: Growth and Development.* 2d ed. New York: Praeger, 1983.

————. "Import Substitution and Industrialization in Latin America." *Latin American Research Review* 7, no. 1 (Spring 1972): 95–122.

Baer, Werner, and Paul Beckerman. "Indexing in Brazil." *World Development* 2, no. 10–12 (October–December 1974): 35–47.

————. "The Trouble with Index-Linking." *World Development* 8, no. 9 (September 1980): 677–703.

Balassa, Bela, et al. *Toward Renewed Economic Growth in Latin America.* Mexico City: El Colegio de México, 1986.

Baloyra, Enrique, ed. *Comparing New Democracies: Transition and Consolidation in Mediterranean Europe and the Southern Cone.* Boulder, Colo.: Westview Press, 1987.

Baloyra, Enrique, and John Martz. *Political Attitudes in Venezuela.* Austin: University of Texas Press, 1979.

Barandiarán, Edgardo. "Nuestra crisis financiera." *Estudios Públicos* 12 (Spring 1983): 89–107.

Bardón, Alvaro, Camilo Carrasco, and Alvaro Vial. *Una década de cambios económicos: La experiencia chilena 1973–1983.* Santiago: Editorial Andrés Bello, 1985.

Barros de Castro, Antonio, and Francisco Eduardo Pires de Souza. *A economia brasileira em marcha forçada.* Rio de Janeiro: Paz e Terra, 1985.

Barzelay, Michael. *The Politicized Market Economy: Alcohol in Brazil.* Berkeley: University of California Press, 1986.

Basáñez, Miguel. *La lucha por la hegemonía en México, 1968–1980.* Mexico City: Siglo Veintiuno Editores, 1981.

Bates, Robert. *Markets and States in Tropical Africa: The Political Basis of Agricultural Policies.* Berkeley: University of California Press, 1981.

Bates, Robert, and Da-Hsiang Donald Lien. "A Note on Taxation, Development, and Representative Government." *Politics and Society* 14, no. 1 (1985): 53–70.

Baumann Neves, Renato, and Helson C. Braga. *O sistema brasileiro de financiamento às exportações.* Rio de Janeiro: IPEA/INPES, 1986.

Beccaria, L., and R. Carciofi. "The Recent Experience of Stabilising and Opening Up the Argentinian Economy." *Cambridge Journal of Economics* 6, no. 2 (June 1982): 145–65.

Behrman, Jere. *Foreign Trade Regimes and Economic Development: Chile.* New York: Columbia University Press, 1976.

————. *Macroeconomic Policy in a Developing Country: The Chilean Experience.* Amsterdam: North-Holland, 1977.

Bergsman, Joel. *Brazil: Industrialization and Trade Policies.* London: Oxford University Press, 1970.

Berlinski, Julio. "Dismantling Foreign Trade Restrictions: Some Evidence and Issues on the Argentine Case." In *Trade, Stability, Technology, and Equity in Latin America.* Edited by Moshe Syrquin and Simon Teitel, 57–68. New York: Academic Press, 1982.

Bitar, Sergio, and Eduardo Troncoso. *El desafío industrial de Venezuela.* Buenos Aires: Editorial Pomaire, 1983.

Blank, David Eugene. *Politics in Venezuela.* Boston: Little, Brown and Company, 1973.

———. *Venezuela: Politics in a Petroleum Republic.* New York: Praeger, 1984.

Bonelli, Regis. "Concentração industrial no Brasil." *Pesquisa e Planejamento Econômico* 10, no. 3 (December 1980): 851–84.

Bouzas, Roberto, ed. *Entre la heterodoxia y el ajuste.* Buenos Aires: Grupo Editor Latinoamericano, 1988.

Braga, Helson. *Estrutura de Mercado e Desempenho da Indústria Brasileira: 1973/75.* Rio de Janeiro: Editora da Fundação Getulio Vargas, 1980.

Bresser Pereira, Luiz Carlos. *Development and Crisis in Brazil, 1930–1983.* Boulder, Colo.: Westview Press, 1984.

———. *Economia brasileira.* São Paulo: Brasiliense, 1982.

———. *O colapso de uma aliança de classes: A burguesia e a crise do autoritarismo tecnoburocrático.* São Paulo: Brasiliense, 1978.

Brothers, Dwight. "El financiamento de la formación de capital en México, 1950–1961." *Comercio Exterior* 13, no. 12 (December 1963): 901–10.

Bruno, M., G. Di Tella, R. Dornbusch, and S. Fischer, eds. *Inflación y estabilización: La experiencia de Israel, Argentina, Brasil, Bolivia y México.* Mexico City: Fondo de Cultura Económica, 1988.

Buarque de Holanda Filho, Sergio. *Estrutura industrial no Brasil: Concentração e diversificação.* Rio de Janeiro: IPEA/INPES, 1983.

Bueno, Gerardo. "The Structure of Protection in Mexico." In Bela Balassa et al. *The Structure of Protection in Developing Countries,* 169–202. Baltimore: Johns Hopkins University Press, 1971.

Calvo, Guillermo. "Fractured Liberalism: Argentina under Martínez de Hoz." *Economic Development and Cultural Change* 34, no. 3 (April 1986): 511–33.

Campero, Guillermo. *Los gremios empresariales en el período 1970–1983: Comportamiento sociopolítico y orientaciones ideológicos.* Santiago: Instituto Latinoamericano de Estudios Transnacionales, 1984.

Campero, Guillermo, and René Cortázar. "Actores sociales y la transición a la democracia en Chile." *Colección Estudios CIEPLAN* 25 (December 1988): 115–58.

———. "Lógicas de acción sindical en Chile." *Colección Estudios CIEPLAN* 18 (December 1985): 5–37.

Canak, William. "The Peripheral State Debate." *Latin American Research Review* 19, no. 1 (1984): 3–36.

Canitrot, Adolfo. "Discipline as the Central Objective of Economic Policy: An Essay on the Economic Programme of the Argentine Government since 1976." *World Development* 8 (1980): 913–28.

———. "Teoría y práctica del liberalismo: Política antiinflacionaria y apertura económica en la Argentina, 1976–1981." *Desarrollo Económico* 21, no. 82 (July–September 1981): 131–89.

Cardoso, Fernando Henrique, and Enzo Faletto. *Dependency and Development in Latin America.* Berkeley: University of California Press, 1978.

Cardoso, Fernando H., and Bolivar Lamounier, eds. *Os partidos e as eleições no Brasil.* Rio de Janeiro: Paz e Terra, 1975.

Carone, E. *A Republica Nova (1930–1937).* São Paulo: DIFEL, 1976.

———. *O Estado Novo (1939–1945).* São Paulo: DIFEL, 1977.

Carrillo Castro, Alejandro, and Sergio Garcia Ramírez. *Las empresas públicas en México.* Mexico City: Miguel Angel Porrúa, 1983.

Carvalho Pereira, José Eduardo de. *Financiamento externo e crescimento econômico no Brasil: 1966/73.* Rio de Janeiro: IPEA/INPES, 1974.

Castro de Resende, Gervásio. "Setor externo e agricultura." *Literatura Econômica 5,* no. 3 (May–June 1983): 299–318.

Collier, David, ed. *The New Authoritarianism in Latin America.* Princeton: Princeton University Press, 1979.

Comin, Alexandre, and Geraldo Müller. *Crédito, modernização e atraso.* Cadernos CEBRAP 6. São Paulo: CEBRAP, 1985.

Corbo, Vittorio. "Reforms and Macroeconomic Adjustments in Chile during 1974–1984." *World Development* 13, no. 8 (1985): 893–916.

Corbo, Vittorio, and Jaime de Melo, eds. *Scrambling for Survival: How Firms Adjusted to the Recent Reforms in Argentina, Chile, and Uruguay.* Washington, D.C.: World Bank, 1985.

Corden, W. M. "Booming Sector and Dutch Disease Economics: Survey and Consolidation." *Oxford Economic Papers* 36 (1984): 359–80.

Cornelius, Wayne. *The Political Economy of Mexico under De la Madrid: The Crisis Deepens, 1985–1986.* Research Report Series no. 43. San Diego: Center for U.S.-Mexican Studies, 1986.

Coronel, Gustavo. *The Nationalization of the Venezuelan Oil Industry.* Lexington: Lexington Books, 1983.

Coronil, Fernando, and Julie Skurski. "Reproducing Dependency: Auto Industry Policy and Petrodollar Circulation in Venezuela. *International Organization* 36, no. 1 (Winter 1982): 61–94.

Corradi, Juan. *The Fitful Republic: Economy, Society, and Politics in Argentina.* Boulder, Colo.: Westview Press, 1985.

Corrêa do Lago, Luiz A., Fernando Lopes de Almeida, and Beatriz M. F. de Lima. *A indústria brasileira de bens de capital.* Rio de Janeiro: Instituto Brasileiro de Economia/Editora da Fundação Getúlio Vargas, 1979.

Cortés Conde, Roberto, and Shane Hunt, eds. *The Latin American Economies: Growth and the Export Sector, 1880–1930.* New York: Holmes and Meier, 1985.

Cuddington, John. *Capital Flight: Estimates, Issues, and Explanations.* Princeton Studies in International Finance no. 58. Princeton: International Finance Section, Princeton University, 1986.

Dahse, Fernando. *Mapa de la extrema riqueza.* Santiago: Editorial Aconcagua, 1979.

Davidoff Cruz, Paulo. *Dívida externa e política econômica: A experiência brasileira nos anos setenta.* São Paulo: Brasiliense, 1984.

De Jesús Martínez, José and Eduardo Jacobs. "Competencia y concentración: El caso del sector manufacturero, 1970–1975." *Economía mexicana* 2 (1980).

De Mateo, Fernando. "La política comercial de México y el GATT." *El Trimestre Económico 55*, no. 217 (January–March 1988): 175–216.

De Pablo, Juan Carlos. "El enfoque monetario de la balanza de pagos en la Argentina: Análisis del programa del 20 de diciembre de 1978." *El Trimestre Económico 50*, no. 198 (April–June 1983): 641–69.

———. *La economía que yo hice*. Buenos Aires: Ediciones El Cronista Comercial, 1986.

Dean, Warren. *The Industrialization of São Paulo, 1880–1945*. Austin: University of Texas Press, 1969.

Derossi, Flavia. *The Mexican Entrepreneur*. Paris: OECD, 1971.

Devlin, Robert. *Debt and Crisis in Latin America: The Supply Side of the Story*. Princeton: Princeton University Press, 1989.

Di Tella, Guido. *Argentina under Peron, 1973–6*. London: Macmillan, 1983.

Di Tella, Guido, and Rudiger Dornbusch, eds. *The Political Economy of Argentina, 1946–83*. London: Macmillan, 1989.

Di Tella, Torcuato. "Working-Class Organization and Politics in Argentina." *Latin American Research Review* 16, no. 2 (1981): 33–56.

Diaz Alejandro, Carlos. "Good-bye Financial Repression, Hello Financial Crash." *Journal of Development Economics* 19 (1985): 1–24.

———. *Essays in the Economic History of the Argentine Republic*. New Haven: Yale University Press, 1970.

———. "Latin America in Depression, 1929–39." In *The Theory and Experience of Economic Development: Essays in Honor of Sir W. Arthur Lewis*. Edited by Mark Gersovitz et al., 334–55. London: George Allen and Unwin, 1982.

———. "Latin American Debt." *Brookings Papers on Economic Activity* 2 (1984): 335–89.

———. "The 1940s in Latin America." In *Economic Structure and Performance: Essays in Honor of Hollis B. Chenery*. Edited by Moshe Syrquin, Lance Taylor and Larry Westphal. New York: Harcourt Brace Jovanovich, 1984.

———. "Some Aspects of the 1982–83 Brazilian Payments Crisis." *Brookings Papers on Economic Activity* 2 (1983): 515–42.

———. "Stories of the 1930s for the 1980s." In *Financial Policies and the World Capital Market*. Edited by Pedro Aspe Armella, Rudiger Dornbusch, and Maurice Obstfeld, 5–35. Chicago: University of Chicago Press, 1983.

Diniz, Eli. "A transição política no Brasil: Uma reavaliação da dinâmica da abertura." *Dados* 28, no. 3 (1985): 329–46.

Diniz, Eli, and Renato Raul Boschi. *Empresariado nacional e estado no Brasil*. Rio de Janeiro: Forense-Universitária, 1978.

Dornbusch, Rudiger. "External Debt, Budget Deficits, and Disequilibrium Exchange Rates." In *International Debt and the Developing Countries*. Edited by Gordon W. Smith and John T. Cuddington, 213–35. Washington, D.C.: World Bank, 1985.

———. "Mexico: Stabilization, Debt and Growth." *Economic Policy* 7 (October 1988): 233–83.

Dornbusch, Rudiger, and Juan Carlos de Pablo. *Deuda externa e inestabilidad macroeconómica en la Argentina*. Buenos Aires: Sudamericana, 1988.

Drake, Paul. *Socialism and Populism in Chile, 1932–1952.* Urbana: University of Illinois Press, 1978.

Echevarría, Oscar. *La economía venezolana 1944–1984.* Caracas: FEDECA-MARAS, 1984.

Economic Commission for Latin America and the Caribbean. *External Debt in Latin America.* Boulder, Colo.: Lynne Rienner, 1985.

Edwards, Sebastian. *Real Exchange Rates, Devaluation, and Adjustment: Exchange Rate Policy in Developing Countries.* Cambridge: MIT Press, 1989.

Edwards, Sebastian, and Alejandra Cox Edwards. *Monetarism and Liberalization: The Chilean Experiment.* Cambridge, Mass.: Ballinger, 1987.

Eichengreen, Barry, and Peter Lindert, eds. *The International Debt Crisis in Historical Perspective.* Cambridge: MIT Press, 1989.

Erickson, Kenneth Paul. *The Brazilian Corporative State and Working-Class Politics.* Berkeley: University of California Press, 1977.

Evans, Peter. *Dependent Development: The Alliance of Multinational, State, and Local Capital in Brazil.* Princeton: Princeton University Press, 1979.

Ewell, Judith. *Venezuela: A Century of Change.* London: C. Hurst and Company, 1984.

Eyzaguirre, Nicolás. "La deuda interna chilena, 1975–1985." In *Deuda interna y estabilidad financiera.* Edited by Carlos Massad and Roberto Zahler, 2:341–85. Buenos Aires: Grupo Editor Latinoamericano, 1988.

Fernandez, Roque. "The Expectations Management Approach to Stabilization in Argentina during 1976–82." *World Development* 13, no. 8 (1985): 871–92.

———. "La crisis financiera argentina, 1980–1982." *Desarrollo Económico* 23, no. 89 (April–June 1983): 79–97.

Fernandez, Roque, and Carlos Rodriguez, eds. *Inflación y estabilidad.* Buenos Aires: Ediciones Macchi, 1982.

Ferns, H. S. *Britain and Argentina in the Nineteenth Century.* Oxford: Oxford University Press, 1960.

Ffrench-Davis, Ricardo. "Exports and Industrialization in an Orthodox Model: Chile, 1973–1978." *CEPAL Review* 9 (December 1979): 95–113.

———. "The Monetarist Experiment in Chile: A Critical Survey." *World Development* 11, no. 11 (1983): 905–26.

———. *Políticas económicas en Chile 1952–1970.* Santiago: Ediciones Nueva Universidad, 1973.

Ffrench-Davis, Ricardo, and José De Gregorio. "Orígenes y efectos del endeudamiento externo en Chile." *Nota Técnica CIEPLAN* 99 (August 1987).

Ffrench-Davis, Ricardo, ed. *Relaciones financieras externas y su efecto en la economía latinoamericana.* Mexico City: Fondo de Cultura Económica, 1983.

Fishlow, Albert. "A economia política do ajustamento brasileiro aos choques do petróleo: Uma nota sobre o período 1974/84." *Pesquisa e Planejamento Econômico* 16, no. 3 (December 1986): 507–50.

Fitzgerald, E. V. K. "The State and Capital Accumulation in Mexico." *Journal of Latin American Studies* 10, no. 2 (November 1978): 263–82.

Flynn, Peter. *Brazil: A Political Analysis.* Boulder, Colo.: Westview Press, 1979.

Fontana, Andrés. *Fuerzas armadas, partidos políticos y transición a la democracia en Argentina*. Buenos Aires: CEDES, 1984.

Ford, A. G. *The Gold Standard, 1880–1914: Britain and Argentina*. Oxford: Oxford University Press, 1962.

Foxley, Alejandro. *Latin American Experiments in Neo-Conservative Economics*. Berkeley: University of California Press, 1983.

Frenkel, Roberto, and José María Fanelli, "El Plan Austral: Un año y medio después." *El Trimestre Económico* 54 (September 1987): 55–117.

Frieden, Jeffry. *Banking on the World: The Politics of American International Finance*. New York: Harper and Row, 1987.

———. "The Brazilian Borrowing Experience." *Latin American Research Review* 22, no. 1 (1987): 95–131.

———. "Third World Indebted Industrialization: International Finance and State Capitalism in Mexico, Brazil, Algeria, and South Korea." *International Organization* 35, no. 3 (Summer 1981): 407–31.

Furtado, Celso. *Economic Development of Latin America*. New York: Cambridge University Press, 1970.

Galveas, Ernane. *A política econômico-financeira do Brasil*. Brasília: Banco Central do Brasil, 1982.

———. *Evolução do sistema financeiro*. Brasília: Ministério da Fazenda, 1981.

Galvez, Julio, and James Tybout. "Microeconomic Adjustments in Chile during 1977–1981: The Importance of Being a *Grupo*." *World Development* 13, no. 8 (1985): 969–94.

Garretón, Manuel Antonio. *El proceso político chileno*. Santiago: FLACSO, 1983.

Geddes, Barbara. "Building 'State' Autonomy in Brazil, 1930–1964." *Comparative Politics* 22, no. 2 (January 1990): 217–35.

———. *Politician's Dilemma*. Berkeley: University of California Press, 1991.

Gerchunoff, Pablo, and Carlos Bozzalla. "Posibilidades y límites de un programa de estabilización heterodoxo: El caso argentino." *El Trimestre Económico* 54 (September 1987): 119–54.

Gil, Federico, Ricardo Lagos, and H. A. Landsberger, eds. *Chile at the Turning Point*. Philadelphia: ISHI, 1979.

Gil Díaz, Francisco. "Mexico's Path from Stability to Inflation." In *World Economic Growth*. Edited by Arnold Harberger, 333–76. San Francisco: ICS Press, 1984.

Gil Yepes, José Antonio. *The Challenge of Venezuelan Democracy*. New Brunswick, N.J.: Transaction Books, 1981.

Gómez, Octavio. "Las empresas públicas en México: Desempeño reciente y relaciones con la política económica." *El Trimestre Económico* 49, no. 2 (April–June 1982): 451–79.

Gonzaga M. Belluzzo, Luis, and Renata Coutinho, eds. *Desenvolvimento Capitalista no Brasil*. 2 vols. São Paulo: Brasiliense, 1980, 1983.

Gourevitch, Peter. "International Trade, Domestic Coalitions, and Liberty: Comparative Responses to the Crisis of 1873–1896." *Journal of Interdisciplinary History* 8, no. 2 (Autumn 1977): 281–313.

Gourevitch, Peter. *Politics in Hard Times: Comparative Responses to International Economic Crises*. Ithaca: Cornell University Press, 1986.

Graham, Richard. *Britain and the Onset of Modernization in Brazil, 1850–1914*. Cambridge: Cambridge University Press, 1968.

Green, Rosario. *El endeudamiento público externo de México 1940–1973*. Guanajuato: El Colegio de México, 1976.

Gribomont, C., and M. Rimez. "La política económica del gobierno de Luis Echeverría (1971–1976): Un primer ensayo de interpretación." *El Trimestre Económico* 44, no. 4 (October–December 1977): 771–835.

Gudin, Eugênio, and Roberto C. Simonsen. *A controvérsia do planejamento na economia brasileira*. Rio de Janeiro: IPEA/INPES, 1978.

Gutiérrez r., Roberto. "El endeudamiento externo del sector privado de México: Expansión y renegociación." *Comercio Exterior* 36, no. 4 (April 1986): 337–43.

Haggard, Stephan. "The Newly Industrializing Countries in the International System." *World Politics* 38, no. 2 (January 1986): 343–70.

———. *Pathways from the Periphery: The Politics of Growth in the Newly Industrializing Countries*. Ithaca: Cornell University Press, 1990.

Hamilton, Nora. *The Limits of State Autonomy: Post-Revolutionary Mexico*. Princeton: Princeton University Press, 1982.

Hansen, Roger. *The Politics of Mexican Development*. Baltimore: Johns Hopkins University Press, 1971.

Harberger, Arnold C. "Economic Adjustment and the Real Exchange Rate." In *Economic Adjustment and Exchange Rates in Developing Countries*. Edited by Sebastian Edwards and Liaquat Ahamed, 371–414. Chicago: University of Chicago Press, 1986.

———. "Observations on the Chilean Economy, 1973–1983." *Economic Development and Cultural Change* 33, no. 3 (April 1985): 451–62.

———. "Welfare Consequences of Capital Inflows." In *Economic Liberalization in Developing Countries*. Edited by Armeane M. Choksi and Demetris Papageorgiou, 157–78. New York: Basil Blackwell, 1986.

Hausmann, Ricardo, and G. Márquez. "La crisis económica venezolana: Origen, mecanismos, y encadenamientos." *Investigación Económica* 165 (July–September 1983): 117–54.

———. "Venezuela: Política de estabilización y mercado de trabajo en 1984." *Economía de América Latina* 13 (1985): 145–57.

Herman, Donald L. *Christian Democracy in Venezuela*. Chapel Hill: University of North Carolina Press, 1980.

Herman, Donald L., ed. *Democracy in Latin America: Colombia and Venezuela*. New York: Praeger, 1988.

Hewitt de Alcantara, Cynthia. *Modernizing Mexican Agriculture*. Geneva: United Nations, 1976.

Hewlett, Sylvia, and Richard Weinert, eds. *Brazil and Mexico: Patterns in Late Development*. Philadelphia: ISHI, 1982.

Higgott, Richard A. *Political Development Theory: The Contemporary Debate*. London: Croom Helm, 1983.

Humphrey, John. *Capitalist Control and Workers' Struggle in the Brazilian Auto Industry*. Princeton: Princeton University Press, 1982.

Inter-American Development Bank. *External Debt and Economic Development in Latin America*. Washington, D.C.: IDB, 1984.

IPEA/INPES. *Perspectivas de longo prazo da economia brasileira*. Rio de Janeiro: IPEA/INPES, 1985.

Jacobs, Eduardo. "La evolución reciente de los grupos de capital privado nacional." *Economía Mexicana* 3 (1981): 23–44.

Jacobs, Eduardo, and Wilson Perez Nuñez. "Las grandes empresas y el crecimiento acelerado." *Economía Mexicana* 4 (1982): 99–113.

Jadresic, Esteban. "Evolución del empleo y desempleo en Chile, 1970–1985." *Colección Estudios CIEPLAN* 20 (December 1986): 147–93.

Karl, Terry Lynn. "Petroleum and Political Pacts: The Transition to Democracy in Venezuela." *Latin American Research Review* 22, no. 1 (1987): 63–94.

Kaufman, Robert. "Democratic and Authoritarian Responses to the Debt Issue." *International Organization* 39, no. 3 (Summer 1985): 473–503.

———. *The Politics of Debt in Argentina, Brazil, and Mexico*. Berkeley: Institute of International Studies, 1988.

Kelly de Escobar, Janet, ed. *Empresas del estado en América Latina*. Caracas: Ediciones IESA, 1985.

Kindleberger, Charles. "Group Behavior and International Trade." *Journal of Political Economy* 59, no. 1 (February 1951): 30–46.

King, Timothy. *Mexico: Industrialization and Trade Policies since 1940*. London: Oxford University Press, 1970.

Kosacoff, Bernardo, and Daniel Azpiazu. *La industria argentina: Desarrollo y cambios estructurales*. Buenos Aires: Centro Editor de América Latina, 1989.

Lamounier, Bolivar, ed. *Voto de Desconfiança: Eleições e Mudança Política no Brasil*. Rio de Janeiro: Vozes, 1980.

Lamounier, Bolivar, and Rachel Meneguello. *Partidos políticos e consolidação democrática*. São Paulo: Brasiliense, 1986.

Lamounier, Bolivar, and Alkimar Moura. "Economic Policy and Political Opening in Brazil." In *Latin American Political Economy: Financial Crisis and Political Change*. Edited by Jonathan Hartlyn and Samuel Morley, 165–96. Boulder, Colo.: Westview Press, 1986.

Lara Resende, André. "A política brasileira de estabilização: 1963/1968." *Pesquisa e Planejamento Econômico* 12, no. 3 (December 1982): 757–805.

Leff, Nathaniel. *Underdevelopment and Development in Brazil*. Vol. 1: *Economic Structure and Change, 1822–1947*. London: George Allen and Unwin, 1982.

Lessard, Donald, and John Williamson, eds. *Capital Flight and Third World Debt*. Washington, D.C.: Institute for International Economics, 1987.

Levine, Daniel H. *Conflict and Political Change in Venezuela*. Princeton: Princeton University Press, 1973.

Linz, Juan, and Alfred Stepan, eds. *The Breakdown of Democratic Regimes: Latin America*. Baltimore: Johns Hopkins University Press, 1978.

Lipson, Charles. "The International Organization of Third World Debt." *International Organization* 35, no. 4 (Autumn 1981): 603–31.

Lustig, Nora, ed. *Panorama y perspectivas de la economía mexicana.* Mexico City: El Colegio de México, 1980.

McCoy, Jennifer. "Labor and the State in a Party-Mediated Democracy: Institutional Change in Venezuela." *Latin American Research Review* 24, no. 2 (1989): 35–67.

———. "The Politics of Adjustment: Labor and the Venezuelan Debt Crisis." *Journal of Interamerican Studies and World Affairs* 28, no. 4 (Winter 1986–1987): 103–38.

McDonough, Peter. *Power and Ideology in Brazil.* Princeton: Princeton University Press, 1981.

Maddison, Angus. *Two Crises: Latin America and Asia, 1929–38 and 1973–83.* Paris: OECD, 1985.

Mainwaring, Scott. "The Transition to Democracy in Brazil." *Journal of Interamerican Studies and World Affairs* 28, no. 2 (Spring 1986): 149–79.

Malan, Pedro, Regis Bonelli, Marcelo de P. Abreu, and José Eduardo de C. Pereira. *Política econômica externa e industrialização no Brasil (1939/52).* Rio de Janeiro: IPEA/INPES, 1980.

Mallon, Richard, and Juan Sourrouille. *Economic Policymaking in a Conflict Society: The Argentine Case.* Cambridge: Harvard University Press, 1975.

Malloy, James, and Mitchell Seligson, eds. *Authoritarians and Democrats: Regime Transition in Latin America.* Pittsburgh: University of Pittsburgh Press, 1987.

Mamalakis, Markos. *The Growth and Structure of the Chilean Economy: From Independence to Allende.* New Haven: Yale University Press, 1976.

———. "The Theory of Sectoral Clashes." *Latin American Research Review* 4, no. 3 (1969): 9–46.

———. "The Theory of Sectoral Clashes and Coalitions Revisited." *Latin American Research Review* 6, no. 3 (1971): 89–126.

Mamalakis, Markos, and Clark Reynolds, eds. *Essays on the Chilean Economy.* Homewood, Ill.: Irwin, 1965.

Marcel, Mario, and Patricio Meller. "Empalme de las cuentas nacionales de Chile 1960–1985: Métodos alternativos y resultados." *Colección Estudios CIEPLAN* 20 (December 1986): 121–46.

Mares, David. *Penetrating the International Market: Theoretical Considerations and a Mexican Case Study.* New York: Columbia University Press, 1987.

Marichal, Carlos. *A Century of Debt Crises in Latin America.* Princeton: Princeton University Press, 1989.

Martone, Celso L. *Macroeconomic Policies, Debt Accumulation, and Adjustment in Brazil, 1965–84.* World Bank Discussion Paper no. 8. Washington, D.C.: World Bank, 1987.

Martz, John, and David Myers, eds. *Venezuela: The Democratic Experience.* New York: Prager Publishers, 1977.

Mathieson, Donald. "Estimating Models of Financial Market Behavior during Periods of Extensive Structural Reform: The Experience of Chile." *IMF Staff Papers* 30, no. 2 (June 1983): 352–60.

————. "Inflation, Interest Rates, and the Balance of Payments during a Financial Reform: The Case of Argentina." *World Development* 10, no. 9 (1982): 813–27.

Maxfield, Sylvia. *Governing Capital: International Finance and Mexican Politics.* Ithaca: Cornell University Press, 1990.

Maxfield, Sylvia, and Ricardo Anzaldúa Montoya, eds., *Government and Private Sector in Contemporary Mexico.* San Diego: Center for U.S.-Mexican Studies, 1987.

Meller, Patricio. "Un enfoque analítico-empírico de las causas del actual endeudamiento externo chileno." *Colección Estudios CIEPLAN* 20 (December 1986): 19–60.

Méndez, Juan Carlos, ed. *Chilean Economic Policy.* Santiago: Budget Directorate, 1979.

Mericle, Kenneth S. "Corporatist Control of the Working Class: Authoritarian Brazil since 1964." In *Authoritarianism and Corporatism in Latin America.* Edited by James M. Malloy, 303–38. Pittsburgh: University of Pittsburgh Press, 1977.

Miller, Rory. "Latin American Manufacturing and the First World War: An Exploratory Essay." *World Development* 9, no. 8 (August 1981): 707–16.

Milner, Helen. *Resisting Protection: Global Industries and the Politics of International Trade.* Princeton: Princeton University Press, 1988.

Molina Warner, Isabel. "El endeudamiento externo del sector privado y sus efectos en la economía mexicana." *Comercio Exterior* 31, no. 10 (October 1981): 1140–47.

Montoro Filho, André Franco. *Moeda e sistema financeiro no Brasil.* Rio de Janeiro: IPEA/INPES, 1982.

Moran, Theodore. *Multinational Corporations and the Politics of Dependence: Copper in Chile.* Princeton: Princeton University Press, 1974.

Most, Sanford. *Industrial Revolution in Mexico.* Berkeley: University of California Press, 1950.

Moulián, Tomás, and Pilar Vergara. "Estado, ideología y políticas económicas en Chile: 1973–1978." *Colección Estudios CIEPLAN* 3 (June 1980): 65–120.

Moura da Silva, Adroaldo, and Rudiger Dornbusch. "Taxa de juros e depósitos em moeda estrangeira no Brasil." *Revista Brasileira de Economia* 38, no. 1 (January–March 1984): 39–52.

Mueller, Charles. *Das oligarquias agrárias ao predomínio urbano-industrial.* Rio de Janeiro: IPEA/INPES, 1983.

Muñoz Gomá, Oscar. *Chile y su industrialización.* Santiago: CIEPLAN, 1986.

Muñoz, Oscar. "Chile: El colapso de un experimento económico y sus efectos políticos." *Colección Estudios CIEPLAN* 16 (June 1985): 101–22.

Musalem, Alberto Roque. "Política de subsídios e exportações de manufaturados no Brasil." *Revista Brasileira de Economia* 35, no. 1 (January–March 1981): 17–41.

Naím, Moisés, and Ramón Piñango, eds. *El caso Venezuela: Una ilusión de armonía.* Caracas: Ediciones IESA, 1984.

Njaim, Humberto. "El sistema venezolano de partidos y grupos de influencia." *Politeia* 7 (1978): 181–213.

Nogueira Batista, Paulo, Jr. *International Financial Flows to Brazil since the Late 1960s*. World Bank Discussion Paper 7. Washington, D.C.: World Bank, 1987.

———. *Mito e realidade na dívida externa brasileira*. Rio de Janeiro: Paz e Terra, 1983.

Nogueira Batista, Paulo, Jr., et al. *Ensaios sobre o setor externo da economia brasileira*. Rio de Janeiro: IBRE/FGV, 1981.

Nogués, Julio. "Distorsiones en mercados de factores, empleo y ventajas comparativas en el sector manufacturero argentino." *Ensayos económicos* 20 (December 1981): 23–80.

———. *The Nature of Argentina's Policy Reforms during 1976–81*. Washington, D.C.: World Bank, 1986.

———. "Protección nominal y efectiva: Impacto de las reformas arancelarias durante 1976–1977." *Ensayos económicos* 8 (December 1978): 147–212.

Nuncio, Abraham, ed. *La sucesión presidencial en 1988*. Mexico City: Grijalbo, 1987.

O'Connell, Arturo. "Argentina into the Depression: Problems of an Open Economy." In *Latin America in the 1930s*. Edited by Rosemary Thorp, 188–221. New York: St. Martin's Press, 1984.

O'Donnell, Guillermo. *El estado burocrático autoritario, 1966–1973*. Buenos Aires: Editorial de Belgrano, 1982.

———. *Modernization and Bureaucratic Authoritarianism*. Berkeley: Institute of International Studies, 1973.

———. "State and Alliances in Argentina, 1956–1976." *Journal of Development Studies* 15 (1978–1979): 3–33.

Ortiz, Guillermo, and Leopoldo Solís. "Financial Structure and Exchange Rate Experience: Mexico 1954–1977." *Journal of Development Economics* 6, no. 3 (September 1979): 515–48.

Paiva Abreu, Marcelo de. "Argentina and Brazil in the 1930s: The Impact of British and American International Economic Policies." In *Latin America in the 1930s*. Edited by Rosemary Thorp, 144–62. New York: St. Martin's Press, 1984.

Palma, Gabriel. "From an Export-Led to an Import-Substituting Economy: Chile 1914–1939." In *Latin America in the 1930s*. Edited by Rosemary Thorp, 50–80. New York: St. Martin's Press, 1984.

Pastore, José, and Thomas E. Skidmore. "Brazilian Labor Relations: A New Era?" In *Industrial Relations in a Decade of Economic Change*, edited by Hervey Juris, Mark Thompson, and Wilbur Daniels, 75–113. Madison, Wis.: Industrial Relations Research Association, 1985.

Peñaloza Webb, Tomás. "La productividad de la banca en México, 1980–1983." *El Trimestre Económico* 52, no. 206 (April–June 1985): 465–97.

Pérez Nuñez, Wilson. "La estructura de la industria estatal." *Economía Mexicana* 4 (1982): 115–35.

Petrei, A. Humberto, and James Tybout. "Microeconomic Adjustments in Argentina during 1976–1981: The Importance of Changing Levels of Financial Subsidies." *World Development* 13, no. 8 (1985): 949–67.

Pion-Berlin, David. "The Fall of Military Rule in Argentina: 1976–1983." *Journal of Interamerican Studies and World Affairs* 27, no. 2 (Summer 1985): 55–76.

Platt, D. C. M. "Dependency in Nineteenth-Century Latin America: An Historian Objects." *Latin American Research Review* 15, no. 1 (1980): 113–49.

———. *Latin America and British Trade, 1806–1914.* London: A. and C. Black, 1972.

Platt, D. C. M., ed. *Business Imperialism 1840–1930: An Enquiry Based on British Experience in Latin America.* Oxford: Clarendon Press, 1977.

Porta, Fernando, Miguel Lacabana, and Víctor Fajardo. *La internacionalización financiera en Venezuela.* Buenos Aires: Centro de Economía Transnacional, 1983.

Portocarrero de Castro, Hélio O., ed. *Introdução ao Mercado de Capitais.* Rio de Janeiro: IBMEC, 1979.

Przeworski, Adam. "Some Problems in the Study of the Transition to Democracy." In *Transitions from Authoritarian Rule.* Edited by Guillermo O'Donnell, Philippe Schmitter, and Laurence Whitehead, 3:47–63. Baltimore: Johns Hopkins University Press, 1986.

Quijano, José Manuel, ed. *La banca: Pasado y presente.* Mexico City: CIDE, 1983.

Ramirez, Miguel D. *Development Banking in Mexico: The Case of Nacional Financiera, S.A.* New York: Praeger, 1986.

Ramirez de la O, Rogelio. "Industrialización y sustitución de importaciones en México." *Comercio Exterior* 30, no. 1 (January 1980): 31–37.

Ramírez Rancaño, Mario. *La burguesía industrial: Revelaciones de una encuesta.* Mexico City: Editorial Nuestro Tiempo, 1974.

Ramos, Joseph. *Neoconservative Economics in the Southern Cone of Latin America, 1973–1983.* Baltimore: Johns Hopkins University Press, 1986.

Randall, Laura. *An Economic History of Argentina in the Twentieth Century.* New York: Columbia University Press, 1978.

———. *The Political Economy of Venezuelan Oil.* New York: Praeger, 1987.

Remmer, Karen. "Democracy and Economic Crisis: The Latin American Experience." *World Politics* 52, no. 3 (1990): 315–35.

———. "Public Policy and Regime Consolidation: The First Five Years of the Chilean Junta." *Journal of Developing Areas* 13, no. 4 (July 1979): 441–61.

Remmer, Karen, and Gilbert Merkx. "Bureaucratic-Authoritarianism Revisited." *Latin America Research Review* 22, no. 2 (1987): 3–40.

Reyna, José Luis, and Richard S. Weinert, eds. *Authoritarianism in Mexico.* Philadelphia: ISHI, 1977.

Reynolds, Clark. *The Mexican Economy: Twentieth Century Structure and Growth.* New Haven: Yale University Press, 1970.

———. "Why Mexico's 'Stabilizing Development' Was Actually Destabilizing (with Some Implications for the Future)." *World Development* 6, no. 7/8 (July–August 1978): 1005–18.

Riveros, Luis. "Desempleo, distribución del ingreso y política social." *Estudios Públicos* 20 (Spring 1985): 315–47.

Rock, David. *Argentina, 1516–1982: From Spanish Colonization to the Falklands War.* Berkeley: University of California Press, 1985.

———. *Politics in Argentina, 1890–1930: The Rise and Fall of Radicalism.* New York: Cambridge University Press, 1975.

Rodriguez, Carlos Alfredo. "The Argentine Stabilization Plan of December 20th." *World Development* 10, no. 9 (1982): 801–11.

———. "Políticas de estabilización en la economía argentina, 1978–1982." *Cuadernos de economía* 20, no. 59 (April 1983): 21–42.

Rodríguez F., Miguel. "Auge petrolero, estancamiento y políticas de ajuste en Venezuela." *Coyuntura Económica* (Bogotá), December 1985, 201–27.

Rosenberg, Hans. "The Depression of 1873–1896 in Central Europe." *Journal of Economic History* 13 (1943): 58–73.

Rozo Carlos, et al. *México en la división internacional del trabajo.* Mexico City: CIDE, 1984.

Sachs, Jeffrey D., ed. *Developing Country Debt and Economic Performance.* Vol. 1. *The International Financial System.* Chicago: University of Chicago Press, 1989.

Salgado, René. "Economic Pressure Groups and Policy-Making in Venezuela: The Case of FEDECAMARAS Reconsidered." *Latin American Research Review* 22, no. 3 (1987): 91–105.

Sanfuentes, Andrés. "Los grupos económicos: Control y políticas." *Colección Estudios CIEPLAN* 15 (December 1984): 131–70.

Schvarzer, Jorge. *Martínez de Hoz: La lógica política de la política económica.* Buenos Aires: CISEA, 1983.

Secretaria de Controle de Empresas Estatais. *Empresas estatais no Brasil e o controle da SEST.* Brasília: SEST, 1981.

Selcher, Wayne, ed. *Political Liberalization in Brazil: Dynamics, Dilemmas, and Future Prospects.* Boulder, Colo.: Westview Press, 1986.

Shafer, Robert Jones. *Mexican Business Organizations: History and Analysis.* Syracuse: Syracuse University Press, 1973.

Sigmund, Paul. *The Overthrow of Allende and the Politics of Chile.* Pittsburgh: University of Pittsburg Press, 1977.

Skidmore, Thomas E. *Politics in Brazil, 1930–1964.* New York: Oxford University Press, 1967.

Smith, Peter. *Politics and Beef in Argentina: Patterns of Conflict and Change.* New York: Columbia University Press, 1969.

Smith, William C. "The Political Transition in Brazil." In *Comparing New Democracies.* Edited by Enrique Baloyra. Boulder, Colo.: Westview Press, 1987.

———. "The Travail of Brazilian Democracy in the 'New Republic'." *Journal of Interamerican Studies and World Affairs* 28, no. 4 (Winter 1986–1987): 39–73.

Solís, Leopoldo. *Alternativas para el desarrollo.* Mexico City: Joaquín Mortiz, 1980.

————. *Controversias sobre el crecimiento y la distribución.* Mexico City: Fondo de Cultura Económica, 1972.

————. *Economic Policy Reform in Mexico: A Case Study for Developing Countries.* New York: Pergamon Press, 1981.

————. *La realidad económica mexicana: Retrovisión y perspectivas.* 16th ed. Mexico City: Siglo Veintiuno, 1987.

Sourrouille, Juan, Bernardo Kosacoff, and Jorge Lucangeli. *Transnacionalización y política económica en la Argentina.* Buenos Aires: Centro Editor de América Latina, 1985.

Stallings, Barbara. *Banker to the Third World.* Berkeley: University of California Press, 1987.

————. *Class Conflict and Economic Development in Chile, 1958–1973.* Stanford: Stanford University Press, 1978.

————. "Political Economy of Democratic Transition: Chile in the 1980s." In *Debt and Democracy in Latin America.* Edited by Barbara Stallings and Robert Kaufman, 181–99. Boulder, Colo.: Westview Press, 1989.

Stepan, Alfred. *The Military in Politics.* Princeton: Princeton University Press, 1971.

————. *Rethinking Military Politics: Brazil and the Southern Cone.* Princeton: Princeton University Press, 1988.

————. "State Power and the Strength of Civil Society in the Southern Cone of Latin America." In *Bringing the State Back In.* Edited by Peter Evans, Dietrich Rueschemeyer, and Theda Skocpol. Cambridge: Cambridge University Press, 1985.

Stepan, Alfred, ed. *Authoritarian Brazil: Origins, Policies, and Future.* New Haven: Yale University Press, 1973.

Story, Dale. *Industry, the State, and Public Policy in Mexico.* Austin: University of Texas Press, 1986.

————. *Sectoral Clash and Industrialization in Latin America.* Syracuse, N.Y.: Maxwell School, 1981.

Suzigan, Wilson. *Indústria brasileira: Origem e desenvolvimento.* São Paulo: Brasiliense, 1986.

Suzigan, Wilson, ed. *Indústria: Política, instituções e desenvolvimento.* Rio de Janeiro: IPEA/INPES, 1978.

Tamayo, Jorge. "El papel del sector público en el proceso de acumulación de capital." *Investigación Económica* 23, no. 92 (October–December 1963): 709–47.

Teichman, Judith. *Policymaking in Mexico: From Boom to Crisis.* Boston: Allen and Unwin, 1988.

Tello, Carlos. *La nacionalización de la banca en México.* Mexico City: Siglo Veintiuno Editores, 1984.

Ten Kate, Adriaan, and Fernando de Mateo Venturini. "Apertura comercial y estructura de la protección en México." *Comercio Exterior* 39, no. 4 (April 1989): 312–29.

Ten Kate, Adriaan, and Robert Bruce Wallace. *Protection and Economic Development in Mexico.* New York: St. Martin's Press, 1981.

Thorp, Rosemary, ed. *Latin America in the 1930s.* New York: St. Martin's Press, 1984.

Trebat, Thomas J. *Brazil's State-Owned Enterprises: A Case Study of the State as Entrepreneur.* Cambridge: Cambridge University Press, 1983.

Tsebelis, George. *Nested Games.* Berkeley: University of California Press, 1990.

Tyler, William G. *The Brazilian Industrial Economy.* Lexington, Mass.: Lexington Books, 1981.

———. "Proteção tarifária efetiva recente do Brasil." *Estudos Econômicos* 10, no. 3 (September–December 1980): 47–59.

Valenzuela, Arturo. *The Breakdown of Democratic Regimes: Chile.* Baltimore: Johns Hopkins University Press, 1978.

Valenzuela, J. Samuel, and Arturo Valenzuela. "Modernization and Dependency: Alternative Perspectives on the Study of Latin American Underdevelopment." *Comparative Politics* 10, no. 4 (July 1978): 535–57.

Valenzuela, J. Samuel, and Arturo Valenzuela, eds. *Military Rule in Chile.* Baltimore: Johns Hopkins University Press, 1986.

Velásquez, Ramón, et al. *Venezuela moderna: Medio siglo de historia 1926–1976.* 2d ed. Caracas: Editorial Ariel, 1979.

Vellinga, Menno. *Economic Development and the Dynamics of Class: Industrialization, Power and Control in Monterrey, Mexico.* Assen, Holland: Van Gorcum, 1979.

Vergara, Pilar. "Apertura externa y desarrollo industrial en Chile: 1973–1978." *Desarrollo Económico* 20, no. 80 (January–March 1981): 453–89.

———. *Auge y caída del neoliberalismo en Chile.* Santiago: Facultad Latinoamericana de Ciencias Sociales, 1985.

Villa M., Rosa Olivia. *National Financiera.* Mexico City: Nacional Financiera, 1976.

Villela, Annibal, and Werner Baer. *O setor privado nacional: Problemas e políticas para seu fortalecimento.* Rio de Janeiro: IPEA/INPES, 1980.

Villela, Annibal, and Wilson Suzigan. *Government Policy and the Economic Growth of Brazil, 1889–1945.* Brazilian Economic Studies no. 3. Rio de Janeiro: IPEA/INPES, 1977.

Waisman, Carlos. *Reversal of Development in Argentina.* Princeton: Princeton University Press, 1987.

Wallerstein, Michael. "The Collapse of Democracy in Brazil." *Latin American Research Review* 15, no. 3 (1980): 3–40.

Walton, Gary, ed. *The National Economic Policies of Chile.* Greenwich, Conn.: JAI Press, 1985.

Weintraub, Sidney. "Case Study of Economic Stabilization: Mexico." In *Economic Stabilization in Developing Countries.* Edited by William Cline and Sidney Weintraub, 271–92. Washington, D.C.: Brookings Institution, 1981.

Werneck, Rogério L. Furquim. "Poupança estatal, dívida externa e crise financeira do setor público." *Pesquisa e Planejamento Econômico* 16, no. 3 (December 1986): 551–74.

Whitehead, Laurence. "The Adjustment Process in Chile: A Comparative Perspective." In *Latin American Debt and the Adjustment Crisis.* Edited by Rosemary Thorp and Laurence Whitehead, 117–61. London: Macmillan Press, 1987.

Willis, Eliza. "The State as Banker: The Expansion of the Public Sector in Brazil." Ph.D. diss., University of Texas, Austin, 1986.

Wirth, John. *The Politics of Brazilian Development, 1930–1954.* Stanford: Stanford University Press, 1970.

World Bank. *Brazil: Financial Systems Review.* Washington, D.C.: World Bank, 1980.

Wyman, Donald L., ed. *Mexico's Economic Crisis.* San Diego: Center for U.S.-Mexican Studies, 1983.

Wynia, Gary. *Argentina in the Postwar Era.* Albuquerque: University of New Mexico Press, 1978.

Zahler, Roberto. "Estrategias financieras latinoamericanas: La experiencia del Cono Sur." *Colección Estudios CIEPLAN* 23 (March 1988): 117–43.

————. "The Monetary and Real Effects of the Financial Opening Up of National Economies to the Exterior: The Chilean Case, 1974–1978." *CEPAL Review* 10 (April 1980): 127–54.

————. "Recent Southern Cone Liberalization Reforms and Stabilization Policies: The Chilean Case, 1974–1982." *Journal of Interamerican Studies and World Affairs* 25, no. 4 (November 1983): 509–62.

Zambrano, Luis, Matías Riutort, Charlotte de Vainrub, Chi-Yi Chen. "La deuda externa de Venezuela." *Resumen,* no. 508, 31 July 1983, 19–41.

Zedillo Ponce de Leon, Ernesto. "External Public Indebtedness in Mexico." Ph.D. thesis, Yale University, 1981.

Index

Acción Democrática, Venezuela (AD), 87, 88, 89, 184, 185, 199, 202, 203–4, 206, 217, 222, 223, 224, 228, 229, 234
Alemann, Roberto, 226
Alessandri, Arturo, 147, 148
Alessandri, Jorge, 148, 149
Alfa, 194, 218
Alfonsín, Raúl, 227
Aliança Renovadora Nacional (ARENA), Brazil, 115, 124, 129
Alianza Democrática (AD), Chile, 172, 173, 174
Allende, Salvador, 143, 145, 148, 149, 150, 171, 176
Andean Pact, 156, 185
Angarita, Isaias Medina, 183
Argentina: antimanufacturing bias in, 75, 78–80, 89, 186; balance of payments for, 189, 212, 243; class conflict in, 8, 9, 34, 35, 88–89, 228, 234; deindustrialization in, 8; democratization of, 85, 88, 91, 178, 209, 216, 224–25, 226, 228, 234, 238, 254; economic crisis in, 216, 224–27; economic indicators for conditions in, 52; exchange rates in, 81, 212, 214, 225, 228; exports from, 44, 179, 189, 211; foreign debt of, 75–83, 206–15; GDP of, 46, 77, 82, 84, 207, 209, 226; governing coalitions in, 44, 186; history of political economy in, 186–89, 254; import-competing industry in, 186, 189, 209, 213, 214; imports to, 80, 82, 83, 84; import substitution in, 180, 187, 188, 206, 210, 211, 238; invasion of Falkland Islands by, 64, 87, 226; investments in, 78, 82, 83; labor-capital relations in, 179, 180, 187, 206, 209, 215, 229, 230; literacy rate in, 47; market-oriented policies in, 74, 83, 91, 144, 178, 179, 208, 229, 234; military dictatorships in, 54, 85, 86, 91, 177, 178, 179, 187, 188, 189, 206–7, 209–10, 214–15, 225–26, 241, 255; political conflict in, 50; privatization in, 8; sec-

toral economics in, 38, 89, 186, 190, 206–7, 208, 211, 217, 225, 226, 229, 234; wages and per capita income in, 3, 187, 189, 209, 226
assets: redeployment of, 21; specificity of, 19, 20–22, 32, 33, 40–41, 89, 233, 240; susceptibility of, to policy, 18–19
asset specificity, 19, 20–22, 32, 33, 40–41, 89, 233, 240
Austral Plan, 227
authoritarianism. *See* dictatorships

balance of payments, 69, 243; in Argentina, 189, 212, 243; in Brazil, 102, 128–29, 132; in Chile, 155, 158, 243
Banco Colocadora Nacional de Valores, 166
Banco de Chile, 166, 173
Banco de México, 180
Banco de Santiago, 166, 173
Banco do Brasil, 99, 111
Banco Hipotecario de Chile (BHC), 166. *See also* Vial/BHC
Banco Industrial de Venezuela, 200
Banco Nacional de Desenvolvimento Econômico e Social (BNDES), Brazil, 101, 104, 107, 111, 112, 122, 123, 129
Bank for International Settlements, 78
Betancourt, Rómulo, 184
Bignone, Gen. Reynaldo, 226
boom and bust cycles, 56–57, 58–59
Bradesco, 111, 132
Brazil: balance of payments crises in, 102, 128–29, 132; "big projects" period in, 96, 118–25; class conflict in, 88, 102, 135, 137, 234; debt crisis in, 96, 125–34; democratization of, 85, 87, 88, 91, 95, 96, 97, 125, 129, 131, 134, 137, 234, 238, 254; economic indicators for conditions in, 51, 52; exchange rates in, 81, 119; exports from, 44, 96, 98, 105, 106, 117, 119, 122, 123, 126, 128; foreign debt of, 62, 75–83, 95, 107–15, 116, 119–20, 126, 128–34, 138; foreign

Brazil (*cont.*)
   direct investment in, 105, 116; GDP of,
   77, 82, 84, 101, 105, 110, 117, 123,
   130; government control of foreign capital in, 109, 122–23, 135; government
   subsidies to agricultural sector in, 111–
   12, 115, 122, 128; government subsidies
   to industrial sectors in, 34, 96–97, 99–
   100, 101, 102, 106, 114–15, 118, 119,
   120–22, 125–26, 128, 134, 136, 139–
   40, 234, 254; growth coalition in, 107,
   122–23, 130, 131–32, 133–34; history
   of political economy of, 97–102; imports
   to, 80, 84, 99, 117, 119, 126; import-
   substituting industrialization in, 74, 91,
   96, 101; industrialization in, 7–8, 95,
   96, 98, 99–101, 106–7, 117, 119; investments in, 7, 78, 82, 83, 96, 107, 116,
   119, 120, 129; labor movement in, 90,
   100, 102, 103, 115, 118, 135–36; market-oriented policies in, 105, 116, 136;
   military dictatorship in, 85, 86, 91, 95,
   96, 97, 102, 103–5, 115–17, 123–24,
   134, 177, 241, 255; "miracle" period in,
   96, 115–18; multinational corporate affiliates in, 117; net financial resource
   transfer of, 126; oil imports to, 63, 64;
   political conflict in, 50; political participation in, 102, 129–30; promanufacturing bias in, 75, 78–80, 89; sectoral economics in, 38, 88, 89, 95, 96, 102, 126,
   127, 135, 136, 141–42, 146; terms of
   trade for, 99, 126, 128; wages and per
   capita income in, 103–4
Buarque de Holanda Filho, Sergio, 140,
   141
Bulhões, Octávio Gouvea de, 103, 116,
   118
bureaucratic authoritarianism, 9, 237–38

Cáceres, Carlos, 173
Calabi, Andrea, 141
Cámpora, Héctor, 188
Campos, Roberto de Oliveira, 103, 116,
   118
Canitrot, Adolfo, 210
capital: and labor, 30–31, 33, 34, 90
Carajas (Brazil) mineral zone, 119
Cárdenas, Cuauhtémoc, 221
Cárdenas, Lázaro, 47, 180
Cauas, Jorge, 155, 157

Cavallo, Domingo, 226
Central Bank, Argentina, 210, 226
Chicago boys: in Chile, 155, 157, 243
Chile: antimanufacturing bias in, 75, 78–
   80, 89; balance of payments for, 155,
   158, 243; class conflict in, 8, 9, 34, 35,
   38, 88, 89, 143, 144–45, 146, 150–51,
   156, 228, 234; deindustrialization, 8; democratization of, 85n.19, 86, 143, 145,
   146, 148, 172, 173, 174, 177; economic
   crisis in, 169–74; economic indicators
   for conditions in, 52; exchange rates in,
   81, 147, 159, 162; exports from, 44, 45,
   146, 159–60, 168, 169, 240; foreign
   debt of, 75–83, 143, 156, 158, 160, 161,
   173; GDP of, 46, 77, 82, 84, 145, 146,
   149, 153, 154, 158, 159, 169; *grupos* in,
   157–58, 162, 166–67, 169–70, 175,
   176–77, 246; history of political economy of, 146–50, 254; imports to, 80,
   81, 82, 83, 84, 159–60, 165, 169; import substitution in, 155, 162, 164, 168,
   238; industrialization of, 147, 165; investments in, 78, 81, 82, 83, 149, 161;
   labor-capital relations in, 90, 143, 144–
   45, 149, 161, 162, 163–64, 168, 175–
   76, 177, 234; literacy rate in, 47; market-oriented policies in, 74, 83, 91, 143,
   144, 151, 152, 156–57, 167, 176, 234;
   military dictatorship in, 54, 85, 86, 89,
   91, 143, 144, 145, 150–52, 157, 169,
   173, 174, 175, 176, 177, 241, 255; political conflict in, 50, 171–72, 173, 175,
   241; privatization in, 8, 144, 152, 155,
   160, 164, 165; sectoral economics in,
   151, 152, 158, 176–77; terms of trade
   for, 45, 146–47, 155; wages and per
   capita income in, 147, 148, 153, 154,
   162, 168, 174
class, 29, 30–31. *See also* class conflict
class conflict, 8, 9, 15, 34–35, 41, 53, 89,
   233; in Argentina, 8, 9, 34, 35, 88–89,
   228, 234; in Brazil, 88, 102, 135, 137,
   234; in Chile, 8, 9, 34, 35, 38, 88, 89,
   143, 144–45, 146, 150–51, 156, 228,
   234
coalitions, 25, 40, 51
collective action, 23–24, 28
Comisión Federal de Electricidad (CFE),
   Mexico, 180, 190, 193

Comité de Organización Política Electoral Independiente (COPEI), Venezuela, 87, 88, 89, 184, 185, 199, 202, 204, 206, 216, 222, 224, 228, 229, 234
Communist party: in Brazil, 100; in Chile, 172, 174; in Venezuela, 184
consumer price index (CPI), American, 63, 64
Contreras, Eleazar López, 183
Corporación de Fomento (CORFO), Chile, 147, 155, 160
Costa e Silva, Gen. Artur da, 116, 117
credit-rationing, 55–56, 58
crisis politics, 36–38
Cruz, Paulo Davidoff, 141
Cruzat-Larraín, 166, 167, 174
Cuban Revolution, 103
currency devaluations, 81
Cydsa, 194

Dagnino, José María, 226
de Castro, Sergio, 157, 170
decolonization, 3
default risk, 56
de la Cuadra, Sergio, 170
Delfim Netto, Antônio, 116, 118, 127–28, 130, 132
democracy, 6, 235–36, 237
democratization: in Argentina, 85, 88, 91, 178, 209, 216, 224–25, 226, 228, 234, 238, 254; in Brazil, 85, 87, 88, 91, 95, 96, 97, 125, 129, 131, 134, 137, 234, 238, 254; in Chile, 85n.19, 86, 143, 145, 146, 148, 172, 173, 174, 177; in Mexico, 85, 87–88, 91, 178, 238, 241–42, 254, 255; rise of, 3, 8–9, 36; in Venezuela, 87, 88, 91, 178, 184, 238, 241, 254, 255
dependency theory, 9, 235, 236–37, 238
dependent development theory, 238–39
development: versus economic growth, 4n.2; multiple explanations of, 246–48
developmentalism, 47; in Argentina, 186, 187; in Brazil, 102; in Mexico, 180
dictatorships, military: decline of, 3, 8–9; dynamics of, 28; and economic data, 10; support for, 6. See also military sector
Dutch disease, 73, 165, 183, 240

Echeverría, Luis, 196–97, 217, 219

economic growth: versus development, 4n.2; retardation of, 4–5
economic performance: controlled by government policy, 4–6, 8, 15, 33–34, 67, 70–74, 233, 239, 244–45; impact of international financial flows on, 67–70
Escóbar, Luis, 173
Eurocurrency, 54, 61
Evans, Peter, 238
exchange rates: in Argentina, 81, 212, 214, 225, 228; in Brazil, 81, 119; in Chile, 81, 147, 159, 162; in Mexico, 81, 218, 219, 228; real, 72, 81, 82, 84, 119; in Venezuela, 81, 228
export-competing industry, 206
export-oriented primary producers, 32, 44, 49, 168, 213
Extended Fund Facility agreement, 197

factors. See sectors, economic
Falkland Islands (Malvinas), 64, 87, 226
Federação das Indústrias do Estado de São Paulo (FIESP), Brazil, 106, 131
Figueiredo, João Baptista, 125, 127, 130, 133
foreign direct investment (FDI), 62, 63, 105, 116
free riding, 23, 24
Frei, Eduardo, 148–49
Frente Democrático Nacional (FDN), Mexico, 88, 221
Frondizi, Arturo, 188

Galtieri, Gen. Leopoldo, 226
Galveas, Ernane, 128
game theory, 18, 40
Garretón, Manuel Antonio, 151
Geisel, Gen. Ernesto, 118, 123, 125, 129, 131
General Agreement on Tariffs and Trade (GATT), 217–18, 220
global monetarism, 158, 212, 243
Gómez, Juan Vicente, 183
Goulart, João, 50, 102, 103
governmental stability: affected by economics, 35–38
Great Depression, 45, 98–99, 146–47
gross domestic investment (GDI), 77–78, 117
gross domestic product (GDP): of Argentina, 46, 77, 82, 84, 207, 209, 226; of

gross domestic product (*cont.*)
  Brazil, 77, 82, 84, 101, 105, 110, 117,
  123, 130; of Chile, 46, 77, 82, 84, 145,
  146, 149, 153, 154, 158, 159, 169; impact of foreign capital inflow on, 75; and
  investment efficiency index, 78, 80; of
  Latin America, 46, 48; of Mexico, 46,
  77, 82, 84, 182, 192, 193, 196–97, 198,
  219; of Venezuela, 77, 82, 84, 186, 201,
  204, 205, 222, 223
gross national product (GNP), 145
Guri (Venezuela) hydroelectric power
  plant, 201

Herrera Campins, Luis, 204–6, 222
Hurtado, Miguel de la Madrid, 219

Ibáñez, Gen. Carlos, 147–48
ideology, 39–40, 243
Illia, Arturo, 188
import-competing industry, 168, 186, 189,
  209, 213, 214, 217
import-substituting industrialization (ISI):
  in Brazil, 74, 91, 96, 101; and bureaucratic authoritarianism, 237–38; elements in, 48; in Latin America, 46, 48,
  65, 74, 91
import substitution, 46, 48; in Argentina,
  180, 187, 188, 206, 210, 211, 238; in
  Chile, 155, 162, 164, 168, 238; in Latin
  America, 46; in Mexico, 74, 91, 180,
  181, 182, 183, 192, 196, 229; in Venezuela, 74, 91, 180, 185, 199, 201, 202,
  203, 206, 229. *See also* import–substituting industrialization.
income maximization, 17, 18
individualism, methodological, 18
industrial sector, 32
institutional change, 25–26, 28, 29, 36
institutions: dynamic, 25–26, 28; impact
  of, 38–39, 241–42; static, 25
Instituto de Planejamento Econômico e Social (IPEA), Brazil, 140
interest groups, 5, 6, 7–9, 11, 12, 16, 25,
  26, 38, 40, 41, 233, 240, 245
International Monetary Fund (IMF), 65,
  130–31, 132, 171, 197, 198
investment climate, 31, 34–35; for Brazil,
  103, 125
investment efficiency index, 78, 80

Itaipu (Brazil) hydroelectric power plant,
  119
Itaú, 132

Klein-Saks Mission, 147
Korean War, 46, 47
Kubitschek, Juscelino, 101, 102

labor: and capital, 30–31, 33, 34, 90
Latin America: development of economic
  classes in, 48–49; economic and political
  history of, 43–53; external finance in,
  67; foreign debt of, 59–61, 62–65, 68;
  foreign exchange in, 71; GDP of, 46, 48;
  government control of development in,
  48, 50, 51, 66; import-substituting industrialization in, 46, 48, 65, 74, 91; industrialization in, 44, 46–47, 48–49, 51,
  65–66; international finance in, 53–66;
  international trade in, 43–44, 45–46,
  47–48, 50; literacy rate in, 47; multinational corporate affiliates in, 50, 61; political participation in, 47, 50, 51–53,
  65–66; urbanization of, 46–47, 51;
  wages in, 49
less-developed countries (LDCs): credit-rationing to, 55–56, 58; definition of, 38;
  and dependency theory, 236–37; economic role of the state in, 75; foreign
  debt of, 62–64; impact of American
  monetary tightening on, 64; impact of
  foreign capital inflow in, 68, 175; interest rates for loans to, 54; international
  economic conditions of, 38; and liberalization, 247; and modernization theory,
  235
liberalization, 247–48
Liberal party, Chile, 147.
Lloyd Brasileiro, 99
London inter-bank offer rate (LIBOR), 54,
  55, 63, 64
López Portillo, José, 197, 219
Lüders, Rolf, 170–71, 174
Lusinchi, Jaime, 223

Malvinas. *See* Falkland Islands
Martínez de Hoz, José Alfredo, 209–10,
  211, 212, 214, 215, 225, 226
Marx, Karl, 4–5n.3, 16
Matte, 166
Médici, Gen. Emílio Garrastazú, 116, 117

Meném, Carlos Saúl, 227
Mexican Revolution (1910–1920), 44, 98, 180
Mexico: democratization of, 85, 87–88, 91, 178, 238, 241–42, 254, 255; economic crisis in, 217–22; economic indicators for conditions in, 51, 52; exchange rates in, 81, 218, 219, 228; exports from, 44, 179, 180, 182; foreign debt of, 62, 64, 75–83, 190–99; GDP of, 46, 77, 82, 84, 182, 192, 193, 196–97, 198, 219; government subsidies to industrial sectors in, 34, 178, 180, 181, 189, 193, 195, 216–17, 228, 234, 254; history of political economy of, 180–83, 228–29; imports to, 80, 82, 83, 84, 182; import substitution in, 74, 91, 180, 181, 182, 183, 192, 196, 229; industrialization in, 7–8, 192, 194; investments in, 78, 82, 83, 180, 181–82, 192, 197; labor-capital relations in, 178, 195, 217, 220, 228, 229, 234; market-oriented policies in, 220–21; oil exports from, 63, 64, 80, 179, 190, 197–98, 240; political conflict in, 50; promanufacturing bias in, 75, 78–80, 89; public investments in, 7; sectoral economics in, 38, 88, 89, 90, 179, 195, 198, 229; terms of trade for, 45, 240; wages and per capita income in, 217, 219, 220
military sector, 39. See also dictatorships, military
Mill, John Stuart, 16
Ministry of Labor, Brazilian, 106
modernization theory, 9, 235–36, 237
Monterrey Group, 194
Moraes, Antônio Ermírio de, 131
Morgan-Finansa, 166
Movimento al Socialismo (MAS), Venezuela, 184
Movimento Democrático Brasileiro (MDB), 115, 124, 129
Movimento Democrático Popular (MDP), Chile, 172, 174

Nacional Financiera (Nafinsa), 180, 182, 190, 192, 193
nationalism, 47, 178; in Argentina, 212; in Brazil, 102, 103; in Mexico, 180, 197, 218
neoclassical Marxism, 16
Neves, Tancredo, 133

Obrigação Reajustável do Tesouro Nacionale (ORTN), Brazil, 128
O'Donnell, Guillermo, 237
oil shocks, 62–63, 64, 75, 119, 123, 240
Onganía, Juan Carlos, 188, 207
Organization of Petroleum Exporting Countries (OPEC), 62, 202

Partido de Acción Nacional (PAN), Mexico, 88, 218, 220, 221
Partido de la Revolución Democrática (PRD), Mexico, 88, 221, 229
Partido Democrático Cristiano (PDC), Chile, 148–49, 150, 172
Partido Democrático Social (PDS), Brazil, 129, 130, 133
Partido Frente Liberal (PFL), Brazil, 133, 137
Partido Movimento Democrático Brasileiro (PMDB), 129, 132, 133, 137
Partido Revolucionario Institucional (PRI), Mexico, 50, 87, 88, 89, 91, 181, 183, 184, 195, 197, 217, 218, 220, 221–22, 241–42
Pérez, Carlos Andrés (CAP), 88, 202–3, 204, 205, 206, 224, 227
Pérez Jiménez, Marcos, 184
Perón, Eva, 189
Perón, Juan Domingo, 47, 50, 98, 178, 187–88, 189, 210
Petrobras, 101
Petróleos Mexicanos (Pemex), 190, 193
Pinochet, Gen. Augusto, 88, 151, 157, 169, 170, 171, 173, 175, 241
Plano Nacional de Desenvolvimento (PND), Brazil, 119, 122, 123
policy outcomes, 27–29
political economy, classical, 16
political economy, modern: and actors' group relations with other social institutions, 16, 24–27, 28; actors' policy preferences in, 16, 17, 19–22, 28; and aggregation of actors into groups, 16, 22–24, 28; components of, 16–17; defining actors and objectives in, 16, 17–19; definition of, 15–16; and policy outcomes, 27–29; and political outcomes, 27–29, 35–38
political outcomes, 27–29, 35–38, 83–88, 234

politics: and economics, 26–27, 35–38, 83–88, 233, 245–46, 249, 250–53
Popular Front, Chile, 147
Popular Unity, Chile. *See* Unidad Popular (UP), Chile
populism, 47, 178; in Argentina, 179; in Brazil, 102, 103, 105, 115, 135; in Chile, 149; in Mexico, 178, 180, 189–90, 197, 217, 218, 219, 220, 228; nationalist, 45, 179; in Venezuela, 178, 184, 189–90
postimperialism, 9
preference intensity, 19, 33
price elasticities, 20n.9
prices, relative, 28–29
public choice theory, 16, 17

Quadros, Jânio, 102
quasi-rents, 20–21

Radical party: in Argentina, 187, 188, 225, 226, 227; in Chile, 147
rational-choice Marxism, 16
rational-choice theory, 16, 17–18
rationalist political economy, 16
real exchange rate, 72, 81, 82, 84, 119
Rostow, W. W., 235

Sáenz, Orlando, 163
Salinas de Gortari, Carlos, 221
Sarney, José, 133
sectors: economic, 8, 9, 15, 29–30, 31–32, 33–34, 35, 37, 40–41, 53, 233
sector-specific policies, 20, 21n.11
service sector, 32
Setúbal, Olavo, 132
Sigaut, Lorenzo, 225, 226
Simonsen, Mário Henrique, 118, 127
Simonsen, Roberto, 106
Smith, Adam, 16
social choice theory, 16
Socialist party, Chile, 153, 172
Sociedad de Fomento Fabril (SOFOFA), Chile, 163, 170
Superior War College, Brazilian, 128

Tomic, Radomiro, 149
20 December 1978 Plan, 212–13

Unidad Popular (UP), Chile, 143, 149, 150, 151, 155
Unión Cívica Radical (UCR), Argentina, 186
University of Chicago, Department of Economics, 155
Uruguay, 44, 144
utility maximization, 18, 19

Vargas, Getúlio, 47, 99, 100, 101, 102, 106
Venezuela: democratization of, 87, 88, 91, 178, 184, 238, 241, 254, 255; economic crisis in, 216, 222–24; economic indicators for conditions in, 51, 52; exchange rates in, 81, 228; exports from, 179, 186, 224; foreign debt of, 75–83, 199–206, 223; GDP of, 77, 82, 84, 186, 201, 204, 205, 222, 223; government subsidies to industrial sectors in, 34, 178, 185, 189, 203, 228, 234, 254; history of political economy in, 183–86, 229; imports to, 80, 82, 83, 84; import substitution in, 74, 91, 180, 185, 199, 201, 202, 203, 206, 229; industrialization in, 7–8, 203; investments in, 78, 82, 83, 201–2, 203; labor-capital relations in, 178, 185, 199, 204, 205, 206, 217, 222–23, 228, 229–30, 234; market-oriented policies in, 199; military dictatorship in, 184; oil exports from, 63, 80, 179, 183, 184, 185, 186, 199–200, 205, 224, 240; pro-manufacturing bias in, 75, 78–80, 89; public investments in, 7; sectoral economics in, 38, 88, 89, 179, 185, 199, 229; terms of trade for, 240; wages and per capita income in, 204, 205, 222, 223
Vial, Javier, 170, 174
Vial/BHC, 166, 167, 170, 174, 177
Videla, Gen. Jorge Rafael, 209, 212, 225
Viola, Gen. Roberto Eduardo, 212, 225, 226, 230
VISA, 194
Vitro, 194
Votorantim, 131

Wehbe, Jorge, 226
World Bank, 101
world systems theory, 236
World War I, 44, 98
World War II, 46, 48, 50, 99, 100